The Path of Economic Growth

The Path of Economic Growth

ADOLPH LOWE

Assisted by STANFORD PULRANG

with an appendix by
EDWARD J. NELL

CAMBRIDGE UNIVERSITY PRESS
CAMBRIDGE
LONDON · NEW YORK · MELBOURNE

CAMBRIDGE UNIVERSITY PRESS
Cambridge, New York, Melbourne, Madrid, Cape Town, Singapore,
São Paulo, Delhi, Dubai, Tokyo

Cambridge University Press
The Edinburgh Building, Cambridge CB2 8RU, UK

Published in the United States of America by Cambridge University Press, New York

www.cambridge.org
Information on this title: www.cambridge.org/9780521125338

First published 1976
This digitally printed version 2009

A catalogue record for this publication is available from the British Library

Library of Congress Cataloguing in Publication data
Lowe, Adolph, 1893-
The path to economic growth.

1. Economic development.
2. Economic development – Mathematical models.
3. Industrialization.
4. Industrialization – Mathematical models.
I. Pulrang, Stanford, joint author.
II. Title.
HD82.L69   338′.001′84   75-38186

ISBN 978-0-521-20888-8 Hardback
ISBN 978-0-521-12533-8 Paperback

To my students – my teachers

Contents

Preface   ix

Acknowledgments   xi

PART I   The Basic Model

1 Introduction: Scope and Method   3
2 Patterns of Economic Growth   19
3 A Schema of Industrial Production   24
4 The Circulation of Fixed Capital   35
5 The Circulation of Working Capital   48
6 The Stationary Process in Operation: Structure Analysis   55
7 The Stationary Process in Operation: Force Analysis   62
8 Transition to Dynamic Equilibrium   70
9 Dynamic Equilibrium: Structure Analysis   77
10 Dynamic Equilibrium: Force Analysis   95

PART II   Changes in the Rate of Change
   I. *The Dynamics of Labor Supply*

11 The Setting of the Problem   103
12 A Bird's-Eye View of an Expanding Traverse   109
13 On the Short-Period Variability of the Capital–Labor Ratio   115
14 Adjustment to a Higher Rate of Growth of Labor Supply in a
   Free Market. I. Structure Analysis   123
15 Adjustment to a Higher Rate of Growth of Labor Supply in a
   Free Market. II. Force Analysis   146
16 Adjustment to a Higher Rate of Growth of Labor Supply in a
   Collectivist System   168
17 Some Comments on the Role of Working Capital in the Traverse   176
18 Instrumental Analysis of Decline in the Rate of Growth of
   Labor Supply   182

PART III   Changes in the Rate of Change
II. *The Dynamics of Natural Resources Supply*

19 The Dynamics of Diminishing Returns   209
20 Recycling of Production and Consumption Residuals and the
   Structure of Production   223

PART IV   Changes in the Rate of Change
III. *The Dynamics of Technological Progress*

21 The Scope of the Investigation   235
22 Dynamic Equilibrium Once More   240
23 Nonneutral Innovations: A General Survey   246
24 Pure Labor-Displacing Innovations   256
25 Pure Capital-Displacing Innovations   266
26 Some Comments on Combined Changes in the Input of Labor
   and Capital   272
27 Technical Progress and Diminishing Returns   275

28 Some Concluding Remarks   285

*Appendix: An Alternative Presentation of Lowe's Basic Model
by Edward J. Nell*   289

Glossary of Recurring Symbols   327

Name Index   331

Subject Index   333

Preface

Fifty years ago, in 1925, I published an essay outlining the stages and patterns characteristic for the process of industrialization.[1] This investigation, my first contact with the problem of economic growth, served as the starting point for an ambitious research program concerned with World Industrialization and International Business Cycles, which I conducted during the subsequent quinquennium under the auspices of the Institute of World Economics at the University of Kiel, Germany. Among the studies that issued from this enterprise, the best known are F. A. Burchardt's work on the industrial structure of production,[2] and Walter G. Hoffmann's elaboration and testing of my original hypothesis.[3]

The search for a verifiable model of "cyclical growth" has remained at the center of my own writings[4] as well as of my former activity as Director of Research of the Institute of World Affairs in New York City.[5] All of these partly theoretical, partly historical-descriptive studies fall into the category of "positive" economics. However, increasing doubts as to

[1] Adolph Lowe, "Chronik der Weltwirtschaft," *Weltwirtschaftliches Archiv*, Vol. 22, 1925, pp. 1*–32*.

[2] Summarized in R. Nurkse, "The Schematic Representation of the Structure of Production," *Review of Economic Studies*, Vol. 2, 1935, pp. 232–44, and in Adolph Lowe, "A Structural Model of Production," *Social Research*, Vol. 19, 1952, pp. 135–76. See also Chapter 2, Section II, of this book.

[3] Walter G. Hoffmann, *Stadien und Typen der Industrialisierung*, Jena, 1931, published in English as *The Growth of Industrial Economies*, Manchester, 1958.

[4] See Adolph Lowe, "Some Theoretical Considerations of the Meaning of Trend," *Proceedings of the Manchester Statistical Society*, Manchester, 1935; "The Trend in World Economics," *The American Journal of Economics and Sociology*, Vol. 3, 1944, pp. 419–33; "A Structural Model of Production," *loc. cit.;* "The Classical Theory of Economic Growth," *Social Research*, Vol. 21, 1954, pp. 127–58; "Structural Analysis of Real Capital Formation," in *Capital Formation and Economic Growth*, ed. Moses Abramovitz, Princeton, 1955, pp. 581–634.

[5] Of the pertinent publications of the Institute, I mention Henry G. Aubrey, "Deliberate Industrialization," *Occasional Paper*, New York, 1949, and "Small Industry in Economic Development," *Occasional Paper*, New York, 1951; Wilbert E. Moore, *Industrialization and Labor*, Ithaca and New York, 1951; Hans Neisser and Franco Modigliani, *National Incomes and International Trade*, Urbana, 1953.

the practical applicability of the results obtained gradually convinced me that analytical progress in this field was conditional on a fundamental revision of the method of research.

A different approach was first outlined in my book *On Economic Knowledge.*[6] There, in the eleventh chapter, the reader will find a literary sketch of the manner in which the problem of economic growth can be treated with the help of this particular technique of analysis. The present work is a systematic elaboration of that first attempt, now presenting the issues in both literary and symbolic formulations.

The reasons for adopting a new methodology will be presented in the introductory chapter. Otherwise, as the reader will see, this book is almost totally devoid of controversy and even of neutral discussions of other writings. After having summarized my past work, I trust that this will not be attributed to ignorance or disrespect. I simply believe that our contributions should be judged by what they add rather than by what they detract.

New York   Adolph Lowe
April 1976

[6] Adolph Lowe, *On Economic Knowledge,* New York and Evanston, Ill., 1964 (also Harper Torchbook TB 1526).

Acknowledgments

When the Syndics of Cambridge University Press invited me early in 1970 to write up my lecture notes on the theory of economic growth, I did not expect that this assignment would take me the better part of five years. Apart from some unforeseeable interruptions, the main reason for this slow process of gestation was the well-known experience that what sounds perfectly plausible in the classroom loses some of its apparent validity when put in black and white. Moreover, as even Keynes had to admit in the Preface to his *General Theory*, "It is astonishing what foolish things one can temporarily believe if one thinks too long alone." Therefore, I am thankful for the good fortune that provided me in the later stages of this inquiry with the ideal critic in the person of my friend and former student, Stanford Pulrang.

In speaking of the ideal critic, I am not alluding to the literary judge who is mainly concerned with questioning our basic outlook and its underlying assumptions. His function can be very helpful in the initial stages when we lay out our program. However, once work is in progress, we are in need of another type of evaluator who accepts our frame of reference but checks the inner consistency of the argument, points out alternatives, and in every way acts as the Devil's Advocate. Mr. Pulrang has played this role to perfection. His contribution is important enough to deserve more than this passing reference.

Of a different nature but no less significant in its own right has been the contribution of Professor Nell. Several readers of the manuscript had felt that interest in and comprehension of my exposition would be greatly enhanced if the underlying basic model would be rendered in the symbolic language used in some recent writings in the theory of growth. In the Appendix, Professor Nell has carried out this delicate task with exceptional skill. Not only has he succeeded in faithfully translating my analytical scheme, but in doing so, he has been able to identify essential similarities and differences of my model compared with the analytical apparatus of Hicks, Morishima, von Neumann, and Sraffa. His demonstration will no doubt serve as an effective tool of communication, and I feel deeply obligated to him for the effort he has bestowed on this project.

I am also grateful to Professors Murray Brown and David Laibman for useful suggestions concerning particular chapters. Drs. D. N. Lincoln, E. Lustig, and W. S. Sheldrick have skillfully lifted me over some mathematical hurdles. To all these helpmates, I extend my sincere thanks, while naturally exempting' them from all responsibility for the use I have made of their advice.

I have dedicated this book to my students who were associated with me at various times in several countries during more than half a century. It has been their incessant and relentless questioning which, more than any other outside influence, has determined the direction of my work. If I were to single out a particular name it would, of course, be Robert L. Heilbroner. A close friend for more than 25 years and a highly esteemed colleague, he has once again acted as guardian of my style and also as an expert simplifier. By carefully disentangling a number of rather involved passages, he drew my attention to more than a few lacunae and errors. Thus his contribution has improved the content as well as the form of the book, and I am very grateful for both.

For a second time the Lucius Littauer Foundation has awarded me a grant for the completion of a manuscript, a favor for which I wish to express my genuine appreciation.

Special thanks are due the editorial officers of Cambridge University Press, in particular Luther Wilson and Rhona Johnson and also Edith Feinstein, accomplished copy editor, for their help in improving the text. But that there was any text to improve upon has been the achievement of Ms. Lillian Salzman who has done outstanding work in transforming an almost illegible manuscript into the final draft. It is difficult for me to find the proper words of praise for the intelligence, meticulous care, and good-humored patience with which she has performed a Herculean task.

PART I
The basic model

I

Introduction: scope and method

I

Let me begin by raising the primal question, Is economic growth a subject at all fit for theorizing?

We have only to look at the theoretical work in economics during the last generation to answer the question in the affirmative. Indeed, one might even go so far as to see in the theory of growth the major preoccupation of contemporary economists. For example, two excellent surveys – both presenting only selections from the available material – have assembled more than 400 writings in this field since the end of World War II.[1] Why then another book on this topic?

Possibly my best defense is the verdict by which one of these reports sums up the collective achievements of this immense body of work:

> It would be difficult to claim that any of the models we have discussed goes far toward explaining these differences [to wit: between countries and between periods in rates of growth] or predicting what will happen to them in the future. Given the assumptions common to the models...this is not surprising, and it may be reasonably argued that most model-builders have not been trying to do this anyway. However, the general preoccupation with the case of steady-state growth and also, perhaps, an unduly restricted and oversimplified background concept of the phenomenon to be explained...have drawn the theory into directions which severely limit its direct empirical application and usefulness. (Hahn and Matthews, pp. 889–90)

[1] See F. A. Hahn and R. C. O. Matthews, "The Theory of Economic Growth: A Survey," *Economic Journal,* December 1964, pp. 770–902, and Ronald Britto, "Some Recent Developments in the Theory of Economic Growth: An Interpretation," *Journal of Economic Literature,* December 1973, pp. 1343–66. See also E. Burmeister and A. R. Dobell, *Mathematical Theories of Economic Growth,* New York and London, 1970.

3

The second report echoes the first:

> We must admit that the recent developments outlined here will not
> be of much help in explaining growth patterns in the real world.
> (Britto, p. 1360)

Perhaps I can build an even more forceful argument on the basis of
the skepticism with which Hicks, one of the most eminent workers in the
field, evaluates the major contributions including his own:

> It is the dynamic problem of positive economics – of the actual be-
> havior of an economy, with imperfect foresight – that, when even
> considered in this much detail, becomes so baffling...we cannot de-
> termine the actual path which the economy (even the model
> economy) will follow...[2]

In addition, strong reservations against not only the work actually done
but the very search for a "theory" of growth come from a different quar-
ter. They are voiced by those students of economic growth who aim at
the description of actual growth processes, based on historical and
sociological inquiries. As Abramovitz puts it:

> The study of economic growth presents in aggravated form that
> universal problem of economics and of social science, the distillation
> of dependable uniformities from a process of cumulative change. A
> dependable law implies some stable system of structural character-
> istics (tastes, propensities, motives, physical obstacles, organization,
> law, etc.) which cause a set of recognizable tendencies to emerge in
> the relation among variables. Social structure, however, is notori-
> ously in flux, so that in practice it is some sort of relative stability
> on which we must depend – relative usually to the period of time
> that is relevant. *But the longer the period, the less likely are we to
> find the degree of stability we need* [my italics]. ...The study of
> economic growth, therefore, stands closer to history than do other
> economic subjects...it seems unlikely that, for the foreseeable
> future, the economics of growth can be much more than economic
> history rationalized here and there to a limited degree as uniformi-
> ties in the process of development are established.[3]

These warnings give little encouragement to another attempt to build
a theory of growth. Yet, we should not permit them to distort our historical perspective. Model builders and empiricists alike make it appear

---

[2] John Hicks, *Capital and Growth,* New York and Oxford, 1965, p. 201.
[3] Moses Abramovitz, "Economics of Growth," in *A Survey of Contemporary Economics,* Vol. II, ed. B. F. Haley, Homewood, Ill., 1952, pp. 177–78.

as if we were dealing with a novel problem, brought to our attention mainly by practical concerns that have only recently emerged in developed and, especially, underdeveloped countries. Yet, it is hardly an exaggeration to say that the standard works of the classical economists – Smith, Ricardo, Marx – not only contain but essentially *are* theories of economic growth. Whereas the modern researcher is troubled by the tentative nature of his generalizations, classical economics abounds with laws of secular evolution and with unconditional predictions.

To a generation brought up on systems analysis the classical procedure can be easily explained. For Adam Smith and his followers and, *mutatis mutandis,* also for Karl Marx, all macroeconomic processes were strictly interdependent. They were related through a number of negative and positive feedbacks which permitted the system to grow, but precluded any unforeseeable movement within the system and for the system as a whole. Such feedback relations, say, between the level of real wages and the birth rate or between division of labor and the extent of the market, were the elements from which "laws" of population, of accumulation, and of technical progress could be derived, supplemented by "natural" laws such as the law of diminishing returns on land.

For Smith the ensuing secular evolution is benign over an indefinite future, assuring increasing national wealth which is expected to benefit all social classes. Contrariwise, Marx's general law of capitalist accumulation reveals growing tensions among the social components of the system, leading to its eventual breakdown. But, in spite of the contrast between the two visions, the destructive tendencies that Marx's analysis lays bare appear hardly less determinate than do the equilibrating secular movements in Smith's replica of the free market and, for this reason, both could be presented as unconditional predictions.

Moreover (and this even meets the challenge of the modern empiricists), this "systemic" orientation has broader application than a positive theory of *economic* evolution in the narrow sense. What is distinctive in classical theory is that the models also include the impact of the social and technological environment. In Smith's work as in Marx's this environment is created and continually recreated by the economic processes themselves. More precisely, the factors of production or inputs of today are nothing else than the outputs of yesterday: The stock of capital is the aggregate of prior investments; the supply of labor is the end product of the output of consumer goods or, as in Marx, is drawn from the ranks of a technologically produced reserve army; and the ruling technology itself is a function of the level of output and the competitive struggle. Thus, through a chain of reciprocal relations of cause and effect, the social and technological stimuli that sustain long-term economic motion appear themselves as the product of economic growth, and an all-inclusive theory of socioeconomic evolution emerges that eclipses the most ambitious program of modern empiricists, such as Abramovitz, Kuznets, or Lewis.[4]

We need not dwell on the fatal weaknesses of these earlier constructions, most of which have long been relegated to the textbooks on the history of economic thought. The mere fact that the individual predictions radically contradicted one another, coming in long waves of optimism and pessimism, weakened the credibility of each. The actual course of capitalist development has so far refuted them all.

More important for our purpose is the *analytical critique* that exposed the theoretical fallacies in these models. It directed itself, above all, against the alleged feedbacks from which generalizations and predictions were derived. Each one of them was proven spurious – be it the association of population growth with real wages, the *ex ante* equality of savings and investments, or the treatment of technological change as a function of intrasystemic processes. When finally J. S. Mill acknowledged that the strategic forces that determine labor supply, accumulation, and technical progress must be treated as independent variables, the circular mechanisms – the core of classical economics – were abandoned for good. Economics, hitherto a "body of truths," was transformed into "an engine for the discovery of concrete truth" (Marshall). The unconditional predictions of a Smith or Marx were replaced by an open-ended catalog of conditional inferences, themselves drawn from observations or "basic postulates."

Liberation from the straitjacket of the classical "systems" undoubtedly enlarged the scope of neoclassical theorizing, but only at the price of new fetters. There the empiricist reservations to modern theory hit their target. Unless we deal with the very short run, it is uncertain whether conditional predictions based on observed "data" will ever yield empirically useful results, not to speak of the inferences drawn from abstract postulates. Yet growth models thus constructed are bound to lose contact with the real world. They refer to a time span during which the initial conditions change as a matter of course. So far positive economics has discovered no procedure by which to anticipate such changes.

Moreover, the liberation from the classical shackles has actually not gone far enough. Abramovitz points to the crucial factor when he insists that economists "cultivate a science of pecuniary advantage."[5] Even when disguised as a purely formal "maximum principle," modern analysis of

---

[4] For details, see Adolph Lowe, *On Economic Knowledge*, New York and Evanston, Ill., 1964 (also Harper Torchbook TB 1526), Chs. 6 and 7; henceforth cited as *OEK*.

[5] Abramovitz, *loc. cit.*, p. 178.

production has, indeed, retained the classical profit motive as its sole motivational and behavioral rule.[6] In another context,[7] I have tried to explain how characteristic environmental pressures – mass poverty, unbridled competition, and an untamed spirit of accumulation – combined to evoke some such "extremum" behavior during the early stages of capitalism and, thus, bestowed a high degree of realism on the classical hypothesis. However, in agreement with the conclusions that Boulding, Galbraith, or H. A. Simon have drawn from a wealth of empirical studies, I also stressed the progressive weakening of the aims of receipt maximization and expenditure minimization, as the earlier pressures lessened in modern regimes characterized by rising affluence, imperfect competition and growing social security. In conjunction with the incessant revolutions in technology, there is an ever-widening spectrum of observed behavior[8] that reduces the truth value of economic predictions in proportion with the length of the prediction interval.

Still, when all this is admitted, the superscience to which the empiricists want to entrust the solution of the growth problem hardly holds out any better promise. Even if its explorations should not involve us in an infinite regress, it is difficult to believe that, considering the indeterminacy of the strategic variables, extrapolations of historical and sociological findings could offer a safer guide to valid generalizations than the admittedly precarious procedure of deductive reasoning.

II

Where does this leave us? Unless we somehow recapture the achievements of classical theory – analytical stringency within a framework that makes allowance for the forces of the environment – how can we hope to make any confirmable generalizations about economic growth? Yet, how do we set about designing such a framework?

Let us reflect once more on the misgivings expressed by Hahn-Matthews, Britto, and, above all, by Hicks. If so many astute minds have failed to come up with answers satisfactory at least to themselves, we cannot suppress a suspicion that they may not have asked the right question. Indeed, in anticipating one main result of my further deliberations, I strongly believe that the Mecca of the modern growth theorist does not lie where prevailing opinion looks for it; namely, in "positive" analysis. More specifically, I doubt that the obstacles that have so far impeded the search for

---

[6] For the most recent statement, see Paul A. Samuelson's Nobel Memorial Address, reprinted as "Maximum Principles in Analytical Economics," *The American Economic Review,* June 1972, pp. 249–62.

[7] See *OEK,* Ch. 3.

[8] See Chapter 7.

explanatory and predictive laws and generalizations can easily be over-come. Without prejudging future developments of research, it seems to me that at the present juncture we should base our trust in *prescriptive* rather than *descriptive* analysis. In other words, even if we do not seem to be able to generalize about the actual course of growth processes – especially those emerging from the free play of market forces – we may yet succeed in constructing a theory and in building reality-oriented models that reveal the *means suitable for the attainment of stipulated goals* of secular evolution.[9]

As a matter of fact, this conclusion has been foreshadowed by no less an authority than Hicks himself in the very passage from which previously I quoted only the negative part. After having admitted that "we cannot determine the actual path which the economy (even the model economy) will follow," he continues that "we can say more about its optimum path, about the path which will best satisfy some social objective."

However, before expounding all the implications of this methodological statement, we must, first of all, identify the particular aspects of the many-sided phenomenon of economic growth that require and are amenable to treatment along these lines. This is equivalent to saying that we must spell out the *substantive topic* of our investigation.

In doing so we take our bearings from the striking fact that during the century following the abandonment of the classical model, the lack of an explicit growth theory was hardly noticed. To understand this we must recall one of the main characteristics of this era of industrial capitalism, namely, the large fluctuations in economic activity which, up to the Second World War, placed the study of business cycles at the center of analytical interest.

From the viewpoint of growth the recurrent, long-lasting stretches of underutilization of resouces had a paradoxical effect. A periodic drag on output and income and, hence, on welfare generally, it was, nevertheless, the very presence of large pools of idle resources that greatly facilitated the system's adjustment to changes in aggregate demand and technology. Expansion of individual sectors of production remained unaffected by the state of capacity utilization and employment in other sectors, thus avoiding the frictions and bottlenecks that impede intersectoral shifts of resources – the unavoidable mode of adjustment under conditions of full utilization. Thus, growth became a by-product of the cycle and hardly distinguishable from the latter's phase of recovery.

[9] I have elaborated this procedure and the methodological principles on which it is based in two previous publications. See *OEK,* Chs. 5 and 10, and Robert L. Heilbroner, ed., *Economic Means and Social Ends,* Englewood Cliffs, N.J., pp. 1–36 and 167–99; henceforth cited as *EMASE.*

These conditions have drastically changed during the last generation. Full employment has become the universally adopted aim of public policy in the mature countries, so much so that, until quite recently, even rising rates of inflation were rarely considered as too high a price for its achievement. Although the policy of the "new economics" was nowhere completely successful, where properly applied, it eliminated at least the large fluctuations of the past, and, thus, greatly reduced the degree of underutilization of resources and the duration of their idleness.

Here we encounter a reverse paradox. The greater the success of this policy of stabilization, the smaller the flexibility of the system, and the greater the difficulties in achieving a smooth expansion path. Growth can then no longer feed on pools of idle capital and labor and, more than ever before, becomes conditional on the shift of employed resources and, especially, on capital formation. Furthermore, in the developing countries the situation is not basically different. Though endowed with large reserves of manpower, they sorely lack the real capital necessary for the productive employment of their labor force.

If we go one step further we realize that the root of all these difficulties is *technological*. Obstruction of resource shifts, bottlenecks in production, inelasticity of supply owing to the *longue durée* of capital formation and even more to the large costs of sunk capital, these and most other impediments to smooth expansion are the effect of the *large size and the technical specificity* of inputs. Consequently "fixed coefficients of production" dominate the adjustment processes and, in particular, the adjustment to the major growth stimuli – changes in population, resource supply, and technology.

Such emphasis on the relevance of fixed coefficients in the analysis of growth processes appears at first sight self-contradictory. Customarily we relegate this type of production function to the Marshallian short period; on the other hand, it is the essence of the time span over which growth extends that the stock of real capital and the labor force change in quantity and quality, with large variations in the combinations of both. Later on I shall offer a detailed explanation of why, nevertheless, I base my analysis on the postulate of fixed coefficients.[10] At this point I shall confine myself to a few clarifying remarks.

Obviously I cannot deny that secular analysis is concerned with a sequence of states and processes that differ from one another with respect to the quantity and quality of capital and labor and their combination. What I wish to stress is the fact that, except in the limiting and quite unrealistic case of steady exponential expansion, all these sequences are

[10] See Chapters 11 and 13.

discontinuous. They depict successive but separate levels of "capital formed" and "labor trained," but offer no insight into the intervening processes during which new capital is "being formed" and labor is "being trained."

Now these intervening processes fall, indeed, into the Marshallian short period, because during their course the quantity and quality of the initial capital stock, considered as a factor of production, remains unchanged. Assuming more or less full utilization of this stock – a condition with which, as we saw, mature as well as developing regions are confronted today – additional and possibly different real capital can be formed only with the help of this original stock. Or, in another formulation, the initially prevailing technical coefficients of production can be altered only by a productive process that itself is conditioned by these very coefficients.

The practical as well as the theoretical consequences of this "rigidity" are far-reaching. To the extent to which the technical structure is unalterable in the short period, the prevailing degree of factor specificity determines each stage of the growth path. Therefore, what in retrospect appears as a secular process is, in fact, an abstraction derived from a sequence of short-term movements, the latter being the only "real" processes. We have long been accustomed to this kind of reasoning in statistical trend analysis. It is time to realize that it applies with equal force to the theoretical treatment of growth.[11]

At the same time these considerations illuminate the key position that "real capital" holds in the growth of an industrial economy. It is this factor that, at all levels of industrialization, is responsible for the major bottlenecks when the rate of growth rises, and for waste of available inputs when it falls. For this reason our investigation will center on the *formation, application, and liquidation of real capital.*

Real capital formation or accumulation as our central topic may be further vindicated if we recall the methodological foundations of classical growth theory. Real capital is, indeed, both an input and an output and,

---

[11] I have stated this position originally in the Introduction to my paper on "Structural Analysis of Real Capital Formation," in *Capital Formation and Economic Growth,* Princeton, 1955, pp. 581–634, especially Section 4. In the meantime I received the valuable support of Michal Kalecki in his *Selected Essays on the Dynamics of the Capitalist Economy,* Cambridge (England), 1971, p. 165: "In fact, the long-run trend is but a slowly changing component of a chain of short-period situations; it has no independent entity. . . ." The significance of these short-term processes for a theory of economic growth has been implicitly recognized in Joan Robinson, *The Accumulation of Capital,* London, 1956, Book III, and in Hicks, *loc. cit.,* Ch. XVI, in which he discusses the intermediate processes required to achieve a change in the rate of growth under the heading of "traverse" – a suggestive term which we shall adopt. See also John Hicks, *Capital and Time,* Oxford, 1973, Chs. VII–XII.

thus, is the one productive factor subject to the kind of circular mechanism or feedback relations that were attributed to all factors by classical writers. This characteristic bestows on the analysis of capital problems a degree of stringency not encountered in other economic phenomena directly exposed to the variegated influences of the natural and social environment. It is just because real capital is not an "original" factor but is the result of economic processes in which it participates as one of the determinants that it can serve as the pathway through which the influence of the prime factors and their changes – labor supply, natural resources, savings propensities, and, above all, "embodied" technologies – are channeled into the industrial process. It is this auxiliary but all-comprehending function of real capital that permits us to treat accumulation and decumulation as genuinely economic problems, qualifying our version as an *economic theory of growth*.

III

Having defined our subject matter, we must now turn back to the question of *method*. To restate the conclusions we have drawn from the literature, we feel compelled to doubt the fruitfulness of any "positive" version of growth theory. On the other hand, the empiricist approach does not appear as a more efficient technique for obtaining practically useful generalizations. The solution must, therefore, be sought in the pursuit of prescriptive analysis or, in Hicks's words, in the study of "optimum paths."

Now prescriptive analysis is frequently identified with welfare theory. However, in speaking of the path that will quite generally satisfy "some social objective," Hicks himself points to a wider application because social objectives need not represent states of "welfare" in the customary sense of the term. Mobilization for war, minimization of change even at the cost of freezing output, and as the most extreme case, a scorched earth policy are all possible macrogoals for the attainment of which an "optimum" path may be sought. Nor should the term optimum be interpreted in the narrow sense of some quantitative, not to say, pecuniary maximum, as we do when we speak of a Pareto optimum. Homeostatic processes assuring a traditional standard of living may serve as social objectives no less than the maximization of the flow of consumer goods or of the terminal capital stock (turnpike theory).

This multiplicity of social objectives, coupled with neutrality toward any value judgments, have convinced me that terms such as "normative" or "optimum" should be avoided when defining an alternative approach to positive analysis. What is at stake is quite generally the *search for*

the economic means suitable for the attainment of any stipulated end.
To this procedure I have assigned the label of *instrumental analysis.*[12]

As is true of most methodological issues, the relevance of instrumental
analysis for the solution of growth problems can be understood much
better by its application than by a formal exposition. Therefore the
following comments will limit themselves to a bare minimum, concentrating on the two critical points emphasized previously – stringency of
analysis and social scope.[13]

1. What, first of all, distinguishes instrumental from positive analysis
is the "inversion of the problem."[14] In accord with the hypothetico-
deductive method, positive economic theory in all its variants takes as
given (a) an initial state of the system, (b) behavioral "laws of motion,"
based on generalized observations or on "useful fictions" (Friedman,
Machlup), and (c) constraints of an institutional and technological
nature, including public controls. From these data are derived actual
past states (explanation) and future states (prediction) of the system,
as well as the paths connecting such states with the initial conditions.

Contrariwise, instrumental analysis takes as *given* not only the initial
but also the *terminal* state – the latter being "known" through explicit
stipulation of a macrogoal toward which the system is to move. The
unknowns to be determined are (a) suitable *paths* over which the system
can move toward the macrogoal, (b) *behavioral and motivational patterns*
that set the system on such paths and keep it to them, and, possibly,
(c) public controls suitable to elicit the appropriate motivations. Finally,
the link between data and unknowns is forged by our knowledge of the
pertinent laws of nature and engineering rules, including those *psycho-
logical laws* that relate specific behavior to specific motivations, and
of certain *empirical generalizations* describing the manner in which the
social environment and, in particular, public controls affect motivations.

Thus, in contrast to the deductive procedure of positive analysis that
argues "forward" from behavioral premises to terminal states, instrumental analysis resembles induction by searching "backward" for the
determinants of given states. However, it differs from induction by taking
the terminal states and processes as given, not by observation, but by
stipulation. Methodologically speaking, it falls into the category of

---

[12] I have discussed the relationship of instrumental analysis to other "goal-oriented"
procedures, such as welfare economics and linear programming, in *OEK,*
pp. 261–63.

[13] Readers interested in the logical and methodological ramifications of instrumental
analysis are again referred to my publications listed in footnote 9 of this
chapter.

[14] The expression is taken from J. Tinbergen, *On the Theory of Economic Policy,*
Amsterdam, 1952, p. 14.

"heuristics" which, even though it differs in logical procedure from deductive reasoning, is by no means in conflict with it. Rather, instrumental analysis resembles the mental process by which the premises .of any deductive syllogism are established.

It is true, there are no formal rules of inference, observance of which would perforce guide us to the right answer. The answer must be discovered as one of the possibilities that are implied in the nature of the problem. However, the more strictly we delineate the problem by precisely defining initial and terminal states and the criteria for the selection of the path, the fewer the remaining alternatives and the more determinate the solution. Moreover, the link with engineering rules and the underlying laws of nature confers on the procedure a degree of empirical relevance – the "means" thus derived are true causes of the stipulated effect – that the conclusions of positive theorizing based on "behavioral axioms" sadly lack.[15]

2. Establishing the paths and the behavioral and motivational patterns suitable for the attainment of a preordained economic macrogoal is the primary task of instrumental analysis. Our subsequent investigations will concentrate on these requirements for goal-adequate motion of the system. However, the findings thus obtained will not tell us anything about the real states or processes that materialize through the autonomous motions of the system under investigation, nor about the coincidence or discrepancy of real as compared with goal-adequate states. To assure such coincidence, in many cases another step must be taken, that is, a *practical step of intervention,* geared to adapt economic reality to the design fashioned by instrumental analysis. There lies the importance of *public controls.*

The systemic role of such controls can perhaps best be understood if we place them beside the .circular mechanisms on whose operation the classical theories of growth were founded. Just as those mechanisms were supposed to bring the behavior of the "parts" in accord with the functional requirements of the "whole," so it is the task of instrumental controls to achieve a "fit" with the help of deliberate measures of economic policy – a contrived system taking the place of a self-regulating one.

Although the practical application of such measures transcends the range of scientific inquiry, the discovery of *which controls are goal-adequate in a given context* is part of instrumental analysis proper. Speci-

---

[15] For further clarification, see the references quoted in footnote 9 of this chapter. See also N. R. Hanson, *Patterns of Discovery,* London, 1958, especially Ch. IV, and the writings of G. Polya. Instrumental analysis coincides with what C. S. Peirce (*Collected Papers,* Cambridge, Mass., 1931) has defined as *retroduction.*

fically, a means–ends nexus needs to be established between public controls and the behavioral–motivational patterns which, in a prior stage of instrumental analysis, are found suitable for goal attainment. Here we encounter a special instance of what is called "social causation."[16] With this problem in mind, we have included in the catalog of "data" of instrumental analysis the "empirical generalizations describing the manner in which the social environment, in particular public controls, affect motivations."

It must be admitted that the branch of social psychology concerned with this problem is still in a rudimentary state and that the reliable generalizations so far discovered are few.[17] For this reason, it has rightly been suggested that, at the present state of our knowledge, a pragmatic attitude, willing to experiment with alternative hypotheses is indicated.[18]

3. To the extent to which this final step of instrumental analysis succeeds in devising goal-adequate controls, a definite link is established between the economic core process and its *political environment*. But an even closer tie is constituted from the very outset by the stipulation of the macrogoal.

So far we have left it open to whom such stipulation is to be entrusted. There is, of course, no objection to a growth theorist, pursuing instrumental analysis in the privacy of his study, positing any conceivable terminal state. However, any attempt at validating such a choice on the basis of "objective criteria" has so far failed, and we must be aware that we overstep the conventional boundaries of economics and of science generally when we decide in favor of one among the multitude of possibly conflicting goal states.[19] In practice the goalsetter is a political authority, and his decision acquires at least political legitimacy when it is taken in accord with ruling constitutional principles.

However, before looking more closely at this second channel which, in the context of instrumental analysis, connects the economic domain with its environment, a ghost needs be laid to rest. In tying our analysis to political choices based on intersubjectively undemonstrable value judgments, are we not completely surrendering the scientific objectivity of our investigations?

[16] See Robert M. MacIver, *Social Causation,* Boston, 1942, especially Part III.
[17] For details, see *OEK,* pp. 147–56, and *EMASE,* 26–32, 185–88.
[18] See Robert L. Heilbroner, "On the Possibility of a Political Economics," *Journal of Economic Issues,* December 1970, pp. 19–20. See also Chapter 28 of this book.
[19] The reader will realize that these statements reflect the agnostic position of "scientific value relativism." For a divergent view, see Hans Jonas, "Economic Knowledge and the Critique of Goals," in *EMASE,* pp. 67–87; also see my rejoinder, *ibid.,* pp. 192–99.

Perhaps the best answer to this challenge is a comparison of the instrumental procedure with the engineering processes that led to the production of the atom bomb. No doubt, when the decision was taken to manufacture, not to say to *use* the bomb in the service of certain objectives (no matter what these may have been), the decision makers were thrown back on value judgements, whose wisdom has remained controversial to this day. The technical operations involved in the *making* of the bomb, however, were quite untouched by value considerations. They rested on factors resulting from value-free research, namely a set of engineeing rules that were themselves derived from laws of nature.

In a comparable manner the goals to be subjected to instrumental analysis are the value-laden outcome of a political decision and are as such beyond the concern of the analyst. His work begins only after the macrogoals have been chosen and is confined to the search for suitable means of reaching the objectives. This search is based on analogous laws and rules, the objective nature of which has already been touched upon. Moreover, the instrumental findings lend themselves to empirical falsification in the best tradition of the scientific method.

On the other hand, the metaeconomic significance of the instrumental procedure is that it reconstitutes economics as a chapter in the comprehensive study of man and society. It does so by establishing a firm link between the dimension of political decision making and the dimension of scientific economic inquiry in choosing both a strategy of goal-setting and a tactic of goal-seeking. In other words, instrumental analysis transforms the "pure economics" of postclassical origin into a "political economics."

This phenomenon manifests itself most clearly whenever the quest of the conditions appropriate to the attainment of a macrogoal leads the researcher beyond the boundaries of economic core processes into the wider sociopolitical environment. To be specific, I will anticipate a finding subsequently demonstrated in detail.[20] It concerns the manner in which Balanced Growth can be restored in a market system after some growth stimulus has distorted it. We shall see that "dynamic equilibium" cannot be recaptured within the structure of a laissez-faire market, but requires ongoing public control. Thus, only a change in the initially prevailing social framework, partly substituting centralized for decentralized decision making, can accomplish goal realization.

It should be noted that this manner of reintegrating economics with social science at large must be strictly distinguished from the popular call for "interdisciplinary research." Not only do we lack at present "a

---

[20] See Chapters 14 and 18.

viable language or translation devices by which the different social sciences can be brought into systematic cooperation,"[21] but all the objections raised earlier against the positive approach to economics proper are compounded when more inclusive social analysis is at stake. The instrumental technique is protected from such pitfalls by its emphasis on political control, which either neutralizes the influence of the environmental forces or indicates the manner,in which these forces can be reoriented so as to harmonize with the required behavior of the intrasystemic factors.

One can well argue that instrumental analysis has gained relevance only recently owing to our expanding power of control over the environment at large. Political economics and its instrumental technique are, indeed, geared to an age in which passive submission to inexorable blind mechanisms is gradually being superseded by the deliberate design of the socioeconomic process.

IV

After such strong emphasis on the multiplicity of possible goals on which instrumental analysis can orient itself, and on the large variety of institutional and sociopsychological variables that it can accommodate, my intention to conduct all substantive investigations in a highly simplified frame of reference may come as an anticlimax.

First of all, throughout the book, I shall stipulate *dynamic equilibrium* or *steady growth* as both the initial and the terminal state of the system. But, to quote Hahn and Matthews once more, this is not to imply that I share the "general preoccupation with the state of steady growth." Quite to the contrary, my concern will be with typical *disequilibria* as they arise under the impact of changes in the major growth stimuli – labor supply, supply of natural resources, and technology – and with the *paths* an economic system must pursue in order to resolve such disequilibria.

If I read the literature correctly, neither of these problems has so far found the attention it deserves under the aspect of empirically useful theorizing. At the same time it should be clear that the subsequent investigations are far from attempting an inclusive theory of growth. They are meant to offer no more than a few building blocks for a theoretical edifice that itself is in the early stages of growth.

Perhaps it should also be stressed that steady growth as a frame of reference fits quite well in the historical context in which growth processes take their course at this juncture. To the extent to which the stabilization policies of the mature countries are successful, a state of the system will be approximated of which dynamic equilibrium is a valid abstraction.

[21] See *EMASE*, p. 177.

At the other end of the scale, the lowest level of underdevelopment can be conceived as a type of stationary state. Finally, certain intermediary stages of development, combining full capital utilization with a large supply of idle labor, can be understood as moving from one rate of growth to a higher one.

As far as the *institutional framework* is concerned, account will be taken of free market systems as well as of fully collectivized economies. Mixed types, which predominate in present-day industrial organization, will be taken up whenever the function of controls is discussed. All systems will be treated as closed.

A primary distinction will be made between structure analysis and motor or force analysis. *Structure analysis* studies the configurations in which the elements of an economic system – inputs and outputs, employment and income, savings and investments, etc., – must be arranged if the transformation of the initial into the stipulated terminal state is to be achieved. These configurations have two aspects: one, physical or technical; the other, social. *Technical* relations are concerned with the manner in which resources can be combined; the sequence of stages of production through which natural resources are converted into finished output; the coordination of specific sectors of production to assure steady replacement; and, under conditions of growth, the expansion of material resources. *Social* relations, on the other hand, refer to the dominant type of decision making, centralized or decentralized; the order of ownership; the ruling systems of communication and sanction, for example, based on personalized command or on an anonymous price mechanism. Both types of structural relations operate as constraints on the motion of the respective systems and as such determine the range of feasible *paths* toward the stipulated terminal state.

Structure analysis is only preliminary to *motor or force analysis*. It is the latter that raises economics above the level of a mere engineering science by studying the patterns of behavior and motivation that initiate and sustain the motion of the system along the structurally determined path. These patterns themselves are closely related to the prevailing social structure that defines the institutional framework within which economic activity is to operate. Force analysis has a special significance in market systems, whose goal-adequate performance depends on the interlocking of innumerable microdecisions and on the concordance of these microdecisions with the required macroprocesses.

Part I of our investigation is concerned with the construction of a basic model that reproduces the essential features, structural and motorial, of dynamic equilibrium. In the subsequent parts this model is applied to the study of "changes in the rate of change" of labor supply in Part II, of natural resources in Part III, and of technology in Part IV. Both increases and decreases in the rate of growth will be examined, processes that will prove far from symmetrical. In Part III, we shall also consider the problem of "recycling" resources, an issue that, together with limitations in the general rate of growth, is gaining importance in the context of our ecological concerns.

2

Patterns of economic growth

The most promising way of coming to grips with our problem is through a precise circumscription of the phenomenon of growth. To do so, we must first of all distinguish economic *growth* from economic *change* in general. The wider concept, change, is to refer to any conceivable alteration of an economic system, comprising not only expansions and contractions of aggregate states and processes, but also relative shifts within a constant aggregate as induced, for example, by a change in tastes. Of growth, on the other hand, we shall speak only when the system varies in the aggregate. This gives the term a broader meaning including also decline, covering not only contraction in the absolute sense but also a mere fall in the rate of growth. In order to isolate the particular problems in which we are interested, we shall narrow down this definition even further, excluding from it what, in the wake of Keynesian theory, has been labelled "changes in the level of activity." Whereas the latter describe varying degrees of utilization of a *given* stock of resources, growth as here understood is bound up with *changes* in the *size* or the *productivity* of at least one resource factor.

In much of the literature the concept of growth is used in a still more restrictive sense, as applying only to per capita increases in output or consumption. This definition excludes all processes relating to a mere "widening" of the system – a term familiar in the theory of capital – which refers to processes that extend the structure of production in an isomorphic manner. Considering the importance of these phenomena, for example, for the absorption of an increase in population, with technology unchanged, such a limitation seems unwarranted.

Growth processes as here defined lend themselves to further differentiation according to *growth patterns*. Following Harrod[1] we distinguish between once-over and continuing growth. *Once-over* growth refers to the effect on an economic system of a single change (increase or decrease) in the supply or technical efficiency of one or more basic factors. Examples

[1] See R. F. Harrod, *Toward a Dynamic Economics,* London, 1948, Lecture One.

are a once-occurring influx of immigrants or one particular technical improvement. After such a single act of change has occurred the system is supposed to operate again under the previously prevailing conditions.

By contrast, *continuing* growth is the result of a continuing change in one or more resource factors, representing either *steady* growth with a constant positive or negative rate of change, or *unsteady* growth with varying rates of change. The isolated effect of a constant rate of population increase illustrates the steady pattern, whereas sequences of irregular rises in productivity exemplify the unsteady pattern.

It is noteworthy that, following Harrod's lead, many studies of growth omit the analysis of once-over growth patterns altogether. In Harrod's view these patterns can be "satisfactorily handled by the apparatus of static theory . . . since the familiar static equations define the new position."[2] To the retort that, in addition to the new position, we are also interested in the path over which this position is to be reached, Harrod answers that "this is making much ado about a trivial matter." In fact, the path of a once-over growth adjustment is a very complex phenomenon. It poses, even if in a simplified form, most of the problems that arise during the traverse from one growth path to another one; these problems are our major concern. For this reason the latter could also be defined as "dynamic once-over growth" patterns, superimposing a once-over change on a movement of steady growth.

What requires further clarification is the concept of "steady growth." Taken as a positive concept, that is, as an abstraction from experience, population increase is probably the only phenomenon that approximates the condition of a relatively constant rate of change. Therefore if, as was stated in Chapter 1, steady growth is to serve as our overall frame of reference, the justification of this choice must lie elsewhere.

A terminological clue will be helpful. Steady growth also goes by the name of "dynamic equilibrium," a label that points to a logical kinship with stationary equilibrium. Now in accordance with Marshall's well-known definition, neoclassical economics tends to a positive interpretation of stationary equilibrium as the state "which economic forces would bring about if the general conditions of life were stationary for a run of time long enough to enable them all to work out their full effect."[3] By substituting "undergoing steady change" for "stationary," one might think of adopting Marshall's rendering as an interpretation of dynamic equilibrium. However, any economic equilibrium must be sustained by particular

[2] *Ibid.*, p. 7.
[3] Alfred Marshall, *Principles of Economics*, London, 1927, p. 347.

behavior patterns and, as we pointed out earlier, to take it for granted that actual behavior patterns are generally equilibrating, that is, stable and mutually consistent, is a highly dubious assumption.

Machlup,[4] in accusing Marshall of the fallacy of misplaced concreteness, denies that the equilibrium concept has any operational meaning. He wants it understood as no more than a methodological device in analogy to controlled experiments in the physical sciences. To him equilibrium describes "a constellation of selected interrelated variables so adjusted to one another that no inherent tendency to change prevails in the model which they constitute." If then, in a mental experiment, we introduce a "disequilibrating change," we can derive the "sequence of adjusting changes until we reach a situation in which, barring another disturbance from the outside, everything could go on as it is," that is, "a new equilibrium."

Despite his protestation, by relating the equilibrium concept to the absence of any "inherent tendency to change," Machlup still remains on the level of positive analysis, along with Marshall and his followers. How else than through prior knowledge of the prevailing behavior patterns can we pronounce about the "inherent tendencies of the variables"? Unless we have the right to assume that the particular patterns yielding a state of "no change" are, in fact, operative in the real world, why bother studying deviations from, and adjustment toward, such a state?

II

The legitimacy as well as the usefulness of stationary and dynamic equilibria rest on different foundations. We enter here for the first time the dimension of instrumental analysis. From the instrumental perspective, rather than depicting, on however high a level of abstraction, some empirical state or process or serving as a methodological device, both equilibria describe stipulated macrogoals to be accomplished under very special structural and motorial conditions. We shall subsequently subject the pertinent goals and the conditions of their attainment to a detailed investigation. For the present purpose of definition, enumeration of the main features of these goals must suffice. They have in common the properties of *continuous, full, and efficient utilization* of the available inputs. They differ insofar as in stationary equilibrium the aggregate of inputs or basic resources is treated as constant, whereas in dynamic

---

[4] See F. Machlup, "Equilibrium and Disequilibrium: Misplaced Concreteness and Disguised Politics," *Economic Journal*, Vol. LXVIII, March 1958, pp. 1–24.

equilibrium the aggregate is supposed to grow or decline at a constant rate.[5]

In order to pinpoint the precise structural and motorial conditions of dynamic equilibrium – our future frame of reference – it is preferable to treat this concept not as a datum but as a process to be derived from a state of no growth, that is, from stationary equilibrium. This will lead to important insights into controversial issues such as the "pure" structure of real capital unaffected by growth itself and the nature of profits. However, before we describe the stationary structure of production, our initial datum, a word must be said about the *level of aggregation* appropriate to our investigation.

Obviously all levels of aggregation are not equally suitable for the study of all problems. It is in the nature of relative prices as a set of exchange ratios between individual commodities that the interdependence of such prices can be adequately depicted only in a model as highly disaggregated as the Walrasian. On the other hand, in the theory of income and employment, a two-sector model such as the Keynesian has proved to be an effective tool.

Now the particular problems of growth, which are in the center of our interest, concern matters such as the building up and wearing down of fixed capital, the accumulation and decumulation of working capital, the relationship between these capital stocks and the flows of output, the effect of technical change on capital formation and employment capacity, and related topics. It cannot be denied that each of these problems has also a microeconomic aspect. But our investigation will, on the whole, concentrate on those macroeconomic issues that are independent of the peculiarities of individual units or even industries. For this reason the level of aggregation chosen here is very much higher than the one applied, for example, in input–output analysis. At the same time the Keynesian model is too highly aggregated for our purpose. Dealing with production problems we require a model that depicts not only the "value dimension" of income–expenditure flows and asset stocks but also the "physical dimension" of technically differentiated inputs and outputs. These considerations

---

[5] Our definition implicitly denies that there is "a blind mechanism so constituted that it makes continual trial and error adjustments toward equilibrium," which is the conventional interpretation of Walras's *tâtonnements* (see Professor W. Jaffe's comment in his edition of L. Walras, *Elements of Pure Economics*, Homewood, Ill., 1954, p. 520). Yet it is compatible, for example, with Domar's interpretation of an equilibrium rate of growth as subject to specific requirements in the relationship between the savings and the capital-output ratio (see E. Domar, "Capital Expansion, Rate of Growth, and Employment," in *Essays in the Theory of Growth*, New York, 1957, pp. 70–82), and also concurs with Leontief's open input–output model, in which a stipulated bill of goods functions as the macrogoal.

have resulted in a three-sector schema supplemented by a multistage schema, to the exposition of which we now turn.[6]

[6] In earlier publications (Lowe, "A Structural Model of Production," *loc. cit.*, and "Structural Analysis of Real Capital Formation," (*loc. cit.*), I traced the history of this schema, of which I restate here only the culminating points. Disregarding the general suggestions contained in Quesnay's *Tableau Économique*, we can determine two rather disparate sources for our sector model. One is Marx's schemata of "simple" and "expanded" reproduction, (*The Capital*, Kerr edition, Chicago, 1933, Vol. 2, Ch. XX); and the other is J. B. Clark's (*The Distribution of Wealth*, New York, 1899, Chs. XVIII–XX) "group system of production."

The stage model, which is more familiar to traditional economics, is usually traced back to E. v. Boehm-Bawerk (*Positive Theory of Capital,* London, 1891, Book II, Section IV). It was, however, described much earlier by Karl Marx in *Theorien ueber den Mehrwert,* Stuttgart, 1905, Vol. 1, pp. 198–231 (according to Engels' testimony the book was written between 1861 and 1863), and later also by Clark (*loc. cit.,* pp. 268–75) in a much more adequate fashion. The first synthesis of the two models was undertaken by F. A. Burchardt ("Die Schemata des stationaeren Kreislaufs bei Boehm-Bawerk und Marx," *Weltwirtschaftliches Archiv,* Kiel, Vol. 34, 1931, pp. 525–64, and Vol. 35, 1932, pp. 116–76). The composite model that I have expounded here is an elaboration of Burchardt's schema. It adds the appropriate stock variables to the customary flow variables and, above all, extends the sector analysis by substituting a three-sector model for the two-sector models used by both Marx and Clark. The conditions for such aggregation that avoid distortion of prices and quantities of inputs and outputs have recently been investigated by M. Morishima, *Marx's Economics,* Cambridge (England), 1973, Ch. 8. The major condition, "sector-wise identity of the value-composition of capital," is fulfilled in all our models of the growth process. For an extensive review of the problem, see also H. T. N. Gaitskell, "Notes on the Period of Production," *Zeitschrift fuer Nationaloekonomie,* Vol. 9, 1938, pp. 215–44.

3

A schema of industrial production

If at any point in time we were to undertake a census of an industrial community's wealth in physical terms, we would find four different stocks of real assets: a stock of labor; a stock of natural resources; a stock of durable equipment goods, such as plant, machinery, residential buildings; and a stock of other goods of rather diverse physical forms and economic uses, which needs further specification.

We would find these stocks distributed among a number of productive units whose activity consists in converting, through certain technical processes, portions of some or all of these stocks into new goods. This activity describes what is meant by "production" in the technical sense of the term – the only sense in which we are interested at the moment.

What we have said so far refers to any sociopolitical order of the economic process, market or collectivist or to any of the mixes of these opposites. The only condition that all these orders must fulfill to fit into our picture of the productive process is that they be industrial systems. Provisionally we call *industrial* any process of production that uses, as factors of production, not only labor and materials but a stock of equipment goods. The latter term itself will be defined presently as we undertake a further classification of our basic stocks.

First, we can distinguish between *original* stocks – labor and natural resources, which shall be treated as the ultimate data of the productive process – and *manufactured* stocks, represented by the last two types of goods included in our list.

Second, concentrating on the manufactured stocks in particular, we may subdivide them according to the "degree of completion." We then distinguish between *unfinished* and *finished* goods, with the latter defined as those that are ready for use. Conventionally the group of unfinished goods is subdivided into raw materials and semimanufactured goods, but there is no easy criterion for this distinction. Individual production as a technical process consists of an unbroken chain of operations by which some natural resource is transformed into finished goods. Any caesura made in order to establish technical stages of completion is arbitrary. We shall meet this problem again when we try to set up a "stage model"; for the moment we leave it open. However, in this chain of operations we have to find a place for activities such as transportation and commerce. We shall include them in our definition of production and regard a good as completed only when it has reached its final place and time of use.

Third, in narrowing down our field of vision still further, we can classify the group of finished goods ready for use according to their specific characteristics as either *consumer goods* or *equipment goods*. The former are used up in the households, the latter in the process of production. The term "used up" describes exactly what happens to consumer goods and equipment goods in distinction to what happens to unfinished goods.[1] The latter are "used" but not "used up" during the process of production.

Now the physical appearance of a finished good does not always clearly indicate in which group it belongs. An obvious example is coal. It can serve, on the one hand, as a consumer good in the household and, on the other hand, as an auxiliary material and even as an unfinished good (chemical industry) in production. Still, in any concrete case, it should be possible to establish the role of each good unambiguously.

Fourth, we have so far assumed that the various groups of goods, unfinished and finished, consumer and equipment goods, are currently put to use either in the households or the productive units. This need not be so. Part of the stock of each group may be held as inventories for future use or for precautionary reasons. Important as such inventories are in practice, the level of abstraction of our analysis will allow us to disregard them.

With this terminology we have so far skirted the ambiguous term of *capital* in our system of classification. We cannot, however, dispense with it entirely and must, therefore, define its precise usage.

The difficulties with the concept of capital arise from the fact that it is used in no less than three different meanings which overlap in a complicated manner. Once these differences are clearly recognized, confusion can easily be avoided by adding qualifying adjectives to the main term.

Our first distinction is between real capital goods and money capital funds or, briefly, between real capital and money capital. In agreement with convention we define *real capital* as the aggregate of fixed capital (or equipment goods) and of working capital (or goods in process), that is, as the complex of goods other than natural resources required to carry out continuous production. This aggregate may also be called "producer goods." Real capital in this sense is a condition for the operation of any

[1] The problem of residuals will be taken up in Chapter 20, of this book.

system under whatever order of social organization, once the primitive stage of mere gathering is overcome. *Money capital,* on the other hand, is bound up with market systems. It consists of money funds accumulated for the purpose of acquiring real capital and other productive factors. Money capital in this sense might be regarded as another instrument applied in the productive process of market systems.

Cutting across this "technical" meaning, which attaches to the terms of both real capital and money capital, is the "enterprise" meaning of capital. It refers to the application of any type of good, real capital goods (fixed and working capital) and consumer goods, and also of the funds that constitute money capital, to the purpose of creating a money surplus. Such application of the goods and funds concerned is confined to particular suborders of market systems, namely systems containing at least a core of free enterprise or of "manipulation of market chances," to use Max Weber's term. We are here in an altogether different dimension of the economic process, in which the speculative outlook of the owner or disposer of the respective means takes the place of objective technical requirements. It would certainly clarify matters if both theorists and men of affairs were to use different terms for the specific phenomena falling within the respective dimensions. Because the convention of applying the term capital to both dimensions seems unshakeable, one had better speak of *speculative capital* when referring to the surplus-yielding use of goods and funds.[2]

In summary, we contrast real capital and money capital, on the one hand, with speculative capital, on the other hand, and subdivide real capital into fixed and working capital. We shall furthermore use the term "equipment" synonymously with fixed capital, a term in which we include also "auxiliary goods," such as industrial fuel and lubricants. Working capital, on the other hand, will also be noted as "intermediate goods."

Thus far we have dealt with the types of goods that make up the physical wealth of an industrial community. It will also be necessary for us to distinguish the *productive units* in which these goods are combined with one another and with other factors, or from whose productive activity the goods emanate. In this respect our fundamental distinction is between consumer-good and equipment-good industries.

We have thus far confined the terms consumer good and equipment good to the *finished* products ready to be used up. In now classifying the two basic industrial sectors, it is convenient to extend the meaning of the

---

[2] Our definitions of speculative capital points to the only legitimate use of the terms "capitalism" and "capitalist production." The latter term should never be used to include all economic systems that apply real capital, if confusion of a technical with a social classification is to be avoided.

terms so that they include all stages of production that lead up to the finished good. In other words, our category of consumer-good *industries* includes not only the finished dress ready in the retail store for sale but also the preceding stages of cotton growing, spinning, weaving, manufacturing, and transporting the technically finished product. The same considerations are valid for the inclusion of mining, pig iron production, steel production, etc., in our definition of equipment-good *industries*.

Because the physical distinction between the "goods" belonging to the two groups is blurred, it cannot be expected that, in practice, the respective industrial *sectors* can be clearly defined. For instance, coal mining or chemical production, taken as a whole, fall into both sectors, and it is again only the concrete situation that can tell us where to draw the exact dividing line.

One last important point. For reasons that are central to our argument, I propose further to distinguish between those equipment-good industries that *produce equipment to be applied in the consumer-good industries* and those that *produce equipment for the equipment-good industries themselves*. Even more than is the case in the relation between the consumer-good sector and the equipment-good sector as a whole, the actual productive units within the two subsectors of the equipment-good sector overlap in the type of equipment they produce. As we shall see, this does not reduce the significance for the operation of the system of the relative size of output in these two subsectors.

II

We have completed our survey of what can be called the physical balance sheet of an industrial community. We now shall examine the manner in which the items in this balance sheet operate through time. In other words, we proceed from the analysis of the physical stocks of wealth to the analysis of the *physical flows of production*.

A continuous process of production requires that the industrial sectors, the various stages of completion into which each sector is subdivided, and the portions of each of the four basic stocks of goods and services assigned to the individual productive units in every stage of every sector be arranged in a definite order. We shall call a *schema of production* the model that depicts the reproduction of the principal stocks and flows in the technically required sequence. Our task now is to elaborate such a schema of production in terms sufficiently precise to make the schema a tool for further analysis.

We begin with the technical sequence of production of a particular consumer good, say, a dress. Model I depicts the essential features.

$$N_1 \cup R_1 \cup F_1 \qquad \rightarrow \omega_1 = \text{cotton}$$
$$N_2 \cup R_2 \cup F_2 \cup \omega_1 \rightarrow \omega_2 = \text{yarn}$$
$$N_3 \cup R_3 \cup F_3 \cup \omega_2 \rightarrow \omega_3 = \text{cloth} \qquad\qquad\qquad (I)$$
$$N_4 \cup R_4 \cup F_4 \cup \omega_3 \rightarrow \omega_4 = \text{dress}$$

Our model contains four sets of causal relations, expressed by arrows, between a number of physical magnitudes. The causal relationship signifies no more than that the magnitudes on the right side of the arrows are the productive result or output of the several inputs appearing on the left side of the arrows. Most of the input items are printed in capital letters, indicating that they refer to stocks, whereas the lower-case symbols on both sides of the arrows denote flows. Symbol $\cup$ connecting the inputs indicates that for the purpose of production these items are combined in fixed proportions. Otherwise the symbols used refer to some of the groups of goods and services discussed in Section I. The N's stand for stocks of labor, the term to be understood in the wider sense as comprising all human agents performing productive services; the R's stand for stocks of natural resources, and the F's for stocks of fixed capital or equipment. On the other hand, the flow variables denoted by ω stand for items of working capital or intermediate goods.

The model describes four successive stages, indicated by subscripts, through which a given stock of natural resources, R, is transformed with the help of simultaneously and successively operating stocks of labor, other natural resources, and equipment into a finished consumer good. The stages have been chosen in such a manner that in every stage a qualitatively different type of equipment is applied; say, gin–spindle–loom–sewing machine, which gives the stage order of the production flow an appearance of technical realism. However, the appearance is spurious insofar as a number of other intermediate stages and the later stages of transportation, wholesaling, and retailing are disregarded. More important still, it is only in certain mechanical processes of production that production stages can be so easily distinguished by the various types of equipment used. The situation is quite different, for example, for most chemical processes. This, however, will in no way prejudice our conclusions, so long as we remember that our model, and most of the models that follow, represent flows with the help of "stills," that is, snapshots taken at a moment in time.

Although elements of each one of the basic factor stocks operate in every stage, not only their technical form but also their relative significance differs from stage to stage. This is particularly true of factor R. It plays its main role in the first stage; but, because every plant in the successive stages has to have a location, some R representing land must be included there too. More interesting is the fact that from the second stage on, the output ω of the preceding stage figures as input in the subsequent stage.

It is through this successive shifting of varying forms of intermediate goods, first as output and then as input, that the gradual process of transformation of the natural resource into a finished good, that is, the process of production is realized.

To assure *continuity of such production,* two conditions have to be fulfilled. First, the "active" factors, labor and equipment, have to operate in a technically predetermined manner upon the "passive" factor: natural resources, both in their original form and in their successive transformations as working capital. Second, the stocks of labor, equipment, and natural resources must be continuously replenished in proportion to what they release currently as input flows into actual production. With regard to the renewal of the stocks of labor and natural resources, our economic analysis has nothing to say. It is true that classical theory derives the supply of labor through a "circular mechanism" from the input of consumer goods. However, in accord with conventional theory, we shall treat a continuing supply of labor and of natural resources as "data" for our analysis.

The case is different with regard to fixed-capital goods or equipment. Here we come up against the characteristic, mentioned before, that distinguishes real capital in all its forms from the other factors of production; namely, that real capital is as much an output of the productive process as it is an input. In the present context this amounts to saying that the same model, which we used to symbolize the gradual maturation of a finished consumer good, must also be applicable to the production of an equipment good. By simply changing the nature of the inputs, we arrive at a sequence of stage outputs that reads: ore–pig iron–steel–machinery.

We see at once that this procedure creates a problem. In adding a second-stage model illustrating the production of equipment, we tacitly assume the presence of other equipment goods that can serve as input for the output of fixed capital, and we seem to be involved in an infinite technical regress. To extricate ourselves from this dilemma we might want to look for some kind of fixed-capital good that is produced with the help of labor and natural resources only. However, for us to encounter such an instrument within the total production flow of an industrial system would be unlikely. To find it we should have to go back to the earliest periods of human history when primitive man first picked up a stone to use it as a tool. Were we looking for a schema that depicted the secular technical process through which a primitive system can develop into an industrial economy, some such construction might prove helpful. However, what we want to know is the manner in which, *within an industrial system,* the existing stock of equipment is continuously physically renewed, not to say, expanded.

What is at stake can perhaps be best illustrated by a more elementary example. As a matter of fact, we meet a parallel problem in agricultural production, irrespective of the technical level at which such production is carried out. How can a given output of, say, wheat be maintained over time? Disregarding equipment altogether, we require for this purpose labor, land, and seed wheat. Again we treat labor and land as data; but where do we get seed wheat? This time the answer is simple: We have to put aside from the current wheat output a certain amount to be used in the next season as input.

Now we should realize that this solution rests upon two conditions – an economic and a technological one. The *economic* condition has been generally recognized. It postulates an act of "saving." To maintain the level of output, not to say, to increase it, we have to restrain current consumption and devote part of the currently available stock of goods to production for the future. However, we must realize that in the preceding example such an act of "gross saving" although a necessary, is not a sufficient condition for continuous production. To assure such production, that is, to utilize part of this year's output as next year's input, a technological condition must be fulfilled. The twofold application is possible only because of the *physical identity* of the consumer good, wheat, with the producer good, seed. To put it differently, the second condition for continuous production of wheat is its physical capacity of self-reproduction.

The lesson is obvious. Only if we can find in the mechanical sphere certain instruments that share with wheat and all other organic matter, including the human organism, the capacity for physical self-reproduction, can our problem be solved without historical regress. In other words, we have to look for some type of equipment that is technically suited, in conjunction with other productive factors, to reproduce itself as well as to produce other equipment. What we actually find is not one single such instrument but a comprehensive group of fixed-capital goods which are classified as *machine tools*. They are for industrial production what seed wheat and the reproductive system in animals are for agricultural production. They hold the strategic position in any industrial system, a system that can now be defined more precisely as that stage of economic-technical development in which machines are produced by machines.

It is this consideration which has led me to extend Marx's two-sector schema into a three-sector schema through the subdivision of the equipment-good sector into two subsectors – one producing equipment to be applied in the production of consumer goods, the other producing equipment to be applied in the replacement and (under conditions of growth) the expansion of the equipment operating in either equipment-good subsector. Although, as was stated previously, both types of equipment may be produced in one and the same productive unit, the two types themselves – looms and machine tools – are to be taken as technically specific and nonsubstitutable.[3]

III

We have now collected all the elements with the help of which the main physical and technical conditions for a continuous flow of industrial production can be described. To simplify understanding, I shall illustrate the schema of production valid for the system as a whole by a diagram.

There the order of production has been vertically divided into the two basic sectors: equipment-good industries on the left and consumer-good industries on the right, described as Sector I and Sector II, respectively. The consumer-good sector is represented by one finished good only, whereas the equipment-good sector has been subdivided into two sectors, Ia and Ib. Sector Ia produces the equipment applied in both Subsectors Ia and Ib, whereas Sector Ib supplies Sector II only. Technically this subdivision is relevant only for the final stage, in which the productive process of the equipment-good sector as a whole divides into different types of absolutely specific finished output. All sectors are horizontally divided into four stages as in Model I, representing from top to bottom the successive maturing of natural resources into finished goods.

On both sides of the schema are recorded the productive factors – labor, fixed-capital goods, and natural resources – the continuous application of which maintains the process of production. In each main sector these three factors appear at every stage. They are again denoted, first of all, by capital letters (N, R, F), to show that we start out from a number of given stocks. For the fixed-capital goods the particular physical form is indicated in which these stocks appear in every stage of each sector.

All other magnitudes, indicated by lower-case letters, indicate input flows and output flows over a certain period of time. Among these input flows we have the specific amounts of the three stocks of factors that enter the productive process at each stage during a given period. They represent (as n, r, and f, respectively) the hours of labor, the quantity of natural resources, and the wear and tear of equipment, which constitute the factor inputs over the period. The output flows are represented by shaded rectangles; they show, besides the output effect of the respective stage inputs, at each stage except the first, also the quantity of working capital that is transferred from the preceding stage. The outputs of the last stage are identical with the finished consumer and equipment goods.

[3] The earliest reference to the "power of self-reproduction" on the part of machines, which I have been able to find, is of all places in Samuel Butler, *Erewhon*, London, 1872, Chapter XXIV.

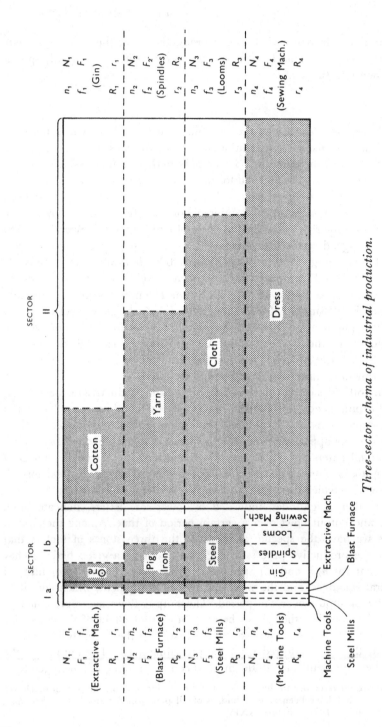

Three-sector schema of industrial production.

The didactic purpose of the schema is to represent the process of production as a number of interdependent flows that are themselves related to the system's basic stocks. Beginning with Sector II, we find there a vertical as well as a horizontal flow. Vertically, natural resources flow in progressive transformation down to the level of finished consumer goods. The continuity of this vertical flow depends, however, on the simultaneous presence of a horizontal flow, from Sector I to Sector II, of certain quantities of finished fixed-capital goods – large enough to replace at least the fixed-capital goods used up in every stage during the vertical flow occurring in Sector II.

A corresponding vertical flow occurs in Sector I. At first glance, however, there is an important difference between the two sectors with regard to the horizontal flow. In Sector II it is a horizontal flow from Sector I that replaces the worn-out equipment. In Sector I the currently used-up equipment is replaced from the output of that sector itself, more precisely, from the output of Subsector Ia. In other words, the horizontal flow consists of a portion of the vertical flow "turned back," that is, it is a circular flow.

This apparent asymmetry disappears if we contemplate the use to which the output of Sector II, that is, of final consumer goods is put. One part of this output is consumed by the human factor, labor, that operates in Sector II, whereas another part is consumed by the same type of factor employed in Sector I. We need not fall back upon the classical hypothesis that labor should be treated as if it were "produced" by the "input" of consumer goods (in the technical sense in which goods are produced) in order to interpret this utilization of the output of Sector II also in terms of a horizontal and a circular flow. Through the former, some consumer goods flow to the labor force employed in Sector I, whereas the latter provides for the labor force operating in Sector II.

It is these horizontal and circular flows that deserve special attention because they are disregarded in the conventional presentations of the productive mechanism. In accord with the Austrian concept of the "structure of production," developed by v. Boehm-Bawerk and popularized by L. v. Mises and F. A. v. Hayek, these presentations concentrate exclusively on the linear "downflows" through which natural resources are transformed into finished goods. As a rule, they fail to recognize the need for a special equipment-good sector. The production or reproduction of equipment is seen as a stage problem for the consumer-good sector, which is equivalent to treating fixed capital as if it were working capital.[4]

---

[4] The logical fallacies implied in this procedure, and the failure of the resulting model to elucidate the relevant problems, have been brilliantly expounded in F. A. Burchardt's paper cited in Chapter 2 of this book.

There are, indeed, as we saw, two vertical downflows in the production process. To keep it in continuous operation, however, two horizontal and two circular flows are required in addition. The former move part of the output of each sector to the opposite sector, whereas the latter channel back to the sectors part of their own finished output. Among them there is a peculiar kind of circular flow within the equipment-good sector, for which there is no parallel in the consumer-good sector. It refers to Subsector Ia where the input of machine tools in the sense defined above reproduces itself as output of the same stage. The analogous processes of self-reproduction relating to labor and organic natural resources fall outside the economic system. The absence of such a process of self-reproduction in the realm of inorganic resources raises for these goods the issue of "scarcity" in a particularly poignant sense.[5,6]

[5] Small wonder that since the eighteenth century this lack of self-replacement of inorganic materials has served as the focus for pessimistic predictions about the future of the industrial system. The further development of synthetic chemistry, by substituting the practically unlimited elements of the chemical realm for the scarce products of geological evolution, and the new technology of recycling the residuals from past production may well banish this spectre for the long-term future (see Chapter 20).

[6] After decades of being completely disregarded the circular processes of reproduction have, under the name of "whirlpools," suddenly acquired excessive popularity. An extreme position is taken by P. Sraffa (*Production of Commodities by Means of Commodities,* Cambridge, England, 1960) who eliminates linear processes of production altogether. Less extreme but still extravagant is the statement, "For the production of coal, iron is required; for the production of iron, coal is required; no one can say whether the coal industry or the iron industry is earlier or later in the hierarchy of production" (Dorfman, Samuelson, and Solow, *Linear Programming and Economic Analysis,* New York, 1958, p. 205; henceforth cited as *Dosso*). Now, it is true that coal, as a "finished equipment good" in the sense previously defined, is required for the production of iron, but the converse is not true. What we require for the production of coal is extractive machinery, in the production of which iron is an intermediate good, itself derived from the natural resource "ore" and transformed into extractive machinery with the help of the truly circular factor "machine tool." One need only to consider an increase in the aggregate demand for coal, that is, growth, in a system in which all real capital is fully utilized. Then we see at once that the critical bottleneck "in the hierarchy of production" arises in the machine tool stage and that only after capacity has been increased there, can the output of ore–steel–extractive machinery and, finally, coal be increased. Failing to pinpoint the true circularities will confuse our understanding of the theory of capital as much as did the linear "imperialism" of the Austrians. See also Chapter 17 of this book.

4

The circulation of fixed capital

So far our schema of industrial production has served as no more than an expository device for a commonsense picture of certain relations between the basic economic stocks and flows. With even a simpler model, J. B. Clark aimed at the same purpose. If his very fruitful suggestions have been eclipsed by the Austrian model of the structure of production, this is probably owing to the fact that Clark did not develop his didactic sketch into an instrument of analysis. This I propose to do now with our schema.

Both the vertical and the horizontal processes described lend themselves to such a transformation, which will provide the tools for our analysis of the capital problems. As a matter of fact, the horizontal processes describe in essence the circulation and, implicitly, also the conditions for the formation of fixed capital, whereas the vertical processes do the same for the working capital. It will be convenient to study the two processes separately and then to combine the results in a comprehensive treatment of the capital problem in a stationary system.

I

Our first step in transforming our schema into an analytical tool consists in consolidating the various stage inputs and outputs of our three sectors, Ia, Ib, and II, in terms of certain aggregates of *finished goods.* One group of such aggregates, the outputs of the three sectors, will henceforth be designated a, b, and z, respectively. This choice of letters is to emphasize the technical propinquity, under the aspect of production, of the finished outputs in the two subsectors of Sector I, from now on also called primary and secondary equipment, as compared with the technical properties of the consumer-good output of Sector II. Likewise the factor inputs (labor, natural resources, fixed-capital goods) in the three sectors will be designated as n_a, n_b, and n_z, and correspondingly for r and f, the subscripts indicating the place of application of each input.

Model II depicts the most general causal relationships between the consolidated inputs and outputs; the symbols are to be interpreted as in Model I.

$$[F_a \cdot d_a = f_{a_t}] \cup n_{a_t} \cup r_{a_t} \rightarrow a_t$$
$$[F_b \cdot d_b = f_{b_t}] \cup n_{b_t} \cup r_{b_t} \rightarrow b_t \qquad \qquad \text{(II)}$$
$$[F_z \cdot d_z = f_{z_t}] \cup n_{z_t} \cup r_{z_t} \rightarrow z_t$$

There is one important difference in the setup of Model II as compared with Model I. Inputs f, n, and r are now expressed as flow magnitudes, indicating the precise amount of each factor stock that "enters" the production flow during period t. Only for factor F is also the previous notation in stock terms maintained because only for fixed-capital goods is the precise relationship between total stock and flow over a given period an economic problem. This is indicated by the addition of variable d, which measures the prevailing rate of depreciation for the capital stock in each sector. Because Model II registers only the output of finished goods, the inputs and outputs relating to unfinished or working-capital goods do not appear. According to prevailing opinion their inclusion would amount to double-counting, a notion that we shall presently examine more closely.[1]

It hardly needs pointing out that consolidation of the physical inputs of individual production units into stage inputs representing entire industries, and the further consolidation of these stage inputs into aggregate sector inputs, raises a difficult aggregation problem. Because we shall presently transpose our model into a price-sum model, in which physically heterogeneous magnitudes become comparable in price terms, we can skirt this problem here. The conclusions that we are going to draw as to certain requirements of a physical nature are unaffected by this omission.

Model II depicts the most general and "loosest" form of an industrial structure. Far from presenting a random assemblage of inputs and outputs, however, it describes an order of these elements, namely, the minimum order required to assure one act of production in each sector. It does not establish any relationship among the inputs and outputs of different sectors – all it tells us is that certain input quantities yield certain output quantities over a stated period.

Much more can be said if we now stipulate that production be *continuous*. This amounts to introducing the first of the three properties – continuous, full, and efficient utilization of available resources – which served us earlier as the definition of an industrial process moving in equilibrium.[2] Utilizing the insight gained into the nature of the various horizontal flows, we can establish the necessary relationship between the outputs of Period 1 and the inputs in a subsequent Period 2, indicating

[1] See Chapter 5, Section II, and Chapter 6, Section I.
[2] See Chapter 2, Section II.

successive periods by prime and double-prime signs:

$$a' \geq f_a'' + f_b''$$
$$b' \geq f_z''$$
$$z' \geq n_a'' + n_b'' + n_z'' \tag{4.1}$$

Inequalities (4.1) represent the conditions that must be imposed on Model II if continuity of production is to be assured. They tell us, first, that at least part, possibly all, of the output of primary equipment produced in Period 1 will be physically required in the subsequent period as fixed-capital input in the two equipment sectors. Second, in the same manner part or even the whole of the output of secondary equipment must subsequently serve as fixed-capital input in the consumer-good sector. These two propositions are, of course, strictly valid only over a span of time covering the full life of the originally available stock of primary and secondary equipment. Such a time span and even longer ones are implied in our stipulation of "continuity." Third, part or even the whole of the output of Sector II during Period 1 must serve to sustain the productive efforts of the various groups of the labor force that operate during Period 2 in the three sectors of the system. The latter statement is physically true under the classical assumption that the output of consumer goods serves to "replace" the input of labor. It can also be interpreted in the wider sense that the output of the consumer-good sector is to be *distributed* among all three sectors *in proportion to* the quantities of homogeneous units of labor input in each of the three sectors. This interpretation underlies all subsequent statements about the relationship between n and z.

A comment is in order with regard to our treatment of *natural resources*. They do not appear in the inequalities 4.1, nor will they appear in subsequent sector models. The reason is that we are dealing here with the technical conditions of "resource replacement." Now, so far as *organic* resources, plants and animals, are concerned, they can and must be reproduced with the help of finished or unfinished goods (seeds, feeds, etc.). To that extent, deductions must be made from total gross output. Output and, in particular, the output of consumer goods, as it appears in subsequent models, must thus be understood as net of such deductions. *Inorganic* resources, on the other hand, have no place in our models since they are, in principle, irreplaceable. Like labor, they appear in the chain of reproduction only as inputs, not as outputs.[3]

---

[3] We arrive at the same conclusion if we stipulate that natural resources, untouched by labor and equipment, are to be treated as free goods. In choosing at this point a substantive justification for their exclusion, we prepare the way for a later discussion of the technology of "recycling" (see Chapter 20), which transforms the provision of basic resources into a genuine production problem.

II

Our next step consists in stipulating a more specific goal for the continuous process of production, thus introducing the second property of our definition of equilibrium. We now demand that all outputs of Period 1 and, disregarding natural resources, only these outputs are to become inputs of Period 2. We stipulate, in other words, that the available stock of labor and equipment be *fully utilized*. We are not yet in a position to introduce also the third property, namely, "efficient" utilization, although our failure to do so leaves the condition of "full" utilization in some respects indeterminate. For our present purposes this indeterminacy is irrelevant. Whatever level of utilization is decided upon, stipulating full utilization implies that this particular level be maintained through time for all resource units available. On this basis we can now establish a model for the *stationary process of reproduction* of finished goods.

1. By introducing into Model II conditions 4.1 interpreted as equalities, we obtain the skeleton of a stationary process both in symbolic and numerical terms[4]:

f	n	o			f	n	o	
$f_a \cup n_a \to a$					$1 \cup$	$20 \to$	5	
$f_b \cup n_b \to b$		(III)			$4 \cup$	$60 \to$	80	(III.i)
$f_z \cup n_z \to z$					$80 \cup$	$320 \to$	200	

where[5]

$$a = f_a + f_b; \qquad b = f_z; \qquad z = n_a + n_b + n_z$$

We can now be more explicit about the significance of the respective equalities. In the original formulation (4.1), they stated the *intertemporal* conditions for the continuity of the economic process by relating outputs and inputs of two successive periods of production. Now they reveal also the *intersectoral* structure within one and the same period. They stipulate, as it were, a production and exchange program that must be fulfilled if stationary equilibrium is to be attained and to be maintained. More precisely, such equilibrium requires not only a trisectoral *production* of specific outputs with the help of specific inputs but also a number of intersectoral *transfers* that must be completed before another period of production can get under way.

[4] Models III and III.i. omit not only the expressions for natural resources but also for the respective capital stocks. The latter have no function in the analysis of a circular flow that, by definition, does not undergo change (see, however, Section III).

[5] The equality $z = n_a + n_b + n_z$ is to be interpreted in the light of previous comments about Equation 4.1.

(a) Sector Ib's output of secondary equipment must be transferred *in its entirety* to Sector II in order to replace the used-up part of the secondary capital stock.

(b) Sector Ia's output must *in part* be transferred to Sector Ib in order to replace the used-up part of the primary capital stock operating in that sector.

(c) Sector II's output must *in part* be transferred to Sectors Ia and Ib in order to replenish the currently absorbed consumer goods.

2. Up to this point we have conducted our investigation in terms of *physical quantities* only. However, we cannot elaborate the production and transfer processes in full, unless we translate the physical relations into *value* or *price-sum* relations. With the help of the simplifying devices of treating the inputs of equipment goods *within* each sector as homogeneous (notwithstanding their absolute specificity as outputs, a and b) and of treating the units of labor inputs as homogeneous all through the system, we can derive the required price ratios from the preceding quantity models.

We begin by stipulating the unit price of the consumer-good output (assuming one good only) as our *numéraire;* that is, we are going to express the unit prices of secondary and primary equipment in terms of the unit price of the consumer good. By further equating the value or price sum of the consumer-good output, z_p, with the aggregate quantity of such output, z_q, we obtain the unit price of 1 for the consumer good. On this basis we can determine the unit price of labor input, the wage unit w, as the ratio of the price sum of consumer-good output, z_p, to total labor input $n_{(a+b+z)_q}$. It amounts in our Model III.i to $w = \frac{1}{2}$.

This now enables us to calculate the respective claims of the three sectors on the output of consumer goods. What is consumed in Sector II itself equals $w \cdot n_{z_q}$ units, amounting in our model to 160 units. This leaves for transfer to the other two sectors (see the preceding condition c) an amount of $z_q - w \cdot n_{z_q} = 40$ units.

This transfer takes place in two stages. First, the aggregate of $z_q - w \cdot n_{z_q}$ is to be transferred to Sector Ib, to be matched by a reverse transfer of the total output of secondary equipment (condition a), $b_q = 80$ units, to replace the worn-out part of the equipment in Sector II. It is from the exchange ratio of these two quantities

$$\frac{z_q - w \cdot n_{z_q}}{b_q}$$

that we derive the price of secondary equipment goods in terms of the price of consumer goods, namely, $40/80 = \frac{1}{2}$.

A similar exchange between consumer goods and primary equipment goods establishes the price of the latter. We know that Sector Ib can retain from its "import" of consumer goods only an amount equal to $w \cdot n_{b_q}$, that is, 30 units, which equal the value of its own labor input. The difference, equal to $w \cdot n_{a_q}$, amounting to 10 units, must be transferred to Sector Ia in order to obtain in reverse transfer the surplus of primary equipment left in Sector Ia, that is $a_q - f_{a_q}$, the amount f_{a_q} required for replacement in Sector Ia itself. The surplus amounts to 4 units, which serves as replacement in Sector Ib. Again, the exchange ratio

$$\frac{w \cdot n_{a_q}}{a_q - f_{a_q}}$$

yields the price of primary equipment goods in terms of the price of consumer goods, amounting to $2\frac{1}{2}$.[6]

3. Models IV and IV.i present our findings in a combined *quantity–price sum* arrangement, which shows for each sector the physical as well as the value order required for the stationary equilibrium of the system as a whole.

$$
\begin{array}{cccc}
f & n & o & p
\end{array}
$$

$$
\text{Ia}\begin{cases} f_{a_q} \cup n_{a_q} \to a_q \\ p_a \cdot f_{a_q} + w \cdot n_{a_q} = p_a \cdot a_q \quad \dfrac{w \cdot n_{a_q}}{a_q - f_{a_q}} \end{cases}
$$

$$
\text{Ib}\begin{cases} f_{b_q} \cup n_{b_q} \to b_q \\ p_a \cdot f_{b_q} + w \cdot n_{b_q} = p_b \cdot b_q \quad \dfrac{z_q - w \cdot n_{z_q}}{b_q} \end{cases} \quad \text{(IV)}
$$

$$
\text{II}\begin{cases} f_{z_q} \cup n_{z_q} \to z_q \\ p_b \cdot f_{z_q} + w \cdot n_{z_q} = p_z \cdot z_q \quad \dfrac{z_p}{z_q} \end{cases}
$$

		f		n		o		p

$$
\text{Ia}\begin{cases} 1 & \cup & 20 & \to & 5 & \\ 2.5 & + & 10 & = & 12.5 & \quad 2.5 \end{cases}
$$

$$
\text{Ib}\begin{cases} 4 & \cup & 60 & \to & 80 & \\ 10 & + & 30 & = & 40 & \quad 0.5 \end{cases} \quad \text{(IV.i)}
$$

$$
\text{II}\begin{cases} 80 & \cup & 320 & \to & 200 & \\ 40 & + & 160 & = & 200 & \quad 1 \end{cases}
$$

In addition, as supplements to the *physical equilibrium conditions* (Equation 4.1) specified as equalities, we obtain the following *inter-*

---

[6] This procedure of deriving equilibrium prices from equilibrium quantities elaborates a clue offered by Sraffa, *loc. cit.*, pp. 3–4.

sectoral price-sum or value equations for stationary equilibrium:

$$f_{a_v} = a_v - f_{b_v} \tag{4.2}$$
$$f_{b_v} = a_v - f_{a_v}$$
$$= n_{a_v} \tag{4.3}$$
$$= z_v - n_{b_v} - n_{z_v}$$
$$f_{z_v} = b_v$$
$$= n_{a_v} + n_{b_v} \tag{4.4}$$
$$= z_v - n_{z_v}$$

In words, the primary equipment required per period in Sector Ia must equal, in physical terms, the surplus of such equipment produced in Sector Ia over and above the requirements for replacement in Sector Ib. Conversely, the primary equipment required per period in Sector Ib must equal, in physical terms, the surplus of such equipment produced in Sector Ia over and above that sector's own requirements. But it must also equal, in value terms, that part of the aggregate output of consumer goods produced in Sector II claimed by the prime factors employed in Sector Ia. This, in turn, equals, in physical terms, the aggregate output of consumer goods minus the requirements of consumer goods in both Sectors II and Ib. Finally, the secondary equipment required per period in Sector II must equal, in physical terms, the output of Sector Ib. However, it must also equal, in value terms, the surplus of consumer goods produced in Sector II over and above that sector's own requirements, a difference that must equal, in physical terms, the joint requirements of consumer goods in Sectors Ia and Ib.[7]

Now it is a property of stationary equilibrium that the same relations that describe the *intersectoral* structure are also valid for the *intertemporal* structure if marked with the appropriate time indicators – an obvious consequence of the fact that the structural order remains unchanged through time. We then have

$$f_{a_v}'' = a_v' - f_{b_v}'' \tag{4.2a}$$
$$f_{b_v}'' = a_v' - f_{a_v}''$$
$$= n_{a_v}'' \tag{4.3a}$$
$$= z_v' - n_{b_v}'' - n_{z_v}''$$
$$f_{z_v}'' = b_v'$$
$$= n_{a_v}'' + n_{b_v}'' \tag{4.4a}$$
$$= z_v' - n_{z_v}''$$

We shall see that this property is absent from the structure of dynamic equilibrium.

[7] It was Marx's great achievement (see Marx, *Capital, loc. cit.,* Vol. II, Ch. 20) to have pioneered in establishing the structural condition expressed in the first relation of Equation 4.4. Because he argued in the context of a two-sector model, the conditions formulated in Equations 4.2 and 4.3, and especially in the second relation of Equation 4.3, remained hidden.

In establishing the price ratio for primary equipment relative to consumer goods we spoke at one point of the "import" of consumer goods into Sector Ib. We could have followed this up by calling *re-export* that part of such import which is forwarded to Sector Ia. Such an analogy between the sectoral transfers and the exchange relations in international trade helps us to understand the true meaning of "structural" relations. In either case the actual exchanges are mediated through behavioral forces, the nature of which changes with the social organization of the system in question. Indeed, for the full understanding of the processes involved, investigation of these forces is indispensable. There are, however, at the same time, purely physical characteristics, defining the technical function of specific inputs in the process of production or the qualitative nature of the goods exported and imported, that must be present if stationary equilibrium or equilibrium in the balance of trade is to be achieved. Moreover, the validity of these physical relations transcends the sociopolitical differences of economic systems and is, thus, independent of the nature of the motorial forces at work. Indeed, for the purpose of attaining the macrogoal of equilibrium, these relations – almost totally disregarded in conventional economics – present the prior problem for both analysis and policy.

A final word must be added concerning the interpretation of Models IV and IV.i and of Equations 4.2–4 in terms of a free market system. In both models, variables f and n represent, on the one hand, price sums or costs of inputs in each sector and, on the other hand, money receipts that accrue, in the form of amortization sums and incomes, to the holders of the respective inputs. In the equations the same symbols represent expenditure for, and receipts from the sale of basic productive factors. Variables a, b, and z on their part denote in the models price sums of output, whereas in the equations they measure aggregates of expenditure and sales receipts.

Far from prejudicing analytical clarity, this change of meaning of the basic variables in successive transactions emphasizes the interdependence of the production–receipt–expenditure flows.[8]

III

From what has so far been said about the structure of stationary equilibrium, it is intuitively clear that such a structure displays not only a num-

---

[8] A similar ambiguity characterizes the basic Keynesian model, which has both a "supply" and a "demand" meaning. In the first interpretation, it refers to aggregate output as composed of consumer and investment goods. In the second interpretation, it refers to aggregate income divided into a part to be spent on consumer goods and another part, called savings, to be spent on investment goods.

ber of physical and price-sum equalities but also that the aggregate inputs and outputs in one sector must stand in a definite quantitative relationship to those of the other sectors. If we can establish these "sector ratios" in precise terms, we gain a simple measure for the distribution of inputs over the system, from which the necessary transfer of certain outputs can be derived.

The relative size of these ratios can be traced to two elements. Whether the equipment-good sector taken as a whole is large or small relative to the size of the consumer-good sector depends, first of all, on the size of the capital input and its productivity. The larger the aggregate capital input and the lower its productivity in terms of output, the larger the quantity of factors that must be employed in the two equipment-good subsectors if steady replacement is to be assured. Thus, one strategic factor in determining the sector ratios is the prevailing *capital–output ratio,* to which the size of the equipment-good sector is directly proportional. The same reasoning applies to the relative size of Sectors Ia and Ib. The larger the capital–output ratio of primary equipment, the larger the share of Sector Ia in the structural order of the system.

Still, these propositions require some qualification. Given the level of capital productivity, what really determines the size of output in every period of production is not the capital stock as a whole but that part currently entering the production flow and in need of replacement. Therefore the size of the equipment-good sector is also proportional to the *rate of depreciation,* and the effect of a high capital–output ratio may well be counteracted by a low rate of depreciation. At any rate, only by considering the combined effect of capital–output ratio and depreciation rate can a measure for the sector ratios be established.

Denoting by k the capital–output ratio in its conventional form of F_v/o_v, that is, the value of the fixed-capital stock divided by the value of output, and using d for the rate of depreciation, we obtain the capital flow-output ratio kd.[9]

$$kd = \frac{F_v \cdot d}{o_v} = \frac{f_v}{o_v}$$

IV

In now elaborating the *stationary sector ratios* with the help of the capital flow–output ratio kd, we denote these ratios themselves, that is,

[9] By combining the capital stock–output ratio with the rate of depreciation we avoid a difficulty that besets the isolated use of the conventional capital–output ratio. The later joins a stock magnitude to a flow magnitude, making the quotient inversely proportional to the time span of observation. Introducing the rate of depreciation, a flow variable that moves directly with

$z/(a + b + z)$, $b/(a + b + z)$, and $a/(a + b + z)$, as $\bar{z}$, $\bar{b}$, and $\bar{a}$, respectively. As a first approximation, we now assume equal capital–output ratios and depreciation rates in all three sectors.

The solution rests on the following consideration. First, since $kd = f/o$, it measures the ratio of the aggregate period input of equipment goods to aggregate output. But stationary equilibrium can be maintained through time only if the same ratio also equals the ratio of the combined output of the two equipment-good sectors to aggregate output, that is, if $kd = \bar{b} + \bar{a}$.[10] Second, by the same reasoning f_z/o measures the ratio of input of secondary equipment to aggregate output, a ratio that must equal $\bar{b}$, that is, the ratio of output of Sector Ib to aggregate output. Thus we obtain:[11]

$$\bar{z} = 1 - (\bar{a} + \bar{b}) = 1 - kd$$
$$\bar{b} = \bar{f}_z = \bar{F}_z \cdot d = k \cdot \bar{z} \cdot d = kd(1 - kd)$$
$$\bar{a} = 1 - (\bar{z} + \bar{b}) = 1 - 1 + kd - kd + k^2 d^2 = k^2 d^2$$

and

$$\bar{z} : \bar{b} : \bar{a} = 1 - kd : kd(1 - kd) : k^2 d^2 \qquad (4.5)$$

time, turns our measure into a timeless coefficient. The measure kd disregards the contribution of working capital, a limitation for which the rationale will be given in Chapter 5, Section I, and in Chapter 6, Section I.

The same procedure can, and will later on, be applied to the determination of the *capital–labor* ratio c that can be equated with F_v/n_v. This makes it easy to transform the two flow coefficients into each other, so that $c = k/(1 - kd)$ because

$$\frac{F_v}{n_v} = \frac{ko_v}{o_v - f_v} = \frac{ko_v}{o_v - kdo_v}$$

Finally determination of either coefficient presupposes that the "value of a capital stock" is a meaningful concept. A further discussion is found in Chapter 6, Section II.

[10] Because $k = F/o$ and $1/d = F/f$, therefore k must always be smaller than $1/d$, or else we would obtain for the output of equipment goods a magnitude that equals or even exceeds total output.

[11] By dividing the right-hand side of Equation 4.5 by $1 - kd$, we obtain for the share of Sector Ia in total output the expression $k^2 d^2/(1 - kd)$, which can be interpreted as the finite value of an infinite series with kd as multiplicant. This fact has been adduced as proof of the Austrian proposition that the contribution of the factor "real capital" can be derived from the assumption of an exclusively vertically organized structure of production of infinite "length" (see, for example, *Dosso*, p. 234). However mathematical convenience can hardly be regarded as a substitute for an economic interpretation of the capital structure in circular terms, as previously demonstrated in Chapter 3. The later interpretation can dispense with the fiction of an infinite process.

By the same procedure we obtain the sector ratios in a system with *unequal* values for k and d in the consumer-good and equipment-good sectors, respectively.[12] This yields

$$\bar{z}:\bar{b}:\bar{a} = \left[\frac{1}{1 - k_{ab}d_{ab} + k_z d_z} \right] [1 - k_{ab}d_{ab}:(1 - k_{ab}d_{ab}) \cdot k_z d_z : k_{ab}d_{ab} \cdot k_z d_z] \quad (4.6)$$

Thus, given the fixed capital flow–output ratios and the depreciation rates for each sector, the shares of the sector outputs in total output (or gross national product) of stationary equilibrium are determined, as is the distribution of primary and supplementary factors over the sectors.

At this point a general comment is in order. The capital flow-output coefficient kd enables us to describe the structure of stationary equilibrium in terms of sector ratios. Presently we shall see that it is possible to translate all stock and flow variables defining stationary equilibrium into multiples of kd and $1 - kd$. When subsequently proceeding to the analysis of dynamic equilibrium, the same coefficient, in combination with certain specifically dynamic variables, will reveal the structure also of a system in steady growth. Finally when we come to studying *changes* in the rate of growth – our ultimate concern – the capital flow–output ratio and the rate of depreciation, combined and in isolation, will serve as keys to the understanding of the most complex processes of traverse.

As a first illustration of the comprehensive use to which the coefficient kd lends itself, starting from the price-sum rows of Model IV, we shall

---

[12] Since the same type of capital stock operates in Sectors Ia and Ib, it seems appropriate to apply there the same coefficients. We then obtain

$$\bar{b} = \bar{f}_z = k_z d_z \cdot \bar{z}$$

$$\bar{a} = \bar{f}_a + \bar{f}_b = k_{ab}d_{ab} \cdot \bar{a} + k_{ab}d_{ab} \cdot \bar{b}$$
$$= k_{ab}d_{ab} \cdot \bar{a} + k_{ab}d_{ab} \cdot k_z d_z \cdot \bar{z}$$

$$\bar{a} - k_{ab}d_{ab} \cdot \bar{a} = k_{ab}d_{ab} \cdot k_z d_z \cdot \bar{z}$$

$$\bar{a} = \frac{k_{ab}d_{ab} \cdot k_z d_z \cdot \bar{z}}{1 - k_{ab}d_{ab}}$$

$$\bar{z} = 1 - (\bar{a} + \bar{b}) = 1 - k_z d_z \cdot \bar{z} - \frac{k_{ab}d_{ab} \cdot k_z d_z \cdot \bar{z}}{1 - k_{ab}d_{ab}}$$

$$(1 - k_{ab}d_{ab})\bar{z} = 1 - k_{ab}d_{ab} - k_z d_z \cdot \bar{z}$$

$$\bar{z} = \frac{1 - k_{ab}d_{ab}}{1 - k_{ab}d_{ab} + k_z d_z}$$

$$\bar{z}:\bar{b}:\bar{a} = \frac{1 - k_{ab}d_{ab}}{1 - k_{ab}d_{ab} + k_z d_z} : \frac{k_z d_z(1 - k_{ab}d_{ab})}{1 - k_{ab}d_{ab} + k_z d_z} : \frac{k_z d_z \cdot k_{ab}d_{ab}(1 - k_{ab}d_{ab})}{(1 - k_{ab}d_{ab})(1 - k_{ab}d_{ab} + k_z d_z)}$$

$$= \frac{1}{1 - k_{ab}d_{ab} + k_z d_z} [1 - k_{ab}d_{ab}:k_z d_z(1 - k_{ab}d_{ab}):k_z d_z \cdot k_{ab} \cdot d_{ab}]$$

now construe an input–output model of the stationary process:

	F	f	n		o	
Ia	k^3d^2	$(kd)^3$	$+\ (kd)^2(1-kd)$	$=$	$(kd)^2$	
Ib	$k^2d(1-kd)$	$(kd)^2(1-kd)$	$+\ kd(1-kd)^2$	$=$	$kd(1-kd)$	(V)
II	$k(1-kd)$	$kd(1-kd)$	$+\ (1-kd)^2$	$=$	$1-kd$	

By stipulating $k = 2$ and $d = \frac{1}{10}$, we obtain the corresponding numerical value model of the sector ratios:

$$
\begin{array}{llll}
\text{Ia} & \dfrac{8}{100} & \dfrac{1}{125} + \dfrac{4}{125} = \dfrac{5}{125} & \\[3mm]
\text{Ib} & \dfrac{32}{100} & \dfrac{4}{125} + \dfrac{16}{125} = \dfrac{20}{125} & \text{(V.i)} \\[3mm]
\text{II} & \dfrac{160}{100} & \dfrac{20}{125} + \dfrac{80}{125} = \dfrac{100}{125} &
\end{array}
$$

By arbitrarily setting the value of aggregate output at some multiple of 1, say, at 250, the stationary structure, that is, the instrumental requirements as formulated in Equations 4.2–4 and 4.2a–4a take on the form of a standard example which, in several dynamic variants, will serve as the basis of more complex calculations:

Ia	20		2	$+$	8	$=$	10	
Ib	80		8	$+$	32	$=$	40	(V.ii)
II	400		40	$+$	160	$=$	200	
System	500		50	$+$	200	$=$	250	

However, in not accounting for the contribution of working capital, Models V and V.i still lack some essential elements the elaboration of which will be our next task.[13]

[13] It will be illuminating to translate Model V into a three-sector input–output matrix. For this purpose we rewrite our flow equations as follows:

$$
\begin{aligned}
kd \cdot a + (1-kd) \cdot a &= a \\
kd \cdot b + (1-kd) \cdot b &= b \\
kd \cdot z + (1-kd) \cdot z &= z
\end{aligned}
$$

By transposing this into the form of a conventional input–output matrix, we obtain

$$
\begin{aligned}
kd \cdot a + kd \cdot b &= a \\
kd \cdot z &= b \\
(1-kd) \cdot a + (1-kd) \cdot b + (1-kd) \cdot z &= z
\end{aligned}
$$

Since all items of such a model represent physical quantities, we can add up the rows, but not the columns. Only by introducing a base price for each physical unit can we transform the columns into cost figures, the sum of which can be compared with the priced outputs or revenues. However, there is certainly no guarantee that, for any arbitrary set of prices, costs and revenues will balance.

In contrast with such indeterminacy, in Models V and V.i the sum of the columns is equal to the sum of rows because, first of all, all items represent price sums. Moreover, as a consequence of the prior stipulation of stationary equilibrium, $kd \cdot b$ equals $(1 - kd) \cdot a$, and $kd \cdot z$ equals the sum of $(1 - kd) \cdot a + (1 - kd) \cdot b$. In other words, our models depict, among all the possible variants, that special case in which total costs equal total revenues. See also *Dosso,* pp. 205–10, 260–64, and Paul A. Samuelson, "Wages and Interest: A Modern Dissection of Marxian Economic Models," *American Economic Review,* December 1957, pp. 884–86.

5

The circulation of working capital

Working capital is one of the neglected issues in neoclassical literature. As a matter of fact, very little of analytical use has been handed down to us even from classical writings. After two false starts by Smith and Ricardo, both trying to find a distinction between "fixed" and "circulating" capital,[1] the latter concept became more and more identified with the "wage fund" and, thus, with one of the most dubious constructs of classical economics. Neither Jevons nor the founders of either the Lausanne School or the earlier Cambridge School had anything substantial to contribute to further clarification.[2] The situation improved only much later, especially through F. W. Taussig's study on *Wages and Capital,* and with Boehm-Bawerk's version of the structure of production, which is really a special model of the circulation of working capital. Once again, J. B. Clark[3] deserves mention. Without going into details, Clark makes the decisive distinction between *active capital goods* that perform an act of "transformation" and "perish in the using" and *passive capital goods* that are being transformed but "mature" rather than being destroyed during the process of production.

The next one to add to clarification was D. H. Robertson, whose famous analogy of the process of production with a sausage machine has helped to give to the notion of an "average period of production" as much meaning as can be bestowed upon it.[4] Of more recent contributions I should like to mention those by Keynes, Neisser, Lundberg, Hicks, and Wyler.[5]

---

[1] See Adam Smith, *Wealth of Nations,* Book II, Ch. I. For David Ricardo (*Principles of Political Economy and Taxation,* Ch. 1, Section 4) the difference hinges on what today would be seen as different degrees of "durability." He, therefore calls it "not essential."

[2] See, for example, the remarkable unconcern with which Marshall (*loc. cit.,* p. 75) takes over the Ricardian concepts through the medium of J. S. Mill.

[3] Clark, *loc. cit.,* Chs. XVII and XIX. Marx's contribution to the problem was previously mentioned in Chapter 2 of this book.

[4] See D. H. Robertson, *Banking Policy and the Price Level,* London, 1926, Ch. V, and *Money,* rev. ed., Cambridge (England), 1928, Ch. V, Par. 7.

[5] See J. M. Keynes, *Treatise on Money, loc. cit.,* Vol. 2, Ch. 28; Hans Neisser, "Lohnhoehe und Beschaeftigungsgrad," *Weltwirtschaftliches Archiv,* October

I

Earlier in our exposition of the schema of production, we identified the stock of working capital goods with the group of unfinished goods which, during the process of production, move to the state of completion as progressively transformed natural resources and are, therefore, also called "goods in process." We saw, however, that the notion of discrete "stages of completion," although useful for didactic purposes, has little operational meaning in view of the continuity of the process of transformation. This creates our first problem when we now try to devise a measure for the *stationary stock of working capital*.

It is at once obvious that we cannot express this stock as the sum of stage outputs as they arise as the result of the business differentiation of a free market system, or as the plant and industry organization of a socialist market system yields them. Needless to say such organizational caesuras are of great importance for both practice and theory. Because the transition from one such stage to the next in any market order is effected through a money exchange, the number of such stages, the price sum of the respective stage outputs, and the aggregate price sum of all stage outputs form important issues in the theory of money. But none of these transaction concepts can serve as a measure for the size of that stock of intermediate goods which is *technically* required for continuous production.

The difficulty can, however, be resolved if we try to measure the stock of working capital by means of inputs rather than of outputs. The procedure can be best understood if we focus attention on the "process of gestation," by which the stationary flow under examination has supposedly been built up.

We assume that the process of transformation of natural resources or of "maturation," as we shall call it from now on, is subdivided into ten distinct transaction stages.[6] We further assume that the working capital goods under consideration spend one day in each stage, during which they undergo transformation through the operation of the active factors, labor and fixed capital. For simplicity's sake we finally assume that the

1932, pp. 415–55; Erik Lundberg, *Studies in the Theory of Economic Expansion,* London, 1937, Ch. III; J. R. Hicks, *A Contribution to the Theory of the Trade Cycle,* Oxford, 1950, pp. 47–51; Julius Wyler, "Working Capital and Output," *Social Research,* Vol. 20, 1953, pp. 91–9; the latter is in many respects the most advanced treatment of the subject.
6 We start out from this assumption in spite of the warning sounded above, because it enables us to demonstrate our procedure by means of simple arithmetic. It will presently be shown that, by concentrating on inputs rather than outputs, we render this assumption innocuous.

aggregate value of these active factors, $n + f$, amounts to $100 in every stage.

On the first day, active inputs to the value of $100 enter the earliest stage and there transform some free natural resource into the intermediate good ω_1. All the subsequent stages are empty at this point of time. On the second day, ω_1 is moved to the second stage and is transformed there, with the help of another dose of $n + f$, into the intermediate good ω_2 which, according to our assumptions, equals the value of $2\omega_1$. However, on the same day another input $n + f$ enters the first stage to produce there another unit of ω_1.

This process continues up to the tenth day when the first finished good equivalent to $10\omega_1$ leaves the flow of production. At this point of time, at which the first period of maturation is completed, a stock of intermediate goods exists in our system that is distributed over the ten stages in the following order:

1. In every stage we find *physical* units, decreasing in numbers from ten in the earliest stage to one in the latest stage, in a progressively more advanced state of technical completion.

2. In accord with this difference in technical completeness, the *values* of successive stage outputs rise steadily from stage to stage, each time by the amount of $100.

3. Thus the aggregate value of all the units of stage outputs amount to $5,500, which equals the aggregate value of all inputs over the whole period of maturation.

From this point on, both the distribution of the physical units over the stages, the individual stage values, and also the aggregate value of the stage outputs remain constant. It is true that from now on every day aggregate inputs to the value of $1,000 enter the system. At the same time, however, outputs to the same value of $1,000 leave the system as finished goods. This is equivalent to saying that the stationary flow, that is, the continuous equality of inputs and outputs is established.

It should be evident that our result is in principle independent of our arbitrary assumption that the flow of maturation be subdivided into ten stages. As long as the aggregate inputs remain constant per time unit, it does not matter in what manner the stage order is differentiated. What does matter is the *degree of continuity* of the active inputs, on which we base our calculation. In order to obtain an adequate picture of the maturation process, we must assume *full continuity* of influx, starting, say, with an "input bundle" to the value of 1¢ per second. We then approach the limiting value of $5,000 for the aggregate of successive inputs and also for the aggregate of the corresponding stage outputs. This limiting value is the actual value of the stock of working capital technically required for the maintenance of the stationary process. We can measure it as the integral of the gestation inputs or, a simpler procedure, by relating it to the current input or output after the stationary flow is fully established. We obtain then for the working capital stock W

$$W = \frac{inp}{2} = \frac{o}{2}.$$

with *inp* and *o* measured over the *average period of maturation*. Here *inp* represents aggregate input, and *o* the aggregate output of finished goods. The period of maturation is an empirical constant that measures the chronological time it takes to transform a unit of natural resources into a finished good. It differs, of course, from sector to sector, and even from industry to industry. Therefore the average period of maturation will be difficult to establish empirically, although the term is unambiguous conceptually.

The factor of $\frac{1}{2}$ enters the preceding expression because we have so far assumed that the inputs are *evenly* distributed over whatever stages our system exhibits. In this special case the *successive* inputs of factors during the period of gestation are one-half the inputs that enter *simultaneously* during the period of maturation once the stationary flow is established. In order to generalize our results, we must admit differences in the distribution of inputs over the stages, or in Wyler's terminology, different "densities" of stage inputs.[7]

Such differences in density do not affect the physical arrangement because, once stationary equilibrium has been attained, the number of physical units must always be the same in each stage if production is to be a continuous flow. They do, however, modify the stage *values* and, thus, also the aggregate value of the required stock of working capital. This value is the greater, the greater the density, that is, the greater the share in aggregate input on the part of the earlier stages, because any output value registered for one stage is carried over to all subsequent stages. In practice the earlier stages are likely to show relatively larger inputs, because the later stages include, for example, commerce, a stage with small input requirements. If we introduce the concept of an average density of a given stationary flow symbolized by ϕ, the preceding measure changes to[8]

$$W = \phi \cdot inp = \phi \cdot o \qquad\qquad (5.1)$$

where $0 < \phi < 1$.

---

[7] Wyler *loc. cit.*, p. 93.
[8] The expression implies equal fixed capital flow–output ratios in all sectors. The more complex expression valid for different ratios can be derived from Equation 4.6 in Chapter 4.

We can further generalize our result by dropping another assumption. Both *inp* and *o* measure flows and have, therefore, a time dimension that has to be made explicit. In Equation 5.1 we have implied that the period of observation over which we measure both the input and the output flows equals the period of maturation. It is sometimes convenient to keep the former period independent of the latter. We then obtain

$$W = \frac{\phi \cdot m}{t} \cdot inp = \frac{\phi \cdot m}{t} \cdot o \tag{5.1.1}$$

where *m* measures the period of maturation, and *t* the period of observation relating to the flow of inputs and outputs.

II

Although little of precise content can be found in the literature about the stock of working capital, the concept as such is generally acknowledged as valid. This is not the case with the notion of a *flow of working capital,* to which we now turn. It might even be said that whenever such a notion comes up for discussion, it is dismissed as superfluous at best and as misleading at worst. Have we not ourselves insisted that working capital goods are nothing but transformed natural resources and, in particular, resources transformed by the addition of units of the active factors labor and equipment? So long as we treat natural resources untouched by labor and equipment as free goods,[9] what special significance can accrue to the concept of a flow of working capital? Would it not be straight double-counting if, in addition to the contribution of those active factors, the contribution of the flow of working capital goods were included in the value of the finished output?

As a matter of fact, "double-counting" is not a self-explanatory concept, but depends on the purpose for which one undertakes counting. Thus we had better restate the purpose of our present analysis. We defined it at the beginning of Chapter 3 as the establishment of the conditions necessary to keep the process of production in a stationary equilibrium flow, and one of these conditions is continuity. Seen under this aspect, the presence of an adequate stock of intermediate goods of varying degrees of completion, and the *continuous replenishment* of this stock or, to use popular language, the continuous refilling of the pipelines, is as much a condition for a continuous production flow as are the replacement of the

---

[9] See our earlier discussion of this issue in Chapter 3.

fixed-capital stock and the availability of labor and natural resources. Thus, if we want to measure the total activity required over a stated period to keep the stationary process of self-reproduction going, we have to include not only that part of productive activity which matures during this period into finished output but also another part that refills the pipelines emptied by the creation of finished output.

Actually in these propositions we only repeat what we illustrated earlier through the interplay of the various flows in our schema of production. There we demonstrated that the output of the productive process is always the result of the cooperation of *four* preexisting stocks, which, over a given period, release part of their "potential energy" into the production flow as "kinetic energy." In a stationary flow this influx of kinetic energy equals the amount of such energy simultaneously expended. Clearly, this includes also that portion which is required to make up for the current utilization of working capital. If for the moment we adopt the classical notion that the input of labor is "replaced" by the output of consumer goods, we can describe a stationary flow in bookkeeping terms by the fact that the inputs of labor, fixed capital, and working capital replace themselves, whereas in physical terms they replace one another jointly.

If thus the concept of a flow of working capital reveals itself as a legitimate and even indispensable tool of analysis, the question arises as to how it can be translated into quantitative terms. Contemplating what happens in the stationary process during one period of maturation, we can say that the stock of working capital initially given moves once through the system. By this is meant that the items actually existent in every stage at the beginning of the process move forward toward completion, while at the same time new items of working capital are created to replace in each stage the items that have moved forward. Were we to take as our period of observation a period of twice the length of the period of maturation, the initial stock of working capital would move twice through the system. Therefore

$$\omega = W \cdot \frac{t}{m}$$

where ω again measures the flow of working capital, and t and m measure, as before, the periods of observation and of maturation, respectively. Because, according to Equation 5.1.1,

$$W = \frac{\phi \cdot m}{t} \cdot o$$

we obtain

$$\omega = \phi \cdot o \tag{5.2}$$

where o, as before, measures the output of finished goods. Equation 5.2 is identical with the expression for the value of the *stock* of working capital referring to the special case when the periods of observation and of maturation are equal, that is, when the stock of working capital moves once through the system.

6

The stationary process in operation:
structure analysis

We have now assembled all the building blocks necessary for a comprehensive structural model of the stationary process. The purpose of this
model is to serve as the basis for the derivation of our true frame of
reference – dynamic equilibrium. However, before we can make the
transition to dynamic analysis, we must fully clarify the economic meaning of the stationary model. By this I refer, first, to its instrumental significance, that is, its relationship to specific macrogoals, and, second, to
its dependence on specific behavioral and motivational patterns that
create and sustain the structural conditions. The present chapter will
discuss the first issue and is to that extent concerned with the deepest
level of structure analysis. The subsequent chapter will take up the
second issue by introducing the basic principles of motor analysis.

I

The comprehensive value model of the stationary flow (Model VI) is the
definitive specification, in terms of sector ratios, of the elementary Model
II.[1] It fulfills all three instrumental conditions of a stationary equilibrium –
continuous, full, and, as we shall presently see, also efficient utilization
of resources.

In analogy with, and as an extension of Model V.ii,[2] a corresponding
numerical model (VI.i) can be constructed by again giving the basic
coefficients specific numerical values: $k = 2$; $d = \frac{1}{10}$; $\phi = \frac{1}{2}$; $m = t$. We
also stipulate again for the aggregate output o_1 of finished goods the sum
of 250 value units.

Models VI and VI.i dynamically modified will serve as starting points
for the analysis of the relevant types of traverse from one growth path
to another. Therefore some comments are in order concerning the analytical suitability as well as the "realism" of the construct, the latter aspect
referring to the values chosen in the numerical model.

The values of the coefficients and of the aggregate of finished goods

[1] See Chapter 4, Section I.
[2] See Chapter 4, Section IV.

MODEL VI

	Capital stocks		Input flows				Output flows		
	F	W	f	n	ω	o_1	o_2	o_3
Ia	k^3d^2	$\phi(kd)^2$	$(kd)^3 +$	$(kd)^2(1-kd) +$	$\phi(kd)^2 =$	$(kd)^2 +$	$\phi(kd)^2 =$	$(kd)^2(1+\phi)$
Ib	$k^2d(1-kd)$	$\phi kd(1-kd)$	$(kd)^2(1-kd) +$	$kd(1-kd)^2 +$	$\phi(kd)(1-kd) =$	$kd(1-kd) +$	$\phi kd(1-kd) =$	$kd(1-kd)(1+\phi)$
II	$k(1-kd)$	$\phi(1-kd)$	$kd(1-kd) +$	$(1-kd)^2 +$	$\phi(1-kd) =$	$1-kd +$	$\phi(1-kd) =$	$(1-kd)(1+\phi)$

MODEL VI.i

	Capital stocks		Input flows			Output flows		
	F	W	f	n	ω	o_1	o_2	o_3
Ia	20	5	2 +	8 +	5 =	10	5	15
Ib	80	20	8 +	32 +	20 =	40	20	60
II	400	100	40 +	160 +	100 =	200	100	300
System	500	125	50 +	200 +	125 =	250	125	375

output have been picked, first of all, in view of their arithmetical properties; as we shall see, they lend themselves easily to dynamic manipulations. Also, because our interest centers on the change in sectoral configurations that reflect the adjustment path to a higher or lower rate of growth, the absolute values of our coefficients are irrelevant. Still, an fixed capital–output ratio of 2, taking the calendar year as period of observation, lies within the empirical range of industrial systems, especially since we relate the fixed-capital stock to its gross output. On the other hand, even if we confine our attention to the industrial segment of the system, it is difficult to establish a meaningful average rate of depreciation, considering the speedy obsolescence of equipment in technologically sensitive industries as compared with the slow depreciation of "structures." Our average rate of 10 percent should be judged in this context.

The models refer to closed systems and disregard governmental activity except when growth processes are studied in collectivist systems – simplifications that do not affect our analytical results. This is not quite true of some other properties of the numerical model that were also introduced in the interest of simplification. I refer, in particular to the assumption of equal capital–output ratios, depreciation rates, and density coefficients in the three sectors. Moreover, the latter has been set at $\frac{1}{2}$ implying equal distribution of inputs over all stages.

The equal distribution of inputs has been chosen so as to enable us to disregard working capital altogether in some of our investigations because, thus conceived, it affects only the absolute size of inputs and outputs without altering their intersectoral relations. Yet, whenever sectoral differences in working capital input do matter, especially in the context of diminishing returns and technological change, they will be taken into account.

Stipulating equal capital–output ratios and, consequently, also equal capital–labor ratios is another matter. This has no justification in reality, but we shall adduce reasons why this simplification is unlikely to affect our results.[3] Again, when studying technological progress, we shall put aside this assumption. We can, of course, as Equation 4.6[4] demonstrates, always transform the results we obtain from our simpler model into more complex constructs.

II

Turning now to the instrumental meaning of our comprehensive stationary model, we remember that, in a preliminary manner, three charac-

[3] See Chapter 8, footnote 10.
[4] See Chapter 4, Section IV.

teristics of resource utilization were stipulated as requirements for any type of equilibrium. Subsequently two of these, continuous and full utilization, were demonstrated as macrogoals implied in the quantitative order of stationary equilibrium. However, no reasons have so far been proffered for the claim that the same order also represents an "efficiency optimum."

1. Degrees of efficiency in resource utilization can be measured only in relation to a predetermined standard. In other words, a "bill of goods" must be stipulated representing the desired level of output and the desired composition. Because our attention is focused on macroprocesses, we can disregard the composition of the output basket – a limitation already imposed by the high level of aggregation of our model. Such exclusive emphasis on the size of aggregate output might then suggest that optimum efficiency is identical with optimum *technical* efficiency, that is, with such combination of resources that will yield "the maximum physically possible permanent level" of net output – a magnitude that, under stationary conditions, coincides with the output of consumer goods.[5]

However, we should not overlook the fact that, under the aspect of growth, optimization criteria other than technical efficiency may be chosen and are, indeed, applied in practice. These include a fixed level of output, temporary overutilization of equipment in the interest of accelerating the rate of growth, preservation of an antiquated technology so as to avoid social dislocation, etc. For reasons to be given when we discuss force analysis, we shall indeed measure efficiency by the quantity of net output. In doing so, however, we must be aware that we perform an act of instrumental choice of one among a variety of possible goals.

2. In the context of a stationary flow of production – constancy of resource input including constancy of technology – our criterion of technical efficiency is satisfied if all members of the labor force are provided with a stock of equipment capable of producing the *maximum physical output attainable* with the prevailing technology. They must be engaged in producing consumer goods, except those who are required to produce the necessary capital replacements. From this it follows that the aggregate gross output must be distributed according to payrolls (consumer goods) and amortization (equipment goods), with no "surplus" remaining. Speaking in terms of a market system, a technically efficient stationary process yields neither profit nor interest. Therefore it is possible to measure all inputs and, in particular, the inputs and even the stocks of real capital, in terms of wage units – in the case of homogeneous labor, even of labor

[5] See Joan Robinson, *Essays in the Theory of Economic Growth*, London, 1964, p. 130, where such physical maximization is stipulated as the "aim of a benevolent planner." The same notion is implied in conventional welfare analysis when, under conditions of scarcity, "more" is always to be preferred to "less." See, for example, *Dosso*, Ch. 14.

units. Therefore both "quantity" and "value" of real capital acquire an unambiguous meaning.

The same result has been derived by Schumpeter for a "circular flow equilibrium," by Keynes for a "quasi-stationary community," and by Joan Robinson for a "state of bliss," all of these constructs being variants of stationary equilibrium as depicted in the foregoing Models VI and VI.i.[6] In each case it has been shown that, starting from a nonstationary situation with positive profits, the joint mechanisms of competition and accumulation are bound steadily to reduce and ultimately to eliminate profits.

The argument has been put most succinctly by Mrs. Robinson:

> In the special case where the total labour force remains constant . . .
> the mechanism may be conceived to work to its logical conclusion.
> *If accumulation is going on* [my italics], a scarcity of labour will
> sooner or later emerge. A rise in the real wage rate and a fall in
> accumulation draws labour out of the investment sector. The rate of
> accumulation falls, but if it is still positive the scarcity of labour
> will sooner or later emerge again; a further rise in wages will further
> reduce the rate of accumulation, and so on, until replacement
> absorbs the whole of gross investment, and the stock of capital
> ceases to increase. All labour is then employed on producing con-
> sumption goods and maintaining capital, wages absorb the whole
> net product of industry, and the rate of profit is zero. This is . . .
> properly described . . . as the state of *economic bliss*, since con-
> sumption is now at the maximum level which can be permanently
> maintained in the given technical conditions.[7]

Now at the *positive level of analysis,* one might doubt the realism of the italicized condition; namely, the continuation of accumulation in the face of falling profits. However, not only is a fall in the *rate* of profit over a long stretch of the accumulation process compatible with a rise in the *volume* of profits but, what is more important, reducing, not to say stopping investment altogether, is bound to reduce profits even further owing to fall in effective demand. Therefore accumulation might well appear as the lesser evil.[8]

[6] See J. A. Schumpeter, *The Theory of Economic Development,* Cambridge (Mass.) 1934, Chs. IV and V; J. M. Keynes, *The General Theory of Employment, Interest and Money,* London, 1936, Ch. 16; Robinson, *Accumulation of Capital, loc. cit.,* pp. 80–3, 150–52. See also Paul A. Samuelson, "Abstract of a Theorem concerning Substitutibility in Open Leontief Models," in Tjalling C. Koopmans, ed., *Activity Analysis in Production and Allocation,* New York, 1951, pp. 142–46, and, more recently, M. Morishima, *Marx's Economics,* Cambridge (England), 1973, p. 115, with reference to *Dosso.*
[7] Robinson, *Accumulation of Capital, loc. cit.,* pp. 81–83.
[8] *Ibid.,* p. 152.

However, in the context of *instrumental reasoning* the objection is irrelevant. Now no more is asserted than the proposition that accumulation up to the point of capital saturation is a *condition* for attaining the state of optimal technical efficiency.[9] At the same time, absence from our models of a profit variable highlights the significance of n as the sole claimant of net income in our models. We have now seen that, in a technically efficient stationary process, implying capital saturation, labor is the only scarce factor.

There is a logical alternative to our concept of stationary equilibrium in Ricardo's notion of a dismal stationary state.[10] This state of "doom," the opposite of our state of "bliss," derives from the assumption of a steady increase in labor supply associated with progressively falling returns on land. Ricardo's construction can be approximated more closely to our model by the stipulation of a constant stock of capital confronting a

[9] It is understood that, in the case analyzed, not only the technological horizon, but also the specific "technique" chosen within this horizon is taken as constant, which is equivalent to stating that the coefficients of production are fixed. Therefore real net output per capita (real wages) rises, not because the capital–output ratio rises (which it does not), but because a steadily increasing proportion of the constant labor force is employed in the consumer-good sector, whereas employment in the equipment-good sector gradually shrinks to the replacement level. (See the arithmetical example in Robinson, *loc. cit.*, pp. 82–83.)

However, the deduction is valid also if there is a 'spectrum of techniques," that is, if the coefficients of production are supposed to vary with changes in the factor price ratio. It then conforms with neoclassical capital theory and its "parable," according to which a rising capital–labor ratio is associated with rising per capita output, rising real wages, and falling profits. In this context, however, our proposition must defend itself against objections that have recently been raised under the heading of "switches" in technique and "capital reversing." (For an excellent survey of the discussion, see G. C. Harcourt, *Some Cambridge Controversies in the Theory of Capital*, London, 1972.)

By interpretating the accumulation process as a *requirement* for the attainment of the state of optimum efficiency rather than as a mechanism actually at work, our argument is, in fact, immune to such objections. But as a contribution to the current debate it should be stressed that, *within the limits of a constant supply of labor* (an assumption also underlying the neoclassical parable), the steady movement toward economic bliss can be upheld even as an empirical proposition, as long as accumulation of profits continues at all. Temporary blocks obstructing progressive "mechanization," which arise whenever a more labor-intensive technique promises higher profits, can easily be overcome in a stationary process. Any attempt to introduce such techniques is bound to increase competition for the constant stock of labor and, thus, to raise wages – ultimately to the point at which more capital-intensive techniques regain superior profitability, so that the movement toward capital saturation can resume its course. This, incidentally, seems also to be the gist of Mrs. Robinson's discussion of what she calls the "perverse case" (Robinson, *loc. cit.*, pp. 147–48).

[10] See Ricardo, *loc. cit.*, Chs. 4 and 5.

steadily increasing flow of labor. The terminal state will then be one in which wages have fallen to the "replacement" level, whereas aggregate net output beyond that level accrues as profit to the owners of capital.

This model of doom is not without relevance for the study of subsistence economies.[11] By stipulating as our efficiency criterion an output maximum, we have excluded its premises.

[11] See W. A. Lewis, *Economic Development with Unlimited Supply of Labor,* The Manchester School of Economic and Social Studies, May 1954, and Samuelson, "Wages and Interest," *loc. cit.,* pp. 889–904.

7

The stationary process in operation: force analysis

I

Taken by themselves the structural relations of our model, equalities and sector ratios, cannot be identified as specifically referring to economic, or, more generally, social events. They would equally well describe the course of some mechanical process. By linking them with particular macrogoals, we have taken the first step of moving our investigation into the dimension of social analysis. However, only by taking another step, in which the processes formalized in our model are demonstrated as the outcome of deliberate human actions, shall we arrive at a true, even if highly abstract, replica of economic phenomena. This demonstration is the task of force analysis.

Still, this second and indispensable step must not be misunderstood as transcending the instrumental viewpoint. In other words, *force analysis too is goal-oriented,* in the sense of searching for behavioral and motivational patterns that are suitable to the attainment of a stipulated goal, rather than for patterns that actually prevail in any given situation. The immediate goal which now serves as our yardstick is the maintenance of the structural relations – stationary equilibrium relations – which themselves have been derived from the originally stipulated macro goals. Thus our first problem is the discovery of the *behavior patterns* on the part of the elementary producing and consuming units required to assure the maintenance of the structural equilibrium conditions once they have been realized.[1] This will be followed by the elaboration of *motivational patterns* which, in turn, are required to sustain the suitable behavior patterns. The entire procedure is a good illustration of the "regressive" nature of instrumental analysis.

It was emphasized earlier[2] that the basic technical structure of industrial systems transcends the differences in sociopolitical organization, so

---

[1] Movements that *establish* stationary equilibrium are *dynamic* processes. To accomplish this, quite different behavior patterns are required, an issue with which we shall be concerned in a later context.

[2] See Chapter 1.

that, for example, the structural conditions embodied in our models of stationary equilibrium are equally applicable to systems of laissez-faire and of full collectivism. *This neutrality with regard to social relations disappears in force analysis.* But before investigating the behavior patterns germane to different socioeconomic systems, we must spell out the precise functions of motivated behavior in a stationary process.

Stated in terms so general that they apply to all types of systems, this function can be defined as the *control* of the *physical-technical processes* of production and distribution in accord with a stipulated goal. This implies not just action in general but coordinated action on the part of the decision-making units of the economic group under investigation. Such coordination is possible only on the basis of a *particular social structure* embodied in *rules of communication* and *sanction*. What is to be communicated are the desires, and the intention to act accordingly, on the part of the economic units, and also the responses of each unit to the desires expressed by other units. The rules of sanction, on the other hand, refer to the rewards and penalties resulting from compliance or noncompliance with the communicated signals.

The ensemble of these rules represents the channels through which the behavioral forces create what on the level of structure analysis appears as macrostates and macroprocesses. Although the outcome as conceived in terms of a technical structure may be one and the same, the rules of communication and sanction, according to which this outcome is to be accomplished, differ radically in different forms of socioeconomic organization. To take the opposite extremes in the spectrum of possible organizations, in a collectivist system both communication and sanction assume the form of centralized command, whereas, in a system of pure laissez-faire, communication as well as sanction are carried out by the decentralized manipulation of a price order. This difference in social structure has far-reaching consequences for force analysis in the two systems.

II

Under *collectivism,* communication takes the form of a central "Plan," describing the officially designated wants of the community and the resources available for their satisfaction. In doing so the Plan stipulates not only a comprehensive macrogoal but also the manner in which the means are to be allocated to the various stages and sectors of the productive process. Such allocation of the means must obviously be based on a full understanding of the technical structure of the system and its constancy or change through time. In other words, the Plan can be regarded as a highly complex variant of our simple model of production, and structure analysis is, therefore, an indispensable tool for the Plan's establishment.

However, realization of the Plan on the part of the executants depends on their response to the information so communicated. In assessing their behavior the role of these agents as subordinate functionaries of a centralized order ruled by command is decisive. In principle, this role does not leave them any freedom to deviate from the stipulations of the Plan; and plan-adequate performance is further enhanced by the prevailing rules of sanction. However, for a scientific evaluation of the planning procedure, it is essential to realize that the commands implied in the promulgation of the Plan, as well as the rewards and penalties associated with its faithful and competent execution, or mismanagement or sabotage, bear a *political-administrative* character and fall outside the region of economic considerations. Therefore it is fair to state that in a regime of "pure" collectivism the task of *economic* analysis is confined to the elaboration of the relations that determine the technical structure.

III

The situation just described changes radically when we turn to the interplay of the strategic forces in a *free-market system*. It follows from the absence of any controlling authority that there both communication and sanction are completely depersonalized. Interaction is, in principle, confined to individual decisions to buy or not to buy, to sell or not to sell, made overt "to whom it may concern" by offering or charging higher or lower prices and by increasing or decreasing the quantities demanded or supplied. Such anonymity of the signals in no way reduces the clarity of the messages they contain, or the efficacy of the sanctions they imply, so long as the signals themselves are unambiguous. For example, this is the case if, within a given social structure, a price rise is interpreted as indicating deficiency of provision and, at the same time, as the promise of a pecuniary reward for compensating action, whereas a price fall suggests excess provision coupled with pecuniary losses for those responsible for the glut.

Elementary as these considerations are, they contain the clue to the understanding of the *behavioral patterns* required to sustain the structure of stationary equilibrium. Of course, because inputs and their transformation into outputs as well as the intersectoral shifts of certain outputs occur in a uniform sequence, one might conclude that suitable behavior was assured by simple *routinization*. Still, our confidence in such routinization must be backed up by the knowledge of other (though latent) behavioral forces, suitable to return the system to the equilibrium path if it should ever be displaced from it. In other words, we look for an *instrumental analog* to the conventional *stability conditions* of stationary equilibrium. For this purpose consider the following behavioral models:

Instrumental behavioral models for a stationary process

$$\begin{cases} (1) & \pm D \rightarrow \pm p \rightarrow \mp D \rightarrow \mp p \\ (2) & \pm S \rightarrow \mp p \rightarrow \mp S \rightarrow \pm p \end{cases} \qquad \text{(VII)}$$

$$\begin{cases} (1) & \pm D \rightarrow \mp p \rightarrow \mp D \rightarrow \pm p \\ (2) & \pm S \rightarrow \pm p \rightarrow \mp S \rightarrow \mp p \end{cases} \qquad \text{(VIII)}$$

where D and S stand for quantity demanded and supplied, respectively, and p for price; the $+$ and $-$ symbolize increase and decrease, and the arrows link stimuli and responses. In view of what was said earlier about the "message" conveyed by changes in D, S, and p and about the sequential interplay of the actions symbolized in D, S, and p, the four sequences of stimuli and responses previously described exhaust all consistent behavioral combinations capable of leading the system, after an initial displacement, back to its former equilibrium.

These four *behavioral sequences* can be subdivided in two ways. One may place together the cases in which the adjustment is initiated by a change in initial quantity either demanded or supplied. The subdivision chosen uses another and, as will be presently seen, more informative criterion. In the sequences included in Model VII prices are stipulated to vary directly with the quantity demanded and inversely with the quantity supplied; and the quantity demanded is to vary inversely with price, whereas the quantity supplied is to vary directly with price. In contrast with this chain of reactions, in the sequences of Model VIII, prices are stipulated to vary inversely with the quantity demanded and directly with the quantity supplied, whereas the quantity demanded is to vary directly and the quantity supplied inversely with price. As a stimulus–response mechanism designed to counteract displacements from stationary equilibrium, these latter sequences are as effective as the conventional ones, although the rationale for such behavior as seen from the viewpoint of the actors may not be immediately obvious.

Still, in a free-market system such a rationale is a condition for any behavior pattern to materialize. In other words, it is necessary that such behavior, whatever its significance for the attainment of a macrogoal, be suitable for the attainment of the *micro*goals pursued by the individual marketers. Secretary Wilson's famous dictum that what is good for General Motors is good for the United States is a caricature of an important insight: Only if the managers of General Motors regard what is good for the United States also as good for their corporation, can they be expected to behave in a macro-suitable manner.

IV

Our analysis now moves back a step, namely, to the study of the *motivational patterns* that are suitable for creating behavior patterns in accord with our two models described. Any economic decision that reveals itself in overt behavior is the resultant of two motivational components – a *purposive* and a *cognitive* one. The purposive strand, which we define as action directive, refers to the microgoal that a marketer wishes to attain. The cognitive strand, denoted as expectations, assesses the factual context in which the prospective action is to take place. In particular, expectations are concerned with the present "state of the market" and any changes that are likely to occur over the time span marketers consider as relevant for their decisions.

In speaking of *action directives* a possible misunderstanding must be excluded. This can be best illustrated by the purposive motivations of a consumer. His "ultimate" purpose is the acquisition of a basket of goods in accordance with his scale of preferences. This ultimate purpose, concerning the "what" of his buying, needs to be distinguished from the considerations that rule his *behavior in the act of bargaining:* the intent of maximizing his purchases for a given expenditure, or of buying a "normal" basket in agreement with a conventional living standard, or of buying expensively rather than cheaply (conspicuous consumption), and so on. We generalize these "modes" of action for both buyers and sellers by stating that they may prefer the cheapest, the dearest, the nearest, or a habitual market.

It is these modes of action to which the term action directive is to refer. We can then label the major action directives as follows:

1. Conventional extremum principle, elliptically called "profit motive," which directs action toward maximization of pecuniary receipts and minimization of pecuniary expenditures

2. Reverse extremum principle, also called "charity principle," under the rule of which marketers maximize the receipts and minimize the expenditures of their exchange partners

3. Homeostatic principle, which directs action, in Boulding's formulation, toward the maintenance rather than the increase of the present value of assets

4. Finally, what can be called "striving for intangibles" such as power, prestige, security, or goodwill, the common characteristic being the absence of any quantitative standard of measurement

If we now ask which of these action directives are compatible with behavior as described in Model VII, the answer is unambiguous: *only the conventional extremum principle.* Under the rule of this principle the successive acts described there are not only proper signals for the next step but also effective sanctions, rewarding, for example, p responses that move directly with D and inversely with S, and punishing other responses with pecuniary losses (and similarly for D and S responses to movements of p). None of the other action directives can be satisfied by the price–quantity movements of Model VII. The latter are clear violations of the charity principle, and certainly the price movements are incompatible with homeostasis, let alone with any striving for intangibles.

Regarding Model VIII, it clearly depicts behavior as impelled by the *charity principle.* Such interpretation seems to deprive the model of practical relevance, were it not that it is open to quite another interpretation, which we will take up presently. First we must discuss the role of expectations.

Compared with action directives, *expectations* – the diagnosis and prognosis of the context of economic actions as seen from the aspect of the potential actor – are highly volatile phenomena. This volatility and the variety of cognitive constituents, namely past experience, present information, and hunches about the future, which combine into what may be called "commonsense predictions," have until recently excluded expectations from the arsenal of operational concepts. Through the work of Keynes and, especially, of Hicks and Lange, this defect has been overcome. We now have in the concept of "elasticity of expectations" a tool of classification that permits us to use this second motivational strand side by side with action directives for the explanation of price–quantity relations.

We shall employ the concept of elasticity of expectations in the conventional manner, speaking of *inelastic* expectations when a change in present prices leads to a less than proportional change in expected future prices, with the limiting case of "zero" elasticity or static expectations. Conversely, *elastic* expectations prevail when a change in present prices induces a more than proportional change in expected future prices. With *unit* elasticity the change in expected prices is proportional to the present change. We speak of *positive* elasticity when the direction of the change in the expected price is the same (up or down) as that of the present price. Conversely, elasticity is called *negative* when a present rise in price leads to the expectations of a future fall, or, in the case of elastic expectations, to the expectation of a reversal of the prevailing trend.

The only modification we are going to introduce concerns the *extension of the concept from prices to quantities.* In other words, we shall be interested not only in the effect of a change in present prices on expected future prices but also in the effect of a change in present quantities demanded or supplied on expected future quantities demanded or supplied. We shall see that there the difference between positive and negative elasticities of expectations plays the dominant role.

Now, given the conventional extremum principle as action directive, which type of expectations will create behavior in accord with the sequences described in Model VII? The answer is again unambiguous: The elasticity of both quantity and price expectations must be *zero*. This means, first, that, even when responding to a present rise (fall) in the quantity demanded by raising (reducing) their prices, sellers will have to expect the quantity demanded to fall back (rise) to the original level. Second, both buyers and sellers will have to regard the price rise (fall) as temporary only and will, therefore, in anticipation of a return of price to its original level, reduce (raise) the quantity demanded and leave the quantity supplied unchanged. Third, such reduction (increase) of the quantity demanded to the original level must be taken as permanent by the sellers, who accordingly reduce (increase) their price to the original level. The same conditions are valid if the initial displacement arises from a change in the quantity supplied.

It can easily be seen that no other set of expectations will have the same effect. Positive elasticity of quantity expectations, although it stimulates the original price rise (fall), precludes the subsequent return of prices to the equilibrium level. Negative elasticity of quantity expectations prevents both the initial price rise (fall) and the subsequent price fall (rise), whereas elastic price expectations prevent the return of the quantity demanded to the original level.

It is also evident that the same set of expectations combined with the reverse extremum principle yields the sequences of Model VIII. However, we obtain an alternative and more realistic interpretation of Model VIII if we stipulate as action directive the *conventional extremum principle* combined with *negative quantity* and *price* expectations. This setup explains, for example, why a rise in the quantity demanded should be answered by a fall in price and, especially, why such a price fall should induce a reduction in the quantity demanded followed by a restoration of the original price level.

The latter example is a clear refutation of the challenge of behaviorism. To the question: why bother with motivations instead of relying on overt behavior? we must answer that, without knowledge of the underlying motivational pattern, the meaning of behavioral sequences remains indeterminate and behavior patterns unpredictable. This shows clearly when only one of the motivational strands changes, for instance, a shift from inelastic to elastic expectations.

At a later stage of our investigation Model VIII will prove essential for the analysis of certain "traverse" processes. For our immediate concerns, we shall select Model VII as our behavioral-motivational paradigm. From this model we conclude that *persistence of stationary equilibrium is assured if the conventional extremum principle represents the dominant action directive and if both quantity and price expectations have zero elasticity.*

One may well ask whether, in linking the structural equilibrium conditions to specific patterns of the underlying behavioral and motivational forces, regressive analysis has completed its task, or whether those patterns themselves can be traced back to more fundamental factors. In another context I have tried to relate the conventional extremum principal (from now on labeled for short "extremum principle") to certain natural, institutional, and technological "pressures" that prevailed during the era of early capitalism and to establish a connection between the degree of market flexibility and the state of information, on the one hand, and the prevailing type of expectations, on the other hand.[3] Obviously such hypotheses fall in the realm of positive analysis. For the purpose of elucidating no more than the *requirements* for the maintenance of stationary equilibrium, we can dispense with any further regress. On the other hand, we shall subsequently realize that efficient traverses from a given level of the rate of growth to higher or lower levels are conditional on specific measures of public control – a proposition that relates the required behavioral and motivational forces to a factor emanating from the political environment.

[3] See *OEK*, Ch. 3.

8

Transition to dynamic equilibrium

I

We are ready for the next step, the transformation of our stationary model into a model of dynamic equilibrium or steady growth. As we said earlier,[1] dynamic equilibrium is to serve us as the frame of reference for our study of particular growth processes. However, because it is itself a phenomenon of growth, rather than stipulate dynamic equilibrium as a datum, we shall derive it from a state having no characteristics of growth. Our model of stationary equilibrium fulfills this function perfectly because, although displaying a zero growth rate, it shares with dynamic equilibrium essential properties such as continuous, full, and most efficient utilization of resources. By simply substituting for a constant flow of resources so utilized, a steadily changing (increasing or decreasing) flow, the dimension of growth is introduced. For the time being we shall confine ourselves to studying steady growth in the narrower sense of the term, namely, the effects on the system of an *increase* in resource supply. The quite asymmetrical effects of a decrease will be taken up separately.

Provisionally our concept of dynamic equilibrium coincides with that of the "golden age" in Mrs. Robinson's terminology. It presupposes that productive capacity rises through time in proportion to the rate of increase in labor supply plus the rate of capital-requiring increase in productivity.[2] A further condition is the "neutrality" of technical improvements, that is, only such improvements are admissible which, at a constant rate of profit or interest, do not alter either the capital–output ratios or the rates of depreciation in any one of the sectors.[3]

---

[1] See Chapter 2.
[2] See Robinson, *Accumulation of Capital, loc. cit.*, pp. 99, 123. The proviso refers to the fact, detailed by me in Chapter 22, that contrary to prevailing opinion, *steady* capital-requiring increases in productivity are actually incompatible with dynamic equilibrium. We shall disregard this fact, arguing along conventional lines, until we take up the dynamics of technological change in Part IV. Such disregard will not affect our findings up to that point. At the same time we are interested in pointing out, in Chapters 9 and 10, certain internal inconsistencies of the conventional approach.
[3] See R. F. Harrod, *loc. cit.*, pp. 23, 26. Because Harrod deals only with net

Our next task consists in studying the structural relations and motorial forces that perpetuate dynamic equilibrium once it has been established. It will help us to understand the problem if we begin by investigating the *process of transition* from stationary to dynamic equilibrium.

II

Assume an aggregate quantity of fixed capital and labor capable of producing a certain aggregate output. Our sector ratios[4] indicate the proportions according to which the aggregate inputs and outputs are to be distributed over the three sectors so as to assure the reproduction of the uniform structure characterizing a stationary process. In particular, the size of the two equipment-good sectors is determined exclusively by their function of replacing worn-out productive capacity.

It stands to reason that the same function must also be fulfilled in dynamic equilibrium. In addition, the equipment-good sectors must also provide *new* productive capacity capable of absorbing the steady increment in labor supply and productivity. Consequently, from the pool of aggregate resources of real capital and labor, the two equipment-good sectors together now claim a higher proportion,[5] and, for the same capital–output ratios and depreciation rates, the ratio of Sector I to Sector II in dynamic equilibrium must always exceed that prevailing in stationary equilibrium.

Such a shift of factor employment toward the equipment-good sector is a universal structural characteristic of the transition from stationary to dynamic equilibrium. The motorial forces, *on the other hand,* that bring about this shift differ radically in different sociopolitical organizations. In a *fully collectivist system,* they are embodied in the command of the planning authority and in the ensuing performance of the subordinate agents, guarded by the prevailing rules of sanction. Again this mechanism

magnitudes, he does not refer to depreciation rates. In recent years a number of different definitions have been offered for the concept of technical neutrality. For a survey see, for example, Robinson, *Essays, loc. cit.,* pp. 112–13. The one chosen in the text, first propounded by Harrod, will prove especially suitable for our dynamic analyses centering on capital formation. Its analytical superiority generally has been pointed out by Joan Robinson (*Economic Heresies,* New York, 1971, pp. 125–29).

[4] See Chapter 4, Section IV, Equations 4.5 and 4.6.
[5] The proposition holds for the aggregate of the two equipment-good sectors as well as for Sector Ia taken by itself. Whether it is also true of Sector Ib taken by itself depends on the rate of growth. For very high rates of growth, Sector Ib may well shrink, because its size is strictly geared to that of Sector II which, in turn, is inversely related to the rate of growth. More of this in the following.

bears a political administrative character and lies outside the competence of the economist. All the greater is his involvement when the transitional process is to be elucidated in a *free-market system*.

Assuming that, to begin with, the same quantities of resources are employed in both stationary and dynamic equilibrium, the shift of a segment of these resources to the equipment-good sector will not change the aggregate *receipts* of the input factors. However, if continuous and full employment is to prevail, *expenditure* of these receipts must change in such a fashion that, in proportion to the required change in output, demand for consumer goods falls, whereas demand for equipment goods rises. There are in a free market system three mechanisms that can bring about such a qualitative change in expenditure: voluntary saving, involuntary saving, and forced saving. Each one of these types of saving in combination with the investment of the saved sums may produce the necessary changes. For our present purposes it suffices to clarify the operation of the first two mechanisms.

1. In the conventional discussion of dynamic processes the mechanism of *voluntary net saving* holds pride of place. It presupposes a decision on the part of some or all recipients of income to spend part of their receipts not on consumer goods but to apply the saved part, directly or indirectly, to the purchase of equipment or working-capital goods. Provided that the amounts continually saved and invested neither exceed nor fall short of what is required in order to build the additional capacity for the simultaneous absorption of the steady increment in labor supply and productivity, factor receipts will remain what they were in stationary equilibrium. All that the rise in productivity will alter are the quantities demanded and supplied in each one of the three sectors.

Of course, this is true only so long as the savers do not ask for a special remuneration in the form of interest – a remuneration that can be paid by the borrowers only from their own net receipts. However, under the conditions stated, namely, a stationary starting point and an amount of savings and investments sufficient for complete simultaneous absorption of the factor increment, all their net receipts consist of managerial wages. In other words, in the state assumed there are no investors' surpluses from which interest charges could be paid and, so long as this state of *dynamic capital saturation* continues, there are no prospects for any such surplus ever to arise. Only if both savings and investments fall short of the capacity requirements for simultaneous absorption, thus creating a state of *capital scarcity*, will the undersupply of capacity create profits for the borrowers and the opportunity for the lenders to receive interest. Or to put it even more pointedly, profits as continuing receipts, and interest payments derived from them, are conditional on capital scarcity in the sense of the aggregate supply of real capital falling short at any moment of the capacity required for the steady absorption of the resource increments.[6]

2. Another mechanism that does create profits during the transition from stationary to dynamic equilibrium operates in the context of *involuntary* saving. To describe this mechanism we must specify the sociopolitical framework of the system under examination. It can best be depicted by a "two-strata" market model along the lines described by Mrs. Robinson.[7] We now deal with two distinct personal factors: *workers,* without any access to real capital, who represent the only consumers, and *entrepreneurs,* owning the real capital of the firms, who perform the function of saving and of investing (or hoarding) their receipts, which includes the reinvesting (or hoarding) of amortization. In other words, they are nothing but "self-service stands of capital" (Morishima). For reasons to be spelled out in the following, we confine the initial "dynamic distortion" to an increase in labor supply while technology is kept unchanged.

We start out with the first "batch" of a labor increment entering the market without simultaneous provision of the capacity necessary for its absorption, as voluntary savings and investments would supply it. We now introduce the behavioral and motivational conditions as depicted in Model VII of Chapter 7, namely, the extremum principle as universal action directive, coupled with zero elasticity of quantity expectations. What response to the labor increment will this motorial pattern evoke?

The critical point is the zero elasticity of quantity expectations or, more specifically, the expectation that the labor increment will be transitory, so that return to the stationary supply conditions for resources is imminent. With this expectational setup what will best satisfy the ruling action directive is the maintenance of the prevailing wage–price structure. That is, wages are unlikely to be cut. This, however, implies that aggregate

---

[6] It hardly needs to be said that the statements in this paragraph imply a theory of profit and interest that is still controversial. By disregarding all notions of technical productivity of real capital and of discounting the future, it is based on the elementary idea that, in a competitive market, nothing can have a price unless it is scarce. When applied to the sources of profit and interest, this view of the matter coincides not only with the conception of Schumpeter but also of Keynes: "the only reason why an asset offers a prospect of yielding during its life services having an aggregate value greater than its initial supply price is because it is *scarce*" (*General Theory, loc. cit.,* p. 213; his italics). Or in Mrs. Robinson's formulation: "It is the scarcity of capital goods, not the productiveness of time, which makes income from property possible" (*Accumulation of Capital, loc. cit.,* p. 394). Furthermore, in deriving the rate of interest exclusively from the rate of profit, I am disregarding certain effects of "liquidity preference" which, although important for the course of actual economic processes, are absent in the instrumental framework of dynamic equilibrium.

[7] See Robinson, *Accumulation of Capital, loc. cit.,* p. 68.

demand for consumer goods will not be reduced, nor will any surplus profits be created as a potential source of additional saving and investment. Even if wages were cut, the ensuing surplus would not be invested under the assumed expectational setup.

The situation changes drastically once we modify our expectational requirements by stipulating *positive* elasticity of quantity expectations with regard to the labor increment, namely, the expectation that the increase in labor supply will continue. Now the extremum principle is satisfied, that is, the firm's expenditure will be minimized only if the stationary wage rate is reduced. In a fully competitive labor market such a reduction cannot be resisted by labor. Rather, in view of the prevailing excess supply, the lower wage rate now represents a receipt maximum for the employed workers.

Obviously such a fall in money wages and in aggregate payrolls is bound to create a temporary surplus in the hands of the employers – the mechanical consequence of reduced claims on the available business fund. Whether this surplus will perpetuate itself and will thus provide the finance for the absorption of the labor increment depends on the manner of its disposal.

Assume first the initial surplus to be hoarded. Such reduction of the active money flow must cut output prices proportionally to the reduced wage costs and, disregarding any intermediate distortions owing to individual differences in the capital–labor ratio, we end up with the restoration of the original stationary structure of production. The surplus is eliminated without absorption of the labor increment. Under the impact of additional batches of labor supply, the process described will repeat itself indefinitely.

Now assume, against our original premise, the surplus to be spent by the entrepreneurs on consumer goods. Because their demand now compensates for the fall in labor's demand, the structure of production again remains unchanged. However, not only will absorption be prevented, but, with prices unchanged, the surplus will be perpetuated indefinitely and will even rise with the additional pressure that additional batches of labor supply may exert on the money wage rates of the employed.

Finally, assume the surplus to be invested. This will expand capacity in a manner comparable to what voluntary savings and investments achieve. But there is an important difference. Rather than *anticipating* the need for additional capacity, investors *respond ex post* to the appearance of surpluses properly interpreted by them.[8] Were we to deal with a once-over increase in labor supply, absorption of the increment through subsequent expansion of capacity would, under the behavioral and

---

[8] What form of elasticity of expectation a "proper" interpretation must take will be discussed in the context of changes in the rate of growth.

motorial conditions assumed, restore money wage rates to the stationary level and thus eliminate the surplus. However, because the increase is supposed to be continuous and the entrance of each batch is bound to *precede* the construction of the compensating capacity, the pressure on money wages and, consequently, the presence of a surplus will be permanent.[9]

The label of "involuntary" saving has been chosen for this mechanism because, although on the surface it is the entrepreneurs who voluntarily refrain from consuming their surpluses, it is workers' consumption that is actually reduced in comparison with their level of consumption in the initial state of stationary equilibrium. This reduction in consumption is produced by the operation of forces over which they have no control.[10]

This slow-motion picture of the transformation of a stationary into a dynamic equilibrium through involuntary saving highlights a cardinal difference between this mechanism and the mechanism of voluntary saving. In a general manner it remains true that a surplus exceeding current amortization can accrue to the owners of real capital only as long as the latter is "scarce," that is, as long as the increment of absorptive

[9] The foregoing exposition implies that the capital–labor ratio is fixed, so that employment with the stationary capital stock cannot be increased, and absorption of the increment is conditional on the formation of new real capital. Were we to admit variable coefficients of production, the result in terms of the accrual of a permanent surplus to the owners of real capital at the expense of wage earners would not be different, even if the transitional path from stationary to dynamic equilibrium would be.

According to the neoclassical parable the initial wage fall will then induce utilization of the original capital stock beyond its optimum intensity up to the point where the diminishing marginal productivity of labor coincides with the lower wage rate. The surplus will take the form of the J. B. Clark "residual" which, in accord with our instrumental postulate (see Chapter 6, Section II) is to be invested in new capacity. Nevertheless, the continuous influx of additional labor will perpetuate the reduction of money wages and the corresponding surplus, although the continuous investment of the latter will steadily "widen" the structure of real capital.

[10] This derivation of profits is identical with Marx's derivation of surplus value from the presence of an industrial reserve army (*Capital, loc. cit.,* Ch. 25, Sect. III), except for two modifications. First, it confines the appearance of profits to conditions of growth; the absence of profits in stationary equilibrium was demonstrated previously in Chapter 6, Section II. Second, it disregards the so-called transformation problem, namely, the complications that arise in a system in which different industries operate with different capital–labor ratios. In other words, "surplus value" and "profits" are treated as identical magnitudes. At the level of aggregation on which the subsequent investigations move, such simplification does not affect the result. This is obvious so long as we apply equal capital-output coefficients to the three sectors, which, assuming equal labor productivity, implies equal capital–labor coefficients. The situation changes when it comes to studying the effect of differential technical changes in the three sectors. A further discussion of this appears in Part IV.

capacity lags behind the increment of labor. Whereas in a regime of voluntary saving such a lag is possible but by no means necessary, it acquires systematic significance under conditions of involuntary savings. There excess supply of labor is the sole "cause" of the surplus and of its application to the construction of new capacity and must, therefore, always *precede* the latter. Rather, one might ask whether, under these circumstances, dynamic equilibrium is compatible with the goal of "full" utilization of available resources. Such full utilization may be approximated by stipulating the lag as arbitrarily small – but, in principle, Achilles must not catch up with the tortoise.

At the same time it must be realized that the mechanism of involuntary saving operates only when the increment to be absorbed consists of *labor*. There the mere "availability" of an excess supply can directly affect the price–cost relations of a stationary process. This is not true of *capital-requiring technical improvements,* which can exert such an effect only after they have been embodied in new capacity. Such embodiment, which is synonymous with additional investment, must be accomplished through the medium of *voluntary* saving. In this case the surpluses or profits, which are to induce a positive investment decision, are the anticipated result of the act of investment rather than, as in the case of involuntary saving, its cause.[11]

[11] For a more detailed exposition, see Chapter 21, Section II.

9

Dynamic equilibrium: structure analysis

I

The first problem to be tackled is a model of dynamic equilibrium sufficiently general to depict the technical structure irrespective of any modifications that particular social relations may introduce. From our earlier discussion, we know that the main structural difference of dynamic equilibrium, compared with stationary equilibrium, is a relative shift of inputs from the consumer-good sector to the equipment-good sectors. The required magnitude of this shift, that is, the ratio of net investment to the original level of stationary consumption, is obviously a function of the rate of growth. Starting from the data of the stationary state – the prevailing capital–output ratio(s) and depreciation rate(s) – we can determine the appropriate investment ratio for any given rate of growth of labor supply and neutral improvements.

For this purpose we must, first of all, define the respective rates of growth in operational terms. Thus we define the *rate of growth of labor supply* as

$$\alpha = \frac{n_v'' - n_v'}{n_v'} \quad \text{or} \quad \frac{\Delta n_v}{n_v}$$

namely, the period increment of the flow of labor supply, measured in constant wage units.

For our definition of the *rate of growth of productivity*, we take our bearings from a measure of "value productivity," $e_v = o_v/inp_v$, that is, from the ratio of the value of output to the value of the sums of inputs. Although, in principle, the correct measure, it is operational only as long as the proportions of the various input quantities and prices remain constant. A generally applicable although less precise, expedient is to measure value productivity as "labor value productivity," that is, $e_{n_v} = o_v/n_v$. From this we obtain the rate of growth of value productivity,[1]

$$\pi = \frac{e_{n_v}'' - e_{n_v}'}{e_{n_v}'} \quad \text{or} \quad \frac{\Delta o_v}{n_v \cdot e_{n_v}'} = \frac{\Delta o_v}{o_v}$$

[1] An alternative definition of π is based on the assumption that one and the

The required investment ratio, i, can now be defined as the ratio of the value of net investment, I, to the value of net output:

$$i = \frac{I}{z^* + I} = \frac{I}{z_{st}}$$

where the value of net output is to consist of the sum of consumption in dynamic equilibrium, z^*, plus net investment. For the same aggregate of resources, this sum equals stationary consumption.

Given α, π, k, and d, the net investment required to absorb $\alpha + \pi$ equals[2]

$$I = (\alpha + \pi + \alpha\pi) \cdot ko_{st}$$

On the other hand, stationary consumption z_{st} being equal to $(1 - kd) \cdot ko_{st}$,[3] the required shift of factors from the consumption-good sector to the equipment-good sectors yields a second measure for net investment equal to

$$I = i \cdot (1 - kd) \cdot o_{0st}$$

From these two expressions for I, we obtain[4]

$$i = \frac{(\alpha + \pi) \cdot k}{1 - kd} \tag{9.1}$$

II

In analogy with the procedure applied when studying the structure of stationary equilibrium, we are now going to construct a model of dynamic equilibrium. Again we start out from a pure quantity model in both symbolic (Model IX) and numerical (Model IX.i) terms, indicating the

same output is produced in two successive periods, but in the second period with the help of a smaller input, as in the simplified case of less labor. Denoting the decrement of labor input relative to the original labor input as δ, we obtain

$$\pi = \frac{[o_v/(1 - \delta) \cdot n_v] - (o_v/n_v)}{o_v/n_v} = \frac{\delta}{1 - \delta}$$

We shall make use of this alternative approach in our discussion of the dynamics of technological change.

[2] For realistic growth rates, $\alpha\pi$ is a very small magnitude, and, therefore, it will henceforth be disregarded.

[3] See Chapter 4, Section IV.

[4] As a formal expression, Equation 9.1 equals the Harrod-Domar formula for the equilibrium rate of growth, applied to gross output and substituting the investment ratio for the savings ratio. The latter two ratios must be equal in dynamic equilibrium. Still, by focusing on investment rather than

dynamic nature of the variables by adding an asterisk to the stationary symbols.[5]

f^*	n^*	o^*	net o^*			f^*	n^*	o^*	net o^*	
Ia	$f_{a_q}^* \cup n_{a_q}^* \to a_q^*$		net a_q^*		Ia	$6 + 144 =$		45	30	
Ib	$f_{b_q}^* \cup n_{b_q}^* \to b_q^*$		net b_q^*	(IX)	Ib	$9 + 96 =$		90	60	(IX.i)
II	$f_{z_q}^* \cup n_{z_q}^* \to z_q^*$		—		II	$30 + 160 =$		100	—	

where[6]

$$a_q^* = f_{a_q}^* + f_{b_q}^* + \text{net } a_q^* \qquad b_q^* = f_{z_q}^* + \text{net } b_q^*$$
$$z_q^* = n_{a_q}^* + n_{b_q}^* + n_{z_q}^* \tag{9.2}$$

The dynamic characteristic is the presence of *net outputs* in Sectors Ia and Ib. Their role in the intersectoral structure and, especially, in the intersectoral transfers will become clear when we again translate the physical into value relations. In doing so we follow the procedure applied in the analysis of stationary equilibrium.

We again stipulate the unit price of the consumer-good output as *numéraire* and equate the price sum of z_p^* with the aggregate quantity z_q^*. This yields again in Model IX.i a unit price, p_z^*, equal to 1. The wage unit, w^*, that is, the ratio of the price sum of consumer goods relative to the aggregate quantity of labor input, amounts to $\frac{1}{4}$. The unit price of secondary equipment, p_b^*, equals as before the ratio

$$\frac{z_q^* - w^* \cdot n_{z_q}^*}{b_q^*}$$

in numerical terms $60/90 = \frac{2}{3}$. However, Sector Ib now transfers to Sector II a quantity of secondary equipment larger than is required there

on saving, Equation 9.1 is more general. It applies also to sociopolitical systems that achieve the transfer of resources from consumption to investment by mechanisms other than microdecisions about the level of consumption. It may be also worth noting that, although in Equation 9.1 k appears in isolation, the value of i is, nevertheless, independent of the period of observation, because in steady growth the value of the capital stock rises at the same rate as the value of output, leaving k constant.

Furthermore, in speaking of investment, investment ratios, and, subsequently, of savings ratios, we always refer to net investment and net saving, unless indicated otherwise. Thus these ratios are formed as the quotient of *net* investment and *net* savings over *net* output. We shall find it necessary, however, to relate these ratios themselves to *gross* output, because only in this manner can they be applied to all three sectors. This does not affect the ensuing value of the growth rate, for we apply the same procedure to the capital–output ratio. The value we thus obtain for the growth rate coincides with that achieved by the conventional procedure relating the respective ratios to net output or income.

[5] See Chapter 4, Section II,1.

[6] For the interpretation of the third equality, See Chapter 4, Section I.

for replacement. The difference, amounting in Model IX.i to 60 units, serves to expand Sector II and will be labeled I_z, that is, net investment in Sector II.

To find the unit price of primary equipment, $p_a{}^*$, we must modify the stationary expression

$$p_a = \frac{w \cdot n_{a_q}}{a_q - f_{a_q}}$$

by taking account of the net output in Sector Ia. This yields[7]

$$p_a{}^* = \frac{w^* \cdot n_{a_q}{}^*}{a_q{}^* - f_{a_q}{}^* - [\text{net } a_q{}^* \cdot f_{a_q}{}^*/(f_{a_q}{}^* + f_{b_q}{}^*)]} = \frac{4}{3}$$

These unit prices now enable us to establish a price sum–quantity model for dynamic equilibrium (Models X and X.i), corresponding to Models IV and IV.i for stationary equilibrium.[8,9]

Again we can now supplement the physical equilibrium conditions (9.2) by *intersectoral value conditions:*

$$
\begin{aligned}
f_{a_v}{}^* + I_{a_v} &= a_v{}^* - f_{b_v}{}^* - I_{b_v} \\
f_{b_v}{}^* + I_{b_v} &= a_v{}^* - f_{a_v}{}^* - I_{a_v}
\end{aligned}
$$
(9.3)

$$
\begin{aligned}
&= n_{a_v}{}^* \\
&= z_v{}^* - n_{b_v}{}^* - n_{z_v}{}^*
\end{aligned}
$$
(9.4)

$$
\begin{aligned}
f_{z_v}{}^* + I_{z_v} &= b_v{}^* \\
&= n_{a_v}{}^* + n_{b_v}{}^* \\
&= z_v{}^* - n_{z_v}{}^*
\end{aligned}
$$
(9.5)

Equations 9.3–9.5 describe the strategic transfer or exchange relations among the sectors, which must be carried out at the end of every period of production so as to enable the system to continue its operations. However, in contrast to the "triangular trade" under stationary conditions, the

[7] The quantity of primary equipment to be transferred to Sector Ib, the denominator of the price ratio, now amounts to total output of primary equipment $(a_q{}^*)$ minus replacement requirements in Sector Ia $(f_{a_q}{}^*)$ minus that part of net output in Sector Ia (net $a_q{}^*$) which is required for the proportional growth of Sector Ia. The proportion itself equals the ratio of replacement in Sector Ia to replacement in Sector I as a whole:

$$\frac{f_{a_q}{}^*}{f_{a_q}{}^* + f_{b_q}{}^*}$$

This yields the above expression.

[8] See Chapter 4, Section II.3.

[9] In Model X.i, k is set at 2 and d at $\frac{1}{10}$. The $+$ and $=$ signs refer, of course, only to the value numbers.

	F^*	f^*	n^*	I	o^*	net o^*	p^*
Ia	$F_{a_q}^*$	$f_{a_q}^* \cup$	$n_{a_q}^*$	$\longrightarrow$	a_q^*	net a_q^*	—
	$p_a^* \cdot F_{a_q}^*$	$p_a^* f_{a_q}^* + w^*$	$n_{a_q}^* +$	$p_a^*(a_q^* - f_{a_q}^* - f_{b_q}^*)\dfrac{f_{a_q}^*}{f_{a_q}^* + f_{b_q}^*}$	$= p_a^* a_q^*$	$p_a^*(a_q^* - f_{a_q}^* - f_{b_q}^*)$	p_a^*
Ib	$F_{b_q}^*$	$f_{b_q}^* \cup$	$n_{b_q}^*$	$\longrightarrow$	b_q^*	net b_q^*	—
	$p_a^* F_{b_q}^*$	$p_a^* f_{b_q}^* + w^*$	$n_{b_q}^* +$	$p_a^*(a_q^* - f_{a_q}^* - f_{b_q}^*)\dfrac{f_{b_q}^*}{f_{a_q}^* + f_{b_q}^*}$	$= p_b^* b_q^*$	$p_b^*(b_q^* - f_{z_q}^*)$	p_b^*
II	$F_{z_q}^*$	$f_{z_q}^* \cup$	$n_{z_q}^*$	$\longrightarrow$	z_q^*	—	—
	$p_b^* F_{z_q}^*$	$p_b^* f_{z_q}^* + w^*$	$n_{z_q}^* +$	$p_b^*(b_q^* - f_{z_q}^*)$	$= p_z^* z_q^*$	—	p_z^*

(X)

	F^*	f^*	n^*	I	o^*	net o^*	p^*
Ia	60	6 ∪	144	$\longrightarrow$	45	30	—
	80	8 +	36	+ 16 =	60	40	$\frac{4}{3}$
Ib	90	9 ∪	96	$\longrightarrow$	90	60	—
	120	12 +	24	+ 24 =	60	40	$\frac{2}{3}$
II	300	30 ∪	160	$\longrightarrow$	100	—	—
	200	20 +	40	+ 40 =	100	—	1

(X.i)

transfer of equipment goods from Sector Ia to Sector Ib and from Sector Ib to Sector II now includes equipment intended not only for replacement but also for *net investment* – to be compensated by equivalent quantities of consumer goods.

When discussing the structure of stationary equilibrium, the intersectoral equilibrium conditions could serve us also as *intertemporal* equilibrium conditions, because, within that framework, not only the relative but also the absolute quantities of inputs and outputs are constant. Contrariwise, dynamic equilibrium implies steady growth of all magnitudes from period to period. By treating the supply of labor and its steady changes as a datum, we need not account for its source. However, the steady additions to the capital stock in all three sectors are the result of the productive process in the preceding period. In other words, net outputs in the two equipment-good sectors in Period 1 appear as additions to the respective capital stocks in Period 2 – the true meaning of the investment variables in Period 1.

We begin by rewriting Model X.i, combining the value and quantity numbers into one equation for each sector, with the quantity numbers in parentheses. Moreover, we treat the numbers, as Model X.i shows them, as representing inputs and outputs of Period 1, deriving from them the numerical setup of Period 2. We thus obtain

	F^*	f^*	n^*	I	o^*	net o^*	
Ia	80(60)	8(6)	$+36(144)$	$+16$	$= 60(45)$	40(30)	
Ib	120(90)	12(9)	$+24(96)$	$+24$	$= 60(90)$	40(60)	(X.ii)
II	200(300)	20(30)	$+40(160)$	$+40$	$= 100(100)$	—	

and for the subsequent period

Ia	96(72)	9.6(7.2)	$+43.2(172.8)$	$+19.2 =$	72(54)	48(36)	
Ib	144(108)	14.4(10.8)	$+28.8(115.2)$	$+28.8 =$	72(108)	48(72)	(X.iii)
II	240(360)	24(36)	$+48(192)$	$+48 =$	120(120)	—	

On this background we can now establish the dynamic *intertemporal* equilibrium conditions:

$$f_{a_v}^{*''} = a_v^{*'} - f_{b_v}^{*'} - I_{a_v}' - I_{b_v}' + d \cdot I_{a_v}' = a_v^{*'} - f_{b_v}^{*'} - I_{b_v}' - I_{a_v}'(1 - d) \quad (9.6)$$

$$f_{b_v}^{*''} = n_{a_v}^{*'} - I_{b_v}' + d \cdot I_{b_v}' = n_{a_v}^{*'} - I_{b_v}'(1 - d)$$

$$= a_v^{*'} - f_{a_v}^{*'} - I_{a_v}' - I_{b_v}' + d \cdot I_{b_v}' = a_v^{*'} - f_{a_v}^{*'} - I_{a_v}' - I_{b_v}'(1 - d) \quad (9.7)$$

$$= z_v^{*'} - n_{b_v}^{*'} - n_{z_v}^{*'} - I_{b_v}' + d \cdot I_{b_v}' = z_v^{*'} - n_{b_v}^{*'} - n_{z_v}^{*'} - I_{b_v}'(1 - d)$$

$$f_{z_v}^{*''} = b_v^{*'} - I_{z_v}' + d \cdot I_{z_v}' = b_v^{*'} - I_{z_v}'(1 - d)$$

$$= n_{a_v}^{*'} + n_{b_v}^{*'} - I_{z_v}' + d \cdot I_{z_v}' = n_{a_v}^{*'} + n_{b_v}^{*'} - I_{z_v}'(1 - d) \quad (9.8)$$

$$= z_v^{*'} - n_{z_v}^{*'} - I_{z_v}' + d \cdot I_{z_v}' = z_v^{*'} - n_{z_v}^{*'} - I_{z_v}'(1 - d)$$

One main difference between Equations 9.3–9.5, relating to *intersectoral* equilibrium conditions, and Equations 9.6–9.8, relating to *intertemporal* equilibrium conditions, is the introduction, via variable *d,* of the sectoral *capital stocks* in the second case. This is necessary because the net outputs of primary and secondary equipment in Period 1 are invested in Period 2 as additions to the respective capital stocks. The productive effect of these additions to capital stock shows as additions to the *flow* that operates in Period 2. This is the reason why coefficient *d* appears on the right-hand side of every equality of the equation system (9.6–9.8), and every $f^{*''}$ equals then $f^{*'} + d \cdot I'$. For simplicity's sake we have assumed in our numerical Model X.iii the same rate of depreciation in each sector, amounting to $\frac{1}{10}$. For the rest, comparison of Equations 9.6–9.8 with Equations 9.3–9.5 will make the procedure fully apparent. It should perhaps be stressed once more that in our conception of the dynamic process through time – a moving dynamic equilibrium – the periodic additions to the three capital stocks are to be understood as the consequence of the triangular exchanges that occur at the end of each period, so that, in the subsequent period, production starts with a higher level of inputs.

III

Returning to the intersectoral value structure of dynamic equilibrium, we can now derive, for equal kd's, also the *sector ratios* and the distribution of primary and supplementary factors over the three sectors. All we need to know for this purpose is $k, d,$ and G; symbol G stands for $\alpha + \pi$, the combined growth rate of labor supply and productivity. We use again a bar to indicate the sectoral output *ratios*.

Starting from the sector ratios that characterize stationary equilibrium, we know that, for the same aggregate of resources, the output ratio of consumer goods in dynamic equilibrium, $\bar{z}^*$, lies below the stationary put ratio, $\bar{z}_{st}$, by the amount of required net investment. Therefore

$$\bar{z}^* = (1 - i) \cdot \bar{z}_{st} = (1 - i)(1 - kd)$$

By substituting for i the right-hand side of Equation 9.1, we obtain

$$\bar{z}^* = 1 - k(G + d)$$

In determining the magnitude of $\bar{b}^*$, we remember that b^* is to provide not only for the replacement of f_z^*, but also for an addition to the stock F_z^* of secondary equipment in accord with the prevailing rate of growth.

Thus

$$\bar{b}^* = \bar{f}_z^* + \bar{F}_z^* \cdot G$$
$$= [1 - k(G + d)] \cdot kd + [1 - k(G + d)] \cdot k \cdot G$$
$$= [1 - k(G + d)] \cdot k(G + d)$$

Also

$$\bar{a}^* = 1 - (\bar{b}^* + \bar{z}^*)$$
$$= k^2(G + d)^2$$

so that

$$\bar{z}^* : \bar{b}^* : \bar{a}^* = 1 - k(G + d) : [1 - k(G + d)] \cdot k(G + d) : k^2(G + d)^2 \qquad (9.9)$$

Analogous with Model V,[10] we can now construe a value model[11] of dynamic equilibrium in terms of k, d, and G:

	F^*	f^*		n^*		o^*	
Ia	$k \cdot A^2$	$kd \cdot A^2$	+	$(1 - kd) \cdot A^2$	=	A^2	
Ib	$k(1 - A) \cdot A$	$kd(1 - A) \cdot A$	+	$(1 - kd) \cdot A(1 - A)$	=	$(1 - A)A$	(XI)
II	$k(1 - A)$	$kd(1 - A)$	+	$(1 - kd)(1 - A)$	=	$1 - A$	

where $A = k(G + d)$.

IV

So far our investigation of the intersectoral and intertemporal structure of dynamic equilibrium has moved at the highest level of abstraction, focusing on the technical properties of structure that are valid for any sociopolitical organization. In order to approximate our results to empirical processes, we shall now supplement these purely technical relations with certain *social* relations that specify our findings for collectivist and market systems, respectively. The social relations in question concern the establishment of the rate of growth and the formation of investment decisions.

In a *collectivist system* both the growth rate and the investment ratio are part of the Plan and, thus, the result of collective decision making. Of course, since the two variables are functionally interrelated, the Plan cannot establish one independently of the other. In principle, however, either variable can be selected as independent, provided that the maxi-

---

[10] See Chapter 4, Section IV.

[11] See Chapter 4, Section IV, Equation 4.5. Unless indicated otherwise, we shall henceforth deal exclusively with values, and, therefore, drop subscript v.

mum growth rate chosen must not reduce consumption below the minimum of subsistence. The distribution of the inputs over the sectors follows from the stipulated coefficients of k, d, and G, and are realized by means of command.

A much more elaborate mechanism is at work in a *free market system*. There one cannot speak either of an overall investment ratio or of an aggregate growth rate as subjects of decision making. So far as the growth rate is concerned, it is the unplanned result of innumerable microdecisions on investment. Although the latter integrate themselves *ex post* into what may be called a macroinvestment ratio, this ratio cannot be ascertained *ex ante*. Moreover, in a laissez-faire system, with full resource utilization, the microdecisions on investment are themselves contingent on independent microdecisions on saving, the aggregate of which, a *macrosavings ratio,* is the ultimate determinant of the possible rate of growth.

This is the situation that confronts the student who aims at a positive analysis of empirical market processes. It differs for us who are out to discover the structural conditions of a dynamic market equilibrium for which a certain rate of growth has been *stipulated*. As we saw earlier,[12] from this stipulated datum, together with the technical coefficients k and d, the *suitable* macroinvestment ratio can be derived, to which in dynamic equilibrium an equal macrosavings ratio must correspond. For the reason stated, it seems advisable to conduct our further analysis of the dynamics of market systems in terms of sector ratios and aggregate models that contain the suitable *macrosavings* ratio s rather than, as hitherto stipulated, to aggregate growth rate G. Accordingly, it is necessary to reformulate Equation 9.1 and Model XI.

We take again our bearings from the stationary sector ratios.[13] We now obtain for the output ratio of consumer goods in dynamic equilibrium

$$\bar{z}^* = (1 - s) \cdot \bar{z}_{st} = (1 - s)(1 - kd)$$

Again we have

$$\bar{b}^* = \bar{f}_z{}^* + \bar{F}_z{}^* \cdot G$$

Next, by using Equation 9.1 and substituting s for i, we can replace G by the expression $s(1 - kd)/k$, which yields

$$\bar{b}^* = (1 - s)(1 - kd)[kd + s(1 - kd)]$$

---

[12] See Section I.
[13] See Chapter 4, Section IV, Equation 4.5, and Chapter 9, Section III.

and

$$\bar{a}^* = 1 - (\bar{b}^* + \bar{z}^*)$$
$$= [kd + s(1 - kd)]^2$$

Because

$$(1 - s)(1 - kd) = 1 - [kd + s(1 - kd)]$$
$$\bar{z}^*:\bar{b}^*:\bar{a}^* = 1 - [kd + s(1 - kd)]:$$
$$\{1 - [kd + s(1 - kd)]\}[kd + s(1 - kd)]:$$
$$[kd + s(1 - kd)]^2 \qquad (9.10)$$

V

Before deriving from Equation 9.10 a value model of dynamic equilibrium analogous to Model XI,[14] we are going to differentiate the meaning of our strategic variables in the same manner as we did in our analysis of stationary equilibrium.[15] We then realized that variables f, n, a, b, z, to which we must now add i and s, are open to different interpretations, according to whether the overall model is to describe a structure of production, of receipts, or of expenditure.

So far as the *structure of production* is concerned, the quantity variables of Model X tell us all that can be known. Because the criterion is purely technical, we have on the input side only the flows of fixed capital and labor, whereas the outputs represent physical aggregates of nonsubstitutable finished goods.

The setup changes once we consider our model as a *structure of receipts:* variable f takes on the meaning of *amortization* (am), whereas n acquires the meaning of *payrolls* (pay), and the three outputs now represent *sales receipts* ($sal\ rec$). Even more important is that a third type of receipt appears so long as capital saturation is excluded. Besides amortization and payrolls, we now have *profits* (P) as a third claim on total receipts. However, the share of required amortization is technically fixed, therefore this additional claim can be satisfied only at the expense of payrolls.[16]

Moving on to the *structure of expenditure,* we find that f takes on the meaning of *demand for replacement* ($D\ repl$),[17] n now represents aggre-

---

[14] See Section III.
[15] See Chapter 4, Section II.
[16] The mechanism that achieves such "redistribution" relative to the stationary order of receipts was described earlier as involuntary saving (see Chapter 8, Section II,2.)
[17] This proposition implicitly assumes equality between replacement and amortization, an equality which, in the context of positive analysis, has been called

gate *demand for consumer goods* (*D co*), whereas *a*, *b*, and *z* stand for the aggregate *supply of equipment goods and consumer goods* (*S equ* and *S co*) respectively. In addition, what in the receipt structure appears as profit, turns in the expenditure structure into *net savings* (*Sa*) and, subsequently, into *net demand for equipment goods or* net investment (*I*).[18]

Finally, by defining the *profit ratio* $\bar{p}$ as the ratio of aggregate profits (*P*) to the sum of net receipts, that is, to the sum of profits and payrolls,[19]

$$\bar{p} = \frac{P}{P + pay}$$

we establish for our model of dynamic equilibrium the closest possible relationship among profits, savings, and investment: Profit ratio, savings ratio, and investment ratio must all be equal.

On the basis of Equation 9.10,[20] there follows a combined *receipt–expenditure* model for a dynamic market equilibrium, Model XII, where

$$B = kd + (\bar{p}, s, \text{ or } i)(1 - kd)$$

that is, *B* is equal to the gross profit ratio, the gross savings ratio, and the gross investment ratio.[21]

By setting again $k = 2$, $d = 1/10$, and $\bar{p} = s = i$ equal to $\frac{1}{2}$, we obtain for aggregate output equal to 250, in analogy with Model V.ii, a numerical model for dynamic equilibrium.

> in question for a growing system (see especially E. D. Domar, *Essays in the Theory of Growth*, New York, 1957, pp. 154–94, and writings by Eisner and Harrod). But, as Domar himself points out, the answer depends on the manner in which amortization is calculated and productive capacity is assumed to decline and to be replaced. If both processes move in straight-line fashion, equality between amortization and replacement is assured (*ibid.*, pp. 166–67). Thus, straight-line amortization and replacement are themselves instrumental requirements for dynamic equilibrium, and will be treated as such in our subsequent analyses (see also Chapter 22, footnote 6, of this book).

[18] Equality of aggregate profits with aggregate savings and investments follows from the setup of our two-strata model, in which only wage earners are supposed to consume, whereas saving and investment are functions exclusively performed by the recipients of profits. Moreover, in accord with our definition of "efficiency of resource utilization" (see Chapter 6, Section II), dynamic equilibrium is bound up with the "golden rule of accumulation."

[19] Obviously, this profit ratio must be strictly distinguished from the *rate of profit* which is the ratio of aggregate profits to the value of the stock of capital.

[20] See Section IV.

[21] The *B* equals *A* in Model XI but, for the reasons stated earlier, it is a more appropriate coefficient in the study of free market systems in which the profit–savings–investment ratio rather than the growth rate is the subject of decision making.

	F^*	$am^* = D\ repl^*$		$pay^* = D\ co^*$		$P = Sa = I$	$sal\ rec^* = S^*$	
Ia	$k \cdot B^2$	$kd \cdot B^2$	$+$	$(1 - \bar{p},\ s,\ \text{or}\ i)(1 - kd) \cdot B^2$	$+$	$(\bar{p},\ s,\ \text{or}\ i)(1 - kd)(1 - B)$	$= B^2$	
Ib	$k(1 - B) \cdot B$	$kd(1 - B) \cdot B$	$+$	$(1 - \bar{p},\ s,\ \text{or}\ i)(1 - kd)(1 - B) \cdot B$	$+$	$(\bar{p},\ s,\ \text{or}\ i)(1 - kd)(1 - B) \cdot B$	$= (1 - B) \cdot B$	(XII)
II	$k(1 - B)$	$kd(1 - B)$	$+$	$(1 - \bar{p},\ s,\ \text{or}\ i)(1 - kd)(1 - B)$	$+$	$(\bar{p},\ s,\ \text{or}\ i)(1 - kd)(1 - B)$	$= (1 - B)$	
Ia	180	18	$+$	36	$+$	36	$= 90$	
Ib	120	12	$+$	24	$+$	24	$= 60$	(XII.i)
II	200	20	$+$	40	$+$	40	$= 100$	
System	500	50	$+$	100	$+$	100	$= 250$	

One final remark needs emphasizing. The introduction of profits has changed the order of receipts and the distribution of output as compared with the stationary arrangement. So long as we assume equal capital–output ratios (which implies equal capital–labor ratios) and equal rates of depreciation in all sectors, however, the values of all outputs and also of all capital stocks can still be measured in wage and labor units, that is, by the quantity of direct and indirect labor required for their production. What is received as profit is a "deduction" from the stationary receipts of labor. Therefore, speaking in the terminology of Joan Robinson, the value order of such a Golden Age cannot differ from that of the state of Bliss.

VI

With the exception of Section II, in which we established a general model of dynamic equilibrium and also the intertemporal conditions for its maintenance through time, we have conducted our investigation under the assumption that coefficients k and d are equal in all three sectors. This is, in particular, true for the determination of the dynamic sector ratios in Sections III and IV. As was stated earlier,[22] most of our analyses of traverses in Parts II and III from one level of growth to another one make use of this simplification. As a matter of principle, however, it is important to know whether *unequal sectoral coefficients* are compatible with dynamic equilibrium. Moreover, such a clarification will prove helpful in assessing the range of analytical validity of the Harrod-Domar formula for steady growth – the most popular tool in contemporary growth analysis.

To begin with, analogous with the parallel sector ratios for stationary equilibrium,[23] we meet no obstacle in establishing dynamic sector ratios with unequal coefficients. In doing so we shall again apply equal coefficients of k and d to the two equipment-good sectors but use a different set for the consumer-good sector. Following the earlier procedure,[24] we obtain

$$\bar{z}^* : \bar{b}^* : \bar{a}^* = \frac{1}{1 - B_1 + B_2} [1 - B_1 : (1 - B_1) \cdot B_2 : B_1 \cdot B_2] \qquad (9.11)$$

where

$$B_1 = k_{ab}d_{ab} + s_{ab}(1 - k_{ab}d_{ab}) \quad \text{and} \quad B_2 = k_z d_z + s_z(1 - k_z d_z)$$

[22] See Chapter 6, Section I.
[23] See Chapter 4, Section IV, Equation 4.6.
[24] See Chapter 4, Section IV, footnote 11.

To illustrate the interrelationship of these symbols, we translate them into an arithmetical model by specifying the coefficients as follows:[25]

$$k_{ab} = 2, \; d_{ab} = 0.1, \; s_{ab} = 0.25; \; k_z = 5, \; d_z = 0.05, \; s_z = 0.666$$

By setting arbitrarily the aggregate value of the three capital stocks equal to 360 units, we obtain

	F^*	am* = D repl*	pay* = D co*	$P =$ $Sa = I$	sal rec* $= S^*$	net sal rec* = net S^*
Ia	48	4.8 +	14.4 +	4.8 =	24	12
Ib	72	7.2 +	21.6 +	7.2 =	36	24
II	240	12 +	12 +	24 =	48	—
System	360	24 +	48 +	36 =	108	36

and for the subsequent period

Ia	52.8	5.28 +	15.84 +	5.28 =	26.4	13.2
Ib	79.2	7.92 +	23.76 +	7.92 =	39.6	26.4
II	264	13.20 +	13.20 +	26.40 =	52.8	—
System	396	26.4 +	52.8 +	39.6 =	118.8	39.6

We inspect first the numbers for Period 1. Because the model is derived from Equation 9.11, the intersectoral relations are of necessity fulfilled: Aggregate payrolls equal the output value of consumer goods, and aggregate amortization plus aggregate profits equal the output value of equipment goods. Furthermore, the output value of secondary equipment equals amortization and investment in the consumer-good sector. In other words, "instantaneous" dynamic equilibrium is realized. But *what about dynamic equilibrium through time?* By inspecting Period 2, we find again intersectoral equilibrium and, what is more important, comparison of the strategic variables in both periods confirms the fulfillment of the intertemporal conditions (9.6–9.8) – the numerical model presents a true dynamic equilibrium.

Can we draw from this example the general conclusion that dynamic

[25] To assume different savings ratios in different sectors is, in principle, incompatible with our overall assumption of involuntary savings, because the latter are to be understood as deductions from a uniform stationary wage rate. As the only purpose of the present model is to demonstrate the compatibility of different sectoral coefficients with dynamic equilibrium through time, we therefore stipulate as an exception that all savings be *voluntary* with the further proviso that the propensities to save differ in the equipment-good sectors relative to the consumer-good sector. It stands to reason that no such difficulty arises in the case of different k's and d's.

equilibrium through time is compatible with any arbitrary choice of the strategic coefficients *k, d,* and *s?* Another glance at the numerical model gives a clue to the answer. Although the critical coefficients differ, as between the two equipment-good sectors and the consumer-good sector, the rate of growth is the same in all sectors, amounting to 10 percent – a characteristic the significance of which is intuitively clear. Whatever the internal structure of each sector may be, steady growth can prevail only if all sectoral inputs and outputs and, thus, also aggregate output grow at the same rate, that is, when

$$G = \frac{s(1 - kd)}{k} = G_{ab} = \frac{s_{ab}(1 - k_{ab}d_{ab})}{k_{ab}} = G_z = \frac{s_z(1 - k_z d_z)}{k_z}$$

where *k, d,* and *s* are weighted averages of the sectoral coefficients. Therefore the intertemporal conditions and, thus, dynamic equilibrium through time are fulfilled only if[26]

$$\frac{s_{ab}(1 - k_{ab}d_{ab})}{k_{ab}} = \frac{s_z(1 - k_z d_z)}{k_z} \tag{9.12}$$

VII

We are now ready for a critical examination of the Harrod-Domar formula for steady growth, which we encountered before in establishing the equilibrium investment ratio.[27] By transposing terms and extending the frame of reference from net to gross output, the formula reads

$$G = \frac{s(1 - kd)}{k}$$

1. Our first question concerns the range of validity of the formula. Its elegant simplicity has been purchased at the price of total aggregation and, to gauge its significance, we must take into account the sectorally disaggregated values of *k, d,* and *s.* The most favorable but least informative alternative is sectoral equality of the coefficients – a constellation for which the formula appears universally valid.[28] This is no longer true, as

---

[26] The numbers of the coefficients in the preceding arithmetical model were, of course, chosen with Equation 9.12 in mind. The reader can easily convince himself that variation of any number that is not "compensated" by another variation violates condition 9.12 and, consequently, the conditions for inter-temporal equilibrium.

[27] See Section I, footnote 4.

[28] We shall presently see that, even for this constellation of the coefficients, the formula to be valid requires a further qualification.

our preceding investigation has demonstrated, if the sectoral coefficients differ. Equation 9.12 comes into play; this limitation can be detected only if the conventional formula is properly disaggregated. We have here an instance in which our tripartite schema proves its analytical superiority.

2. However, Equation 9.12 is not the only limiting condition for the validity of the formula. Even if the sectoral coefficients are equal, so that condition 9.11 is automatically fulfilled, dynamic equilibrium through time is assured only if not merely the *ratio* $s(1 - kd)/k$, but also the *absolute values* of the coefficients forming that ratio remain constant through time.

What is at stake can again be illustrated by two arithmetical models, both starting with the same aggregates of inputs and outputs and growing at the same rate, $s(1 - kd)/k$. Each has the same coefficients in each sector, but the set of coefficients itself differs between the two models. By assuming first $k = 2$, $d = 0.1$, $s = 0.5$, we obtain

	F^*	am*		pay*		P		o^*	net o^*
Sector Ia	180	18	+	36	+	36	=	90	60
Sector Ib	120	12	+	24	+	24	=	60	40
Sector II	200	20	+	40	+	40	=	100	—
System	500	50	+	100	+	100	=	250	100

and for the subsequent period

Sector Ia	216	21.6	+	43.2	+	43.2	=	108	72
Sector Ib	144	14.4	+	28.8	+	28.8	=	72	48
Sector II	240	24	+	48	+	48	=	120	—
System	600	60	+	120	+	120	=	300	120

Now, if we set $k = 1$, $d = 0.2$, and $s = 0.25$ but retain the initial value of total inputs and outputs, which is 250, then

Sector Ia	40	8	+	24	+	8	=	40	20
Sector Ib	60	12	+	36	+	12	=	60	30
Sector II	150	30	+	90	+	30	=	150	—
System	250	50	+	150	+	50	=	250	50

and for the subsequent period

Sector Ia	48	9.6	+	28.8	+	9.6	=	48	24
Sector Ib	72	14.4	+	43.2	+	14.4	=	72	36
Sector II	180	36	+	108	+	36	=	180	—
System	300	60	+	180	+	60	=	300	60

Because the two models considered by themselves have equal coefficients, all complications bound up with unequal coefficients are eliminated. Moreover, as both models enjoy the same growth rate of 20 percent it should be possible to move from Period 1 of the first model to Period 2 of the second model without encountering any obstacle, always provided that equality of the growth rate is the only condition for steady growth. However, we have only to inspect the respective *capital stocks* in the two models to understand how different values of the coefficients – even if in combination they yield the same growth rate – affect the respective sectoral structures. To be specific, in order to move from the setup of Period 1 of the first model to the setup of Period 2 of the second model, not only must the inputs be reshuffled among the sectors, but large parts of capital stock and labor be laid idle. Conversely, were we to move from Period 1 of the second model to Period 2 of the first model, a process of capital formation would have to intervene before the desired equilibrium could be attained. In other words, in either case, adjustment is conditional on a complicated "traverse."

In summary, we can say that in the recent discussion about the conditions of steady growth, we can distinguish between three levels of progressively more restrictive conditions. One extreme is represented by the traditional neoclassical approach that disregards all aspects of specificity, in particular specificity of fixed capital. On this assumption steady growth once attained cannot be disturbed: Any changes in d or s can be absorbed in the short run by compensating changes in k.

Harrod and Domar take on an intermediate position. They treat k as independent of changes in s and, thus, take capital specificity into account. They disregard, however, all divergences between the capital stocks of the two systems whose s/k ratio may well be the same. Therefore, so long as the s/k ratio is constant, they assume that steady growth is assured.

We have been compelled to introduce a still more restrictive condition. Not only the fraction of the growth ratio but both the numerator and the denominator must remain constant, expressing constancy of the sector ratios of capital stocks over time. Only then do we obtain a genuinely "moving" equilibrium.

Thus we have arrived at the conclusion that the requirements for dynamic equilibrium are much stricter than conventional analysis – neoclassical as well as post-Keynesian – makes them appear. However although the choice of suitable equilibrium paths is much more limited, dynamic equilibrium *once attained* is inherently more stable than the same convention asserts. In what has been said, the issue of stability has already been touched upon. To gain full insight, we must now supplement our structure analysis with an exposition of the forces suitable to sustain an equilibrating dynamic process.[29]

[29] A comment is in order concerning the mathematical technique applied in the foregoing analyses. The informed reader may wonder why, in establishing the structural conditions of dynamic equilibrium, I have not, in line with representative writings in the field, availed myself of differential calculus (see, for example, Domar, *loc. cit.*, Ch. III), instead of using elementary algebra in the form of sector ratios, intersectoral equalities, and so on. The reason is that our study of dynamic equilibrium is only the preparation for the subsequent inquiry into dynamic *dis*equilibria, as they arise in the context of traverse analysis. The nonlinear nature of the latter makes the application of calculus very difficult, even when a general solution is not altogether precluded. This will make it necessary to have recourse to simpler techniques, and it seems only logical to apply, in the interest of consistency, the same techniques to the underlying frame of reference.

IO

Dynamic equilibrium: force analysis

I

On investigating the motor forces that sustain stationary equilibrium, we came up with a simple solution to the problem. In a collectivist system, we saw that the suitable behavior patterns are implied in the prescriptions of the Plan. On the other hand, the motivations that are to elicit such behavior on the part of the executants lie outside the realm of economics in the region of political-administrative control. In a free market system, on the other hand, the proper guide to stabilizing behavior appears to be an action directive aiming at maximizing pecuniary receipts and minimizing pecuniary expenditures, combined with zero elasticity of both quantity and price expectations.

When the stability of dynamic equilibrium is at stake, we can, so far as collectivism is concerned, only restate what was said about the stationary case. In a free market order, on the other hand, we find a significant change of required behavior, a change already apparent when we were discussing the transition from stationary to dynamic equilibrium.[1] This change is ultimately grounded in a difference in quantity expectations. Whereas under stationary conditions the goal of adjustment is the recovery of the initial position of quantities and prices, steady growth, although compatible with unvarying prices, requires a steady increase in all quantities, such as inputs and outputs, employment, savings, and investments. Referring to the two behavioral models outlined earlier,[2] the stabilizing response to a change in price – itself induced by a change in the quantity demanded – can no longer be an inverse change in the quantity *demanded*, but must now be a direct change in the quantity *supplied* and, conversely, for initial changes in the quantity supplied. This, however, presupposes that, again guided by the extremum principle as action directive, quantity expectations of both buyers and sellers must take on positive or, more precisely, unit elasticity. In other words, both partners in market transactions are now to expect that the rate of change of the strategic quantities will be maintained indefinitely.

[1] See Chapter 8, Section II.
[2] See Chapter 7, Section III.

It was already indicated that this type of quantity expectation is fully compatible with zero elasticity of price expectations, implying that unit prices of commodities and factors as well as profit ratios are expected to remain constant. Such constancy presupposes, of course, an increase in the active money flow in accord with the prevailing rate of growth, which is brought about either through an institutional mechanism or through reliance on commodity money the production of which must obey the same rule of steady growth.

As in the stationary case, behavior in line with this new motivational setup will be confirmed by subsequent experience. Or, in Harrod's formulation, the actual rate of growth then coincides with the warranted rate, which "will leave entrepreneurs in a state of mind in which they are prepared to carry on a similar advance."[3] And dynamic equilibrium will be stable so long as actual motivations take on the required form.

II

Such an optimistic evaluation of steady growth contrasts sharply with prevailing opinion. Dating back to the earliest discussion of the problem in Harrod's celebrated "Essay,"[4] the so-called knife-edge nature of dynamic equilibrium is supposed to transform even small deviations from the steady path into large cumulative processes of inflation or deflation.

It is impossible and, for our purposes, unnecessary to survey the immense body of writings that this instability proposition has provoked during the last thirty years.[5] Our interest centers on two fallacies, which are shared by almost all contributions to the debate and which can be exposed by examining any one of them. We choose for this demonstration the step-by-step description of the process of destabilization in Kurihara's introductory tract.[6]

We start out on an equilibrium path as defined by the conventional growth formula. We now introduce a *fall in the savings ratio* – that ratio which is required for the steady absorption of the accruing resource increments. What will happen?

The act of undersaving is equivalent to an act of overconsumption, that is, demand for consumer goods rises. Existing capacity in the consumer-

---

[3] See Harrod, *Toward a Dynamic Economics, loc. cit.*, p. 82.
[4] See R. F. Harrod, "An Essay in Dynamic Theory," *Economic Journal*, March 1939, pp. 14–33.
[5] For a comprehensive survey, see Hahn and Matthews, *loc. cit.*, especially Sections I and III, 5.
[6] See Kenneth K. Kurihara, *Introduction to Keynesian Dynamics*, New York, 1956, pp. 198–211.

good sector, however, cannot satisfy this rise in the quantity demanded. As a consequence, demand for secondary equipment must rise. Thus:

> this increase in the "derived" demand for capital-goods creates a state of short capacity in capital-goods industries as well. *A deficiency of capital all around* [my italics] gives rise to an upward trend of the marginal efficiency of capital and hence to steadily profitable investment opportunities, thus tending to leave the economy in a persistent state of buoyancy. This means that the propensity to invest at full employment is persistently greater than the propensity to save at full employment, with the net result that the economy, once displaced out of progressive equilibrium by the initiating shock...is likely to find itself staying put on a divergent path of chronic inflation. (Kurihara, pp. 203–4)

Detailed examination of this argument is important, not only for the purpose at hand. It will once again reveal the significance of a three-sector as opposed to a two-sector model for the analysis of dynamic adjustment processes.

There are no objections to the initial steps of Kurihara's argument. With a fall of savings the demand for consumer goods is likely to rise, as is the demand of consumer-good industries for additional equipment. But is it true that this excess demand creates a "deficiency of capital all around"?

It does create such a deficiency in Sector Ib, which produces the equipment for the consumer-good industries. However, Sector Ia clearly suffers the reverse fate. The fall in savings which, in our equilibrium model, is equivalent to a fall in investment, means that demand for the output of Sector Ia is bound to fall. In other words, the rise in demand for additional capacity to be produced in Sector Ib is systematically related to a fall in demand for capacity produced in Sector Ia and with the partial displacement of the equipment operating there. Now, remembering the perfect substitutability of the capital stocks in the two equipment-good sectors, we realize that capacity in Sector Ib can be increased without delay by simply shifting part of the displaced capacity in Sector Ia to the production of the required secondary equipment. Therefore, even if there are no other forces at work to counteract the initial fall in savings (a premise needing closer scrutiny), what happens is by no means a "Wicksellian" cumulative inflation, but a simple shift of factors between the two subsectors of the capital-good industry. That this compensatory process should have been overlooked in the conventional discussion of the problem is not surprising. It remains invisible so long as analysis proceeds on the basis of a one- or two-sector model, in which the two subsectors, Ia and Ib, are treated as one global unit.[7]

However, what happens if the savings ratio *increases?* The answer can be found by comparing the two models set forth in footnote 7. Now we must start out with the numbers for the first period of the second model and compare them with those referring to the second period of the first model. It is at once obvious that, although the output of consumer goods

[7] Our arithmetical example will help us to illustrate the required intersectoral shift among the capital stocks of Sector Ia and Sector Ib. As a starting point, we use the same values for the critical coefficients ($k = 2$, $d = 0.1$, and $s = 0.5$), in the same numerical setup of outputs that served us in Chapter 9, Section VII,2. Thus we have

	F^*	am^*		pay*		P		o^*	net o^*
Ia	180	18	+	36	+	36	=	90	60
Ib	120	12	+	24	+	24	=	60	40
II	200	20	+	40	+	40	=	100	—
System	500	50	+	100	+	100	=	250	100

and for the subsequent period

Ia	216	21.6 +		43.2 +		43.2	=	108	72
Ib	144	14.4 +		28.8 +		28.8	=	72	48
II	240	24	+	48	+	48	=	120	—
System	600	60	+	120	+	120	=	300	120

Now we write down a second model with k and d and initial aggregate output unchanged, but with s reduced from 0.5 to 0.25, and we obtain

Ia	80	8	+	24	+	8	=	40	20
Ib	120	12	+	36	+	12	=	60	30
II	300	30	+	90	+	30	=	150	—
System	500	50	+	150	+	50	=	250	50

and for the subsequent period

Ia	88	8.8 +		26.4 +		8.8	=	44	22
Ib	132	13.2 +		39.6 +		13.2	=	66	33
II	330	33	+	99	+	33	=	165	—
System	550	55	+	165	+	55	=	275	255

To visualize the shift of equipment from Sector Ia to Sector Ib as required by the *fall* in the savings ratio, we must compare the first period in the first model with the second period in the second model. Then we see that Sector Ib, indeed, is in need of an additional 12 units of real capital, which are easily supplied from the excess of 92 units now available in Sector Ia. It stands to reason that, with constant k and d, any fall of the savings ratio is accompanied with a shrinkage of the *aggregate* capital stock in the equipment-good sector relative to the size of the capital stock in the consumer-good sector. Therefore, for equal aggregate outputs, the excess of capital in Sector Ia must always suffice to cover the deficit in Sector Ib.

falls by 20 percent, as does the stock of secondary equipment, the aggregate size of the primary capital stock rises by 80 percent, that is, by 160 units. There is nowhere any excess supply from which this excess demand could be satisfied, and the rise in the savings (and investment) ratio can be accommodated only after an intervening process of capital formation has provided the necessary addition to primary equipment. In other words, adjustment to a *fall* in the savings ratio is *asymmetrical* with adjustment to a *rise* in the savings ratio. The doubts of prevailing opinion concerning the stability of the growth path appear to be justified in the latter case.

Fortunately, the alarm is without cause. Just as the literature on the subject, we have so far disregarded a factor that puts a stabilizing mechanism into operation after all. What is at stake is the consequence of a change in the savings ratio for the *absorptive capacity* of the system. In the initial period representing dynamic equilibrium, the actual rate of growth is in accord with the "natural" rate, that is, with the rate determined by the rise in labor supply and capital requiring improvements. If the savings ratio falls or rises, this concurrence is disturbed. In the former case, the accruing new capacity falls short of what the factor increment requires. As a consequence, in every subsequent period part of the labor increment cannot be absorbed, creating a situation analogous with the one discussed under the heading of involuntary saving.[8] As long as the motorial conditions and, especially, the expectations stipulated earlier remain in force, rising unemployment – by inducing money wages to fall – will recreate savings to be profitably invested in the absorption of the idle resources.

This time the effect of a rise in the savings ratio operates in a perfectly symmetrical manner. The actual rate of growth tends to outrun the natural rate, stimulating rising demand for labor (rising money wages) and a corresponding reduction of savings. Thus, neither undersaving nor oversaving can move the system to a different level of dynamic equilibrium; the mechanism of involuntary saving and dissaving will always restore the original level. Under the motorial conditions stated, which, as we saw previously, are the same as those assumed by Harrod, dynamic equilibrium displays genuine stability, and dislocations from equilibrium evoke forces that will pull the system back to the equilibrium path.

In exposing the flaws that vitiate the conventional treatment of the stability of dynamic equilibrium, we have been moving at the positive level of analysis. Therefore, it is only fair to admit that, once the stipulated motorial conditions are relaxed, *in*stability of dynamic equilibrium can be easily demonstrated. For instance, one may well argue that the

[8] See Chapter 8, Section II.

growing pool of unemployed associated with a fall in the savings ratio will induce elastic wage and price expectations and thus create destabilizing behavior. However, such motorial considerations are not the basis on which prevailing opinion establishes its pessimistic conclusion. Rather, it insists on a structural mechanism set in motion by scarcity or excess of real capital, burdening dynamic equilibrium with "inherent" instability. This is a proposition for which no valid grounds can be found.

Summing up our critical examination of the Harrod–Domar model in this and the preceding chapter, we conclude that the *structural* conditions for steady growth are much more severe than conventionally described but that, once steady growth has been achieved, its inherent stability is considerably greater than conventional analysis makes it appear.

PART II
Changes in the rate of change

*I. The dynamics of
labor supply*

I I

The setting of the problem

I

We have finally reached the foot of the mountain. The structural and motorial analyses pursued in Part I have served the purpose of tooling up. The analytical instruments previously elaborated are now to help us in investigating a selected group of problems which can all be subsumed under the general heading of "changes in the rate of change." More precisely, we shall be concerned with the "traverses" that lead, under the impact of a change in the rate of increase or decrease of one of the basic resource factors (labor, natural resources, technology), from an initial dynamic equilibrium to a terminal dynamic equilibrium at a higher or lower rate of resource utilization.

Part II deals with the traverses as engendered by changes in the rate of change in *labor supply,* whereas Part III takes up the question of diminishing returns of *natural resources* and, in addition, the technique of recycling residuals. Part IV studies some of the processes by which changes in the rate of *productivity* can be absorbed.

Two decades ago I discussed some of these problems in the framework of stationary rather than dynamic equilibrium.[1] For didactic purposes we shall occasionally take our bearings from this simpler frame of reference. However, it stands to reason that analysis within a dynamic framework not only presents a more general case from which the stationary adjustment processes can be derived by setting the initial and the terminal rates of growth equal to zero, but it has also greater empirical relevance. Although actual economic processes do not pursue the course of dynamic equilibrium either, a dynamic framework includes from the outset variables such as saving, investment, and profit that are crucial for the study of the traverses in which we are interested.

Still, a dynamic framework poses a methodological problem of its own which should be faced from the outset. In speaking of *traverses* as our main field of study, we have in mind the path that connects two dynamic equilibria defined by different rates of change. Now, dynamic equilibrium

---

[1] See Lowe, "Structural Analysis of Real Capital Formation," *loc. cit.,* pp. 581–634.

itself pursues a path, the successive steps of which display a steady change in resource utilization. What then is the justification for singling out the special paths in which a *change* in the rate of change manifests itself as the core problem of our investigation?

The answer to this question goes to the root of growth analysis. It has already been indicated in the original circumscription of our central topic as the formation, application, and liquidation of real capital,[2] and can now be set out in more specific terms. It was then stated that, with one important exception, all growth processes are, in principle, *discontinuous*. This was to emphasize the fact that, even if the growth *stimuli* – changes in labor supply and productivity – are themselves continuous, the complementary real capital can be provided for only in discontinuous spurts. An exception to this is dynamic equilibrium where the rate of increase of the stimuli is *constant*. In this case, as we saw, the structure of production and, in particular, the structure of the equipment-good sectors is arranged in such a manner that a net addition to existing working places occurs continuously and in accord with the additional demand arising from increments of labor supply and, in prevailing opinion, also of productivity. Although Model XII depicts only the ratios of the *final-good aggregates*, it is intuitively clear that the same continuous expansion of output occurs in the *stages of production within each sector*, steadily adjusting the supply of working capital to the rising demand. In a word, in dynamic equilibrium, real capital formation in proportion with the steady increase in prime factors is part of the current process of production and can be taken for granted.

The situation is radically different if the rate of change of the prime factors or growth stimuli *increases* or *decreases*. In either case the currently supplied stock of real capital deviates from the stock demanded. In the former case it creates excess demand that can only be met by an additional process of capital formulation and, in the latter, excess supply with the critical consequence of a partial liquidation of the existing stock of real capital. Both processes interrupt the steady motion of dynamic equilibrium, which can be resumed only after the capital shortage or capital glut has been eliminated. Because in the real world changes in the rate of change of the growth stimuli are the rule, actual growth processes present themselves not as continuous paths, in analogy with dynamic equilibrium, but as sequences of capital accumulation or capital decumulation, that is, as a chain of discrete short-term processes of which the long-term growth trend is no more than an abstraction. This abstraction is a useful tool for *measurement*, for example, of the rate of growth or of the input–output levels at different points of time. However, if we

[2] See Chapter 1, Section II.

want to understand the *causal mechanism* that brings about these rates and levels, we must focus on the short-term processes, the tidal waves set in motion by the variations of the growth stimuli.

Now, if real economic growth manifests itself in a succession of irregular short-term processes, what analytical function is left for the steady long-term motion of dynamic equilibrium? It would at best be an accident if the spontaneous interaction of the growth stimuli created dynamic equilibrium as the initial condition from which further analysis could proceed. Even more dubious is the presumption that the response to additional growth stimuli will automatically lead a real system in the direction of some new dynamic equilibrium. Why then choose dynamic equilibrium as the overall frame of reference for our investigations?

There is, indeed, no justification for such a procedure, so long as we move at the level of *positive analysis,* trying to predict "the actual path which the economy (even the·model economy) will follow." Granting the logical elegance of such operations, "it would be blatantly obvious that they would be no more than exercises."[3] Any purport we can bestow on the study of traverses from one to another level of dynamic equilibrium can only be *instrumental;* namely, the demonstration of the structural and motorial changes required, or at least suitable, for the achievement of a stipulated goal, which, in this case, is the return, after the passage through characteristic disequilibria, to a renewed dynamic equilibrium. But what empirical meaning can we attribute to this goal?

This question can be easily answered if we remember that the traverses from one level of dynamic equilibrium to another one depict the successive movements of an economic system toward a new structure in which *rising or falling rates of resource supply are efficiently balanced.* We shall label this structure "balanced growth,"[4] and the general subject of this inquiry can be defined as a search for the conditions under which economic growth can be balanced. Dynamic equilibrium, both as an initial and a terminal state, describes the structural and motorial orders in which such a balance of growth has been achieved.

One of the conditions for balanced growth is the *efficient* absorption of newly accruing resources. The meaning of efficiency was earlier defined as referring to the maximization of taste-adequate physical outputs.[5] However, now our interest focuses on the intermediate positions through which the system moves from one state of balanced growth to another one, that is, on the *adjustment path,* and, therefore, we need an additional criterion

---

[3] See Hicks, Capital and Growth, *loc. cit.,* p. 201.
[4] The term "balanced growth" is used here in a sense different from the one bestowed on it by its originators, Samuelson and Solow. For a later version, see *Dosso,* Ch. 12; see also *OEK,* pp. 291–93.
[5] See Chapter 6, Section II.

for efficiency. This would not be the case if there was always but one path that connected the initial and the terminal position of the system. As a rule, however, there are several such paths. For example, one path maximizes speed of adjustment, another minimizes waste of resources, and a third minimizes the impact on consumption during the interval of capital formation. Some of these paths are mutually exclusive, and to make a choice among them can be accomplished only if, in a given case, a *path criterion* is stipulated, the degree of approximation to which then measures the efficiency of the chosen traverse.

II

Having established the legitimacy of our basic model as the initial position from which the dynamics of balanced growth can set forth, it may be helpful to make explicit some additional characteristics of the model, which have so far been passed over. We shall continue to operate with composite *outputs* in all three sectors – outputs that display absolute specificity. They are supposed to be produced in homogeneous productive units of equal size with equal capital–output ratios and amortization rates. These outputs are balanced by composite *inputs* consisting of homogeneous units of labor (which also include all *increments* of labor supply) and, within each sector, of homogeneous units of fixed and working capital goods. As a first approximation, we assume full mobility of labor over all three sectors, whereas real capital is mobile – in fact, homogeneous – only between the two equipment-good sectors. All through Part II, natural resources are treated as free goods, available in homogeneous units of equal grade; the influence of diminishing returns will be treated separately in Part III.

Throughout Part II the known technological horizon will be taken as constant. Moreover, the coefficients of production will be regarded as fixed once equipment goods are put into operation, so that there are no substitution possibilities between total labor input and the existing capital stock. This is not to deny that such substitution possibilities exist *ex ante,* that is, before investible funds have been sunk into real capital goods. This problem will occupy us in Part IV in the context of technological change. What is excluded by our assumption are technical "spectra," namely, "the fact that in any state of knowledge a great variety of methods are technically feasible, offering different rates of output per man *with different types of equipment,* [my italics] and that the choice between them depends on their relative profitability at the ruling levels of costs and prices."[6] Professor Robinson, to whom we owe the most elaborate

[6] Robinson, *The Accumulation of Capital, loc. cit.,* p. 101.

discussion of such technical spectra, has expressed serious doubts about the realistic significance of the entire construct.[7] However, in the light of our concerns, an analytical objection must be raised. As Professor Robinson explicitly states, transition from one technical spectrum to another is conditional on the prior provision of a "different type of equipment," that is, on the physical transformation of real capital. Therefore, admission of variability of the technical coefficients in this sense would still involve us in technical problems of capital formation similar to those that the assumption of fixed coefficients poses.

In drawing this conclusion, we reject once more the hypothesis of unlimited malleability of real capital. On the other hand, there are, indeed, possibilities for short-period variations of the capital–labor ratio, which, within limits, do admit of absorption of a labor increment *without prior formation of real capital*. These variations are a real challenge to our procedure and will, for this reason, be extensively discussed in Chapter 13.

III

To conclude these introductory remarks, a word needs be added on the *social structures* that affect our investigation of traverse processes. In establishing our Basic Model, we have distinguished between certain technical features of the model that transcend all social differentiation and other characteristics that vary according to whether we use the model for the interpretation of stationary and dynamic equilibria in a collectivist system or in a free market. Among the latter characteristics is the two-strata model defined earlier,[8] describing the social structure underlying our analysis of market processes. We now put further limits on this model by postulating a closed system of strict laissez-faire and pure competition in both the commodity and factor markets.

As was to be expected in a study of equilibria, the difference in social organization revealed itself mainly at the level of motorial analysis, when the behavioral and motivational patterns to sustain equilibrium had to be determined. Henceforth, however, with path analysis in the foreground, some difference between a collectivist and a market organization will already appear at the structural level proper, that is, when the objective range of the system's possible motions is to be discovered, independent of the motorial conditions that set the system on one of the possible paths and keep it there.

Contrary to a widely held opinion, we shall discover that the combination of decentralized decision making with a highly developed industrial

[7] *Ibid.,* pp. 101 (Note 1), 151, 156.
[8] See Chapter 8, Section II.

technology, namely, the social and technical conditions typical for modern markets, imposes stricter constraints on goal-adequate motion than does the same form of industrial organization when steered by centralized decision making. This is equivalent to saying that, because of fewer alternatives, the instrumental solution of the traverse problems is more determinate in a free market, whereas, because of the large number of feasible traverses, the prospects of attaining the goal are more favorable in a collectivist system.[9]

[9] Because from now on all our analyses will be placed in a dynamic framework (except when a stationary context is explicitly noted), we shall no longer mark our variables by an asterisk.

12

A bird's-eye view of an expanding traverse

The chapters to follow display a somewhat technical character, describing in symbolic terms the adjustment path from a given level of dynamic equilibrium to a higher or lower level and, in particular, the expansion, contraction, and relative shifts of the sectors of production. Although the mathematics is quite elementary and the results obtained in most cases confirm our intuitive hunches, it may be helpful to introduce these exercises by a literary survey of the strategic processes. We shall confine ourselves here to surveying the consequences of an *increase* in the rate of labor supply. Knowing that in all such instances it is the formation of real capital that is at the center, we shall first consider the formation and application of additional fixed capital, to be followed by inspection of the changes in working capital.

I

The traverse movements affecting *fixed capital,* which serve to absorb an increase in the rate of labor supply, can be subdivided into four phases: partial liberation of existing capacity; augmentation of primary equipment output; augmentation of secondary equipment output; and augmentation of consumer goods output. We shall now explain the rationale for this sequence of movements and briefly describe the main characteristics of each phase.

1. *Partial Liberation of Existing Capacity.* On intuitive grounds the most appropriate place for the absorption of an increase in the labor increment seems to be the consumer-good sector. Not only would absorption there offer employment, but it would also create the additional output required to provide for the increment at the original level of per capita consumption. However, in a regime of full resource utilization with fixed coefficients of production, such absorption in the consumer-good sector requires additional secondary equipment, an addition that can only come from the equipment-good sector (Sector Ib). Yet, under the stated technical conditions, Sector Ib cannot supply additional output either unless it has

increased its own equipment stock. Such an increase must be obtained from Sector Ia, which produces and replaces what we called primary equipment. However, in the prevailing state of dynamic equilibrium, the capital stock of Sector Ia is also fully utilized – partly in replacing the wear and tear and in expanding the equipment in Sector Ib, and partly in replacing its own wear and tear and providing for its own expansion. Thus our problem of absorbing the labor increment reduces to the question, By what procedure can the output of primary equipment, over and above current replacement and net investment demands, be increased so that both Sector Ib and Sector II can increase their original capital stocks?

One might, first of all, think of temporarily not replacing the capital stock in Sector Ia and of transferring the surplus thus obtained to Sector Ib. Indeed, I shall argue below that such "cannibalization" of capital stocks can overcome certain bottlenecks in a collectivist system.[1] The social structure of a free market, however, lacks the institutional controls to enforce such an expedient. Moreover, this particular type of cannibalization would not really help, because a fall in the rate of replacement and net investment in Sector Ia itself would make the system shrink rather than expand.

The bottleneck can be broken only if the other part of Sector Ia's current output, which has so far served to *replace* the wear and tear and to *expand* the capacity of Sector Ib, is curtailed, and if the productive capacity thus gained is directed to the capital stock in Sector Ia for further self-augmentation. Such a reorganization within Sector Ia can just as well, and perhaps even more instructively, be viewed as a rearrangement of production within Sector Ib. Instead of concentrating on replacing and steadily expanding the capital stock in Sector II, Sector Ib can now be regarded as turning partly to "Sector Ia-like" activity, by using part of its stock of primary equipment, including part of the replacements it receives from Sector Ia, for the production of more primary equipment. In either interpretation what matters is *a shift in the physical aggregate that the two equipment-good sectors produce,* in the direction of less secondary and more primary equipment. In any case, the rate of replacement and expansion of secondary equipment must fall, with the paradoxical result that, in order ultimately to *increase* the output of consumer goods, such output must, to begin with, be *reduced.*

We are at this stage not interested in the mechanisms – collectivist command and voluntary, involuntary, or forced savings – that may bring about such a reduction of consumer-good output. They are part of the motorial analysis of the adjustment process. However, it is now clear why we describe this first phase of the traverse as a "liberation of existing capac-

[1] See Chapter 16.

ity." Specifically, in order to get the expansion process under way, the capacity that is located in Sector Ib, must be freed in part from its original task of replacing and expanding capacity in Sector II. This liberated capacity is now to be used to expand Sector Ia. At this stage we enter the second phase.

2. *Augmentation of Output of Primary Equipment.* It is essential to realize from the outset that augmentation of primary equipment, which amounts to self-augmentation, is a cumulative process. Each unit of primary equipment that is produced with the help of the original stock becomes part of the primary capital stock of the subsequent period. The proper amount of such self-augmentation depends, of course, on the size of the change in the rate of growth of labor supply, for the absorption of which the new capital stock is to be built. We shall discover that approximation of self-augmentation to this ideal limit is much more easily achieved in a collectivist than in a free market system. In other words, the danger of either "overbuilding" or "underbuilding" the new stock of primary equipment and, thus, of creating a peculiar type of waste will prove inherent in the structural setup of a free market.

3. *Augmentation of Output of Secondary Equipment.* Once the addition to primary equipment has been made, the third phase of the traverse begins. It consists in diverting an appropriate part of the newly built primary equipment from further self-augmentation to the expansion of secondary equipment. This again proves to be a rather intricate task, especially in a free market system. The reason is that during the second phase the stock of primary equipment is geared to the cumulative expansion of such *stock*. However, once the required limit of expansion has been reached, the bulk of the new stock must be shifted to Sector Ib for the augmentation of secondary equipment. Or, what amounts to the same, output and capital stock in Sector Ia must adjust themselves to the *replacement* and *steady expansion,* at the higher rate, of the additional equipment now operating in Sectors Ia and Ib.

4. *Augmentation of Consumer-Good Output.* Adjustment will come to an end and the traverse will be completed when the expanded secondary equipment is applied in Sector II for the expansion of the output of consumer goods. As we shall see, it is during this and the preceding phase that the labor increment is finally absorbed.

The question arises whether phases 2, 3, and 4 need be separated by such sharp caesuras. Let us take, for example, the very first unit of additional primary equipment, which is produced in phase 2 by self-augmentation of the original stock. Could it not be at once devoted to an increase of secondary equipment, an addition that could then be manned without delay for the production of additional consumer goods, and so on in continuous sequence? In other words, for the "horizontal" expansion of one sector after another, could we not substitute a process of "vertical" expansion in which successive "layers" would be added in all three sectors?

Indeed, this is the case from a purely technical point of view, and a collectivist system can proceed in this manner. It should, however, be realized that the costs of the traverse in terms of required adjustment time would by no means be reduced by this procedure. In the sequence of horizontal phases, as just described, the entire increment of labor must forego consumption up to the beginning of phase 4. In the vertical sequence, some members of the increment will receive consumer goods as early as in phase 2, but only at the expense of others who will have to wait all the longer. Moreover, as will be shown, what is a matter of choice for a collectivist system is by no means so in a free market. Strict separation between the phases has been chosen in our expository model, because it depicts what is the structurally inescapable sequence in a system with decentralized decision making.

II

So far our attention has focused entirely on the expansion of fixed capital goods in their completed form as finished goods. However, to reach that state, additional natural resources will have to undergo a technical process of transformation into intermediate goods of progressively higher degrees of completion, a process that creates the additional working capital required. It will now be briefly shown in what manner such *formation of working capital* is to be accomplished during the four phases of the adjustment process outlined for the formation of fixed capital. For this purpose we shall make use of the stylized set of goods on which we built earlier our general schema of production.[2]

1. Liberation of Some Existing Working Capital Goods. Reduction of output of consumer goods, with which the traverse starts, is bound also to liberate a quantity of *intermediate* goods in Sector II, proportionate with the fall in utilization of secondary equipment. To the extent to which these intermediate goods are specific, in the sense of being inapplicable to the production of equipment goods, the amounts already in the pipelines when

[2] See Chapter 3, Section II.

the output reduction starts, will stand idle up to the beginning of phase 4 when the production of consumer goods is fully resumed. This is not true of the intermediate goods in Sector Ib. Although we postulate absolute specificity of *finished* primary and secondary equipment, the unfinished goods from which emanate both types of equipment goods (ore, pig iron, steel) are nonspecific and may be employed in either equipment-good sector. Therefore, the working capital liberated in Sector Ib can at once be utilized in the augmentation of primary equipment.

2. *Augmentation of Working Capital Goods for Expansion of Primary Equipment.* This reapplication of working capital liberated in Sector Ib initiates the second phase. In precise terms, the first act of self-augmentation of primary equipment concerns the use of working capital goods, formerly applied to the production of secondary equipment, for the production of additional primary equipment. In other words, ore, pig iron, steel, which were hitherto processed into cotton gins, spindles, looms, and sewing machines, must now be turned into extractive machines, blast furnaces, steel mills, and, ultimately, machine tools. Only with the appearance of such *new primary equipment* are the conditions fulfilled for the general self-augmentation of primary equipment. This self-augmentation must follow a predetermined sequence: first more extractive machinery to provide additional ore; then more blast furnaces to provide additional pig iron; then more steel mills to provide additional steel; and finally culminating in another batch of machine tools. Thus, the self-augmentation of primary equipment occurs in a steady interplay with the expansion of the appropriate working capital goods, that is, together with a continuous expansion of the pipelines in Sector Ia.

3. *Augmentation of Working Capital Goods for Expansion of Secondary Equipment.* The third phase of the traverse devoted to the expansion of secondary equipment requires an analogous expansion of the stock of working capital in Sector Ib. In view of the physical identity of these intermediate goods with those that serve the expansion of primary equipment, all that is necessary is that further quantities of ore, pig iron, and steel will now be manufactured into additional gins, spindles, looms, and sewing machines.

4. *Augmentation of Working Capital for Expansion of Consumer Goods.* The traverse comes to an end when the increments of secondary equipment to be applied in the successive stages of Sector II are put to work in expanding the output of cotton, yarn, cloth, and, ultimately, the finished consumer good, namely, dresses.

It is intuitively clear that the quantitative relations denoting the expansion of working capital through the successive stages in each sector are strictly determined by the technical order of the productive process and are, for this reason, the same in a collectivist system as in a free market. We shall subsequently illustrate these relations with a numerical example.[3]

III

Earlier we commented[4] on the fact that our formal treatment of dynamic equilibrium confines itself to simple algebraic operations supplemented by numerical examples, to the exclusion of differential calculus which, at first sight, appears to be a much more efficient tool for path analysis. In defense of our procedure, it was said that, for the sake of systematic continuity, we wished to treat the problems posed by dynamic equilibrium with the same formal technique that would prove suitable for the analysis of dynamic disequilibria.

Our provisional survey of some of the latter problems, arising during the traverse from one level of dynamic equilibrium to a higher one, has given substance to this apology. To describe with the aid of differential equations the contortions that any economic system must undergo during such an adjustment process – converse sectoral expansions and contractions, sectoral variations occurring at different rates of change, switches from one sector to another one, to mention only a few – requires mathematics of such complexity that any formal advantages would have to be purchased at the sacrifice of analytical transparency. Moreover, in view of the nonlinear nature of most of these processes, it is very doubtful whether a general solution can be obtained at all.

At the same time it must be admitted that our procedure, which subdivides continuous processes into discrete periods for which sector ratios and other structural conditions are established, resembles comparative statics rather than genuine dynamics and has its own pitfalls of misrepresentation that need to be watched. Whether its mathematical simplicity and analytical clarity vindicate this choice of technique can only be judged on the basis of its results.

[3] See Chapter 17.
[4] See Chapter 9, footnote 29.

13

On the short-period variability of the capital–labor ratio

Even our brief survey of the major problems that arise during the adjustment of any economic system to a higher rate of growth of labor supply points up the significance of our assumption as to the fixity of the technical coefficients and, in particular, of the capital–labor ratio. It is this assumption that places capital formation in the center of analysis by excluding employment of the labor increment on the preexisting capital stock, thus calling for highly complex shifts among the sector inputs and outputs. Subsequent investigation of the motorial conditions for the successful accomplishment of these shifts will reveal additional complications. Most of these difficulties, both real and analytical, might be circumvented if the capital–labor ratio could be varied in the short period and the labor increment simply be distributed over the three sectors, thus expanding not only employment but also output in the appropriate proportions. Therefore, to demonstrate the limits of any such solution, a more detailed exposition than has so far been given is in order.

What we are now concerned with has nothing to do with the spectrum of techniques in the sense discussed earlier.[1] Whatever their intrinsic merits, such variations of the capital–labor ratio are of a long-period nature insofar as they require the previous formation or transformation of real capital and, thus, cannot escape the contortions of the adjustment path described. What is now at stake are the possibilities of utilizing the initial capital stock in its given form and, thus, of reducing absorption to a short-period process in the strict Marshallian meaning.

I

In examining such a possibility we must start from the commonsense experience that, in practice, the capital–labor ratio, now seen in this restricted context, is never rigidly fixed. There are at least three instances in which considerable variability seems to prevail: underutilization of the available capital stock; a margin between the optimum and the maximum

[1] See Chapter 11, Section II.

utilization of the initially given equipment; and the working of this equipment over more than one shift.

The three cases are not of equal significance for our investigation. *Underutilization* of the capital stock has been implicitly excluded by our starting out from dynamic equilibrium. For our purposes the relevant change in the capital–labor ratio is related to *expansion* of output and, thus, of employment *beyond the point of optimum efficiency* – the latter marks the limit of the firm's activity in dynamic equilibrium. Building on the conventional microeconomic diagram, we move to the right of the intersection of the average and the marginal cost curves. And we shall see that *additional work shifts* can be conceived as special cases of "moving beyond the production optimum," especially when they are applied to the system at large.

Now, in practice, the feasible margin for such expansion of output and employment varies considerably among different fields of production. Although it is wide in nonmechanized agriculture and in retailing, the technical margin for expansion is quite narrow in most manufacturing industries. Moreover, rapidly diminishing marginal returns and, thus, rapidly rising marginal costs keep the economically exploitable margin within still narrower limits; though, within these limits, lower returns enhance employment.

However, the major limitation to such expansion is bound up with the very fact of "moving to the right". By using the available equipment at more than its optimum intensity, we raise the effective rate of wear and tear, thus increasing the required rate of replacement. Not only does this adversely affect production costs and, thus, the profitability of expansion, but it brings home the fact that expansion of this kind in one sector depends on the available margin of expansion in other sectors that are to provide capital replacement.

To state the problem in literary terms, we assume that, to begin with, the new labor increment, over and above the steady increase prevailing in the initial dynamic equilibrium, will in part be employed in the consumer-good sector. Rising replacement demands in that sector make it necessary that another part be employed in the sector producing secondary equipment, to be followed by a corresponding increase of employment and output in the sector producing primary equipment. It stands to reason that the latent capacity in the latter sector holds the strategic position. Even if the initial expansion of output in all three sectors provides a considerable *one-time* expansion of employment, *continuous* absorption, as required by a permanent increase in the growth of labor supply, is possible only if the increment of output in Sector Ia, due to the initial one-time expansion, *exceeds* the increments of replacement required in both equipment-good sectors. Only if we are left with a *permanent surplus of primary equipment,* can moving to the right accommodate the capital requirements of continuous growth.

II

Can we form a precise conception of the addition to absorptive capacity and, thus, to employment that such moving to the right can provide? For this purpose we introduce some of our earlier simplifying assumptions, namely, equal capital–output ratios and depreciation rates in every sector, coupled with the stipulation that the technical margin for expanding output from the given capital stock also be the same in every sector. We shall further distinguish between the *direct* one-time addition to capacity and employment in all three sectors due to expansion of output derived from the initial capacity, and *indirect* additions to output and employment based on a surplus of output in Sector Ia which may stem from the direct addition.

Our first concern is to find a measure for the *direct increments of employment.* This is easily done when we remember that moving to the right raises aggregate output from the dynamic equilibrium level o_0 to o', which implies a reduction of the capital–output ratio from k_0 to k'. Disregarding for the time being the effect of diminishing returns on employment, we can determine n', the size of employment after expansion, from the necessary equality of o'/n' with o_0/n_0. We thus obtain

$$n' = \frac{o'}{o_0} \cdot n_0 = \frac{F_0/k'}{F_0/k_0} \cdot n_0 = \frac{k_0}{k'} \cdot n_0$$

and the direct increment of employment amounts to

$$\Delta n_{\text{dir}} = \frac{k_0 - k'}{k'} \cdot n_0 \tag{13.1}$$

In order to facilitate comparison of the direct increment with the indirect increment of employment, we express n_0 in terms of the initial capital stock divided by the initial capital–labor ratio c_0; the latter can itself be related[2] to k_0 as

$$c_0 = \frac{k_0}{1 - k_0 d_0}$$

This yields

$$\Delta n_{\text{dir}} = \frac{(k_0 - k')(1 - k_0 d_0)}{k_0 k'} \cdot F_0 \tag{13.1.1}$$

[2] See Chapter 4, footnote 9.

Equations 13.1 and 13.1.1 measure the size of the direct increment of employment, always provided that moving to the right is technically possible. Whether such expansion is, in fact, possible depends on the size of d', that is, on the new higher rate of depreciation. Because the rate of depreciation moves inversely with the capital–output ratio, we can establish a simple rule: Only sô long as the rate of increase of d does not exceed the rate of decrease of k, that is, so long as $k'd' \leq k_0 d_0$, can output and employment be raised above the initial level. If $k'd'$ is larger than $k_0 d_0$ the additional output of primary equipment is too small to meet the higher replacement requirements.

As previously stated, such direct increment of employment, if feasible at all, is a one-time affair. It depends exclusively, as Equation 13.1 shows, on the relative size of k_0 and k', and, because it involves all three sectors, its size can be considerable even for small expansions of output. Making use of the numerical model for dynamic equilibrium introduced earlier[3], which has $k_0 = 2$, and assuming that o' is no larger than $11/10$ of o_0, we obtain $k' = 20/11$ and a direct increment of employment of 10 percent. With $o' = 12/10$, the increment rises to 20 percent. If in addition we take account of diminishing returns and assume a fall in return to 80 percent, then the direct increment of employment in the second example rises to 25 percent.

From this we can conclude that the direct employment gain owing to moving to the right more than suffices to absorb any empirically relevant *once-over* increase in labor supply. We must remember, however, that we are concerned with *steady* absorption of a *permanent* addition to the rate of increase of labor supply. Even if this addition amounts to no more than 2–3 percent, it stands to reason that the new absorptive capacity created by direct output expansion will be exhausted after a few periods of production with rising increments of labor supply. Therefore, the answer to the question whether moving to the right can serve as an *effective substitute for new capital formation also under conditions of continuous growth* depends on the *size and the persistence through time of indirect increments of employment.*

III

From what has so far been said, it is intuitively clear that the presence of any *indirect increments of employment* is conditional on a *surplus of primary equipment* left after the increase in the replacement requirements of the two equipment-good sectors has been met by the direct expansion of output in Sector Ia. This can be expressed in symbolic terms as follows.

[3] See Chapter 9, Section V, Model XII.i.

We start from the strategic equality between inputs and outputs in dynamic equilibrium, namely,

$$a_0 = \frac{F_{a_0}}{k_0} = d_0 \cdot F_{a_0} + d_0 \cdot F_{b_0} + I_{a_0} + I_{b_0}$$

Denoting any surplus of primary equipment due to direct expansion by ΔF_{a_0}, we obtain the new equality

$$\Delta F_{a_0} = \frac{F_{a_0}}{k'} - d'F_{a_0} - d'F_{b_0} - I_{a_0} - I_{b_0}$$

Because

$$F_{b_0} = F_{a_0} \cdot \frac{1 - k_0 d_0(1 - s) + s}{k_0 d_0(1 - s) + s}$$

or in simplified notation[4]

$$F_{b_0} = F_{a_0} \cdot \frac{1 - B}{B}$$

Therefore

$$\Delta F_{a_0} = \frac{F_{a_0}}{k'} - d'F_{a_0} - \frac{1 - B}{B} \cdot d'F_{a_0} - (I_{a_0} + I_{b_0})$$

$$= \frac{B - k'd'}{k'B} \cdot F_{a_0} - (I_{a_0} + I_{b_0})$$

Now

$$I_{a_0} + I_{b_0} = a_0 - f_{a_0} - f_{b_0}$$

$$= \frac{F_{a_0}}{k_0} - d_0 \cdot F_{a_0} - d_0 \cdot \frac{1 - B}{B} \cdot F_{a_0}$$

$$= \frac{B - k_0 d_0}{k_0 B} \cdot F_{a_0}$$

and we obtain for the surplus of primary equipment

$$\Delta F_{a_0} = \left[\frac{B - k'd'}{k'B} - \frac{B - k_0 d_0}{k_0 B} \right] \cdot F_{a_0}$$

We must be aware that the foregoing expression measures the *gross* surplus of primary equipment, which, when applied to further production,

---

[4] See Chapter 9, Section V, Model XII.

must be divided between the two equipment-good sectors in accord with the prevailing sector ratios. The true measure of indirect expansion is represented by the *net* surplus that can be *added* to the capital stock in Sector Ia in the subsequent period. This yields the measure for the indirect expansion of the primary capital stock following the first period of production

$$\Delta F_{a_0} \text{ (net)} = \left[\frac{B - k'd'}{k'} - \frac{B - k_0 d_c}{k_0} \right] \cdot F_{a_0} \tag{13.2}$$

Finally, in order to determine the increment of employment that this period addition to primary capital stock can provide, we must reduce the expression obtained in Equation 13.2 by the inverse of the new capital–labor ratio,[5]

$$c' = \frac{k'}{1 - k_0 d_0}$$

This yields, in analogy with Equation 13.1.1 which states the direct increment of employment,

$$\Delta n_{\text{indir}} = \frac{1 - kd}{k'} \left[\frac{B - k'd'}{k'} - \frac{B - k_0 d_0}{k_0} \right] \cdot F_0 \tag{13.3}$$

Choosing again operational values for the various coefficients ($k_0 = 2$–3; $d_0 = 1/10$–$1/15$; $s = 1/20$–$1/10$)[6] and setting the range of direct expansion of output at 20 percent, the margin for the indirect increment of employment in Sector Ia (with $k' = 5/3$–$9/4$ and $d' = 1/9$–$1/14$) is about 2 percent that of the original level of employment – a result that can be generalized for the system as a whole. By again considering diminishing returns with a reduction of the initial rate of return to 80 percent, the period increment of employment rises to about $2\frac{1}{2}$ percent.[7,8]

---

[5] The denominator expressing the labor–output ratio remains constant so long as returns are constant.

[6] The savings ratio enters via the symbol B.

[7] Because the net surplus in Sector Ia is to be added to the original stock F_{a_0} and will produce another net surplus in the subsequent period, expansion of F_{a_0} and the indirect increment of employment are subject to a multiplying process. However, as our numerical example shows, the multipliers are for all practical purposes close to 1 and can for this reason be disregarded.

[8] Transition to a second or even third shift will not basically alter our result. Although gross output in Sector Ia is likely to expand much more, *net* output will not follow suit because of the sharply rising replacement demand in all sectors. As a consequence the critical difference, $k_0 d_0 - k'd'$, cannot rise much above the values commensurate with mere moving to the right. There is, in addition, a practical reason that militates against the adoption

What then is the final result of all this? We have seen that the *direct increment* provides a large one-time addition to the aggregate employment opportunities prevailing in dynamic equilibrium. Yet, because the margin thus created is fixed once and for all, it can at best serve as a temporary expedient when it comes to the steady absorption of a permanent increase in the rate of growth of labor supply. Therefore, the long-term burden of absorption falls on the *indirect increment,* which accrues indefinitely in every period of production.[9] So long as the increase in labor supply over and above the level of dynamic equilibrium equals, or is smaller than, the increase of indirect absorptive capacity, moving to the right can indeed act as a substitute for new capital formation, as earlier defined.

At the same time we have seen that, for practically relevant values of the critical coefficients, the secondary increment is quite small. In mature industrial countries, the margin is probably wide enough to accommodate upward changes in the rate of population increase, coupled with standard rises in the participation rate of the working population. However, it is more than doubtful that, in addition, the steadily rising capital requirements of technological improvements can thus be taken care of, let alone the need to expand the system's capital stock in order to "compensate" technological unemployment.[10]

The limitations are even stricter in underdeveloped regions where otherwise, in view of the prevailing overall scarcity of capital, such an expedient would be especially beneficial. However, in these areas, the latent capacity of the already small equipment-good industry is much narrower, whereas overutilization is bound to raise the rate of replacement much more steeply. Thus if, within the technological limits discussed, variability of the capital–labor ratio cannot satisfy the rising capacity requirements of a fully industrialized system, it certainly cannot effectively contribute to industrial development.

of a multishift organization of production for the system as a whole. Whatever may be true of manufacturing industries generally, already today iron and steel and chemical production operate under a three-shift system. Both these are strategic stages in the production of equipment goods, so that any sharp rise in replacement requirements is bound to create a capital shortage that can only be overcome by new capital formation.

[9] The role of the direct increment in the absorption of, say, a rise of the equilibrium rate of increase of labor supply from 4 to 6 percent can be visualized as follows: In the early periods such an increase by 2 percent permits only very small moves to the right, that is, a' and k' will hardly differ from the original a_0 and k_0. This means that indirect capacity derived from such a small expansion will be negligible, and the burden of absorption rests during this phase entirely on the direct employment effect. This will gradually change with successive moves to the right so that, once the direct increment nears exhaustion, a' has risen and k' has fallen sufficiently to make it possible for the secondary increment to take over.

[10] For details, see Chapters 23 and 24.

IV

Our negative result might yet be called in question. Why confine expansion of the capital stock in Sector Ia to the *net* surplus of the extended output, instead of using the entire *gross* surplus for such extension? Such a procedure would expand the rise in employment capacity in this sector by a factor of 2 or 3, depending on the relative size of the two equipment-good sectors. True, as a consequence, the capital stock in Sectors Ib and II could no longer be proportionally expanded, resulting in falling real wages, because n rises steadily in the face of a constant output of consumer goods. However, in the meantime the steady self-augmentation of output in Sector Ia will gradually build up a capital stock of primary equipment, sufficient not only to restore the shrinkage of the capital stock in Sector Ib but also to adjust the total capacity of the system to the higher growth rate.

The argument is well taken – only it demonstrates the opposite of what it was intended to prove. It describes a process of *new capital formation* in analogy to our exposition in Chapter 12. Although it starts, as it were, at the "top" of the structure of production by at once applying the surplus output of Sector Ia to self-augmentation (only the second phase in our prior analysis), it leads as a secondary consequence to a temporary reduction of per capita consumption (our starting phase). In a word, although it is initiated by a variation of the capital–output ratio, this procedure amounts to the gradual formation of a new capital stock and may, thus, be considered as an alternative to our scenario.

The reason why we have chosen the latter is very simple. Even if a collectivist system can be thought as directing the plants operating in Sector Ia toward self-augmentation from the outset, a market system lacks the motorial forces and, thus, the mechanism that could guarantee this type of investment. Why this is different in an adjustment process that starts at the "bottom" of the structure of production, as conceived by our model, is a topic to which we now turn.

14

Adjustment to a higher rate of growth of labor supply in a free market

I. Structure Analysis

The present chapter, which is supplemented in Chapter 18 by the study of a *decline* in the rate of growth of labor supply, contains the core of our investigations. Although it concentrates on a change in the rate of labor supply but disregards changes in the rate of return and in technology, it will set the pattern for describing, in slow motion and in quantitative precision, the sectoral contortions of the traverse that lead from an initial level of dynamic equilibrium to a higher level. Because in this chapter we try to reproduce the complexity of the actual phenomena, analysis of these contortions will prove a very intricate undertaking. To facilitate understanding, we shall carry it out in several stages of decreasing abstraction.

Following the procedure outlined in our literary presentation of the traverse, we shall build up in Sections II–IV a Primary Model that insulates the strategic sectoral shifts, as an initial growth stimulus sets them in motion, from other events occurring at the same time. The subsequent sections will integrate these events into a more complex Secondary Model. In Chapter 15, we shall underpin our structure analysis by a complementary force analysis and also illustrate the findings symbolically expressed in the present chapter with a numerical example.

I

Assume a market system reduced to the two-strata organization defined earlier, moving in dynamic equilibrium with a growth rate α of labor supply.[1] Assume further that the dynamic process of growth can be subdivided into finite periods.[2] At the beginning of one of these periods an additional increment α' of labor is supposed to enter the system. This new increment, to be understood in analogy with the original α as a percentage

---

[1] See Chapter 9, Model XII. By substituting, in accord with the Harrod-Domar formula, $k\alpha/(1 - kd)$ for $\bar{p}$, s, and i, respectively, Model XII is then a precise description of our initial state.

[2] These periods, which represent the time units in our models, will subsequently be identified with the period of maturation of primary equipment and will apply to the calculation of all flow magnitudes, in particular of k, d, and s.

addition to the existing stock of labor, is supposed to perpetuate itself so that the total growth rate of labor supply per period rises from α to $\alpha + \alpha'$.

How must the structure of dynamic equilibrium be modified so as to assure the efficient absorption of increment α'? To put it differently, because formation of a complementary addition to real capital is the essential condition for absorption, by what sequence of adjustment processes can such capital formation be accomplished most efficiently?

In stressing the efficiency of the process of capital formation we implicitly assert that there is more than one feasible adjustment path. Therefore, we need *path criteria* if one of these feasible paths is to be selected as the most efficient.[3] We stipulate as our path criterion: *maximum speed of adjustment constrained by the condition that malinvestment must be avoided*. The latter constraint implies that the capital newly formed is equal to the capital required for absorption, so that the new capital stock is neither "overbuilt" nor "underbuilt." We shall discover that a free market system, which is our socioeconomic frame of reference in this chapter, is, in principle, incapable of accomplishing such a "target" capital formation except by chance. Consequently, the traverse in which these conditions are fulfilled serves mainly as a standard by which the relative inefficiency of actual adjustment processes can be gauged.

From our bird's-eye view of an expanding traverse, we know that the adjustment path can be subdivided into several phases. It will now be our task to analyze each one of these phases in full detail and to establish in each phase the structural relations that agree with our path criterion.

II

We begin with what was defined earlier as the phase of *partial capacity liberation*. As we know, the capacity to be liberated will permit the self-augmentation of primary equipment.[4] This liberation, we have seen, is conditional on a reduction of output in Sector Ib, which, in turn, requires that the replacement and investment demand of the consumer-good sector be curtailed. This, however, will happen only if, as a first step, the supply of consumer goods is reduced.

In a free market the only mechanism that initiates a fall in the aggregate supply of consumer goods is a reduction of aggregate demand, that is, a rise in voluntary or involuntary savings.[5] In what follows we are going

---

[3] See Chapter 11, Section I.
[4] See Chapter 12, Section I.1.
[5] See Chapter 8, Section II. We disregard for the time being a third alternative, forced savings or credit inflation up to the limit of the "inflation barrier." This issue is considered in Chapter 15 in the context of motorial analysis.

to choose *in*voluntary savings as the initiating cause because, as we shall show, this is the case most favorable to targeted capital formation, and its failure to achieve an efficient traverse can serve us as *argumentum a fortiori*.

However, involuntary savings are not the original source of distortion of dynamic equilibrium. These savings themselves derive from a rise of profits, which, in turn, is due to a general fall of money wages, itself induced in the present case by the competitive impact of increment a' in the labor market. This yields us a measure for the aggregate of new involuntary savings, namely, the difference between the aggregate wage bill in the initial dynamic equilibrium and in the state in which the wage fall has been realized. The additional savings ratio s' can thus be expressed as

$$s' = \frac{\Sigma w_0 - \Sigma w_{00}}{y_0}$$

where the subscripts refer to dynamic equilibrium and the state after the wage fall, respectively, and y_0 stands for aggregate income in the initial dynamic equilibrium.

Now, in order to determine the size of the capacity to be liberated in Sector I, we must remember our path criterion according to which the traverse is to proceed at maximum speed. Such speed will be attained only if both the newly accruing savings symbolized by s' and also the original savings, symbolized by s, are applied to the self-augmentation of primary equipment. In the original dynamic equilibrium the latter savings had to be distributed over all three sectors in proportion with the prevailing sector ratios, thus assuring steady proportionate expansion. By our present assumption we "freeze," so to speak, the system at large at the level of growth it has attained when the new labor increment first appears. We then have, as it were, two subsystems: one that performs the intermediate act of building up additional capital stock through investment of aggregate savings, and the other that maintains the output of consumer goods at the level attained when the investment process began. The latter subsystem can be conceived in terms of a stationary structure of production in which a constant flow of consumer goods is steadily reproduced with the help of a constant flow of equipment goods.

This then is the set-up that our Primary Model depicts, concentrating on the intersectoral shifts on which adjustment to growth depends rather than on the growth process itself. Only after the intermediary process of capital formation has been completed, is the system in its entirety to resume the proportional expansion of all three sectors in accordance with the new higher growth rate and, thus, to recapture dynamic equilibrium. To the solution of this task our Secondary Model will be employed.

Against this background the size of capacity liberated in Sector I as a consequence of the aggregate of available savings may be ascertained as follows. The initial stock of secondary equipment in dynamic equilibrium amounts to

$$F_{z_0} = (1 - s)(1 - kd) \cdot ko_0$$

The additional savings, expressed as s', will reduce the utilized stock to

$$F_z' = (1 - s - s')(1 - kd) \cdot ko_0$$

By applying the stationary sector ratios, we obtain for the quantity of primary equipment necessary to maintain (no longer to expand) the reduced secondary capital stock

$$F'_{(a+b)} = \frac{kd}{1 - kd} (1 - s - s')(1 - kd) \cdot ko_0$$

Then the liberated primary capital stock amounts to $F_{(a+b)_0} - F'_{(a+b)}$, that is, to[6]

$$
\begin{aligned}
F_{(a+b)}(\text{lib}) &= [B - kd(1 - s - s')] \cdot ko_0 \\
&= (s + s' \cdot kd) \cdot ko_0
\end{aligned}
\tag{14.1}
$$

It is this quantity of the system's primary equipment that is available for self-augmentation, and at first sight it appears as if we were ready to move on to the second phase. Closer examination, however, reveals that further and very important sectoral changes are bound to occur during the liberation phase.

According to our initial assumption of the impact of the labor increment on the general wage level, demand for consumer goods has fallen.[7] However, at this stage of the adjustment process, production of consumer goods is still unchanged, causing excess supply. Our motorial exposition in the next chapter will demonstrate in detail how the firms' losses resulting from this excess supply will induce a fall of output and, thus, lead to a reduction in the utilization of the original capital stock in Sector II – the very reduction required to liberate the strategic capacity in Sector I.

Yet, contraction does not end at this point. The fall in output cannot

---

[6] For the meaning of B as symbolizing the ratio of primary capital stock to total capital stock in dynamic equilibrium and its equivalence with the expression $kd + s(1 - kd)$, see Chapter 9, Model XII and footnote 21.

[7] In Chapter 8, Section II, we have disposed of the notion that the fall in money wages will necessarily be followed by a fall in prices, so that "real" demand

but help create unemployment in part of the labor force originally operating in the consumer-good sector and, as a consequence, a further fall in demand for consumer goods (below that caused by the initial wage fall). Further losses and more curtailment of supply and of employment will ensue. Even if we disregard the additional pressure on unit wages that the growing number of unemployed is likely to exert, we are obviously faced with a "downward multiplier" process, during which, first, the supply of consumer goods and, then, the supply of secondary equipment are forced to adjust to a steadily shrinking demand.

Is there a *rock bottom,* that is, a lower limit for the contraction? The answer is affirmative because contraction is confined to outputs of Sectors II and Ib, whereas Sector Ia, according to our instrumental stipulation, is not affected by it. Rather the original stock and, thus, the output of primary equipment are supposed to remain unchanged and even to expand once self-augmentation gets under way. It is this fact together with our knowledge of the size of the two savings ratios, s and s', that enable us to calculate the rock-bottom level of the system's output in Keynesian fashion.

For our purpose, we must, in contrast with the Keynesian procedure, apply *gross* magnitudes to both investment and savings. This yields for investment an amount equal to the original sum of outputs in Sectors Ia and Ib, or[8]

$$I_{gr} = a_0 + b_0 = [kd + s(1 - kd)] \cdot o_0 = B \cdot o_0$$

Gross savings amount to net savings (original and those arising from the wage fall) plus amortization, that is, to

$$Sa_{gr} = [kd + s(1 - kd) + s'(1 - kd)] \cdot o_0$$

and then the gross savings ratio is

$$s_{gr} = kd + s(1 - kd) + s'(1 - kd)$$

which is henceforth denoted as B'.

Thus, for the rock bottom level of output, o_{00}, we obtain

$$o_{00} = \frac{kd + s(1 - kd)}{kd + s(1 - kd) + s'(1 - kd)} \quad \text{or} \quad \frac{B}{B'} \cdot o_0$$

will be maintained. It was shown that such a price fall presupposes that the initial and all subsequent surpluses accruing to the firms as a consequence of the wage fall will be hoarded; this condition is excluded by our instrumental stipulation of self-augmentation. See also Chapter 15, Section II.

[8] For an explanation of the bracketed expression, see again Chapter 9, footnote 21.

The corresponding *sector ratios at rock bottom* can be derived from the *original dynamic sector ratios.*[9] We obtain first

$$z_{00} = (1 - B') \cdot o_{00} = (1 - B') \cdot \frac{B}{B'} \cdot o_0$$

A complication arises concerning b_{00} and a_{00}. One might be tempted to equate b_{00}, in analogy with b in dynamic equilibrium, with the expression

$$b_{00} = (1 - B') \cdot \frac{B}{B'} \cdot B' \cdot o_0 \quad \text{or} \quad (1 - B') \cdot B \cdot o_0$$

In doing so, however, we would overlook the basic difference pointed out before between steady growth and the traverse toward a higher rate of capital formation. In the former case the savings arising in the consumer-good sector are to be invested in the sector producing *secondary* equipment to assure proportionate expansion. In the latter case, however, the criterion of maximum speed of adjustment requires that all savings, s as well as s', in whatever sector they may arise, be invested in the sector producing primary equipment to initiate the process of self-augmentation. For this reason the foregoing expression for b_{00} must be reduced, and we obtain

$$b_{00} = (1 - B') \cdot B \cdot o_0 - (s + s')(1 - kd) \cdot z_{00}$$

$$= \left[(1 - B') \cdot B - (s + s')(1 - kd)(1 - B') \cdot \frac{B}{B'} \right] \cdot o_0$$

$$= (1 - B') \cdot \frac{B}{B'} [B' - (s + s')(1 - kd)] \cdot o_0$$

and, conversely

$$[a_{00} = \left[B'^2 \cdot \frac{B}{B'} + (s + s')(1 - kd)(1 - B') \cdot \frac{B}{B'} \right] \cdot o_0$$

$$= \frac{B}{B'} [B'^2 + (s + s')(1 - kd)(1 - B')] \cdot o_0$$

The rock bottom sector ratios then reduce to

$$\bar{z}_{00} : \bar{b}_{00} : \bar{a}_{00} = 1 - B' : (1 - B')[B' - (s + s')(1 - kd)] :$$
$$B'^2 + (s + s')(1 - kd)(1 - B') \tag{14.2}$$

We must be aware that in carrying the process of downward cumulation through to the rock bottom level, we have introduced a simplifying and

[9] See Chapter 9, Equation 9.10.

realistically debatable assumption. We have implied that contraction of employment in Sectors II and Ib down to rock bottom will occur *before* the countervailing force of expanding employment through self-augmentation of primary equipment makes itself felt. Let us repeat that we are at this point not concerned with the actual behavior of firms in the respective sectors, nor with the conditions required to elicit a particular behavior. The problem is a structural one: namely, whether it is technically feasible for the expansion of output in Sector Ia to start at a time and to proceed at a rate that will create compensatory employment and income for those workers who are displaced in Sectors II and Ib owing to the initial fall in consumption.

The answer depends, on the one hand, on the size of such labor displacement in Sectors II and I, respectively, relative to the size of liberated capacity in Sector I and, on the other hand, on the relative speed of contraction and expansion of these two sectors. Obviously, potential new employment in the equipment-good sector cannot be larger than the liberated capacity permits and, thus, not larger than labor displacement in the same sector. Therefore full reemployment can be achieved only if unemployment in the consumer-good sector is zero. This, however, is equivalent to assuming that output of consumer goods will not contract at all – a violation of our basic condition for the process of capital formation to start. Therefore, even the speediest possible expansion of primary equipment cannot prevent some initial unemployment and, thus, some contraction of aggregate output.

Whether such contraction cumulates and, if so, whether it can be stopped before rock bottom is reached depends on the rates of expansion of primary equipment and of contraction of consumer goods, respectively. Comparison of these rates is complicated by the fact that we deal here with two dynamic processes that relate to quite different "periods." Expansion of primary equipment is tied to a technically given *period of maturation,* whereas contraction of demand for and, thus, of production of consumer goods depends on the institutionally determined *income period* of wage earners. Under prevailing arrangements the latter is likely to be much shorter than the former, so that expansion can overtake contraction only somewhere along the way to rock bottom.[10] On the other hand, an institutional changeover to advance payments of annual wages would alter the picture in favor of compensation. At any rate, in line with our assumptions, expansion is bound to win out – at the latest when

[10] This pessimistic conclusion would be reinforced if we were to admit a further fall in unit wages as a consequence of unemployment growing with every successive income period. Because the actual wage elasticity of labor supply is difficult to estimate, the influence of this factor has been disregarded in the numerical example of Chapter 15.

rock bottom is reached and self-augmentation of primary equipment takes over as the only dynamic force left.

III

Self-augmentation of primary equipment and the ensuing restoration of the original level of employment – the events that define the *second phase* – can be described in terms of an upward multiplier process in which successive doses of investment induce a general rise of income and output. Under our assumption of perfect mobility of labor, expansion of primary equipment is performed by the labor displaced in Sectors II and Ib. Even if we were to disregard the movement toward rock bottom, absorption of the increment of labor a' would have to wait until the displaced part of the original labor force is reemployed. To that extent, expansion of primary equipment is carried out with the help of resources, namely, liberated capital stock and displaced labor, *available within the original system.* The question arises, *Under what conditions can the terminally required addition to primary capital stock be accomplished by such "expansion from within"?*[11]

Once the labor force operating in the initial dynamic equilibrium has been brought back into employment, *aggregate output* at the point of maximum expansion from within equals the original output *in value terms.* This, however, is not true of the *commodity form* of the new output and, thus, of the relative size of the sectors. Capital stock and output in Sector Ia have increased, whereas output and, consequently, utilization of the capital stock in Sector II are reduced by the initial increase in savings. Capital stock and output in Sector Ib, finally, are also diminished by the effect of s', but have shrunk further as a consequence of the freezing of output in Sector II. Actually, the *sector ratios* in this new position are the same as at rock bottom, as all sectors have expanded from there in strict proportionality.

Now, in order to ascertain whether self-augmentation of primary equipment up to this point has provided the required addition to primary capital stock, we must have a measure for both these magnitudes. The first can be easily calculated. It equals the difference between the stock in the new position and its original size. The latter amounts to

$$F_{(a+b)_0} = k \cdot (a_0 + b_0) = B \cdot k o_0$$

Now, reemployment of the displaced labor force raises the original pri-

---

[11] The significance that the completion of self-augmentation during the process of expansion from within has for our path criterion of avoiding malinvestment will be discussed presently.

mary equipment stock in proportion with the rise of aggregate output from rock bottom to the point of maximum expansion from within, that is, by the ratio of o_0/o_{00}, or

$$F_{(a+b)} \text{ (max exp)} = B \cdot ko_0 \cdot \frac{o_0}{o_{00}} = \frac{B \cdot ko_0 \cdot o_0}{B \cdot o_0/B'} = B' \cdot ko_0$$

Therefore addition to primary equipment through self-augmentation up to the point of maximum expansion from within amounts to

$$\Delta F_{(a+b)} \text{ (max exp)} = (B' - B) \cdot ko_0 = s' \cdot (1 - kd) \cdot ko_0 \qquad (14.3)$$

Now it is essential to realize that, in a free market system, an addition to primary equipment equal to the right side of Equation 14.3 is not only the *maximum* addition that can be accomplished with the original stock of labor but also the *minimum* addition that *must* be produced if the original stock of labor is to be fully reemployed. This is equivalent to stating that self-augmentation of primary equipment must under no circumstances be stopped before maximum expansion from within is reached.

Furthermore, only if what can and must be added up to this point happens to equal the *required* addition, will the adjustment be targeted, that is, avoid both over- and underbuilding of primary equipment. If the required addition is produced *before* maximum expansion from within is attained, even though, for the reason stated, self-augmentation must not be stopped before this point is reached, we are faced with *over*building. If, on the other hand, the actual addition to primary equipment at this point is *less* than the required addition, self-augmentation must continue – a self-defeating process perpetuating *under*building. To start such a process, part of increment α' must now be employed. This implies rising aggregate income and rising aggregate demand for consumer goods, pressing for an expansion of such output. As a consequence, part of the newly constructed stock of primary equipment will be drawn away from further self-augmentation to the production of additional secondary equipment – the condition for satisfying the increased demand for consumer goods. Thus, underbuilding cannot be compensated.[12]

It is now clear that only by elaborating the conditions under which the *actual* addition to primary equipment at the point of maximum expansion from within equals the *required* addition can we decide whether

[12] To clinch the argument certain motorial propositions concerning the propensity to consume and the variation of prices must be introduced. We shall return to the problem in Chapter 15.

an efficient traverse, as previously defined, is feasible in a free market system.

IV

We shall answer this question first in the context of our Primary Model, which describes the sectoral shifts induced by the appearance of a labor increment, disregarding any other changes that occur during the adjustment process. We can now be more explicit about the nature of such changes. If adjustment is not instantaneous but requires one or more periods of production, the realistic case, then additional batches of the labor increment will enter the system, the absorption of which is conditional on more capital formation. We shall deal with this complication in our Secondary Model. For the time being we shall avoid it by, indeed, treating self-augmentation up to the point of maximum expansion from within as an instantaneous process. This will permit us to establish the conditions for the efficient absorption of the original labor increment.

Under these circumstances, how large is the required addition to primary capital stock? To determine its size we fall back on our formulation of the equilibrium sector ratios in terms of the steady rate of growth of labor supply, α, and the rate of depreciation.[13] Thus, the required addition to the original primary capital stock for the purpose of absorbing, besides a steady influx of α, also a steady influx of α' is

$$
\begin{aligned}
\Delta F_{(a+b)} \text{ (requ)} &= [k(\alpha + \alpha' + d) - k(\alpha + d)] \cdot ko_0 \\
&= \alpha' k^2 o_0
\end{aligned}
\tag{14.4}
$$

Making use of Equation 14.3 we obtain as a *first necessary condition* for targeted expansion that the actual expansion of primary equipment must equal the required expansion or

$$
s'(1 - kd) \cdot ko_0 = \alpha' k^2 o_0
$$

or

$$
s'(1 - kd) = \alpha' k
\tag{14.5}
$$

The reader will notice that Equation 14.5 is identical with the Harrod-Domar condition for steady growth, but it is to be interpreted quite differently. Equation 14.5 determines that particular growth rate, expressed as growth rate α' of labor supply, which accords with the actual addition to primary capital stock at the point of maximum expansion from within.

[13] See Equation 9.9 in Chapter 9, Section III.

To realize the significance of this piece of information, we must remember that the *actual* addition to capital stock, $s'(1 - kd) \cdot ko_0$, was found *without any reference* to the change in the system's growth rate, α'. Indeed, had we based the expansion process on *voluntary* savings issuing from innumerable independent microdecisions, there would be no systematic relation whatever between the two critical magnitudes s' and α'. It is, after all, in order to establish such a relationship that we have conducted this analysis in terms of *involuntary* savings. Our savings ratio s' is the result of a general fall in money wages caused by increment α' of labor supply. Equation 14.5 now helps us to establish the particular value of the wage elasticity of labor supply on which targeted expansion of real capital depends. By rewriting Equation 14.5 as

$$s' = \frac{\alpha' k}{1 - kd}$$

and by substituting $(\Sigma w_0 - \Sigma w_{00})/y_0$ for s',[14] we obtain a *second structural condition* for targeted expansion:

$$\Sigma w_{00} = \Sigma w_0 - \frac{\alpha' k}{1 - kd} \cdot y_0 \tag{14.6}$$

If s' is the result of voluntary saving, the equality postulated in Equation 14.6 can materialize only accidentally. In a regime with involuntary savings, in which a systematic relationship does exist between the rate of growth of labor supply and the level of money wages, there is still no autonomous market mechanism capable of assuring that the actual coefficient of wage elasticity is the required one, so long as the former arises from the uncontrolled wage bargains of the contracting parties.

Even if the condition formulated in Equation 14.6 is fulfilled, it is only another necessary but by no means sufficient condition for targeted expansion. Obviously, savings are only indirectly related to real capital formation. The connecting link is, of course, investment, so that targeted expansion is fully assured only if, in addition to conditions 14.5 and 14.6, a *third structural requirement* is fulfilled, namely,

$$s'_{\text{ex ante}} = i'_{\text{ex ante}} \tag{14.7}$$

so that

$$i'(1 - kd) = k\alpha'$$

[14] See Section II.

The ensemble of Equations 14.5–14.7 formulates, in the context of the Primary Model, the necessary and sufficient conditions for targeted expansion of primary equipment – the second phase of the traverse. We shall postpone the elaboration of the adjustment processes falling in the third and fourth phase until we have applied our findings to the more realistic framework of our Secondary Model. But even for the simplified Primary Model, it has become clear that, without public control of the wage bargain and of investment decisions, targeted expansion can be achieved by chance only. This result will be confirmed when, subsequently, the motorial conditions for targeted capital formation will be examined.

V

For didactic reasons, that is, mainly in order to bring the basic intersectoral shifts into bold relief, our Primary Model has abstracted the expansion process from the influence of "time." However, far from really being the instantaneous result of the initial growth stimulus, the addition to primary capital stock at the point of maximum expansion from within is the outcome of one or more periods of production. In other words, self-augmentation claims, as a rule, a number of periods of maturation during which, contrary to the assumptions underlying the Primary Model, *the dynamic stimuli α and α' continue to operate*. In every such period of maturation an additional batch of $\alpha + \alpha'$ enters the system without, as the very term of maximum expansion "from within" indicates, the absorption of any of these batches while self-augmentation proceeds. As a consequence, a *stock of idle labor* accumulates, equal to the sum of *increasing* additions per period. Obviously, dynamic equilibrium cannot be restored before this backlog of labor has also been absorbed. In order to procure the capital stock necessary for such absorption, self-augmentation of primary equipment must either be carried *beyond* the point of maximum expansion from within or it must proceed *at a rate sufficiently large* to build the entire stock required on the way up to this point.

In order to attack this problem we need, first of all, a measure in terms of periods of maturation, of the time it takes to achieve maximum expansion from within. To this effect we take our bearings from the size of the capacity originally liberated in Sector I as the joint effect of $s + s'$. As we know, it amounts to

$$F_{(a+b)} \text{ (lib)} = (s + s' \cdot kd) \cdot ko_0 \tag{14.1}$$

Disregarding again for the time being the backlog of labor, we now ask: How many periods of maturation are technically required to raise the output of this liberated capacity to the level of the additional stock of primary equipment required as we established it for the Primary Model? The required addition itself amounts to

$$\Delta F_{(a+b)} \text{ (requ)} = \alpha' k^2 o_0 \tag{14.4}$$

On this basis we can establish the following equality:

$$(s + s' \cdot kd) \cdot ko_0 \cdot \bar{R}^\gamma = (s + s' \cdot kd) \cdot ko_0 + \alpha' k^2 o_0$$

where $\bar{R}$ symbolizes the rate of self-augmentation, and γ the number of maturation periods required. From this we obtain

$$\gamma = \frac{\log \left[1 + \alpha' k/(s + s' \cdot kd)\right]}{\log \bar{R}} = \frac{\log \left[1 + \alpha'(1 - kd)/(\alpha + kd\alpha')\right]}{\log \bar{R}} \tag{14.8}$$

Then $\bar{R}$ can be derived[15] from our standard variables k and d as

$$\bar{R} = \frac{k(1 - d) + 1}{k} \tag{14.9}$$

so that γ is a function of the system's data, α, α' (or s, s'), k, and d.

Now all this changes drastically once we take into account the fact

---

[15] The expression for $\bar{R}$ is found in the following manner:

	Capital stock	Gross output	Net output
Period 0	F	F/k	$F/k(1 - kd)$
Period 1	$F + (F/k)(1 - kd)$	$(F/k^2)[k(1 - d) + 1]$	$(F/k^2)[k(1 - d) + 1](1 - kd)$
	$= F\dfrac{k(1 - d) + 1}{k}$	$F/k\dfrac{k(1 - d) + 1}{k}$	$F/k\dfrac{k(1 - d) + 1}{k} \cdot (1 - kd)$
	$= F \cdot R$		
Period 2	$F\dfrac{k(1 - d) - 1}{k} + F/k \cdot \dfrac{k(1 - d) + 1}{k} \cdot (1 - kd)$		
	$= F\dfrac{k(1 - d) + 1}{k} \cdot \dfrac{k(1 - d) + 1}{k}$		
	$= F\dfrac{[k(1 - d) + 1]^2}{k^2}$		
	$= F \cdot \bar{R}^2$		

etc.

Note the difference between gross output and net addition to stock. This follows from the assumption that, after each period of self-augmentation, part of gross output equal to future replacement requirements will be set aside. For the rationale of this assumption, see Chapter 9, footnote 17.

that additional batches of α and α' enter the system during the interval measured by γ, requiring for their absorption additional capital formation. To determine this addition, we must first ascertain the size of this intermediary influx, α''. It amounts to

$$\alpha'' = [(1 + \alpha + \alpha')^\gamma - 1] \cdot n_0$$

and the total addition to primary equipment required rises to

$$\Delta F^+_{(a+b)} \text{ (requ)} = \{\alpha'k + [(1 + \alpha + \alpha')^{\gamma+} - 1] \cdot B'\} ko_0 \qquad (14.10)$$

where $\Delta F_{(a+b)}$ (requ), in contrast with $\Delta F_{(a+b)}$ (requ) in Equation 14.4, stands for the addition to required stock *inclusive* of what is necessary to absorb the labor backlog, and γ^+ for the corresponding number of maturation periods.

On this basis we can stipulate a new equality:

$$(s + s' \cdot kd) \cdot ko_0 \cdot \bar{R}^{\gamma+} = (s + s' \cdot kd) \cdot ko_0 + \alpha'k^2o_0 + [(1 + \alpha + \alpha')^{\gamma+} - 1] \cdot B' \cdot ko_0$$

It stands to reason that γ^+ must be larger than the original γ. It amounts to

$$\gamma^+ = \frac{\log \left\{ \dfrac{1 + \alpha'k + [(1 + \alpha + \alpha')^{\gamma+} - 1] \cdot B'}{s + s'kd} \right\}}{\log \bar{R}} \qquad (14.11)$$

Equation 14.11 is a transcendental equation for which no general algebraic solution exists. Still from the general form of the equation some conclusions of economic importance can be drawn. First, γ^+ is directly proportional to the size of α' and inversely proportional to the size of s'. Therefore there is no assurance that any solution exists for arbitrarily chosen values of these two variables, that is, for values that do not obey condition 14.6. For instance, with a very small savings ratio and a large increment of labor supply, γ^+ may approach infinity, that is, capital formation cannot catch up with the new growth rate.

Second, so long as $s + s'$ is kept at a level sufficient to absorb α' alone, capital formation cannot be confined to expansion from within when we take the backlog also into account. We commented already on the obstacles that stand in the way of overcoming such underbuilding.[16] Therefore the question arises, whether or not, by an *appropriate increase in the savings ratio,* the stock of primary equipment can be raised, within the

---

[16] See Section III.

limits set by maximum expansion from within, to such an extent that targeted expansion can after all be achieved with maximum speed.

VI

Let us restate our problem. We are searching for the conditions under which, during the process of maximum expansion from within, a stock of primary equipment can be built that will be large enough to absorb the *permanently increased period flow* of labor as well as the *interim stock* of labor that accumulates while the new capital stock is being constructed. This can only be achieved if from the outset the savings–investment ratio is raised above the level of $s + s'$ or $i + i'$. It is this new larger savings ratio s_1 that we have to determine.

In the interest of efficiency, self-augmentation of primary equipment must be confined to the process of maximum expansion from within also in this Secondary Model. Therefore γ^*, as we shall designate the number of maturation periods required to achieve such self-augmentation (to distinguish it from other values, such as γ^+, that γ assumes when self-augmentation proceeds beyond maximum expansion from within), must coincide with the original γ, as derived in Equation 14.8.

Under these conditions, the addition to primary capital stock required for total absorption changes to

$$\Delta F^*_{(a+b)}(\text{requ}) = \{\alpha'k + [(1 + \alpha + \alpha')^{\gamma *} - 1] \cdot B'\} \cdot k_{0_0} \qquad (14.10.1)$$

To build this addition to the original stock of primary equipment during γ^*, the appropriate savings ratio, s_1, must rise to $s + s' + s''$, where s'' is to take care of the stock required to absorb α'', the labor backlog. By using Equation 14.5, which has served us to determine s' in terms of the required addition to primary equipment in the context of the Primary Model, we obtain

$$s'' = \frac{[(1 + \alpha + \alpha')^{\gamma *} - 1] \cdot B'}{1 - kd}$$

Then the total savings ratio s_1, suitable to absorb the entire labor increment of α, α', and α'', amounts to

$$s_1 = \frac{k(\alpha + \alpha') + [(1 + \alpha + \alpha')^{\gamma *} - 1] \cdot B'}{1 - kd} \qquad (14.12)$$

In analogy with Equation 14.6, we can again relate the new savings ratio s_1 to the level $w_{0_0_0}$ to which the targeted wage rate must fall if the larger savings are to materialize. We have then

$$\Sigma w_{000} = \Sigma w_0 - \frac{k\alpha' + [(1 + \alpha + \alpha')^{\gamma*} - 1] \cdot B'}{1 - kd} \cdot y_0 \qquad (14.6.1)$$

Now an important qualification must be added to the range of validity of both s_1 and w_{000}. Both are limited to the expansion process that leads from the initial dynamic equilibrium to the point of maximum expansion from within. Once this point is reached and the primary capital stock necessary to accommodate the higher growth rate as well as to "mop up" the stock of labor accumulated in the interim has been constructed, the increase in the growth rate reduces again to $\alpha + \alpha'$ per period, and the savings ratio must fall back to the level of $s + s'$. In other words, to carry through targeted expansion of primary equipment in accord with the Secondary Model we require, to begin with, a savings ratio that exceeds the level appropriate to terminal equilibrium – a ratio that, however, must be switched to that lower level once maximum expansion from within is reached. As will be shown more specifically in Chapter 15, a free market system lacks any mechanism by which either of the two levels could be attained spontaneously and at the right point in time.

VII

With these comments we have already entered the *third phase* of the traverse during which the stock of *secondary equipment* is to be adjusted to the higher rate of growth. Unless we introduce a very special stipulation (to be discussed presently), this adjustment is bound to create new complications. As is the case with primary equipment, additions to the stock of secondary equipment must, as a rule, be newly built. However, such construction may also require for its completion one or several periods of maturation during which again new batches of α and α' enter the system. And dynamic equilibrium cannot be restored before an additional stock of primary and secondary equipment is built capable of absorbing these new labor increments. In other words, analogous with $\alpha'' \cdot n_0$, the intermediate stock labor that accumulates during the construction of the addition to *primary* equipment, another intermediary stock of labor, $\alpha''' \cdot n_0$, collects, and s_1 as determined in Equation 14.12 no longer suffices to provide the totality of additions to capital stock required.

There are, in principle, two ways to solve this problem.[17] One alterna-

---

[17] A third possibility, namely, to extend the construction of primary equipment beyond the point of maximum expansion from within, is foreclosed because it contradicts our path criterion of avoiding malinvestment. See Section III.

tive consists in raising s_1 to a level of s_2, large enough to accommodate absorption also of α'''. The other alternative introduces a further restrictive condition, namely, the condition that the secondary capital stock in the new dynamic equilibrium be no larger than it was in the original dynamic equilibrium. Under these conditions, the savings ratio need not be increased further, and, once maximum expansion from within is reached, no more is needed than to reactivate part or all of the original equipment that stood idle during the traverse because of the intermediary reduction of consumption.

The *first alternative* – raising the savings ratio – is the general solution. However, it is complicated by the fact that we are now faced with two different spans of maturation: Besides γ, the number of maturation periods required to produce the addition to *primary* equipment, there is a span measured by what we are going to call β, the number of maturation periods required to produce the addition to *secondary* equipment. Contrariwise, using the *second alternative*, one may dispense with any investigation relating to the construction of additional secondary equipment. By simply reactivating available, although "latent," quantities of such equipment, the traverse is taken directly from maximum expansion from within to the terminal dynamic equilibrium.

VIII

The present section is devoted to a detailed examination of the *first alternative*. We shall try to determine the level of a savings ratio large enough to provide the total capital stock required for absorbing α, α', α'', and α''' in terminal equilibrium, taking into account the necessary additions to both primary and secondary equipment.

1. Again it will be helpful to deal with this problem in stages. Therefore, we shall, first of all, ascertain the number of maturation periods, β_1, required to construct the addition to secondary equipment made necessary by the interim influx of $\alpha + \alpha'$ $(= \alpha'')$ *during the process of maximum expansion from within, disregarding any subsequent influx occurring while the secondary equipment itself is being built.*

For this purpose we must first establish the addition to secondary equipment required for the attainment of such a "provisional" terminal equilibrium – provisional because it still disregards the additional requirements arising from the existence of α'''. Then we must determine the size of the stock of primary equipment available for producing this addition to secondary equipment and, in particular, the period output of this stock. By dividing this period output of secondary equipment into the magnitude of required secondary equipment, we shall obtain β_1, the number of maturation periods required to carry out the *provisional* expansion of the secondary capital stock,[18] namely,

$$\beta_1 = \frac{[(1 - B')(1 + \alpha + \alpha')^{\gamma*} - (1 - B)]}{B'(1 + \alpha + \alpha')^{\gamma*} - kd} \cdot k \tag{14.16}$$

2. As determined in Equation 14.16, β_1, measures the number of maturation periods necessary to construct the secondary equipment re-

[18] We present here a step-by-step derivation of β_1, by which symbol we denote "provisional" β, thus stressing its connection with s_1, because both refer to α, α', α'', with the provisional exclusion of α'''.

We start out from the size of the secondary capital stock in the original dynamic equilibrium as

$$F_{z0} = (1 - B) \cdot ko_0$$

To raise F_{z0} to the provisional level, we must, first of all, substitute $1 - B'$ for $1 - B$ to allow for the adjustment of the stock of secondary equipment to the permanent increase in the growth rate. To this we must add an amount equal to

$$[(1 + \alpha + \alpha')^{\gamma*} - 1] \cdot (1 - B') \cdot ko_0$$

in order to provide secondary equipment also for the temporary backlog of labor. By marking the provisional variables with a bar, we obtain

$$\bar{F}_z = \{(1 - B') + [(1 + \alpha + \alpha')^{\gamma*} - 1](1 - B')\} \cdot ko_0$$
$$= (1 - B')[1 + \alpha + \alpha')^{\gamma*}] \cdot ko_0$$

In calculating the *addition* to the original stock that needs to be *produced*, we must remember that the original stock is fully available. One part has been partly utilized and steadily replaced during the process of expansion from within. Another part, amounting to $(s' + s'')(1 - kd) \cdot ko_0$, has been kept idle, but is capable of immediate reactivation. Thus the addition to secondary equipment that must be produced reduces to

$$\bar{F}_z \text{ (to be produced)} = [(1 - B')(1 + \alpha + \alpha')^{\gamma*}] - (1 - B)] \cdot ko_0 \tag{14.13}$$

The actual production of this addition to secondary capital stock coincides with the "unfreezing" of the system. Once maximum expansion from within is reached and all the primary capital required for the provisional terminal equilibrium is available, all three sectors resume expansion. In other words, absorption of the labor increment $\alpha + \alpha'$ begins with the production of new secondary equipment, maximum expansion from within having led to the reemployment of the original labor force.

The addition to secondary equipment, as determined in Equation 14.13, must be produced with the help of primary equipment available at the point of maximum expansion from within. How much of the primary capital stock available at this point should be employed in this task? Remembering our path criterion of maximum adjustment speed, the entire stock available is to be assigned to it, minus only the quantity required for the steady required to take care of $\alpha + \alpha' + \alpha''$, that is, of the new permanent influx plus the interim influx of labor during the process of self-augmentation of *primary* equipment. We know, however, that true dynamic equilibrium requires us also to accommodate α''', the labor influx accompanying the construction of secondary equipment.

placement of this stock. Now, the total primary capital stock available at the critical point amounts to the initial stock plus the addition due to self-augmentation in accordance with Equation 14.10.1, that is, to

$$\bar{F}_{(a+b)} = \{B + k\alpha' + [(1 + \alpha + \alpha')\gamma^* - 1]B'\} \cdot ko_0$$
$$= B'(1 + \alpha + \alpha')\gamma^* \cdot ko_0 \tag{14.14}$$

After setting aside the quantity of primary equipment required for steady replacement, what is available for the production of secondary equipment amounts to $\bar{F}_{(a+b)} \cdot (1 - kd)$, which produces a period gross output equal to

$$\bar{b}_{gr} = \frac{1 - kd}{k} \cdot B'(1 + \alpha + \alpha')\gamma^* \cdot ko_0$$

However, considering the need for steady replacement of all capital stocks in use, only $\bar{b}_{net}$ can serve the expansion of secondary equipment, that is, $\bar{b}_{gr} - \bar{J}_z$; $\bar{J}_z$ representing the replacement requirements in the consumer-good sector. Expressing $\bar{J}_z$ in the same variables in which we have expressed $\bar{b}_{gr}$, we obtain

$$\bar{J}_z = [o_0 - (\bar{a} + \bar{b})] \cdot kd$$
$$= [o_0 - B'(1 + \alpha + \alpha')\gamma^* \cdot o_0] \cdot kd$$
$$= [1 - B'(1 + \alpha + \alpha')\gamma^*] \cdot kd \cdot o_0$$

and we find for the difference between $\bar{b}_{gr}$ and $\bar{J}_z$

$$\bar{b}_{net} = \left\{ \left[\frac{1 - kd}{k} \cdot B'(1 + \alpha + \alpha')\gamma^* \right] - [1 - B'(1 + \alpha + \alpha')\gamma^*] \cdot d \right\} \cdot ko_0$$
$$= \left[\frac{B'(1 + \alpha + \alpha')\gamma^* - kd}{k} \right] \cdot ko_0 \tag{14.15}$$

By dividing the right-hand side of Equation 14.13 by the right-hand expression of Equation 14.15, we finally obtain

$$\beta_1 = \frac{[(1 - B')(1 + \alpha + \alpha')\gamma^* - (1 - B)] \cdot k}{B'(1 + \alpha + \alpha')\gamma^* - kd} \tag{14.16}$$

A moment's reflection tells us that Equation 14.16 is not quite accurate. It is based on the assumption that $\bar{b}_{net}$ is constant over the entire range of expansion of $\bar{F}_z$. This cannot be the case because, with the gradual increase of $\bar{F}_z$, replacement claims on $\bar{b}_{gr}$ rise, so that $\bar{b}_{net}$ shrinks from period to period. However, under the conditions assumed (application of the entire net stock of primary equipment to the expansion of secondary equipment), β_1, the number of maturation periods required for this purpose, is small, and the inaccuracy of Equation 14.16 is minor.

Now β_1 enables us to determine α''', from which we can derive, first s''', the additional savings ratio required to absorb α''', and then, s_2, the overall savings ratio that assures the completion of an efficient traverse.

In determining α''' we must remember that the traverse has already passed through γ maturation periods before α''' makes its appearance. More precisely, the first batch of α''' enters the system during the period after the aggregate labor force has increased from the original n_0 to $(1 + \alpha + \alpha')^{\gamma*} \cdot n_0$, the quantity entering during the process of self-augmentation of primary equipment. During β_1, the labor force rises further to a total of

$$(1 + \alpha + \alpha')^{\gamma*+\beta_1} \cdot n_0$$

and the labor *increment* during β_1, then amounts to

$$\Delta n_{\beta_1} = [(1 + \alpha + \alpha')^{\gamma*+\beta_1} - (1 + \alpha + \alpha')^{\gamma*}] \cdot n_0$$

Consequently, the rate of increase of labor supply during β_1 equals

$$\alpha''' = [(1 + \alpha + \alpha')^{\gamma*+\beta_1} - 1] - [(1 + \alpha + \alpha')^{\gamma*} - 1]$$

With the help of Equation 14.5, we derive the additional savings ratio s''' required to absorb α''' as

$$s''' = \frac{[(1 + \alpha + \alpha')^{\gamma*+\beta_1} - 1] - [(1 + \alpha + \alpha')^{\gamma*} - 1] \cdot B'}{1 - kd}$$

In analogy with Equation 14.12, we obtain for the overall savings ratio

$$s_2 = \frac{k(\alpha + \alpha') + [(1 + \alpha + \alpha')^{\gamma*+\beta_2} - 1] \cdot B'}{1 - kd} \tag{14.17}$$

where β_1 the provisional measure for the number of maturation periods required to produce the addition to secondary equipment, rises to the definitive measure β_2, so that

$$\beta_2 = \frac{[(1 - B')(1 + \alpha + \alpha')^{\gamma*+\beta_1} - (1 - B)] \cdot k}{B'(1 + \alpha + \alpha')^{\gamma*+\beta_1} - kd} \tag{14.16.1}$$

3. Application of the suitable overall savings ratio s_2 to the self-augmentation of primary equipment also assures the appropriate production of secondary equipment over time span β_2. Thus, we seem to be ready to enter the final phase of the traverse – the adequate expansion of the

output of consumer goods. However, a last hurdle must first be taken. In order to invest the traverse with maximum speed, we have stipulated that, once maximum expansion from within has been attained, the entire then available stock of primary equipment (minus replacement requirements) be "switched" to the production of secondary equipment.[19] It is obvious, however, that a capital stock in Sector Ib thus temporarily maximized is much too large for terminal equilibrium. Therefore, as soon as the terminally required stock of secondary equipment has been produced, part of the primary capital stock now operating in Sector Ib must be "switched back" to Sector Ia, and at the same time the savings ratio must be reduced from its traverse level of s_2 to its new equilibrium level $s + s'$ in accordance with the new growth rate $\alpha + \alpha'$.[20]

4. Finally, we are able to write down the magnitudes of the three capital stocks and also the sector ratios valid for terminal dynamic equilibrium:

$$\left. \begin{array}{l} F_{a_t}{}^* = B'^2(1 + \alpha + \alpha')^{\gamma * + \beta_2} \cdot k o_0 \\ F_{b_t}{}^* = B'(1 - B')(1 + \alpha + \alpha')^{\gamma * + \beta_2} \cdot k o_0 \\ F_{z_t}{}^* = (1 - B')(1 - \alpha + \alpha')^{\gamma * + \beta_2} \cdot k o_0 \end{array} \right\} \tag{14.18}$$

Furthermore, the sector ratios, both for capital stocks and outputs, reduce to

$$F_{z_t}{}^* : F_{b_t}{}^* : F_{a_t}{}^* = \bar{z}_t{}^* : \bar{b}_t{}^* : \bar{a}_t{}^* = 1 - B' : B'(1 - B') : B'^2 \tag{14.19}$$

This result offers the occasion for a more general comment. In comparing the sectoral structure of a terminal equilibrium capable of steadily absorbing a higher rate of growth with the structure appropriate to absorb an initially lower rate, we find that the only difference consists in the substitution of term B' in place of the original B – terms that reflect the respective growth rates or, what amounts to the same, the respective savings ratios. Is this intuitively obvious result worth the effort we invested in following the tortuous path that connects the initial with the terminal state?

Nothing illustrates better the contrast between conventional growth analysis (best exemplified by the Harrod-Domar model) and our own approach than the answer to this question. If all we are interested in is the establishment of sectoral structures that *formally correspond* to different rates of growth, then our effort was misspent. In a Harrod model that is sectorally disaggregated in the manner described earlier,[21] we can im-

---

[19] See preceding footnote 18.
[20] For the rationale of the reduction of the savings ratio, see Section VI.
[21] See Chapter 9, Section IV.

mediately read the effect that a rise in G must have on the initial savings ratio and, thus, on initial B if dynamic equilibrium is to prevail. The answer is quite different if our interest focuses *on the path* itself. But for what reason other than academic pedantry, should we be interested in the slow motion picture of a path, the terminal state of which can be established much more easily?

The answer is implied in our initial warning that the efficient traverse explored here (and thus also the ensuing terminal state) represents no more than an ideal standard by which the *inefficiency of actual traverses* can be gauged. Neither of the two critical savings ratios, s' or s_2 can be expected to materialize from the uncontrolled interplay of free market forces. Nor can their translation into equivalent investment ratios be taken for granted. This depends on rather exceptional conditions of which more will be said presently. There is no mechanism that guarantees either the "forward switch" or the "backward switch" of primary equipment in the right proportions, or the reduction of the savings ratio to its long-term level of $s + s'$ once all the required additions to the system's capital stock have been constructed.

Were one to conclude from these reservations that both the conventional and the instrumental approach are no more than intellectual games far removed from the real world, one would overlook the important lesson that path analysis of the type undertaken here teaches about the actual handling of empirical growth processes. It highlights, as was just indicated, the zones of danger on the traverse where the system is likely to miss its equilibrating course and, thus, it becomes an indispensable tool for the control of actual economic growth. This is a function of instrumental path analysis for which no equivalent can be found in conventional dynamics – a function whose significance will emerge even more clearly when we supplement our structural investigation by a motorial analysis.

IX

However, we must first offer some comments on the second alternative concerning the adjustment of the stock of secondary equipment to the new growth rate.[22] As was stated earlier, this procedure rests on the special stipulation that the secondary capital stock in terminal dynamic equilibrium be no larger than the same type of stock in the original dynamic equilibrium. In symbolic terms: F_z (term) $\leq F_{z_0}$ or

$$(1 - B') \cdot ko_{\text{term}} \leq (1 - B) \cdot ko_0$$

[22] See Section VII.

This amounts to stipulating that any addition to the *active* stock of secondary equipment, over and above the level to which it is reduced by the initial rise in savings and the temporary freezing of the system, must come through reactivation of part or all of the secondary equipment that is being kept idle during the preceding phases of the traverse.

From this it follows that the terminal adjustment of secondary equipment is, indeed, instantaneous, because β is zero. To determine the size of the terminal stocks, we must modify Equation 14.18 by eliminating β_2 as exponent. The sector ratios as shown in Equation 14.19 remain unaffected.

How are we to evaluate the two alternatives? By dispensing with the special stipulation concerning the terminal level of the secondary capital stock, the first alternative presents the more general solution. Still, with a view toward maximizing the speed of adjustment, the second alternative proves superior because it eliminates the time span represented by β. The same would be true if we were to choose as our path criterion "minimum reduction of the level of consumption during the traverse." Because there is no α''' to absorb, the interim savings ratio reduces to the lower level of s_1,[23] and consumption settles at a correspondingly higher level. On the other hand, if the terminal level of secondary equipment is below the original level, both these gains – higher speed and higher interim consumption – mature but must be paid for with the permanent waste of part of the original stock.

[23] See Equation 14.12 in Section VI.

15

Adjustment to a higher rate of growth of labor supply in a free market

II. Force Analysis

In discussing stationary and dynamic equilibrium, we set forth the reasons why instrumental analysis remains incomplete unless the study of economic structures is supplemented by the determination of the behavioral and motivational patterns that support the structure in question – in a word, by force analysis.[1] In particular it was shown that force analysis gains special importance in free market systems owing to their social organization. What then are the motorial requirements for a targeted traverse such as the one explored in the preceding chapter?

We know that market behavior must ultimately orient itself by the variations of prices and of demand and supply quantities in both the commodity and factor markets. We also know that the signals from such variations issue from the prevailing micromotivations: action directives and expectations. Therefore, our task is now to establish those price and quantity patterns and those patterns of the underlying motivational forces that are suitable to guide the system along the contorted path that raises it to a higher rate of growth.

When first taking up the motorial issues arising in a free market,[2] we designed two behavioral models that displayed alternative processes assuring the stability of stationary equilibrium. These models, modified by what was subsequently discovered about the stability conditions of dynamic equilibrium,[3] will play a major role in explaining the behavioral and motivational patterns required for an efficient adjustment of the system to a *change* in the rate of growth.

We are now going to study the motorial requirements for a targeted traverse in accord with our four-phase schema of the adjustment process. In doing so we shall disregard what was previously called the Primary Model and shall proceed directly to the more realistic Secondary Model in its most complex form.[4]

---

[1] See Chapters 7 and 10.
[2] See Chapter 7, Section III.
[3] See Chapter 10, Section I.
[4] See Chapter 14, Sections VI–IX.

I

Three events occurring during the phase of *capacity liberation* call for motorial underpinning: (1) the origin of savings, (2) the liberation of resources and its relationship to an investment decision, and (3) the movement toward rock bottom brought to a halt by the countervailing movement of incipient self-augmentation of primary equipment. We shall treat each in turn here and in the next two sections.

In discussing the Primary Model that describes the traverse, regardless of the complications arising during the adjustment process, we took our bearings from the premise of *involuntary* savings.[5] The reason for this was that, because this type of savings depends on the size of the labor increment, a link can be established between the original stimulus of change and the response suitable for its accommodation.

It is true that this link has proved rather tenuous, because a free market offers no mechanism capable of assuring that the actual wage bargains achieve the required relationship between labor increment and wage reduction. Still, in the case discussed previously the particular wage elasticity with respect to labor supply, which is the condition for an efficient traverse, referred to an increase in labor supply *actually experienced*.

The present case under investigation, the Secondary Model, is quite different. Now an efficient traverse is conditional on a much larger savings ratio (earlier labeled s_2), which is to accommodate not only the premanent flow increment of labor currently observable but also two interim stocks that will accumulate in the future while capital formation proceeds. Without means of knowing at this stage the length of the adjustment process as measured by our parameters γ^* and β_2,[6] the marketer cannot form even the vaguest estimate of the increment of labor supply for which ultimately employment must be provided. Although it remains an instrumental requirement for an efficient traverse, a wage reduction yielding a profit ratio equal to s_2 is most unlikely to occur and, at best, only by chance.

For this reason it seems futile to search for the motorial requirements that would assure an adequate reduction of money wages. Even if we take the extremum principle of action on both sides of the wage bargain for granted, it is impossible to stipulate meaningful expectations, unless a scientific observer were to predict and to publicize the varying states of the labor market on the basis of our structure analysis. Then positively elastic quantity expectations would be in order over the time span of

---

[5] See Chapter 14, Section II.
[6] See Chapter 14, Sections VI and VIII.

investment in primary equipment; that is, the aggregate of labor seeking employment should be expected to rise more than in proportion to the current rise.

It hardly needs pointing out that, under a regime of *voluntary* or *forced* savings, the motorial problem would be even more difficult. In either case the decision, to postpone consumption or to borrow investible funds, will be a function of anticipated rather than actual profits. This anticipation of profits is derived from the expectation of rising prices, which present experience does not justify in advance of a positive investment decision.

II

From our structure analysis we know that the next step on the way to resource liberation is a reduction in the quantity of consumer goods demanded. In our two-strata model such reduction is, to begin with, a mechanical consequence of the wage fall irrespective of any motorial considerations. However, in order to have demand for consumer goods permanently curtailed, the surpluses created in the firms by the general fall in money wages must be invested. If they are consumed, aggregate demand for consumer goods remains on the initial level, and nowhere will any capacity be liberated. The same is true if these surpluses are hoarded. Under our assumption of perfect competition, prices of commodities and factors will then adjust to the reduced level of aggregate spending, and again real demand for consumer goods will be unchanged. In other words, prompt investment of the involuntary savings is the precondition for a permanent reduction in demand for consumer goods that adversely affects output, thus liberating capacity throughout the system. *What then are the motorial requirements for a positive investment decision?*

In order to ascertain these requirements in all their complexity, we must first clarify the long-term behavioral consequences of such a decision. They amount to an increase in demand for additional equipment (and for working capital, which we disregard for the time being) on the part of firms in *all three sectors* of the system. This follows from what structure analysis has taught us, namely, that terminal equilibrium, after the absorption of all labor increments, exhibits a proportionate expansion of primary and secondary equipment and of consumer goods. Moreover, our stipulation, following our path criterion of maximum speed, that up to the point of maximum expansion from within, all savings must be invested in Sector Ia, cannot alter this. The motivations on the part of the actors in the other sectors, on which such a decision is based, are still concerned with the expansion of their own firms.

Once again we take the rule of the extremum principle for granted. The critical factor here consists of the expectations that will eventually make such behavior appear as receipt-maximizing and expenditure-minimizing.

To determine these underlying expectations, let us survey the "field," that is, the wage–price–quantity order that prevails in each one of the three sectors at the time when the decision has to be taken. We have an increase in the quantity of labor supply which has led to a reduction of the unit price of labor. Commodity quantities and prices in all sectors are still at the initial level of dynamic equilibrium. But the future level of consumer-good prices must be regarded as uncertain until the investment decision is taken – a positive decision leading to their reduction. In the face of this price–quantity constellation, we must now strictly distinguish between expectations that are *likely* to be formed and expectations that are *required* to assure a positive investment decision.

As far as the latter expectations are concerned, we already know that the elasticity of quantity expectations with respect to labor supply must be positive, that is, the increment must be expected to perpetuate itself, and even to increase. As a corollary, the present fall in wages must be regarded as permanent and constant. It stands to reason that positively elastic wage expectations, that is, the expectation of a further fall, would, under the aspect of expenditure minimization, counsel postponement of investment.

With regard to price expectations in the commodity field, we must differentiate among prices of primary equipment goods, of secondary equipment goods, and of consumer goods. Both zero and positive elasticity of price expectations in the *primary equipment-goods* sector are conducive to investment – the former under the aspect of expenditure because they anticipate that a major cost item of investment will, in the face of rising demand, remain constant; the latter under the aspect of receipts because equipment goods considered as output now offer rising surpluses over costs. However, the crux of the price expectation problem concerns *consumer goods*.

On the basis of common sense, future expansion of secondary equipment, that is, present investment in Sectors II and Ib, must at this juncture be regarded as violating the extremum principle. As was already stated, the price trend of consumer goods is uncertain at best; it is only certain that prices must fall in case of a positive investment decision, which definitely reduces demand for the output of Sector II. This is bound to be followed by a reduction of supply and by partial idleness of the *existing* stock of secondary equipment. Thus, investment in additions to secondary equipment can only compound an already threatening state of excess supply – unless such excess supply and the concomitant fall of output and prices of consumer goods is regarded as *temporary* only, to be followed by an increase in demand for these goods even beyond the level of the initial demand.

Thus we arrive at the conclusion that a positive investment decision on the part of the firms of Sector II and, indirectly, also of Sector Ib, is justified only if the elasticity of both quantity and price expectations relating to consumer goods is *negative;* that is, if, in the face of a present price fall, higher output and higher prices of such goods are expected because a future increase in demand is anticipated. This leads us back to Model VIII in our original exposition of equilibrating behavior patterns.[7] In that model falling prices are to induce rising supply – a behavior that, at first sight, appears to be incompatible with the conventional extremum principle. However, as the case under examination shows, the apparent contradiction disappears if we admit negative elasticity of price and quantity expectations. Such "perverse" behavior then becomes the very precondition for the required positive investment decisions on the part of the firms in Sectors II and Ib.

Finally, this expectational constellation justifies an assumption that must have puzzled the reader all through our analysis of the structural requirements. It concerns that part of the equipment stock in the consumer-good sector which is made idle through the fall of consumption and, in our designing of an efficient traverse, is to be kept idle in the hope that it can be reactivated during the course of actual absorption of the labor increment.[8] What incentive should there be for any firm to keep this stock idle and to continue, as we have stipulated, with steady replacement of the active part of that capital stock, instead of simply substituting the idle part for the worn-out portions? The answer is now clear. With negative elasticity of price and quantity expectations prevailing in Sector II, reactivation of the idle part of the sector's capital stock is seen as accelerating the desired increase of secondary equipment – an advantage that would be lost by its premature utilization.

Nothing of what we have so far said tells us anything about the *likelihood* of such behavoir materializing in a laissez-faire system. On the contrary, falling quantities and prices, the current market signals and the only source of information in such a system, point in the other direction. Indeed, these factors suggest investment *delay* if not capital *liquidation,* and all the more so because the market constellation under examination creates what, on other occasions, has been defined as the "solidarity

[7] See Chapter 7, Section III.
[8] See Chapter 14, Section VIII.

dilemma."[9] It arises whenever an investment is "autonomous" rather than price induced, without at the same time assuring the investor of technical superiority over his competitors. In such cases, profitability depends on the presence of a series of complementary investments which, directly or through the multiplier effect on aggregate consumption, create reciprocal demand for the output of the investors under consideration. Moreover, it stands to reason that such a solidarity dilemma also obstructs a positive investment decision on the part of the firms in the equipment-good sectors, whose additional output must be sold to firms in the consumer-good industries. In a word, we meet here with a second obstacle on the way to an efficient traverse, graver even than the uncertain relationship between wage fall and profits, because its consequences are not just under- or overbuilding but a total paralysis of the adjustment process.

III

Let us now examine the motorial requirements for the downward multiplier process terminating in a rock-bottom limit with an arithmetical example. Besides obtaining a test for the formal apparatus developed in the preceding chapter, we shall thereby gain an intuitive insight into the *dis*equilibrating movements that characterize not only the contraction toward a rock bottom but the entire traverse. Therefore, the same numerical schema is to serve us as guide through all the contortions of the adjustment process.

One main difference of this arithmetical model from the algebraic model, with the help of which we described the structure adjustments, consists in the introduction of genuine *values* or *price sums* side by side with the original quantity expressions. It is in the discrepancy between values and quantities, and, thus, in changes of unit prices, that disequilibrium manifests itself. Moreover, it is these very price changes on which the behavior of producers and consumers is supposed to orient itself.

It is true that throughout our investigation, both structural and motorial, the underlying quantities have been "priced" in some sense. Such pricing, however, has so far had only an index function for the purpose of making physically different magnitudes comparable and thus permitting aggregation.[10] In the remainder of this chapter, however, we shall supplement these indexed quantities with a set of genuine relative price sums of sectoral inputs and outputs. This will permit us to vary the underlying unit prices with changes in the quantities demanded.

The arithmetical schema outlined in the Appendix of this chapter

[9] See *OEK*, pp. 88, 280, 303.
[10] See Chapter 4, Section II.

depicts a combined production–receipt–expenditure model,[11] in which each item – capital stocks, factor inputs, gross and net outputs – appear in double entry, namely, as an indexed quantity and as a price sum, denoted by the subscripts q and p, respectively. Thus we have, for example, a number for physical replacement (f_q), as well as for amortization or replacement demand (f_p), or for physical output (o_q), as well as for sales receipts $(sal\ rec)$. In order to highlight the subsequent divergence in the movement of quantities and prices, the numbers for quantities and price sums have initially been set equal.

So far as the actual numbers are concerned, the model is a variant of our original dynamic equilibrium model.[12] The physical aggregates of inputs and outputs are the same. What has changed is the initial profit–savings–investment ratio, which has been reduced from $1/2$ to $1/10$, with a corresponding change in sector ratios. Given our standard coefficients $k = 2$ and $d = 1/10$, a savings ratio of $1/10$ can accommodate a steady rate of increase in labor supply of 4 percent. It is further assumed that at the end of Period 0, this rate rises to 6 percent, requiring for absorption an additional savings ratio $s' = 1/20$. Consequently, the new long-term savings ratio required after the traverse is completed, amounts to $s + s' = 3/20$.

Now we know that also to absorb the two interim stocks of labor that accumulate during the traverse, an interim savings ratio of s_2 is required which exceeds $s + s'$. According to Equation 14.17, ratio s_2 equals roughly $1/5$. This magnitude is based on the size of γ^* and β_2, both of which have been set equal to 1.[13] Thus the addition to labor supply over γ^* and β_2 periods amounts to ca. 25 units – the influx over two maturation periods. An addition to total capital stock of ca. 62 units is required to be divided between primary and secondary capital stock in a proportion that raises the original ratio of $B:1 - B$ to the terminal ratio of $B':1 - B'$, that is, in the proportion of $40:22$.[14]

Our schema is subdivided into a number of periods that represent

[11] See Chapter 9, Section V.

[12] See Chapter 9, Model XII.i.

[13] The coefficients γ^* and β_2 calculated from Equations 14.8 and 14.16.1, respectively, amount to 0.92 and 0.54. How are we to interpret these decimals? Logically there are two alternatives. Illustrating the problem with the value for γ^*, we can say either that the total available capital stock will be employed over 0.92 period or that only 0.92 of the available capacity will be employed over a full period. Because with a given technology the period of maturation is fixed once and for all, therefore only the second interpretation makes economic sense. This, however, implies that both γ^* and β_2 must be raised to the next-highest integer, so that both amount to 1. The far-reaching consequences for the determination of the size of the labor influx during the two construction spans are obvious.

[14] See Equation 14.18.

periods of maturation. However, for a full understanding of the strategic price changes, it will be necessary to register three short-term events – the fall in money wage rates, the rise in investment demand, and the intersectoral shifts following such a rise – that occur between Period 0 and Period 1. They will be labeled accordingly.[15]

PERIOD 0

Period 0, our starting point, represents an arbitrarily chosen stage in a long-term process of equilibrium growth. As was already stated, the steady rate of growth of labor supply has been set at 4 percent, for the steady absorption of which a savings ratio of 1/10 is required. Aggregate output amounts to 250 units, with aggregate income equal to 200 units, of which 180 units represent payrolls and 20 units represent profits.[16]

INTERPERIOD I

We now assume that, at the end of Period 0, the rate of growth of labor supply rises from 4 to 6 percent, causing a fall of aggregate payrolls from 180 to 160 units and, thus, raising aggregate profits (= savings) from 20 to 40 to the level of $s_2 = 1/5$. We are aware that, empirically speaking, this assumption is arbitrary,[17] but, because we have recognized it as an indispensable condition for an effective traverse, we establish it by fiat.

All quantities remain unchanged. The system is, nevertheless, in disequilibrium because of two price-sum distortions. Whereas the price sum of consumer-good output is also unchanged (at the level of 180), aggregate payrolls – the expenditure equivalent – have fallen to 160. Conversely, aggregate profits have risen to 40 with investible net output being unchanged at 20. It is these disequilibria that, under the conditions stated

---

[15] To simplify calculation, we have confined our arithmetical terms to first decimals. This has led to small inaccuracies, showing in slight discrepancies between the numerical values of systematically equal items.

[16] In Period 0 the initial dynamic equilibrium yields a net output of 5.6 units in Sector Ia, and of 14.4 units in Sector Ib. If dynamic equilibrium were to continue, these net outputs would raise the three capital stocks proportionally, thus continuing steady growth at 4 percent. However, in line with our path criterion of maximum speed, we have decided to "freeze" the general process of growth and to apply the aggregate of savings and, thus, all net outputs to Sector Ia during the course of self-augmentation. This will become apparent in Period 1. In order to simplify our exposition, we shall disregard all net outputs in Period 0. Although we thus exaggerate the magnitudes of the primary and secondary capital stocks that must be built during the transition, and also the size of γ^* and β_2 as well as the required size of the savings ratio s_2, this omission does not affect the adjustment process systematically. A different situation will face us when we study a fall in the rate of growth in Chapter 18.

[17] See Section I.

previously in Section II, initiate both the process of self-augmentation and the shrinkage of consumer-good output toward the rock bottom level.

INTERPERIOD II

In the same manner in which we treat the wage fall and the compensating rise of profits as instantaneous events, we regard also as instantaneous the *decision* on the part of the receivers of the additional profits to invest these profits in Sector Ia along the lines discussed in Section II. So too we assume instantaneous *price effects* caused by the rising demand for equipment goods and the falling demand for consumer goods. There is still no quantity change. However, it is essential that we follow up in full detail the price changes induced by the aforementioned demand changes.

Starting with Sector II, we know that profits have increased there above their equilibrium level by 14.5 units, which are supposed to be invested in Sector Ib, raising sales receipts there to 64.9 units. In order to expand output, Sector Ib must invest this gain plus its own additional profit of 4 units in Sector Ia, with a similar effect on sales receipts there. In fact, sales receipts in Sector Ia rise to the level of 39.6 units, because the profit increment of 1.5 units in Sector Ia itself must also be invested there. Output is so far unchanged, and, therefore, the ensuing higher unit prices in Sector Ia raise the prices of both capital stocks and amortization in both equipment-good sectors in the same proportion, that is, by ca. 100 percent, whereas capital stock and amortization in Sector II rise in proportion to the price rise of output in Sector Ib by ca. 29 percent.

These price changes of inputs in conjunction with the changes in sales receipts strongly affect the relative profitability of the three sectors. As a consequence of the general wage fall, the profit rate rose in all three sectors from its equilibrium level of 4 to 8 percent. It has now risen in Sector Ia to about 24 percent, whereas it has fallen in Sector Ib to about 6 percent. Most important, however, Sector II shows an actual loss of 1.5 units, because the reduction of the sector's wage bill can no longer compensate for the rise in amortization costs in conjunction with the fall in sales receipts.[18] This is the price–profit constellation on the basis of which the further decisions of the firms must be based. They are reflected in the setup of Interperiod III.

[18] The revaluation of the original input prices seems to create a monetary problem. Sales receipts from aggregate output have risen from the initial 250 units to 264.4, although no rise in the circulating medium has been stipulated. The solution lies in an increase in the velocity of circulation. The additional profits of Sector II circulate twice – first as demand increment in Sector Ib, then as demand increment also in Sector Ia.

INTERPERIOD III

So far as the firms in Sector II are concerned, this decision can only go in the direction of contracting output and employment. This is for once not a question of expectations but, barring a credit system, a "mechanical" necessity. The losses sustained reduce the available business funds below what would be required to maintain the earlier input–output level. This is shown in the figure for o_{z_q} which is reduced from 180 to 160 units. However, it is significant that unit prices of consumer goods, sal rec/0_q, although below the break-even level of 1, begin to rise again above the lowest point of 0.89 reached in Interperiod II, indicating a convergence of the downward movement to a lower limit.

Conversely, surplus profits earned in Sector Ia confirm the motivational setup that induced the original investment decision, thus stimulating demand for additional capacity. Such capacity is now available in Sector Ib, in which the demand for the original output is bound to fall with the contraction of Sector II. This capacity with the corresponding capacity in Sector Ia form the liberated stock of primary equipment on the presence of which self-augmentation depends. In physical terms, it amounts to 36.8 units, which in our model have been transferred to F_{a_q} together with the related labor force.

The general conclusion can be drawn that it is *the price-determined profits in Sector Ia and the equally price-determined losses in Sector II that set the adjustment mechanism in motion.* These profits and losses themselves are the result of the original investment decision and the underlying behavioral and expectational patterns.

PERIOD 1

Over a number of intermediate stages, resembling in all essentials the setup of Interperiod III, rock bottom is finally reached as depicted in Period 1 of our model. The convergence to a lower limit of aggregate output and employment is indicated by the fact that equality is restored between the demand for and the supply of consumer goods both in terms of sales receipts and of transacted quantities. In this way, the break-even level of consumer-good prices is also restored. All the while transfer of primary equipment to Sector Ia has been progressing, whereas in Sector Ib the output level has adjusted to the demand for replacement, f_{z_p}, in Sector II.

We still must establish the motivational conditions that justify the behavior as depicted by the price–quantity variations in Period 1. So far as the firms of Sector Ia are concerned, adoption of the extremum principle and of positive elasticity of quantity and price expectations will elicit the required actions leading to self-augmentation. At the same time, the ensuing levels of prices and output quantities and, above all, the steadily rising profits fully justify the expectations held and, thus, assure their perpetuation.

The situation is quite different when we analyze the motorial conditions necessary for a gradual fall in the rate of contraction of Sectors Ib and II and its convergence to a rock bottom limit. We saw earlier that a positive investment decision on the part of the firms in these sectors requires negative elasticity of price and quantity expectations; that is, in the face of a present price fall, there is the expectation of rising prices and quantities in the future. Only rigid adherence to such expectations, but modified in the direction of growing inelasticity, will gradually reduce the rate of shrinkage and finally establish a rock bottom.

IV

Our next task concerns the upward movement toward *maximum expansion from within,* which follows or, in favorable cases, checks the downward movement toward rock bottom. Progressive investment in Sector Ia now dominates the system's aggregate and sectorial expansion, gradually bringing about the reemployment of the displaced part of the original labor force. In this way, the net output of primary equipment is raised from the 31 units produced in Period 1 to the required level of 40 units.

These processes are conditional on a particular motorial setup. In Sector Ia no more is required than the persistence of the action directive and the expectations that induce continuous investment during the downswing phase, namely, the extremum principle coupled with positive elasticity of price and quantity expectations. In Sectors Ib and II, however, the negative price and quantity expectations required to establish rock bottom must now turn into positive expectations, more precisely, into the anticipation of rising quantities demanded at break-even prices. Once the upward movement gets under way, these motorial conditions should easily materialize, because the results of the ensuing behavior will fully confirm them.

The overall result of such proportional expansion is registered in the next period.

PERIOD 2

First, by inspecting sector ratios, we find that capital stock and output of primary equipment have increased above the initial level – the former by ca. 40 units, that is, by addition of the amount of equipment required for terminal equilibrium.[19] Capital stock and output in Sector II have decreased by the same amount.

What attracts notice, however, is the restoration of equality between quantities and price sums at the initial level. To understand this adjustment, we must remember that the divergence between the two measures was caused in Interperiod II by excess demand – first for secondary, and, subsequently, for primary equipment. It is the function of self-augmentation of primary equipment to eliminate this excess demand by a gradual increase in supply accompanied by a gradual fall in price. Once maximum expansion from within is achieved over γ^* maturation periods, the quantity of primary equipment supplied equals the quantity demanded, and prices fall back to the equilibrium level for which p/q was set equal to 1. This price fall must be reflected in the valuation of the stocks of primary equipment and the price of their respective amortizations; it also reduces the output price in Sector Ib and, thus, prices of capital inputs and outputs in Sector II to the initial level.

What is the motorial justification for this general price adjustment? To clarify it we must slightly modify what was previously said about the expectational constellation suitable for the upward movement. We had stipulated quite generally positive elasticity of quantity expectations for all three sectors. This needs now to be specified by the further stipulation that quantity expectations be inelastic; that is, for any present increase in output quantity, a smaller increase should be expected in the future, with zero elasticity once maximum expansion from within has been attained. The same qualification applies to price expectations, with the further condition that the rate of price decrease remains in step with the rate of cost decrease.

V

From our structure analysis, we know that the next step on the traverse must be a "forward switch" of primary equipment from Sector Ia to Sector Ib so that the stock of secondary equipment can be expanded to the required level.[20] The number of maturation periods β_2 required to achieve such expansion has been calculated on the assumption that the entire stock of primary equipment available at this point (minus replacement requirements) be devoted to this purpose. Period (3) depicts the sectoral order for the first maturation period relating to such expansion of secondary equipment, after the stipulated switch has been performed.

[19] See Section III.
[20] See Chapter 14, Section VIII.

PERIOD 3

Net output produced during this period in Sector Ib amounts to 40 units of secondary equipment. We know[21] that the addition to be produced amounts to 22 units, so that the actual period output emanating from the total available stock of primary equipment exceeds the required one by almost 100 percent. To put it differently, only 0.54 of the available primary stock is required to raise the secondary stock to the terminal level – precisely the value we have obtained for β_2.[22]

Once all production requirements with regard to both the primary and the secondary capital stock have been fulfilled, we approach a new dynamic equilibrium, depicted as Period 4.

PERIOD 4

In order to attain terminal equilibrium, three additional steps must be taken:

1. That part of secondary equipment which was kept idle during the traverse must now be reactivated. It amounts to 40 units, namely, the difference between the initial quantity operating in Period 0 and the quantity operating in Period 3.

2. Of the primary equipment operating during Period 4, an amount equal to 21.6 units must be switched back to Sector Ia.

3. The savings ratio s_2, which prevailed throughout the traverse, must be reduced to the long term level of $s + s'$, equaling 3/20.

The model as depicted in Period 4 reflects all three readjustments. It also shows that the system has now achieved a growth rate of 6 percent, which was the initially postulated goal.

Finally, what are the motorial requirements that assure, first, transition from Period 2 to Period 3 and, afterward, from Period 3 to Period 4?

1. The decisive step, after maximum expansion from within has been attained, is the shift of net investment from further self-augmentation of primary equipment to the expansion of secondary equipment, that is, to the expansion of output in Sector Ib. What are the signals on which investors' behavior can orient itself, and what are the motivations that guide such behavior into goal-adequate channels?

We saw that, in Period 2, prices in all three sectors fell back to the equilibrium level. We must now add that the same is true of profit rates,

---

[21] See Chapter 14, Section VIII, Equation 14.13.
[22] See preceding footnote 13.

which are again at the level of 8 percent reached in Interperiod I. Thus, at first sight, it appears that, under the aspect of the extremum principle, the prevailing price–profit constellation offers no inducement for any shift of investment toward Sector Ib. The picture looks different when we focus on the *rate of change* of the profit rate during the upward movement from rock bottom to maximum expansion from within. Then we realize that, in Sector Ia, the profit rate fell from 24 to 8 percent, whereas it rose in Sector Ib from ca. 6 to 8 percent, and in Sector II from 4 to 8 percent. Obviously, there is no longer any incentive further to invest in the production of primary equipment, but investment in secondary equipment appears attractive provided that the elasticity of quantity and price expectations in the consumer-good sector is positively elastic.

The first consequence of such an investment decision is a price rise of this output (another "interperiod" event that we have not registered). The ensuing rise of profits in Sector Ib creates then an incentive for the forward switch, that is, for the application of the total primary equipment stock (minus replacement requirements) to the production of secondary equipment.

As a matter of fact, the forward switch must occur before maximum expansion from within has been reached. As it stands, Period 2 shows a net output of primary equipment amounting to 40 units. If self-augmentation were to be pushed to this point, we would be faced with overbuilding of primary equipment, because the stock increment in Sector Ia plus the net output referred to far exceed the required addition. Therefore, Period 2 has only a "virtual" significance as a limit of expansion. In reality, the forward switch must occur as soon as the required addition to primary equipment has been built. It must be *applied* in the sectoral proportions as shown in Period 3.[23]

2. Transition from Period 3 to Period 4 requires rather complex motorial conditions. So far as *reactivation* of the idle equipment stock in Sector II is concerned, we must be aware that, as soon as the net output of secondary equipment in Period 3 appears as capital input in Sector II, aggregate employment rises, that is, absorption of the labor increment starts. With the simultaneous fall in the savings ratio, aggregate demand for consumer goods and, thus, for secondary equipment rises even more than in proportion to employment. Then, if positive elasticity of quantity and price expectations with regard to the output of consumer goods is assumed, it is likely that reactivation will begin.

---

[23] What seems to be a structural complication is mainly owing to the fact that our model describes a continuous process in terms of discrete periods of maturation.

The *fall in the savings ratio* itself can be related to the easing of pressure on money wages in proportion to the gradual absorption of the labor increment. As was the case, however, when we initially stipulated a wage fall yielding the required profit–savings ratio, the implied wage elasticity of labor supply is by no means empirically assured.

Finally, the "backward switch" of primary equipment from Sector Ib to Sector Ia can be traced to the reapportioning of savings once Sector II expands. During Period 3, savings were invested in their entirety in Sector Ib. From then on they have to be distributed in equilibrium proportions over the three sectors, also bringing about equilibrium distribution of primary equipment among the two equipment-good sectors. These events can only occur provided that the elasticity of quantity and price expectations is positive in Sector Ia and negative in Sector Ib.[24]

VI

We have reached the point where a summing up of our motorial findings seems in order. In doing so we shall also draw the final conclusions from our structure analysis. Actually the two approaches are inseparable.

First of all, motorial analysis has revealed the significance of a functioning price mechanism for an efficient traverse. To the extent that the direction and intensity of price variations (and related profit variations) are goal-adequate, that is, tend toward a new dynamic equilibrium, they operate as a perfect signal system on which the decisions of the firms can orient themselves even in the complex crisscross of counter-

[24] A word must be added about a numerical representation of the "second alternative" of an efficient traverse, discussed in Chapter 14, Sections VII and IX. We remember that this alternative is based on the stipulation that the stock of secondary equipment in terminal equilibrium be no larger than the original stock. It stands to reason that with this assumption Period 3, during which, in the model described in the Appendix of this chapter, secondary equipment is constructed, can be dispensed with. Thus, terminal equilibrium is reached directly from Period 2 – maximum expansion from within. All that is required is the switching of an appropriate part of primary equipment from Sector Ia to Sector Ib.

We must be aware, however, that the values of some strategic magnitudes are affected by stipulating the indicated relationship between the original and the terminal stock of secondary equipment. Because there is no construction span for secondary equipment, β disappears from our measures – not only of the terminal capital stocks but also of the interim savings ratio, which now equals s_i as established in Equation 14.12. In the numerical setup of our model, s_i amounts to 7/40. Correspondingly, the required addition to *primary* equipment, now represented by Equation 14.10.1, falls to ca. 30 units. Then, assuming equality between initial and terminal secondary equipment, total capital stock rises from the original 500 units to 360 plus 170 = 530 units. These indications should suffice for the interested reader to construct a numerical model of the entire adjustment path, in analogy with the one described in the appendix of this chapter.

vailing sectoral movements. A superficial observer might conclude from this that the decentralized mechanism of a laissez-faire system is ideally adapted to the successful solution of all traverse problems.

On the contrary, our attempt to bring into the open the motivational requirements that underlie such a functioning price mechanism has shown the fallacy of such a conclusion. It would be correct only if the mechanism at work was ruled by "objective laws," independent of varying action directives and, above all, of the expectations of the economic actors. In fact, neither the action directives nor the particular expectations that assure goal-adequate behavior can be taken for granted. The price mechanism is anything but a mechanical tool.

We need not confine ourselves to such a general reservation. What both our structural and our motorial analyses have revealed are quite specific hurdles in the course of the traverse that the uncontrolled actions of free marketers are unlikely to negotiate. Referring to the most difficult obstacles, we recall once more the initial wage bargain that was charged with establishing the one and only efficient savings ratio, the requirement of a rise in investment in the face of falling quantities and prices of output, the "solidarity dilemma," the necessity of timely braking both the contraction and the expansion of output, the forward switch and, subsequently, the backward switch of primary equipment, and the ultimate reduction of the savings ratio to a level that accords with the long-term increase in labor supply. In each instance, commonsense evaluation of profit and loss chances suggests goal-*in*adequate interpretation of available information and price signals, diverting action in the wrong direction if not blocking it altogether.

Even graver are the difficulties in a traverse that is based on voluntary savings, when there is no systematic connection at all between the rate of growth of labor supply and the prevailing savings ratio. In this practically most common case, under- and overbuilding of primary equipment are equiprobable.

We shall not enter into a detailed analysis of either of these failures of an efficient traverse,[25] although they represent the realistic alternatives to Balanced Growth; consider, for instance, the large fluctuations in aggregate activity that have characterized economic growth during the era of uncontrolled capitalism. Nor is it the task of this essay to study measures of public control appropriate to counteract deviations of the traverse from its efficient course.[26] Our task is simply to demonstrate the direction of this course and its precariousness when left to the play of autonomous market forces.

[25] The nature of these distortions has been indicated in Chapter 14, Section III.
[26] For a brief discussion of these issues, see *OEK*, Ch. 11, Sections 11–13.

Appendix to chapter 15

Traverse toward dynamic equilibrium with a higher rate of growth of labor supply, illustrated on a numerical price sum-quantity schema (quantities in parentheses).

(F_q)	F_p	(f_q)	f_p	Pay rolls	P	Sal. rec.	(o_q)	Net sal. rec.	$\left(\begin{array}{c}\text{Net}\\o_q\end{array}\right)$	Rate of profit
			INITIAL DYNAMIC EQUILIBRIUM							
Period 0										
(39.2)	39.2	(3.9)	3.9 +	14.1 +	1.6 =	19.6	(19.6)	5.6	(5.6)	⎫
(100.8)	100.8	(10.1)	10.1 +	36.3 +	4.0 =	50.4	(50.4)	14.4	(14.4)	⎬ 4%
(360.0)	360.0	(36.0)	36.0 +	129.6 +	14.4 =	180.0	(180.0)	—	—	⎭
(500.0)	500.0	(50.0)	50.0 +	180.0 +	20.0 =	250.0	(250.0)	20.0	(20.0)	
			FALL OF MONEY WAGES—RISE OF PROFITS							
Interperiod I										
(39.2)	39.2	(3.9)	3.9 +	12.6 +	3.1 =	19.6	(19.6)	5.6	(5.6)	⎫
(100.8)	100.8	(10.1)	10.1 +	32.3 +	8.0 =	50.4	(50.4)	14.4	(14.4)	⎬ 8%
(360.0)	360.0	(36.0)	36.0 +	115.1 +	28.9 =	180.0	(180.0)	—	—	⎭
(500.0)	500.0	(50.0)	50.0 +	160.0 +	40.0 =	250.0	(250.0)	20.0	(20.0)	
			FIRST ROUND OF INVESTMENT DEMAND							
Interperiod II										
(39.2)	78.0	(3.9)	7.8 +	12.6 +	19.2 =	39.6	(19.6)	11.8	(5.6)	ca. 24%
(100.8)	200.0	(10.1)	20.0 +	32.3 +	12.7 =	65.0	(50.4)	18.5	(14.4)	6.3%
(360.0)	464.0	(36.0)	46.4 +	115.1 +	−1.5 =	160.0	(180.0)	—	—	—
(500.0)	742.0	(50.0)	74.2 +	160.0 +	30.4 =	264.6	(250.0)	30.3	(20.0)	

FIRST ROUND OF SECTORAL EXPANSION AND CONTRACTION

Interperiod III							
(76.0)	152.0	(7.6)	15.2 + 24.6 + 36.2 = 76.0	(38.0)	48.1	(24)	ca. 24%
(64.0)	127.0	(6.4)	12.7 + 20.3 + 8.3 = 41.3	(32.0)	—	—	6.5%
(320.0)	413.0	(32.0)	41.3 + 102.3 + 4.0 = 147.6	(160.0)	147.6	(24)	1%
(460.0)	692.0	(46.0)	69.2 + 147.2 + 48.5 = 264.9	(230.0)	48.1	(24)	

ROCK BOTTOM

Period 1							
(90.2)	180.0	(9.0)	18.0 + 28.9 + 43.1 = 90.0	(45.1)	62.1	(31)	ca. 24%
(49.8)	99.0	(5.0)	9.9 + 15.9 + 6.3 = 32.1	(24.9)	—	—	6.3%
(248.8)	321.0	(24.8)	32.1 + 79.6 + 12.7 = 124.4	(124.4)	124.4	—	4%
(388.8)	600.0	(38.8)	60.0 + 124.4 + 62.1 = 246.5	(194.4)	62.1	(31)	

MAXIMUM EXPANSION FROM WITHIN

Period 2							
(116.0)	116.0	(11.6)	11.6 + 37.1 + 9.3 = 58.0	(58.0)	40	(40)	8%
(64.0)	64.0	(6.4)	6.4 + 20.5 + 5.1 = 32.0	(32.0)	—	—	
(320.0)	320.0	(32.0)	32.0 + 102.4 + 25.6 = 160.0	(160.0)	—	—	
(500.0)	500.0	(50.0)	50.0 + 160.0 + 40.0 = 250.0	(250.0)	40	(40)	

EXPANSION OF SECONDARY EQUIPMENT

Period 3							
(36.0)	36.0	(3.6)	3.6 + 11.6 + 2.8 = 18.0	(18.0)	40	—	8%
(144.0)	144.0	(14.4)	14.4 + 46.1 + 11.5 = 72.0	(72.0)	—	(40)	
(320.0)	320.0	(32.0)	32.0 + 102.3 + 25.7 = 160.0	(160.0)	—	—	
(500.0)	500.0	(50.0)	50.0 + 160.0 + 40.0 = 250.0	(250.0)	40	(40)	

TERMINAL DYNAMIC EQUILIBRIUM

Period 4							
(57.6)	57.6	(5.8)	5.8 + 19.6 + 3.4 = 28.8	(28.8)	10.8	(10.8)	6%
(122.4)	122.4	(12.2)	12.2 + 41.7 + 7.3 = 61.2	(61.2)	22.9	(22.9)	
(382.0)	382.0	(38.2)	38.2 + 129.9 + 22.9 = 191.0	(191.0)	—	—	
(562.0)	562.0	(56.2)	56.2 + 191.2 + 33.6 = 281.0	(281.0)	33.7	(33.7)	

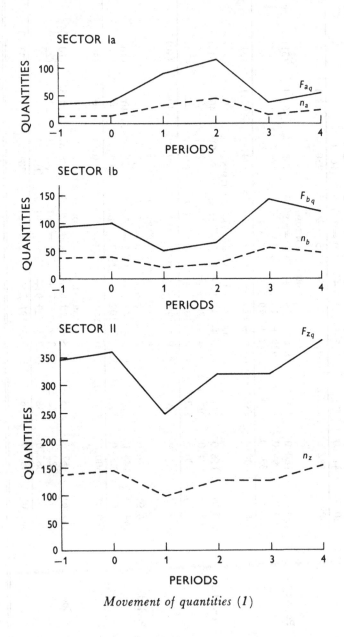

Movement of quantities (1)

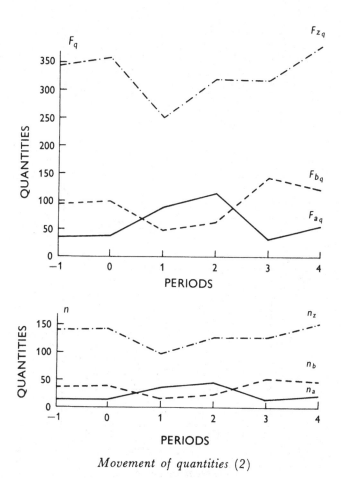

Movement of quantities (2)

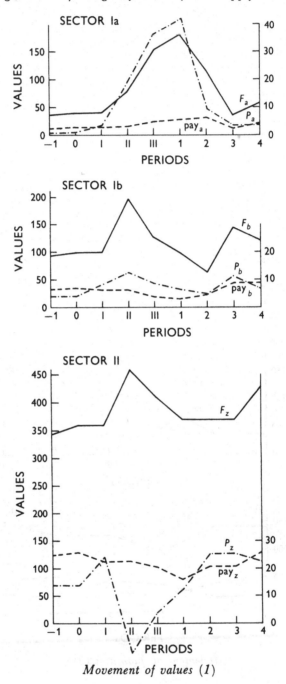

Movement of values (*1*)

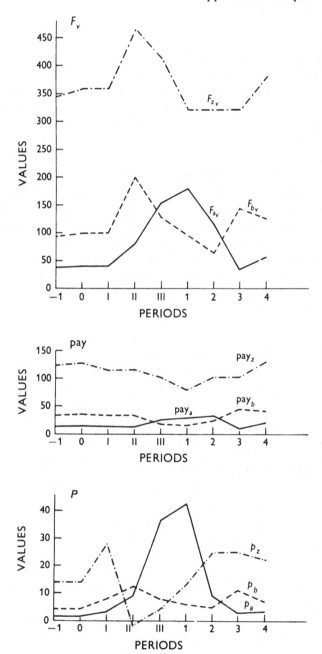

Movement of values (2)

16

Adjustment to a higher rate of growth of labor supply in a collectivist system

It is an overall thesis of this book that, at the level of instrumental analysis of *structure* and *structural change,* there is no basic difference between a laissez-faire market and a collectivist order. This thesis is fully confirmed by the findings reported in Chapter 14. The main phases of goal-adequate adjustment to a higher rate of growth of labor supply – reduction of consumer demand and the liberation of capacity, the application of such capacity to self-augmentation of primary equipment, and the backward shift of part of the capital stock so augmented for the complementary expansion of secondary equipment – are common features of the traverse in both systems. Thus, our earlier set of equations describing these processes is valid also in the collectivist case.

This is by no means true of the *motorial processes* that generate the structural path. In a collectivist system, not only are the strategic decisions centralized, therefore greatly simplifying coordination, but they are guided by a Plan outlining the future configuration of the overall structure. Hence they are free from the uncertainties that tend to deflect market behavior from the required course. As was emphasized before, collectivist systems have political and administrative problems of their own when it comes to assuring the loyal and effective execution of the directives of the Plan. However, to the extent that these problems can be solved through the proper gratification of bureaucratic incentives, centralized command is likely to overcome the obstacles in the way of an efficient traverse more easily than orientation on *ex post* variations of prices within a free market.[1]

This seems true of practically all impediments that decentralized decision making encounters in pursuing a goal-adequate path.[2] First of all, the rate of growth of labor supply, the initial stimulus, is no longer a factor unknown to the decision makers. An estimate of its size is part of the Plan, and it may even itself be manipulated. Therefore, the critical

---

[1] A collectivist system can, of course, employ a price order for its own purposes as an accounting technique and for the planned manipulation of demand and supply.

[2] See Chapter 15, Section VI.

savings and investment ratios, on which both capacity liberation and self-augmentation depend, can from the outset be adjusted to the new capital requirements. This adjustment is further facilitated because the aggregate savings ratio is no longer the unpredictable result of innumerable individual decisions or the equally unforeseeable outcome of many wage bargains but can be centrally planned by taxation, price fixing of consumer goods, and rationing.

Second, the initial investment decision that sets self-augmentation in motion, is not hampered either by unfavorable expectations or by any solidarity dilemma. Even the downward cumulation of employment and output in the consumer-good sector can be prevented, once planned regulation of living standards cuts the link between the supply of and the private demand for such goods. Finally, the limits to self-augmentation and the subsequent "switch" – both likely occasions for over- or underbuilding in a free market – are preordained in the Plan and put into practice by central control. Indeed, overbuilding can itself be part of the Plan in the interest of reducing the adjustment time of secondary equipment (β).[3]

There is no need for further enlarging on these issues, detailed discussion of which would lead us beyond the boundaries of economic analysis proper. Instead we are going to concentrate on a *structural* problem that can only arise in a collectivist organization and for which there is no feasible analogy in a free market. It concerns the temporary nonreplacement or "cannibalization"[4] of part of the initially available stock of equipment for the sake of speeding up the building of new equipment.

I

We begin with a more specific definition of what is to be understood by a collectivist system. The main features relevant in the present context are public ownership of the means of production, in particular of equipment goods and working capital goods; conscription of labor; and central direction of factors and commodities in accord with a preestablished Plan. For simplicity, we shall again argue within the framework of a two-strata model, but the role of independent firms is now taken over by the

[3] When speed of adjustment alone is the criterion of efficiency, for example, in wartime, overbuilding of primary equipment is an appropriate method because self-augmentation raises primary capacity at a geometric rate, whereas secondary output can rise only at an arithmetic rate – an advantage which of course may have to be paid for by subsequent wastage of part of the primary equipment stock.

[4] The suggestive term for the phenomenon under examination has been coined by Professor Ernest Bloch.

hierarchic organization of plant managers, administrators of industrial sectors, and the agents of the overall Plan.

The problem under consideration was alluded to in our earlier Bird's-Eye View of an Expanding Traverse.[5] Nonreplacement of part of the initial capital stock was then mentioned as a possible means of overcoming the bottleneck that impedes the rapid expansion of primary and secondary equipment. In other words, that part of initially available capacity which previously served the steady replacement and expansion of the capital stocks in all three sectors might be used in its entirety for self-augmentation, within the obvious limits set by progressive wear and tear.

As we saw, a rise in savings, voluntary or involuntary, indirectly achieves the same purpose, by reducing the demand for output and, as a consequence, for the capacity to produce it. Because in this case capacity liberation is a function of the reduction in consumption, it is narrowly restricted by the necessity of currently maintaining a minimum standard of living. If for the sake of argument we assume that voluntary and involuntary savings together must not reduce the prevailing level of consumption by more than 25 percent, capacity liberation at its maximum is confined to the same ratio. On the other hand, by temporarily stopping all replacements, the liberated capacity can be raised to 100 percent – a result that could only be achieved through the savings mechanism if consumption were to cease altogether.

Of course, the output of consumer goods is bound to shrink even under cannibalization. However, the shrinkage is gradual, amounting per period to no more than what is enforced by the actual wear and tear of the capital stock, measured by the rate of depreciation. Therefore, if the required addition to capital stock can be produced over a time span during which actual consumption can be kept at or above a stipulated minimum level, adjustment to the new terminal equilibrium can be speeded up considerably, although the final adjustment must now include the restoration of the cannibalized part of the capital stock.

The reasons why such expansion through cannibalization of the existing equipment can be carried out only in the framework of a collectivist system are *motorial*. There are, in principle, no structural impediments to the same procedure in a free market, but there is no mechanism that could enforce it. Rather, nonreplacement of worn-out equipment, when judged *ex ante,* contradicts the extremum principle and also the type of expectations on which expansion builds. In addition, increasing the speed of adjustment at large has no part in forming the individual investor's

[5] See Chapter 12, Section I.

action directive, and the need for subsequent restoration of the cannibalized equipment deprives such capital consumption of any prospect of profitability. Furthermore, if in the face of all the impediments discussed earlier firms decide to invest, they will do so on the basis of expectations that suggest full maintenance of the present capital stock.[6]

Although cannibalization does not alter the sequence of phases that describe the traverse, it modifies them in a manner worthy of detailed exposition. The remainder of this chapter is devoted to its discussion.

II

In principle, three different types of cannibalization are conceivable: capital consumption confined to the two equipment-good sectors, capital consumption confined to the consumer-good sector, and capital consumption in all three sectors simultaneously. Of these alternatives, the first is *prima facie* the most attractive, because it seems to permit the maintenance of the initial per capita consumption. But this impression is deceptive.

Cannibalization of primary equipment is actually self-defeating, because it reduces the initial capacity for self-augmentation by precisely the amount that nonreplacement temporarily adds, so that the liberation of primary capacity is the same, whether the initial stock is steadily replaced or left to dwindle. On the other hand, cannibalization confined to Sector II is sufficient to achieve the aim of freeing the total capacity in Sector Ib for self-augmentation, over the time span during which the stipulated minimum standard of consumption can be maintained. This then is the setup we are going to investigate under the aspect of a possible speeding up of the traverse. Our first task is to find a measure for this critical time span in terms of the new, reduced, consumption level and for the rate of depreciation of the capital stock in the consumer-good sector.

For simplicity's sake we assume that the capital stock in Sector II has an "equilibrium" age distribution and undergoes straight-line depreciation. Consequently, in every period of production an amount equal to the initial stock times the period rate of depreciation wears out, to be replaced under normal conditions by part of the simultaneous period output of secondary equipment. We further assume that the Plan stipulates a fraction μ, say 80 percent, to which the initial level of consumption is to be

---

[6] One might be inclined toward a different conclusion with regard to firms in the consumer-good sector, which are confronted with excess capacity. However, such excess capacity is only temporary, its reactivation being assured once expansion reaches down to the consumer-good sector. In addition, if in practice such capital consumption occurs, it is in the service of loss-reducing contraction rather than of profitable expansion.

reduced by means of rationing. It is understood that, independent of the actual output in a given period, aggregate consumption is to be kept in each period at the level of $\mu \cdot z_0$, and any surplus output is temporarily stored. Over how many periods of production can the reduced consumption level $\mu \cdot z_0$ be maintained, considering that output falls by $d \cdot z_0$ in every period?[7]

Because output declines at a steady rate, the standard level of $\mu \cdot z_0$ can be expressed as

$$\mu \cdot z_0 = \frac{z_0 + z_{\lim}}{2}$$

where $z_{\lim}$ measures the limit to which output of z may fall without prejudice to the average consumption level of $\mu \cdot z_0$. From this we obtain

$$\mu = \frac{1}{2} + \frac{1}{2} \frac{z_{\lim}}{z_0}$$

Now $z_{\lim}$ also equals $(1 - \Pi \cdot d) \cdot z_0$ where Π stands for the maximum feasible number of cannibalization periods – our unknown. This yields

$$\mu = \tfrac{1}{2} + \tfrac{1}{2}(1 - \Pi \cdot d)$$

and

$$\Pi = \frac{2(1 - \mu)}{d} \tag{16.1}$$

Given a reduction of consumption to 80 percent of the initial level, and $d = 1/10$, Π amounts to 4.

The maximum number of cannibalization periods (Π) compatible with a stipulated level of aggregate consumption is the "critical time span" (CTS), because on its size depend the alternatives open to the planning authorities as to the manner in which the traverse is to be carried out. If the required addition to the system's capital stock can be accomplished within CTS, cannibalization is the more efficient procedure. If, on the other hand, CTS is too short to permit the formation of the real capital required, then also a collectivist system must avail itself of the savings mechanism. Thus, the decision hinges on the time span required for the

---

[7] Both the period of production and the lifetime of the capital stock must be defined in chronological terms if the effect of cannibalization on the speed of adjustment is to be evaluated. For our present purposes, this question can be left open. See, however, footnote 11 in the following.

construction of the addition to capital stock and output. We now have to establish a measure for the minimum length of this time span.

III

This *minimum period of construction* (MPC) is obviously a function of the period of maturation of output in the three sectors. We know from the discussion of the Secondary Model[8] that construction of the required addition to capital stock is likely to take several periods of maturation, for the sum of which we have introduced the symbols γ and β, respectively. No such multiplying factor need be added for the output of consumer goods because, once the necessary addition to secondary capital stock is available, the complementary increase of consumer goods can be produced in one period of maturation.[9]

We then obtain

$$\text{MPC} = \gamma \cdot m_a + \beta \cdot m_b + m_z$$

or, by equating m_b with m_a,[10]

$$\text{MPC} = (\gamma + \beta)m_a + m_z \qquad (16.?)$$

Now in what manner is MPC related to CTS? At first sight one might presume that the entire period of construction must fall within the critical time span if cannibalization is to be feasible. Further reflection, however, tells us that the situation is more favorable. The true condition for the feasibility of cannibalization is the certainty that, after the passage of CTS, the output of consumer goods can continue at or above the stipulated minimum level. To assure this, Sector Ib must at this point have added sufficient secondary equipment to maintain the capital stock operating in Sector II at the required level or to raise it to that level.

In the most favorable case, namely, a low degree of cannibalization and a large expansion of primary equipment, β reduces to 1, and MPC amounts then to $\gamma + 2$. Thus we obtain the general feasibility condition for cannibalization as

$$\Pi \geq \gamma + 2 \qquad (16.3)$$

[8] See Chapter 14, Section V.
[9] For the interpretation of a period of maturation and, in particular, of a sectoral average period of maturation as an empirical constant, see Chapter 5, Section I.
[10] This is justified because all the stages of production except the last are identical in the two sectors. Even the maturation periods of the last stage, which in both sector refers to the production of machinery, are unlikely to differ much. In this manner, m_a provides *the measure in which all coefficients with a time dimension*, such as k and d, *must be expressed.*

that is, the critical time span must not fall below the number of maturation periods required to build the addition to primary equipment, plus two additional periods of maturation.

To determine γ, we make use of the results obtained when we discussed the Secondary Model depicting a rise of the rate of growth in a free market system. We found there[11]

$$\gamma^+ = \frac{\log\left\{\dfrac{1 + \alpha'k + [(1 + \alpha + \alpha')^{\gamma^+} - 1]\cdot B'}{s + s'kd}\right\}}{\log \bar{R}} \tag{14.11}$$

Now it is important to realize that, in the present context, the value of γ differs from the preceding expression in two respects. First, the liberation effect of cannibalizing F_z far exceeds that of any realistic savings ratio. It includes the entire stock of primary equipment operating in Sector Ib and thus equals a savings ratio of 1. For this reason the right side of Equation 14.11 changes to

$$\frac{\log\{[B'(1 + \alpha + \alpha')^\gamma]/B\}}{\log \bar{R}}$$

The second change goes in the other direction. Augmentation of primary equipment must now take care not only of the requirements imposed by the rise in the rate of growth of labor supply, but it must also restore the cannibalized part of the stock of secondary equipment. The latter amounts to the period depreciation of that stock, multiplied by the number of maturation periods, γ, necessary to produce the required addition to primary equipment. It amounts to

$$F_z\,(\text{cann}) = (1 - B)\cdot d\cdot \gamma \cdot k o_0$$

Now the task facing the planners is twofold. Not only must the cannibalized part of the stock of secondary equipment be restored, but the aggregate stock of such equipment must be raised to the level required for a new dynamic equilibrium, that is, to the level of

$$F_z\,(\text{requ}) = (1 - B')(1 + \alpha + \alpha')^\gamma \cdot F_{z_0}$$

Thus, the amount of secondary equipment actually to be built equals the terminal amount minus what is left after cannibalization, that is,

$$F_z\,(\text{to be built}) = [(1 - B')(1 + \alpha + \alpha')^\gamma - (1 - B)(1 - d\cdot\gamma)]\cdot k o_0 \tag{16.4}$$

[11] See Chapter 14, Section V.

The additional primary capital stock required to raise the stock of secondary equipment to the terminal level then amounts to[12]

$$F_b \text{ (requ)} = Bk_{0_0} \cdot \bar{R}^\gamma = \{B'(1 + \alpha + \alpha')^\gamma k_{0_0}$$
$$+ \frac{1}{\beta}[(1 - B')(1 + \alpha + \alpha')^\gamma - (1 - B)(1 - d \cdot \gamma)]\}k_{0_0}$$

and

$$\gamma = \log \frac{\left\{ \dfrac{B'(1 + \alpha + \alpha')^\gamma + (1/\beta)[(1 - B')(1 + \alpha + \alpha')^\gamma - (1 - B)(1 - d \cdot \gamma)]}{B} \right\}}{\log \bar{R}}$$

$$(16.5)$$

Equation (16.5) is another transcendental equation, and all we can say in general terms is that, for any value of γ that equals or is smaller than $\text{II} - 2$ (see Equation 16.3), cannibalization is a feasible procedure. We arrive at a more definite result if we change our approach and try to determine the maximum rate α' of a labor increment that can be absorbed within the critical time span. By substituting in Equation 16.5 for the unknown γ its known maximum feasible value $\text{II} - 2$, we can solve the equation for α'. Thus, we obtain the maximum increment of labor supply that can be absorbed through cannibalization of the stock of secondary equipment.

Speaking in practical terms, cannibalization as a technique for capital formation presupposes the presence of a considerable stock of equipment to begin with. Therefore, it is of little help where a substitute for a low savings ratio is most needed – in the underdeveloped regions. It is worth noting that such cannibalization played a significant role in the early stages of the accelerated industrialization of the Soviet Union[13] – a clear proof that, judged by its capital structure, Czarist Russia was by no means an undeveloped country.

[12] Factor β appears in the denominator because the quantity of primary equipment necessary to build the required addition to secondary equipment is inversely related to the number of maturation periods required for such construction.
[13] See Alexander Erlich, *The Soviet Industrialization Debate,* Cambridge, Mass., 1960.

17

Some comments on the role of working capital in the traverse

It was stated earlier that, with very few exceptions, the role of working capital in a stationary or dynamic structure of production has been neglected in modern literature.[1] This is especially true of *changes* in a given stock of working capital and their integration with the overall process of adjustment to a higher rate of growth.[2] We have briefly dealt with the problem in the context of our Bird's-Eye View of an Expanding Traverse, and shall now supplement these general comments by a schematic exposition of the step-by-step movements illustrated again in a numerical model. However, to facilitate understanding, we shall, first, discuss the salient points in literary terms.

I

Let us visualize the situation at the moment when expansion and, in particular, expansion of the initial stock of working capital is to begin. The influx of a new increment of labor supply and the concomitant appearance of additional savings have reduced the aggregate demand for consumer goods, displacing part of the labor force in Sector II and reducing demand for the output of Sector Ib, thus liberating part of the capital stock in Sector Ib for producing finished output other than secondary equipment. Assuming that a positive investment decision is forthcoming, this changed output in Sector Ib will henceforth consist of primary equipment, the embodiment of self-augmentation.

Now, this description in terms of sectoral aggregates is quite appropriate so long as our interest centers on the changes of *finished* output in the two equipment-good sectors – primary or secondary equipment. It is no longer adequate once we direct our attention to what is to happen to the *intermediary* outputs, namely, working capital goods, through which the finished output is gradually built up in *successive stages of production.*

---

[1] See Chapter 5.
[2] For an exception, see Erik Lundberg, *Studies in the Theory of Economic Expansion, loc. cit.,* Ch. III, especially the reference in paragraph 6 to the work of Alf Johansson.

Rather we must now spell out the specific changes in fixed and working capital goods that must occur in each stage of the diminished Sector Ib and of the extended Sector Ia, if an increase in the finished output of primary equipment is to become technically possible.

Thus, when speaking of liberated capacity in Sector Ib, we now refer to parts of the fixed capital stock and its output, namely, working capital goods, in each stage of this sector. Or to use the concrete terms of our original schema,[3] there are now in Sector Ib not only free machine tools – the fixed capital stock of the final stage – but, in ascending sequence, free steel mills, blast furnaces, and extractive machinery and, no less important, free steel, pig iron, and ore. We know from our original exposition of an industrial order of production[4] that it is the twofold serviceability of each one of these fixed and working capital goods for the ultimate production of primary as well as of secondary equipment that makes expansion at large at all possible. Moreover, it is the mere act of increasing savings, by reducing demand for secondary equipment and the proportionate inputs and outputs of its higher stages of production, that makes part of the *original* stocks of extractive machinery, of blast furnaces, of steel mills, and of machine tools, as well as part of the *original* output of ore, pig iron, and steel (all of which formerly served in the production of gins, spindles, looms, and sewing machines) now available for producing more extractive machinery, blast furnaces, steel mills, and machine tools.

Only after a *shift* has occurred in the utilization of *initially existing capacities and earlier outputs* – a shift that actually transforms part of Sector Ib into an extension of Sector Ia – can genuine self-augmentation begin. It must start in the earliest stage where the new extractive machinery can now raise the output of ore to be transferred as additional working capital good to the second stage, to increase there, through the operation of new blast furnaces, the output of pig iron, and so forth, until in the final stage the new machine tools transform additional steel into still more extractive machinery, blast furnaces, steel mills, and machine tools.[5,6]

---

[3] See Chapter 3, Section II, and Chapter 12, Section II.

[4] *Ibid.*

[5] It was emphasized repeatedly that the process of self-augmentation as such does not initiate absorption of the new labor increment, because the workers employed in expanding output in Sector Ia are, up to the point of maximum expansion from within, taken from the pool of unemployed present in Sectors Ib and II.

[6] Apologies are due the reader who feels that the preceding slow-motion description of the expansion process labors the obvious. That this is not so can be demonstrated by the example of Johansson (as quoted by Lundberg; see preceding footnote 2.) Johansson too insists that expansion proceeds in

II

The attached numerical model (see the Appendix to this chapter) illustrates these intrasectoral shifts within each stage and the circular or, rather, spiral motion through which, subsequently, rising stage outputs produce finished outputs. These outputs, in turn, acting as stage inputs, further expand output in every stage. Compared with our earlier numerical models the present one is highly simplified. First, to avoid the complications arising from changing rates of growth of labor supply and changing savings ratios, we start out from stationary equilibrium, into which we introduce a once-over increase of the current rate of labor supply. Second, we shall study the effect of such a change only for the two equipment-good sectors, with particular emphasis on what occurs in Sector Ia. The results thus obtained can be directly applied to the expansion of working capital goods in Sectors Ib and II. Third, expansion is supposed to be based on an increase of savings rather than on cannibalization, so as to make the discussion applicable to both a free market and a collectivist system. Finally, we shall limit ourselves to a description of structural events, because the underlying motorial conditions coincide with those we have established for the expansion of the stock of fixed capital.[7]

By inspecting the model, we see that production of equipment goods has been horizontally divided in accordance with our basic schema into Sectors Ia and Ib. However, contrary to our earlier representation, we have now also divided the physically homogeneous inputs of labor, primary equipment, and working capital goods among each sector pro rata with their contribution to the final output. Thus, in particular, the *inputs* of extractive machinery, blast furnaces, and so on, appear in both sectors, and it is only in the last stage that *outputs* differ physically. This will make it possible to describe the intrasectoral shifts occurring during the process of expansion by decreasing the numbers in the right-hand part of the schema and by increasing them in the left-hand part.

> linear fashion from the earliest to the latest stage, because "as no stocks exist that can be used in the later stages of production, an increase of production must necessarily start in the first stage" (*loc. cit.*, p. 70). However, in this quotation, he is apparently concerned only with the *outputs* in successive stages, not with the *capital stocks* that are to produce these outputs. Nonetheless, if there were no free capacity available in the first stage, brought about by additional saving (voluntary, involuntary, or forced), how could production be increased anywhere – unless workers extracted the ore, in good Austrian fashion, with their bare hands? For this reason, what needs stressing is the strategic function of a reduction in the output of consumer goods for the *technical* feasibility of expansion in an equilibrating system.

[7] See Chapter 15, Section II.

In each sector the process of production has been subdivided into four stages illustrating the successive transformation of the basic raw material (ore) into primary or secondary equipment, respectively. We assume that the quantities of labor and equipment operating in each stage, disregarding natural resources, are equal so that the output change in each stage is due to the continuous increase in working capital embodying the input of labor and equipment in the earlier stages. As has been mentioned before, the increase in labor input in Sector Ia is, from Period 2 on, achieved by the shift of unemployed labor first from Sector Ib and then from Sector II.

The model describes the process of expanding working capital in Sector Ia over four periods, each period covering the processes successively occurring in each of the four stages and required for the production of finished output. It starts out from a stationary equilibrium (*Period 0*), in which the available capital and labor resources are divided between the two equipment-good sectors in the ratio of 1:4. The figures are chosen so that again $k = 2$ and $d = 1/10$. At this stage the function of production in Sector Ia is exclusively one of replacing used-up equipment in both Sectors Ia and Ib, so that the net output in Sector Ia must be zero.

Period 1 registers the effect of an increase in labor supply and of a concomitant appearance of savings. For purposes of vivid illustration, a savings ratio of $\frac{1}{2}$ has been chosen. As the consequence of the fall in aggregate consumption, demand for the output of Sector Ib (secondary machinery) has been reduced by half, as has also the supply, freeing half the capacity of the capital stock in each stage of Sector Ib. The freed capacity is now utilized in terms of Sector Ia, with the important consequence that final output there rises to 30 units, whereas aggregate replacement demand in both sectors still stands at 10, leaving a net output in terms of primary machinery amounting to 20.

This net output appears in Period 2 as input, raising the capital stock in every stage of the already extended Sector Ia from 15 to 20 – the beginning of self-augmentation proper. In this manner, net output in the final stage is raised to 28 units. From then on, the process continues in analogous fashion. Incidentally, given the above figures for k and d, the rate of growth of self-augmenting primary equipment equals $\frac{2}{8}$, a rate that equals $\bar{R} - 1$, which is the rate of net self-augmentation established previously.[8]

As the model indicates, inputs and outputs in Sector Ib remain unchanged from Period 1 on, up to the period in which self-augmentation of primary equipment comes to an end, and the switch occurs. The switch

[8] See Chapter 14, Section V.

itself indicates not only the beginning of the expansion of secondary equipment, but also of the concomitant increase of working capital in Sector Ib. Or, rather, it is the increase of the latter that enables the expansion of the former to take place, that is, via the reverse shift of existing capacity and the use of the stage outputs for producing the final output, namely, secondary machinery. Replacement demands in Sector Ib must, of course, be met by Sector Ia, as is the case all through the traverse.

III

As was said earlier, there is no need for discussing the motorial conditions that assure the appropriate adjustment path in a free market system in any detail. As we saw, rising demand for additional primary equipment – the essence of a positive investment decision – sets the price mechanism in motion, creating price rises for the output of the production stages in an ascending sequence, resulting in the highest price gain for the output of the earliest stage, namely, ore. With the price and quantity expectations as established in the preceding,[9] the incentive of receipt maximization will draw the idle capacity of the stock of extractive machinery, which the fall in demand for consumer goods has created in the earliest stage of Sector Ib, into production in Sector Ia, followed by a proportionate expansion of the later stages induced by the same incentive. The same set of motivations assures the application of the additional output of the final stage, Sector Ia type of machinery, as inputs in the respective stages, until the rise in supply of all types of primary equipment meets the rise in demand and price gains disappear.

[9] See Chapter 15, Section II.

Appendix to chapter 17

A numerical model of the growth of working capital

	Sector Ia							Sector Ib					
	F	f	n	ω	o	net o	(product)	F	f	n	ω	o	(product)
Period 0													
Stage I	(Ex.M.5)	0.5 +	2 +		= 2.5		ore	(Ex.M.20)	2 +	8 +		= 10	ore
Stage II	(Bl.F.5)	0.5 +	2 +	2.5	= 5.0		pig iron	(Bl.F.20)	2 +	8 +	10	= 20	pig iron
Stage III	(St.M.5)	0.5 +	2 +	5.0	= 7.5		steel	(St.M.20)	2 +	8 +	20	= 30	steel
Stage IV	(M.T.5)	0.5 +	2 +	7.5	= 10.0	0	Ex.M. Bl.F. St.M. M.T.	(M.T.20)	2 +	8 +	30	= 40	jenny spindle loom sewing machine
Period 1													
Stage I	15	1.5 +	6 +		= 7.5			10	1 +	4 +		= 5	
Stage II	15	1.5 +	6 +	7.5	= 15.0			10	1 +	4 +	5	= 10	same
Stage III	15	1.5 +	6 +	15.0	= 22.5			10	1 +	4 +	10	= 15	
Stage IV	15	1.5 +	6 +	22.5	= 30.0	20		10	1 +	4 +	15	= 20	
Period 2													
Stage I	20	2 +	8 +		= 10								
Stage II	20	2 +	8 +	10	= 20								same
Stage III	20	2 +	8 +	20	= 30								
Stage IV	20	2 +	8 +	30	= 40	28							
Period 3													
Stage I	27	2.7 +	10.8 +		= 13.5								
Stage II	27	2.7 +	10.8 +	13.5	= 27								same
Stage III	27	2.7 +	10.8 +	27.0	= 40.5								
Stage IV	27	2.7 +	10.8 +	40.5	= 54	39.2							

Abbreviations: Ex.M., extractive machinery; Bl.F., blast furnaces; St.M., steel mills; M.T. machine tools.

18

*Instrumental analysis of decline in
the rate of growth of labor supply*

In defining the topic of this book and, in particular, the meaning we are
going to attach to the notion of growth,[1] we spoke of the formation,
application, and liquidation of real capital. Up to this point we have
dealt with growth only in the narrower sense of steady or unsteady
expansion, and the problems we encountered there were exclusively related
to the formation and application of fixed and working capital. Now the
time has come for a closer look at the structural and motorial problems
of *capital liquidation,* as posed by a *fall* in the rate of growth.

In a general way the issue has a long history, reaching back at least
to Ricardo's concern with the approach of the system to a "stationary
state."[2] However, apart from the effect on income distribution, one
searches in vain for a detailed description of the *path* that is to lead to
this terminal state, not to speak of the change in the intersectoral relations within industry, which such a process is bound to bring about.
Although the secular fall in accumulation holds a strategic place in
Marx's vision of capitalist development, the schemata of reproduction,
his main theoretical tool from which our own structural analysis is derived, were used by him only for demonstrating processes of expansion.

After a lapse of decades, interest in the problem of decline was revived
in the so-called maturity controversy during the thirties.[3] The discussion,
which moved entirely at the level of positive analysis, was at best incon-
clusive, and this all the more so because it centered on the *premises* – falling rate of population increase, slackening of technical progress – rather
than on the *inferences* to be drawn. On the other hand, in the ecological
discussions of recent years, the notion is spreading that a planned reduction of the growth rate, if not the complete cessation of growth, may well
be a precondition for the survival of the industrial system in all its socio-

---

[1] See Chapter 1, Section II, and Chapter 2, Section I.
[2] See, David Richardo, *Principles of Polictical Economy and Taxation,* Sraffa edi-
    tion, Cambridge, 1951, pp. 108–9, 120–21. See also Adam Smith's passing
    reference to a similar tendency in the *Wealth of Nations,* Modern Library
    edition, New York, 1937, p. 94.
[3] See Benjamin Higgins, *Economic Development, Principles, Problems, and Poli-
    cies,* New York, 1959, pp. 167–98, and the literature cited there.

political forms. Without entering into the merits of such a prognosis, we can say that an inquiry into the structural and motorial conditions of a decline in the rate of growth is today of more than academic interest.

At first sight one might be tempted to perceive the structural analysis of such a decline as the symmetrical opposite to that of a rise in the rate of growth. A moment's reflection, however, will tell us that this cannot be so. What is supposed to "decline" is not the system's aggregate activity, but only its *rate* of growth. We are, in other words, still in the *dimension of expansion,* and it is intuitively clear that restoration of balanced growth requires a *relative shift* in the inputs and outputs of our three sectors *rather than an overall reduction.*[4]

In accord with our procedure when we studied expansion, we shall, to begin with, offer a general survey of the successive stages through which the system will have to pass in order to adjust to a fall in the rate of growth of labor supply. This will be followed by a detailed analysis of the sectoral movements within each stage. In a first approach, we shall again study the structural characteristics in isolation, and then supplement our results by a motorial analysis. The latter will confirm the widely held presumption according to which the social structure of uncontrolled industrial capitalism is much better equipped to deal with expansion than with contraction.

In order to be able to choose among several adjustment paths that offered themselves in the case of an expanding traverse, we stipulated, besides the overall goal of balanced growth, a particular *path criterion.* The standard path was then seen as one that permitted maximum speed of adjustment constrained by the condition that malinvestment or capital waste was to be avoided. More precisely, the additional capital stock required for adjustment was neither to be overbuilt nor underbuilt. We

---

[4] Some of the issues we are going to encounter, in particular the required shift of inputs from the production of primary equipment to the production of consumer goods, have been discussed in the context of business cycle analysis, more specifically, in the exposition of the so-called overinvestment theories (see Gottfried Haberler, *Prosperity and Depression,* New York, 1946, Ch. 3, esp. par. 12). See also the detailed analysis of intersectoral shifts as occurring in a "strong boom," in John R. Hicks, *A Contribution to the Theory of the Trade Cycle,* Oxford, 1950, esp. Chs. VIII and X, and my critical comments in *A Structural Model of Production, loc. cit.,* pp. 168–73.

Of course, decline in the literal sense, that is, absolute reduction in the supply of one or more factors, would also have to be part of an all-inclusive study of growth. We omit it here because its empirical significance appears minor for the time being. However, it should be noted that even the path of such absolute contraction is by no means symmetrical with the expansion path of a steady or rising rate of growth because, as we shall presently see, the problems posed by overall capital liquidation, in particular the motorial problems, differ essentially from those related to capital formation.

shall discover in due course that this constraint cannot be applied to our present problem because it is in the nature of a falling rate of growth that part of the initial capital stock must prove redundant. So we shall confine our path criterion to postulating *maximum speed of adjustment.*

I

Given a market system in dynamic equilibrium expanding at a rate of growth of labor supply equal to α^+,[5] and assuming that at the beginning of a stated period α^+ reduces to α, so that $0 < \alpha < \alpha^+$, what are the phases of the traverse through which the system is to pass in order to attain a new level of dynamic equilibrium?

1. Liberation of Some Existing Capacity in Sector Ia. It is intuitively clear that steady absorption of the lower growth rate requires a lower rate of net investment. This is equivalent to stating that, in order to assure full utilization of the still growing resources, the sector ratios must change in the direction of a relative contraction of the growth Sector Ia and a relative expansion of the consumer-good Sector II. Disregarding for the time being all motorial problems, we do not encounter any *technical* difficulties in reducing the output of primary equipment. All that is necessary for this purpose is displacement of some of the prime factors and part of the capital stock operating in Sector Ia. Expansion of the output of consumer goods, on the other hand, is not so easily achieved. Even if we were to stipulate perfect mobility of all factors other than equipment so that not only labor but also working capital now idle in Sector Ia could be transferred without modification to the consumer-good sector, there would be, to begin with, no additional stock of secondary equipment on which these factors could be employed. So the primary adjustment problem concerns the *expansion of secondary equipment.*

Such expansion is conditional on a prior increase of the capital stock operating in Sector Ib. We know that this stock is technically identical with the capital stock operating in Sector Ia, part of which has been made idle by the fall in the investment ratio. Thus, far from obstructing goal-adequate adjustment, the original displacement of primary equipment

---

[5] The above symbols are chosen so as to permit comparison with the respective symbols applied to an expanding traverse in Chapters 14 and 15, especially with the numerical examples introduced there. Symbol α was used then to denote the initial, lower growth rate, which was raised by additional α' to the new growth rate $\alpha + \alpha'$. In what follows the initial growth rate is denoted by α^+, whereas the new, lower growth rate is symbolized as α. Then the former α', the difference between the higher and the lower growth rate, can be expressed as $\alpha^+ - \alpha$.

reveals itself as the very precondition for a feasible traverse. Furthermore, in analogy to the terminology used when studying a rising rate of growth,[6] we may speak of "liberation" of existing capacity, although in the earlier instance this capacity was located in Sector Ib whereas it is now located in Sector Ia.

2. Augmentation of the Output of Secondary Equipment. The second phase consists in the application of idle primary equipment to the augmentation of secondary equipment, that is, to an increase in the output of Sector Ib. In contrast with the events characteristic for an increase in the rate of growth, it is now not a question of "self-augmentation" of primary equipment and, thus, of a geometric increase of output from period to period. Rather, this adjustment process now resembles the procedure through which, in the third phase of an expanding traverse after the switch has occurred, Sector Ib achieves its proportional increase. Again a switch is at stake, and, as we shall presently see, a major problem will be to ascertain the proper amount of primary equipment that is to be transferred to the construction of the permanent addition to secondary equipment.

3. Augmentation of Consumer-Good Output and Final Adjustment of the Capital Stocks in the Two Equipment-Good Sectors. At first sight the events occurring during the third phase do not seem to present particular difficulties. Given, as a result of the augmentation phase, an appropriate amount of additional secondary equipment, output of consumer goods can now be expanded to the goal-adequate size. However, whether in this manner balanced growth can be restored depends on whether inputs and outputs have attained their equilibrium size not only in Sector II but also in Sectors Ia and Ib.

Looking first at Sector Ib, its new equilibrium size is determined by the requirements of Sector II, which arise from the demand for steady replacement and for net investment in accord with the new rate α of the increase in labor supply. A situation is conceivable in which an amount of primary equipment and of the concomitant other factors can be transferred from Sector Ia to Sector Ib during Phase 2, which just equals the stock of resources *permanently* required in Sector Ib. However, as a more detailed exposition will show, for all but minor reductions in the rate of growth of labor supply, the required addition to secondary equipment far exceeds what the *terminally* adequate stock of resources can produce

---

[6] See Chapter 12, Section I.

in Sector Ib in one period of maturation. So we are faced with the choice between either temporarily raising the capital stock in Sector Ib above its terminally required level or using more than one period of maturation for the construction of the terminally required capital stock in Sector II.

We now realize the significance of our criterion for an efficient path, namely, maximum speed of adjustment. This criterion is satisfied only if, in Phase 2, input and output in Sector Ib are expanded to a level that reduces the construction of the required addition to secondary equipment to the smallest number of maturation periods technically feasible, namely, one. Because, however, the size of Sector Ib appropriate for completing the traverse with maximum speed normally exceeds the size compatible with the steady renewal and expansion of the capital stock in Sector II after the traverse has been completed, Phase 3 must bring about a "backward switch" to Sector Ia of some of the resources transferred to Sector Ib in Phase 2.

This brings us finally to the question of what size of Sector Ia is in accord with the new level of balanced growth. Take the extreme case in which the entire stock of primary equipment originally employed in Sector Ia will, in the interest of speedy adjustment, be transferred to Sector Ib. As we just realized, part of this stock must subsequently be retransferred to assure the steady replacement and expansion of the new equilibrium stock of primary equipment operating in both Sectors Ib and Ia. Nonetheless, whatever the size of the prior transfer to Sector Ib, some part of the original stock of primary equipment operating in Sector Ia cannot be reemployed. We shall see that such "waste" of primary equipment, which is inseparable from a fall in the rate of growth, creates serious motorial impediments to the restoration of balanced growth.[7]

II

For didactic reasons, it seems expedient from the outset to illustrate the step-by-step analysis of the traverse through a numerical schema. In analogy with our earlier procedure,[8] the Appendix to this chapter reproduces a *price-quantity schema* in which the successive steps of adjustment to a lower rate of growth can be read. For the structural problems with which this and subsequent section are concerned, only the *quantity* figures are relevant; they are again placed in parentheses.[9]

[7] See Section IV.
[8] See the appendix to Chapter 15.
[9] For the symbols used in the schema and the underlying methodology, see Chapter 15, Section III. In order to facilitate comparison, some of the numbers

PERIOD 0

Period 0 describes a dynamic equilibrium with a growth rate α^+ of labor supply equal to 6 percent. The savings–investment ratio, which absorbs the steady influx, amounts to $s^+ = 3/20$ – precisely the conditions that prevail in the terminal equilibrium as elaborated earlier for a rise in the rate of growth. We now stipulate that the rate of growth falls to $\alpha = 4$ percent. In accord with the general condition for growth equilibrium, the corresponding savings–investment ratios must then fall to $k\alpha/(1 - kd)$,[10] that is, to $1/10$. In other words, only if savings and investments are simultaneously reduced in proportion with the fall in the growth rate, can a new level of dynamic equilibrium be established. This, in turn, is equivalent to saying that consumption must be raised in inverse proportion to the fall in savings. For this shift within aggregate spending, we apply to our model the terms appropriate to a free market system, by equating the rise in consumption with an increase in wage rates and aggregate payrolls at the expense of profits that, as we remember, in our two-strata schema equal savings and investment.

INTERPERIOD I

Interperiod I depicts this shift of profits to wages, which at the same time creates an excess demand for consumer goods, amounting to 10 units. To balance this excess demand the capital stock in Sector II must be expanded, which, in turn, requires an expansion of output in Sector Ib. We know from our general survey of the traverse that such expansion of output and, prior to this, of the capital stock in Sector Ib is conditional on a shift of part of the capital stock in Sector Ia which has been made idle through the fall in the rate of investment. In order to find out how much primary equipment must be shifted to Sector Ib for the traverse to conform to our efficiency criterion of minimizing adjustment time, we must first establish a measure for the required increase in secondary equipment:

$$\Delta F_z \text{ (requ)} = F_z - F_{z_0}$$

where F_z stands for the secondary capital stock adjusted to the lower growth rate. Expressed in terms of the sector ratios prevailing in the two

chosen here correspond to those used in the earlier schema. A characteristic difference is that the numbers depicting initial Period 0 in the present schema coincide with the numbers of terminal Period 4 in the earlier schema, whereas initial Period 0 in the former schema portrays the numbers of present terminal Period 2.

[10] See Chapter 9, Section III.

equilibria, we obtain[11]

$$\Delta F_z \text{ (requ)} = [(1 - B) - (1 - B')] \cdot k o_0$$
$$= (B' - B) \cdot k o_0 \qquad (18.1)$$

In the numerical setup of Period 0 this amounts to 20 units. The initial output of Sector Ib must grow by this same amount if the output of consumer goods is to be raised to the new level at the maximum speed that is technically feasible. Moreover, the stock of primary equipment operating in Sector Ib must rise by k times the expression of Equation 18.1, which measures at the same time the amount of primary equipment that must be shifted from Sector Ia to Sector Ib.

However, this result is valid only if, in analogy with the Primary Model describing adjustment to a rising rate of growth of labor supply,[12] we isolate the traverse to a higher level of consumption from any other changes occurring simultaneously or, what amounts to the same, if we treat the traverse as a timeless process. In reality, at the very minimum *two periods of maturation* must elapse before the additional output of consumer goods becomes available – one devoted to the construction of the required addition to secondary equipment, and the other to its application. During this interval the influx of labor into the system continues, although at the lower rate of α. Therefore, the new position of dynamic equilibrium will be reached only when capital stock and output in Sector II are raised by an amount that can accommodate both the rising demand of the initially employed and the demand of the labor increment accruing during the adjustment process.

When discussing an increase in the rate of growth, we treated the intricacies of time-bound adjustment in a more complex Secondary Model. Although the structural sequences describing the path of a fall in the rate of growth are hardly less entangled, we shall from the outset make use of an analog to the earlier Secondary Model.

PERIOD 1[13]

The structural characteristics of this model are described in Periods 1 and 2 of the attached schema. It demonstrates the approach to a new dynamic equilibrium in which the aggregate output of consumer goods

[11] Compare Chapter 14, Section II. There symbols B and B' were used to denote the respective growth factors expressed in terms of the savings ratio. It was also pointed out in the preceding footnote 5 that the growth rates α and α^+ fully correspond to the growth rates α and $\alpha + \alpha'$ as applied in Chapter 14, so that the symbols B and B' retain their original meaning.

[12] See Chapter 14, Section II.

[13] Interperiod II concerns only motorial analysis. See Section IV.

is raised to the level corresponding to the lower growth rate. Because this output is now also to accommodate the demand for the intermediate labor influx, the required addition to the initial capital stock operating in Sector II must exceed the magnitude determined in Equation 18.1. It now amounts to

$$\Delta F_z \text{ (requ)} = F_z \text{ (term)} - F_{z_0}$$

where F_z (term) stands for the quantity of secondary equipment actually required in terminal equilibrium.

Subsequent to the upward adjustment of wages in Interperiod I, terminal equilibrium is reached in our model over two periods. The function of Period 1 is to provide, partly through a shift of primary equipment from Sector Ia to Sector Ib, an addition to the output of Sector Ib that will raise in Period 2 the capital stock in Sector II and, consequently, the output of consumer goods, to the new equilibrium level.

We begin by establishing a measure for the required addition to secondary equipment under the new conditions. To do so we must first determine F_z (term), the total stock of secondary equipment required in terminal equilibrium. It equals

$$F_z \text{ (term)} = (1 - B)(1 + \alpha)^2 \cdot ko_0 \tag{18.2}$$

amounting in our model to 389.4 units. The expression in the first parentheses multiplied by ko_0 measures the addition to secondary equipment required to raise the consumption of the initially employed labor to the new level. This then is to be multiplied with the expression in the second parentheses, registering a twofold influx of α. By subtracting from this expression the amount of secondary equipment available in the initial stage, we obtain

$$\Delta F_z \text{ (term)} = [(1 - B)(1 + \alpha)^2 - (1 - B')] \cdot ko_0 \tag{18.3}$$

amounting to 49.4 units. In what manner is this addition produced?

a. First of all, we notice that in Period 0 the system, while still operating under the former higher growth rate, produces in Sectors Ia and Ib a net output above replacement demand. In Sector Ia this net output amounts to 9.6 units of primary equipment which, had the original growth rate been maintained, would have been distributed among the two equipment-good sectors at the prevailing equilibrium ratio for the purpose of steady expansion. However, our general survey of the traverse to a lower rate of growth has already taught us that the shrinkage of the growth rate is bound up with the permanent displacement of part of the original capital stock. From this it follows that a further addition to this stock by such net output would only raise the amount of redundant primary equipment, which will remain idle once a new dynamic equilibrium is reached. For this reason we shall, as we did before,[14] disregard the presence of such initial net output while we study the structural requirements of adjustment. We shall return to the issue when we take up the motorial conditions.[15]

The situation is quite different with the simultaneous net output in Sector Ib, which amounts to 20.4 units of secondary equipment. Rather investment of this net output in Period 1 is the first step in overcoming the prevailing deficit of secondary equipment. In this way the capital stock in Sector II is raised in Period 1 to 360.4 units, utilization of which is accompanied by a rise of savings to 14.4 units.

b. To accommodate these savings plus the higher replacement demand of 36 units in Sector II, an output of 50.4 units would have to be produced in Sector Ib during Period 1. This, however, would raise the capital stock of Sector II in the subsequent Period 2 only to 374.8 units, following an investment equivalent to the savings that accrue in Period 1. Yet, from Equation 18.3, we know that the terminal capital stock in Sector II must rise to 389.4 units, requiring an expansion of the output of Sector Ib in Period 1 by another 14.6 units to a total of 65 units. Such output requires a stock of primary equipment operating in Sector Ib of 130 units, that is, an excess of 21.2 units over and above the capital stock of 108.8 units available there initially.

c. At this critical point the shift of primary equipment from Sector Ia to Sector Ib comes into play, that is, 21.2 units of primary equipment that so far were engaged in self-reproduction are now to be employed in producing additional secondary equipment. Therefore, the capital stock remaining in Sector Ia is reduced to 30 units. However, as inspection of Period 1 of our schema shows, we have registered for Sector Ia an active capital stock of only 29.6 units. This is a small discrepancy, which, nevertheless, is not due to numerical inaccuracy but has a systematic significance which we are going to discuss presently.

First, however, let us examine the structure of production as exhibited by the model of Period 1. In accord with the increment of $\alpha = 4$ percent, aggregate inputs and outputs have risen by 4 percent. Otherwise we are confronted with a quite lopsided structure. Aggregate demand for consumer goods, 187.2 units, still exceeds aggregate supply, 180 units, although the difference has narrowed compared with Interperiod I. Net

---

[14] See Chapter 15, Section III.
[15] See Section IV.

output in Sector Ib exceeds savings in Sector II by 14.6 units, and although we know that this amount is necessary to raise in Period 2 the capital stock of Sector II to the new equilibrium level, we must ask how such net investment is financed. We find the answer when we inspect the setup of Sector Ia. Instead of producing in Period 1 a net output equivalent to the savings that accrue in the two equipment-good sectors, the actual output of 14.8 units does not even suffice fully to replace the depreciated part of primary equipment. The amortization funds thus freed, amounting to 1.2 units, plus the not otherwise investible savings of 6.2 units, accruing in the two equipment-good sectors, plus an additional "price gain" in Sector II (the origin of which will be explained in Section IV) form, together with the savings of Sector II, the pool out of which the net output in Sector Ib in the amount of 29 units can be financed for investment in Sector II in Period 2.

However, we now ask, could the output deficit in Sector Ia not be reduced by utilizing the entire stock of primary equipment left over after the transfer of part of it to Sector Ib (to which even the idle net output of such equipment in Period 0 could be added)? What limits the utilization of more of the available primary equipment is the size of the available *labor force*. As was said before, the model as depicted in Period 1 is adjusted to an increase of labor by α, that is, by 8 units, requiring an addition to aggregate capacity of 20 units. Therefore, any capacity exceeding the aggregate of 520 units must stand idle, at least temporarily. Nor can the problem be evaded by an intersectoral shift of capacities, because the size of capacity in Sector II is determined by the net output of Sector Ib in Period 0, and the size of capacity in Sector Ib is fixed by the capacity requirements of Sector II in Period 2. In fact, we encounter there the first manifestation of a structural displacement of primary equipment.

PERIOD 2

Let us move on to Period 2. It depicts the model of a fully adjusted dynamic equilibrium in all three sectors. A labor force equal to the original 200 units multiplied by $(1 + \alpha)^2$, amounting to 216.3 units, is employed on a capital stock amounting to 541 units, in accord with the original capital–labor ratio of 5:2. Demand for consumer goods equals supply, and net output in the two equipment-good sectors equals the respective savings. As is necessary in an equilibrium, inputs and outputs of Sector Ib have been reduced to a level that assures, besides the *current replacement* of secondary equipment, its *further growth* in accord with current savings, but not beyond, as was the case in Period 1. This contraction has freed 21 units of primary equipment for retransfer to Sector Ia.

However, as the figure for the stock of primary equipment employed in Sector Ia shows, only 12.8 of the retransferred units can actually be used, and the aggregate of primary equipment now employed in both equipment-good sectors falls from the original 160 to 151.4 units, making at first sight 8.4 units idle. We must remember however, that, in Period 1, 1.2 units (14.8–16) of the original stock could not be replaced. This deficit, which can now be made up from the excess of 8.6 units, reduces the idle quantity of primary equipment in Period 2 to 7.4 units – not counting the idle net output of 9.6 units in Period 0. Still, the terminal equilibrium into which the otherwise efficient traverse ends, achieving adjustment at the technical minimum of two maturation periods, is marred by the existence of a considerable quantity of idle primary equipment, the effect of which will show when we study the motorial conditions for a successful traverse.[16]

III

Our detailed literary exposition illustrated by a numerical schema has presented us with a concrete picture of the contortions through which the system must pass in order to reach terminal equilibrium. However, for the interdependence of the strategic variables to become fully transparent, a more formal treatment is necessary.

We shall confine ourselves to establishing general measures for only two magnitudes, but magnitudes on the size of which the feasibility of an efficient traverse depends. The first concerns the required *size of capital stock and output in Sector Ib during Period 1,* which we shall label F_{b_1} and b_1, respectively. Our concern is, in particular, with the net amount of b_1 (over and above the amount devoted to amortization) that, according to our stipulation, is to raise the capital stock in Sector II to the level of terminal equilibrium in one more period of maturation. We know that, to that end, part of and, in the extreme case, all primary equipment

---

[16] One might conceive of the following procedure for the purpose of reducing the terminal redundancy of primary equipment. It consists in not renewing that part of the capital stock which operates in Sector Ib during Period 1. It amounts to 13 units in our schema, the "consumption" of which would cut down waste to 3.8 units. By choosing different values for some of our variables, we might come up with combinations in which capital waste disappears altogether. We have disregarded this eventuality in our schema because its realization depends on special motorial conditions – centrally planned capital consumption – that are incompatible with the working of a free market system.

initially available in Sector Ia needs to be shifted to Sector Ib. We thus obtain as the first feasibility condition for an efficient traverse[17]

$$F_{(a+b)_0} \geq F_{b_1} \text{ (requ)} \tag{18.4}$$

that is, the terminally required stock of secondary equipment can be produced in one period of maturation only if the initially available *total* stock of primary equipment at least equals the stock of primary equipment temporarily required in Sector Ib. The significance of this condition can be seen from the fact that, if $F_{(a+b)_0}$ turns out to be smaller, construction of the terminally required stock of secondary equipment will take more than one period of maturation, during which new units of a enter the system, raising in each such period the size of the required stock in Sector II.

1. What then is the efficient size of F_{b_1}? It obviously equals $k \cdot b_1$, and our task consists in finding a general expression for the efficient size of b_1, the output of secondary equipment in Period 1. This output must equal the required addition to capital stock in Sector II, minus that part of such addition which is already available in Period 1, plus the replacement demand of Sector II in Period 1, or

$$b_1 \text{ (requ)} = \Delta F_z \text{ (term)} - (b_0 - d \cdot F_{z_0}) + d \cdot F_{z_1}$$

By substituting the right-hand expression of Equation 18.3 for ΔF_z (term), and by using again the symbols B and B',[18] we obtain

$$\begin{aligned} b_1 \text{ (requ)} &= [(1 - B)(1 + \alpha)^2 - (1 - B')] \cdot ko_0 \\ &\quad - [B'(1 - B') - kd(1 - B')] \cdot o_0 \\ &\quad + d[(1 - B') \cdot k + B'(1 - B') - kd(1 - B')] \cdot o_0 \\ &= \{(1 - B)(1 + \alpha)^2 \cdot k \\ &\quad - (1 - B')(1 - d)[B' + k(1 - d)]\} \cdot o_0 \end{aligned} \tag{18.5}$$

Then F_{b_1} equals the right-hand expression of Equation 18.5 times k. Because $F_{(a+b)_0}$ equals $B' \cdot ko_0$, the *feasibility condition for an efficient traverse,* formulated already in general terms in Equation 18.4, can now be specified as

$$B' \geq (1 - B)(1 + \alpha)^2 \cdot k - (1 - B')(1 - d)[B' + k(1 - d)] \tag{18.4.1}$$

Given an initial structure in dynamic equilibrium, the chances for an efficient traverse to a new dynamic equilibrium with a smaller rate of

---

[17] If we were to include the net output of primary equipment that accrues during Period 0, Equation 18.4 would change to

$$F_{(a+b)_0} + \text{net } a_0 \geq F_{b_1} \text{ (requ)}$$

In what follows we shall disregard this modification.

[18] See preceding footnote 11.

growth improve the smaller the fall in the rate of growth, because the smaller is the required addition to the stock of secondary equipment – a condition that is intuitively obvious.

2. However, we must now ask, What will happen if the condition formulated in the inequality 18.4.1 is not fulfilled, that is, if F_{b_1}(requ) exceeds the aggregate of $F_{(a + b)_0}$? We then find ourselves in a situation similar to the one described in the Secondary Model with the help of which we illustrated an increase in the rate of growth.[19] The required addition to secondary equipment now requires more than one period of maturation. With the extension of the adjustment process in Sector Ib, however, the goal of adjustment, that is, the required size of the terminal stock of secondary equipment, is also extended. This concomitant extension occurs because in every period of maturation another batch of labor supply enters the system at the rate of α, the absorption of which demands a proportional increase in capital stock. In order to determine this extended stock of secondary equipment necessary for attaining a new terminal equilibrium, we must know the number of maturation periods required to this end.

At this point we can make use of certain findings obtained in Chapter 14.[20] We denoted by β the number of maturation periods needed for the production of the required stock of secondary equipment and found as a general expression

$$\beta_1 = \frac{\text{requ } \Delta F_z \text{ (to be produced)}}{\text{net } b \text{ after switch}}$$

This relationship is directly applicable to our problem, although the denominator now acquires a different meaning. Concerning the numerator, we are again not interested in the required total addition to secondary equipment, but only in the difference between the terminal stock and the stock already available in Period 1. By using Equation 18.5, we obtain for this magnitude

$$\Delta F_z \text{ (requ)} = \{(1 - B)(1 + \alpha)^{\beta+1 \cdot} k - (1 - B')[B' + k(1 - d)]\} \cdot o_0$$

In determining the denominator we must remember that the quantity of primary equipment switched from Sector Ia to Sector Ib now includes the total initial stock operating in Sector Ia. Thus, we obtain

$$\text{gross } b_1(\text{max}) = \frac{F_{(a+b)_0}}{k} = B' \cdot o_0$$

[19] See Chapter 14, Section VIII.
[20] *Ibid.*, especially Equation 14.16.

and

$$\text{net } b_1 \text{ (max)} = [B' - kd(1 - B')(1 + \alpha^+)] \cdot o_0$$

This finally yields[21]

$$\beta_1 = \frac{(1 - B)(1 + \alpha)^{\beta_1+1} \cdot k - (1 - B')[B' + k(1 - d)]}{B' - kd(1 - B')(1 + \alpha^+)} \tag{18.6}$$

Again we are confronted with a transcendental equation. As in the previous case, however, a limiting condition can be established. Nonfulfillment of this requirement will prevent once and for all the attainment of any terminal equilibrium. The latter can be obtained only if

$$\text{net } b_1 \text{ (max)} > \alpha \cdot F_{z_1} \tag{18.7}$$

that is, if the net output of secondary equipment over and above replacement demand in Period 1 exceeds the quantity required for absorption of the labor increment entering in Period 1. Otherwise no secondary equipment is left for the reshuffling of the system's capital stock in favor of Sector II, as is required by the fall in the rate of growth.[22]

3. Our second problem concerns the *size of the primary equipment that remains idle* once the capital stock in Sectors II and Ib have been adjusted to the requirements of steady growth at the lower growth rate α. To have a precise measure for the magnitude of this glut is interesting not only on structural grounds, but it will help us to gauge the threat to the stability of what otherwise appears as a system moving toward a new dynamic equilibrium.

At first sight the solution appears to be quite simple, and the searched for measure presents itself as the difference between the larger initial

---

[21] Two properties of Equation 18.6 require comment. First, the exponent in the numerator amounts to $\beta_1 + 1$, because the size of the terminal capital stock in Sector II refers to Period 2 when another batch of labor has entered the system. Second, the expression for replacement in the denominator has α^+ rather than α as multiplicand, because the size of F_{z_1}, to which the replacement demand refers, is determined by the net output of Sector Ib in Period 0, when the higher growth still prevails.

[22] Equation 18.7 is not quite accurate, since net b_1(max) falls from period to period because of rising replacement demands, whereas $\alpha \cdot F_z$ rises from period to period in absolute terms, requiring a steady increase in the capital stock necessary for its absorption. For this reason, net b_1(max), although of sufficient size at the start of the expansion of secondary equipment, may yet be too small to carry expansion to its terminal conclusion, and Equation 18.7 is at best a necessary, but not a sufficient condition for a successful traverse. On the other hand, the net output of primary equipment accruing in Period 0 can serve as a capacity reserve to raise net b(max) in such cases.

capital stock and the smaller terminal stock in the two equipment-good sectors. However, we must remember from our literary exposition[23] that there is a problem of temporary "consumption" of primary equipment, whenever that part of the capital stock which stays in Sector Ia during Period 1 – while another part is temporarily transferred to Sector Ib – proves too small to assure full replacement. This "deficit" is bound to increase, on the one hand, with the ratio between transferred and total stock of primary equipment and, on the other hand, with the number of maturation periods over which the transfer must be extended. It is quite conceivable that, with a large β, that is, a large number of maturation periods for secondary equipment, during which the entire initial stock of primary equipment is prevented from self-reproduction, this deficit may acquire a magnitude greater than the difference between the initial and terminal stock of primary equipment. In such a case, an increasing *dearth* rather than a glut of primary equipment is the more likely possibility and, independent of any motorial considerations, dynamic equilibrium may never be restored, unless the rate of growth can be temporarily stopped to permit the rebuilding of an adequate stock of primary equipment.[24]

For these reasons, a glut of primary equipment is a major problem mainly under the conditions of a fully efficient traverse, when the necessary expansion of the secondary capital stock can be carried out in one period of maturation. In this case, the intermediary capital deficit is bound to be small, and we obtain as a measure of capital glut

$$F_a \text{ (term; idle)} = F_{(a+b)_0} - F_{(a+b)_2} - F_{a_0} \text{ (cons)} \tag{18.8}$$

Let us first determine the size of the *capital deficit*. It amounts to

$$F_{a_0} \text{ (cons)} = \frac{F_{(a+b)_0} - F_{b_1}}{k} - d \cdot F(a+b)_0$$

where the first two terms measure the output of primary equipment in Period 1, and the third term the simultaneous depreciation of such equipment. Translated into our customary symbols, we obtain

$$F_{a_0} \text{ (cons)} = [B'(1 - kd) - E] \cdot o_0 \tag{18.9}$$

where E stands for the expression in braces in Equation 18.5, equal to b_1/o_0.

---

[23] See Section III, 2.
[24] Again the net output related to Period 0 can serve as a capital stock reserve.

On this basis we can now specify the size of the capital glut as

$$F_a \text{ (term; idle)} = \{[B' - B(1 + \alpha)^2]k - B'(1 - kd) + E\} \cdot o_0 \qquad (18.8.1)$$

As is to be expected, the glut varies directly with the initial size of the primary capital stock, and inversely with its terminal size and with the ratio of the temporary transfer of primary equipment to Sector Ib.

IV

The major stages in the structural adjustment of any economic system to a fall in the rate of growth exhibit a peristalsis as complex as, though quite different from, that which characterizes the movements through which a rising rate of growth is absorbed. When we now turn to the corresponding *motorial requirements,* we shall find this complexity greatly enhanced. Again we shall concentrate on the particular events that occur in a free market system, referring to procedures of central planning mainly when we discuss certain public policies designed to safeguard the viability of the market mechanism under conditions of decline.

As we have learned, the first stage in an efficient traverse is to accomplish the liberation of some existing capacity in Sector Ia (subsequently to be transferred to Sector Ib) and also to initiate the expansion of Sector II. Now the only behavioral force that may induce such a shift in a free market is the savings–investment mechanism. Therefore, the primary motorial requirement is a simultaneous and proportional adjustment of the savings–investment ratio to the fall in the rate of growth.

Starting from the motorial conditions underlying the original dynamic equilibrium, we know that the suitable motivational setup is defined by the extremum principle coupled with the unit elasticity of quantity expectations and, assuming a proportionate increase in the active money flow, zero elasticity of price expectations.[25] It is difficult to see how, under these conditions, a fall in the rate of growth of labor supply could directly induce either a simultaneous and proportional reduction of voluntary or forced savings or bring about a change in the motivational conditions themselves that would lead to such a reduction. Rather, we should anticipate that savings and investment continue for a while at the initial rate, with the result of growing overinvestment in Sector Ia leading to a deflationary spiral that will stop the traverse in its tracks.

So we are again thrown back upon *involuntary* savings as the initiating mechanism. As we remember, involuntary savings arise from profits that accrue to firms whenever, and so long as, the pressure of excess supply of

[25] See Chapter 10, Section I.

labor reduces unit wages and, thus, aggregate payrolls below the stationary level. It stands to reason that this profit margin must shrink with the easing of pressure owing to a fall in the excess supply of labor from α^+ to α. Thus, we have a systematic interrelation between a fall in the rate of growth and a fall in savings. (The latter is equivalent in our two-strata model to a rise in aggregate consumption.) On this interaction depends the realization of the first stage of an efficient traverse, that is, a reduction of demand for primary equipment and an increase of demand for consumer goods. Whether the rise in payrolls (and thus the fall in aggregate savings) will establish the *precise* investment–consumption ratio required in the new dynamic equilibrium depends, as in the case of a rising rate of growth, on the actual wage bargain. In any case, there is in the real world no additional mechanism that would once and for all fix the wage elasticity of labor supply at the appropriate level and thus preclude over- or underinvestment. In the context of our instrumental analysis, we assume the presence of such an appropriate ratio by stipulating, in analogy with Equation 14.6,[26] the new, higher wage rate as

$$\Sigma w_{00} = \Sigma w_0 + \frac{(\alpha^+ - \alpha)k}{1 - kd} \cdot y_0 \tag{18.10}$$

In examining now the motorial conditions valid for the successive stages of the traverse, we return to our price–quantity schema, but now focussing on the divergencies between quantities and price sums that accompany, and actually direct, the course of the traverse.

PERIOD 0

Little needs to be added to what was said earlier[27] about the initial structure of our model. However, it should be noted that, in accord with the original rate of growth, the rate of profit amounts in all three sectors to 6 percent.

INTERPERIOD I

Passing on to Interperiod I, which registers the isolated effect of the wage rise and the corresponding fall of profits to 4 percent, the schema shows, as already noted, disequilibrium between both aggregate payrolls and output of consumer goods and between aggregate savings and investments. In the former case, demand exceeds supply, and, in the latter case, supply

[26] See Chapter 14, Section IV.
[27] See Section II.

exceeds demand. It is these disequilibria which, assuming goal-adequate action directives and expectations, will initiate the required expansion of secondary equipment. Such expansion is based on investment decisions the rationale of which is revealed when we examine the price effect of the prevailing disequilibria.

INTERPERIOD II

These effects are shown in Interperiod II. The numerical structure depicted there is the result of a sequence of adjustment processes, which we shall follow up step by step.

1. The initiating stimulus is the excess demand for consumer goods, which raises the sales receipts in Sector II from 170 to 180 units, thus creating there a provisional surplus profit of 10 units. Assuming the validity of the extremum principle, coupled with positively elastic quantity and price expectations (expectations that will be justified by the persistence of the shift of purchasing power to the buyers of consumer goods), we can derive an increase in demand for secondary equipment raising, at first sight, sales receipts in Sector Ib by the same 10 units. However, we must remember that output in Sector Ib, which is still determined by the production structure of the initial dynamic equilibrium, does not show an equally large deficit. Its net output of 20.4 units of secondary equipment is actually confronted with an aggregate demand of only 23.6 units – 13.6 units represent the reduced savings (see Interperiod I) and 10 units represent the surplus profits, both in Sector II. Thus net output in Sector Ib falls short of demand by only 3.2 units, by which amount sales receipts are raised there to the level of 57.6 units, creating a surplus profit of 3.2 units and thus raising total profits to 7.6 units equal to a rate of profit of ca. 7 percent.

2. But price adjustments are not yet complete. The price rise of output by ca. 6 percent in Sector Ib is bound to raise the price of replacements in Sector II, reducing there the initial surplus profit from 10 to 8 units to a total of 21.6 units. This still raises the rate of profit in Sector II above the level of 4 percent, prevailing in Interperiod I, to 6 percent.

3. However, the critical sector is Sector Ia, because of its net output of 9.6 units in Period 0. So long as dynamic equilibrium prevailed, this net output served as net investment in both equipment-good sectors in the subsequent period. Not only does such net investment have no objective function once the rate of growth falls, but the profits (savings) in the two equipment-good sectors, which originally formed the money demand for this net output, have been diverted. These profits fell already, under the impact of the wage rise, from 9.7 to 6.4 units (see Interperiod I), and

must now be invested in Sector Ib in order to achieve the required expansion of Sector II. The higher profit rates in both Sectors Ib and II provide the behavioral stimulus for this purpose.

As a result aggregate demand for primary equipment threatens to fall from 25.6 to 16 units, causing a loss of 9.6 units in Sector Ia. Now speaking in positive terms, at this point the system is faced with two alternatives. As long as the excess supply of primary equipment in the amount of 9.6 units remains effective, the loss constellation cannot be overcome. Unit prices of primary equipment must fall, with secondary consequences for the value of capital stock and amortization in both equipment-good sectors. However, such price fall of amortization will further reduce demand for the output of Sector Ia, creating a further price fall – a vicious circle that can only terminate in progressive deflation of capital values and output prices in Sectors Ia and Ib and the total disequilibration of the system.

The second alternative, and the only one compatible with our search for an efficient traverse, is the "removal" of the excess supply of primary equipment during Interperiod II by measures of public control. This will restore break-even prices of primary equipment, but at the same time displace that part of the capital stock and of the labor force which produced the now discarded net output of 9.6 units. These resources, as we know from our structural analysis, must anyhow be transferred to Sector Ib.[28]

PERIOD 1

Proceeding to Period 1, we notice first of all that the net output of 20.4 units of secondary equipment available from Period 0 is now invested, raising the capital stock in Sector II from the initial 340 to 360.4 units. At the same time, output in Sector Ib has risen to 65 units, leaving a net output, available for investment in the subsequent stage, of 29 units. To obtain this result the capital stock in Sector Ib had to be raised from the original 108.8 units to 130, an expansion that has been achieved by switching 21.2 units of primary equipment and the complementary labor force formerly employed in Sector Ia.

1. The motivational setup that induces both the investment of the net output of Sector Ib produced in Period 0 and the expansion of capital stock and output in the same sector during Period 1 is identical with the

---

[28] The figures as shown for Interperiod II represent the state of affairs *before* this shrinkage of Sector Ia has occurred, but after all the price adjustments discussed in the text have been completed.

one that initiated the rising demand for secondary equipment in Inter-period I: positively elastic quantity and price expectations directed by the extremum principle which, in turn, takes its bearings from the profit rates ruling in Interperiod II in Sectors II and Ib. However, with the increase in output in Sector Ib to the size required for an efficient traverse, the gap between the demand for and the supply of secondary equipment characteristic for Interperiod II disappears, as do the surplus profits in Sector Ib. In other words, the discrepancy between quantities and price sums disappears in the temporary equilibrium position attained by Sector Ib at the end of Period 1. Underlying this proposition is the motorial assumption that both price and quantity expectations are not just positive in general, but are positively inelastic, so that, for any present difference between the actual level and the equilibrium level of quantities and prices, a smaller difference is expected in the future, with zero elasticity of expectations once the maturation period is completed.

2. Considering Sector Ia, we notice again the failure of providing an output sufficient to replace the currently used-up capital stocks in Sectors Ia and Ib in their entirety, resulting in capital consumption in the amount of 1.2 units. As was pointed out earlier,[29] this deficit is by no means due to a lack of primary equipment – at this stage no less than 10 units are kept idle – but rather to the absence of complementary labor.

3. A different kind of discrepancy between supply and demand char-acterizes Sector II. There the rise of the capital stock has made it possible to absorb the Period 1 increment of labor supply (amounting at the re-duced rate of α to 8 units), raising aggregate payrolls and, thus, demand for consumer goods to 187.2 units. Although the expansion of capital stock and employment has raised the supply of such goods to 180.2 units, there is still a gap amounting to 7 units, raising sales receipts in Sector II accordingly and leaving there a surplus profit of the same magnitude.[30] Thus total profits and the rate of profit in Sector II are maintained at their previous level.

4. Net output in Sector Ib, that is, the amount of newly produced sec-ondary equipment available for investment in Period 2 amounts, as we saw, to 29 units. Now, from what sources do the corresponding savings arise that are to finance this investment? We asked this question earlier,[31] but did not give a complete answer.

It is now obvious that, as a consequence of the surplus profits of 7 units

---

[29] See Section II, Period 1.
[30] Because the return of prices in Sector Ib to their equilibrium level has also reduced capital values and amortization in Sector II to this level, there is now no drag on these surplus profits, as was the case in Interperiod II.
[31] See Section II, Period 1.

in Sector II, total net savings in Period 1 have risen to 27.8 units, to which the disinvestment of 1.2 units in Sector Ia must be added. At the same time these surpluses in Sector II give assurance that, under the motivational conditions stipulated, all these sums will in fact be applied to the financing of the required investment in the subsequent period.

PERIOD 2

The price-quantity structure of Period 2, in which the new dynamic equilibrium is reached, reestablishes equality between demand and supply at the level of a new dynamic equilibrium in both Sectors II and Ib. The increase of the capital stock in Sector II, equivalent to the net output of secondary equipment in Period 1, makes it possible to expand Sector II in accord with the fall in the growth rate, at the same time absorbing another increment of α which is supposed to enter the system at the beginning of Period 2.

Sector Ib has shrunk to the new equilibrium level by retransferring the larger part of the amount of primary equipment transferred from Sector Ia in Period 1. It is interesting to note that, in spite of the growth of the system by two batches of α, under our numerical assumption the equilibrium output of Sector Ib is hardly larger than the output in the initial equilibrium. Although replacement demand of Sector II has increased, investment demand has shrunk by almost the same amount under the impact of the lower growth rate.

Again the setup of Sector Ia is more complex. There is, first of all, the retransfer of part (as a rule of the larger part) of primary equipment temporarily "borrowed" by Sector Ib from Sector Ia. The demand–supply relations concerning this type of equipment, which prevail in Period 1, are favorable to initiating such a retransfer, to the extent that output of primary equipment has fallen below the replacement demand of the two equipment-good sectors. This induces a price rise in Sector Ia[32] which, under the ruling motorial conditions, makes the return of part of the transferred capital stock to its original use appear profitable.

However, we now face once more a problem for which a laissez-faire market has no solution. It concerns that quantity of retransferred primary equipment which, in the context of an efficient traverse, cannot find employment in the new equilibrium structure of Period 2. As our figures show, the active capital stock in Sector Ia has fallen by almost 20 percent and although part of the remainder takes the place of primary equipment used up but not replaced in Period 1, we are left with a glut of such

---

[32] Omitted in our schema.

equipment, amounting in our example to ca. 14 percent of the original stock employed in Sector Ia or 4.5 percent of the total stock of primary equipment initially employed. If we include the discarded net output of Period 0, the glut rises to 33 and 10 percent, respectively.

As has already been stressed, there is no mechanism that could "neutralize" the effect of this glut, first, on prices and, second, on output of primary equipment, because both quantity and price expectations are likely to turn negatively elastic. In other words, the excess supply of primary equipment is likely to arouse the expectation that prices and production in Sector Ia will be cut at an increasing rate. The secondary consequences for aggregate employment and, thus, for replacement demand as well as for aggregate demand for consumer goods cannot but prevent both Sectors Ib and II from reaching the new equilibrium path, terminating the traverse in a general depression. This, at least, is the outlook for a market system devoid of controls.

V

In summing up our results, we have been able to demonstrate that a structural path can be devised along which a system in dynamic equilibrium can efficiently adjust to a fall in the rate of labor supply. There are, in principle, no economic impediments to the planning directives with the help of which a collectivist order can satisfy the motorial requirements of an efficient traverse, including even reduction, if not complete elimination, of capital waste. This is, however, not true of an uncontrolled market order, which is bound to encounter grave difficulties at the start as well as at the finish of the adjustment process.

The difficulties at the start are the same we have met in our study of a rise in the rate of growth. They concern the establishment of a new equilibrium savings ratio in accord with the lower growth rate – a task for which the microunits lack *ex ante* the necessary information as well as the necessary incentive. To set a market system, which is exposed to a change in the rate of growth, be it expansion or contraction, on the path marking an efficient traverse, public control of both the savings and the investment ratio is required.

Once this has been achieved, the intrinsic forces dominating the dynamic process (extremum principle coupled with positive quantity and zero price elasticity of expectations) are likely to take the traverse successfully through a number of intermediate stages. Unhampered operation of the price mechanism provides the successive signals for receipt-maximizing microactions, which are in accord with the macrorequirements of expanding both the output of secondary equipment aided by the part-transfer of primary equipment, and the output of consumer goods, combined with initiating the retransfer of primary equipment. The hitch occurs when it becomes evident that this retransfer leads to an excess supply of primary equipment, as certainly happens in all cases of low intermediate capital consumption. This is the same as saying that excess supply rises with the approximation of the traverse to full efficiency. Contrariwise, if the construction of the additional secondary equipment claims more than one period of maturation, the danger is a shortage of primary equipment. By inducing destabilizing expectations, the disparity in either case diverts the system from the adjustment path, and there is no autonomous mechanism either to prevent or to counter such diversion.

It is beyond the range of our investigation to examine suitable techniques of public control capable of neutralizing the deflationary effects of a capital glut or of compensating for capital dearth. They do not differ much from the measures that a collectivist system will have to take when confronted with the same problems: overcoming the *glut* by temporary capital consumption coupled with a temporary expansion of consumer-good output, and overcoming the *dearth* by temporary contraction of consumer-good output coupled with additional capital formation. In either case it is unlikely that measures other than direct control of prices, output, and investment can achieve the goal of a new dynamic equilibrium.

Appendix to chapter 18

Traverse toward dynamic equilibrium with a lower rate of growth of labor supply, illustrated on a numerical price sum-quantity schema (quantities in parentheses).

	(F_q)	F_p	(f_q)	f_p	Pay rolls	P	Sal. rec.	(o_q)	Net sal. rec.	(Net) $\binom{}{o_q}$	Rate of profit
Period 0					INITIAL DYNAMIC EQUILIBRIUM						
	(51.2)	51.2	(5.1)	5.1 +	17.4 +	3.1 =	25.6	(25.6)	9.6	(9.6)	
	(108.8)	108.8	(10.9)	10.9 +	37.0 +	6.6 =	54.4	(54.4)	20.4	(20.4)	} 6%
	(340.0)	340.0	(34.0)	34.0 +	115.6 +	20.4 =	170.0	(170.0)	—	—	
	(500.0)	500.0	(50.0)	50.0 +	170.0 +	30.0 =	250.0	(250.0)	30.0	(30.0)	
Interperiod I					FALL OF PROFITS—RISE OF MONEY WAGES						
	(51.2)	51.2	(5.1)	5.1 +	18.5 +	2.0 =	25.6	(25.6)	9.6	(9.6)	
	(108.8)	108.8	(10.9)	10.9 +	39.1 +	4.4 =	54.4	(54.4)	20.4	(20.4)	} 4%
	(340.0)	340.0	(34.0)	34.0 +	122.4 +	13.6 =	170.0	(170.0)	—	—	
	(500.0)	500.0	(50.0)	50.0 +	180.0 +	20.0 =	250.0	(250.0)	30.0	(30.0)	
Interperiod II					PRICE ADJUSTMENT						
	(51.2)	51.2	(5.1)	5.1 +	18.5 +	2.0 =	25.6	(25.6)	9.6	(9.6)	ca. 4%
	(108.8)	108.8	(10.9)	10.9 +	39.1 +	7.6 =	57.6	(54.4)	21.6	(20.4)	ca. 7%
	(340.0)	360.4	(34.0)	36.0 +	122.4 +	21.6 =	180.0	(170.0)	—	—	ca. 6%
	(500.0)	520.0	(50.0)	52.0 +	180.0 +	31.2 =	263.2	(250.0)	31.2	(31.2)	

Appendix to chapter 18 (cont'd)

	(F_q)	F_p	(f_q)	f_p	Pay rolls	P	Sal. rec.	(o_q)	Net sal. rec.	(Net o_q)	Rate of profit
					ABSORPTION OF α_1						
Period 1	(29.6)	29.6	(3.0)	3.0 +	10.8 +	1.0 =	14.8	(14.8)	−1.2	(−1.2)	ca. 3.4%
	(130.0)	130.0	(13.0)	13.0 +	46.8 +	5.2 =	65.0	(65.0)	29.0	(29.0)	ca. 4%
	(360.4)	360.4	(36.0)	36.0 +	129.6 +	21.6 =	187.2	(180.2)	—	—	ca. 6%
	(520.0)	520.0	(52.0)	52.0 +	187.2 +	27.8 =	267.0	(260.0)	27.8	(27.8)	
				ABSORPTION OF α_2 AND RESTORATION OF DYNAMIC EQUILIBRIUM							
Period 2	(42.4)	42.4	(4.2)	4.2 +	15.3 +	1.7 =	21.2	(21.2)	6.1	(6.1)	⎫
	(109.0)	109.0	(10.9)	10.9 +	39.2 +	4.4 =	54.5	(54.5)	15.6	(15.6)	⎬ 4%
	(389.4)	389.4	(38.9)	38.9 +	140.2 +	15.6 =	194.7	(194.7)	—	—	⎭
	(540.8)	540.8	(54.0)	54.0 +	194.7 +	21.7 =	270.4	(270.4)	21.7	(21.7)	

PART III
Changes in the rate of change

*II. The dynamics of
natural resources supply*

19

The dynamics of diminishing returns

The analyses in Part I and II of this essay have been carried out under the explicit assumption that natural resources be treated not only as free goods but as goods available in unlimited quantities of equal grade. Although aware of the fact that, except for certain chemical elements, this latter assumption is unrealistic, we found it useful for the purpose of isolating the dynamic processes induced by the complementary factors labor and technology, when studying steady growth, or by labor alone when studying a special case of unsteady growth. Moreover, unlimited supply of homogeneous natural resources is even a systematic requirement for the steady growth of output quantities. On the other hand, unsteady changes in the rate of labor supply, the subject matter of Part II, and of technical improvements, which we are going to investigate in Part IV, can well be combined with changes in the rate of supply of natural resources and, in the interest of realism, must be so combined.

It is the task of this chapter and the next to discuss two types of changes in the supply of natural resources: One refers to the effect of *diminishing returns* in the realm of natural resources on the adjustment process by which a steady increase in the rate of labor supply is absorbed; the other is concerned with the *recycling of material residuals* created both in production and consumption. The latter type can be seen as an offset of the former, to the extent that it proves possible to reuse the same stock of resources in successive processes of production, and thus to dispense with or, at least, to slow down the progressive depletion of the natural sources of basic materials.

I

Any discussion of the effect exerted by diminishing returns on the growth of an industrial system must begin by clarifying the meaning that this notion assumes in the context of growth analysis. This is all the more necessary as this meaning differs from the interpretation given to the term in conventional microeconomics. There the "law of diminishing returns" is usually related to the "law of variable proportions." A well-known textbook formulates this latter law as follows:

> An increase in some input relatively to other comparatively fixed inputs will cause output to increase; but after a point the extra output resulting from the *same* [my italics] additions of input will become less and less; this falling off of extra returns is a consequence of the fact that the new "doses" of the varying resources have less and less of the constant resources to work with.[1]

Now it is often stated that this law is only a generalization of the pronouncements on agricultural returns, as issued by classical economists from Steuart and Turgot to Ricardo and J. S. Mill.[2] That this is not so has already been stressed by Marshall who stated: "looking at the problem of agriculture not only from the view of the individual cultivator but also from that of the nation as a whole . . . the older economists rightly insisted that . . . land is not on exactly the same footing as those implements of production which man can increase without limit."[3] Now it is important to spell out in precise terms the difference indicated between the classical and the neoclassical interpretation of the law of diminishing returns. The former belongs in the realm of general equilibrium analysis and refers to Marshall's secular period in which all inputs – resources, labor, capital, and technology – undergo simultaneous changes. The latter is a theorem in partial equilibrium analysis, valid for Marshall's short and long periods in which at least one input is considered as constant.

To be specific, let us, for the sake of simplicity, consider the presence of two factors only: land, standing for natural resources generally, and homogeneous bundles of labor plus real capital. Had Ricardo been presented with the formulation of the law in the neoclassical frame of reference, as laid down in the preceding textbook quotation, there is little doubt that he would have accepted it in its full generality, irrespective of whether it was some unit of land or of labor–capital that was treated as the variable factor. However, when he made the law of diminishing returns responsible for a secular tendency of profits to fall toward zero, and of wages to fall toward the subsistence level, he was talking about something entirely different. If we look for an analogy to what he was talking about, it would be "decreasing returns to scale" rather than "variable proportions." In his analysis there is no "fixed" factor – at least up to the point at which further additions of capital and labor will not add to output. Rather, in

---

[1] Paul A. Samuelson, *Economics,* New York, 1973, p. 27.
[2] See, for example, J. A. Schumpeter, *History of Economic Analysis,* New York, 1954, pp. 259–61.
[3] Marshall, *loc. cit.,* p. 170.

the course of secular evolution, successive doses of labor plus capital are supposed to be combined with successive doses of land, but this land is characterized by steadily diminishing fertility or accessibility.[4] Such a secular fall in the productive efficiency of land is a "fact of nature" that can be compensated only by the additional input of other factors. Yet, and here the special "footing" of natural resources comes into the open, no such natural, sociological or technological obstacles exist to prevent successive inputs of *manpower* and *real capital* when combined with equal doses of land from displaying *constant* productive efficiency over the secular period. After all, successive generations of workers and machines cannot be expected to become steadily less productive, and it remains true that in this context the case of natural resources is indeed singular.[5]

It is this Ricardian notion of diminishing returns, applicable to natural resources only, which is relevant in growth analysis. Without committing ourselves to the extreme conclusions for distribution and welfare that Ricardo drew from his premise, we shall make it the basis of our subsequent inquiry.

In order to formulate our problem with full precision, however, we must be aware that, within the context thus circumscribed, there are still two alternatives for diminishing returns to affect growth. One, which finds expression in Ricardo's analysis, includes the premise that, so long as conditions remain stationary, returns remain constant. In other words, with finished output remaining constant from period to period, constant inputs of labor and equipment are supposed to draw unchanged outputs from the given stock of natural resources. Only if period outputs of finished goods are to be *increased* will resources of a lower grade have to be tapped, and then only for the production of the increment.

Such an assessment may well be overoptimistic, especially when we focus attention on inorganic resources, the basis of extractive industries. In order to obtain a *constant* quantity of ore from period to period, it may be necessary to "dig steadily more deeply," and to enlist for this purpose rising quantities of labor and equipment[6] – an effect that will be magnified under conditions of growth.

[4] Even his treatment of the Intensive Margin (Ricardo, *Principles of Political Economy and Taxation, loc. cit.,* pp. 71–72) can best be understood as the successive utilization of "vertical layers" of one and the same acre of land, analogous with the situation for inorganic resources.

[5] For an attempt at an analogous secular interpretation of the law of diminishing returns with reference to capital, see Chapter 27, Section IV.

[6] Under these conditions, Ricardo's "stationary state," in which growth is supposed to find its terminus, will be neither stationary nor the nadir of dismalness. Rather, returns will continue to fall even if population does not grow any more, initiating a steady reduction of population and the concomitant shrinkage of the system as a whole.

In practice both alternatives are likely to combine though, as Mill anticipated, technical progress may balance and even overcompensate either one for an indefinite future.[7] We shall confine our analysis to the more general case of diminishing returns operating in the system at large. We begin our discussion in a stationary framework.

II

Turning now to the *structural analysis* of our problem, we begin by restating our earlier numerical model of stationary equilibrium.[8] In contrast to our earlier procedure, however, the sectors are now arranged in a horizontal row. This is necessary because in each sector we must add, to the row depicting the production of *finished* output, another row describing the production of *raw material* with the help of natural resources exposed to changes in returns. To simplify our exposition we shall continue treating untapped natural resources as free goods, a premise that we shall have to reconsider when in Chapter 20 we shall discuss recycling, that is, the creation of "artificial" resources as an alternative to the use of "natural" resources. Reading the model vertically, we have then in each sector two *stages:* Stage 1 in which natural resources (agricultural land and mines) first enter the system, to be combined with labor and fixed equipment in order to produce the initial working capital good (cotton and iron ore), and a Stage 2 to be understood as the aggregate of all subsequent stages down to the production of the finished output.[9] Therefore Stage 2 registers under f and n all inputs materializing during one and the same period of maturation except those in Stage 1. To obtain the expression for the aggregate period inputs of labor and equipment, we must in Stage 2 add to these inputs either the corresponding inputs in Stage 1 or, what amounts to the same, the output of Stage 1 entering Stage 2 as working capital goods (ω). All magnitudes represent physical quantities.

Our first topic is the effect of diminishing returns on the output of *consumer goods*. This is the simpler case because, under stationary conditions, the repercussions of its effect on the other sectors of the system are confined to a change in the level of real wages, without otherwise affecting the quantities and the stage division of their inputs and outputs. For this reason we can treat this return effect in isolation, a procedure that cannot

---

[7] The joint effect of diminishing returns and technical progress is discussed in Chapter 27.

[8] See Section I of the Appendix to this chapter.

[9] In our original schema of production (see Chapter 3, Section II), we included some units of land in the subsequent stages to account for plant location. This input will be disregarded here.

be applied when we subsequently study the return effect in the equipment-good sectors.

1. If the original rate of return, $\bar{r}_0$, in Stage 1 of the consumer-good sector falls with the beginning of Period 1 to $\bar{r}_1 = \bar{r}_0/2$, what will be the structural consequences?[10] The immediate effect is shown when we move from Period 0 to Period 1. The initial quantity of inputs in Stage 1 now produces only half the former output, reducing the working capital goods available in Stage 2 to one-half. As a consequence labor and equipment actively employed in Stage 2 must also be reduced to half, as will be the output of finished consumer goods. However, 100 units of the equipment stock and 40 units of labor are now idle in Stage 2 and, disregarding for the moment any considerations of technical specificity, can be redistributed over both stages so as once again to raise output of working capital goods as well as of finished goods.

Such redistribution is illustrated in Period 2. It is a precondition for restoring a new level of stationary equilibrium with full resource utilization. Of course, even so the initial level of finished output cannot be reestablished. However, using the numerical stipulations of our model, a fall in returns by one-half reduces finished output in the end only by one-third. As a consequence real wages will have to be reduced by one-third throughout the system.

2. The structural shifts described permit of a general solution. For this purpose, we introduce the following notations: *inp* for aggregate inputs, representing fixed combinations of labor and equipment; *z* for aggregate outputs of consumer goods; superscripts ′ and ″ for the stages of primary and of finished output, respectively; subscripts 0, 1, and 2 for successive periods of production; and, as was already stated, $\bar{r}_0, \bar{r}_1, \ldots$, for the rate of return with the stipulation that $\bar{r}_0 = 1$ and $0 < \bar{r}_1 < \bar{r}_2, \ldots < 1$. We then obtain

$$z_0' = inp_0' \quad \text{and} \quad z_0'' = inp_0' + inp_0''$$
$$z_1' = \bar{r}_1 \cdot inp_0' \quad \text{and} \quad z_1'' = \bar{r}_1 \cdot (inp_0' + inp_0'')$$

Inputs displaced in Period 1 $\equiv inp_{\text{dis}} = (1 - \bar{r}_1) \cdot inp_0''$

Denoting by x and y, the quantities of inp_{dis} to be reassigned to Stage 1 and Stage 2, respectively, we can determine these unknowns on the basis of two known relations:

$$x + y = (1 - \bar{r}_1) \cdot inp_0''$$
$$\frac{x}{y} = \frac{inp_0'}{\bar{r}_1 \cdot inp_0''}$$

[10] See Section II of the Appendix to this chapter.

the latter because the input ratio between the two stages in the new stationary equilibrium must equal the input ratio in Period 1. This yields

$$x = \frac{(1 - \bar{r}_1) \cdot inp_0' \cdot inp_0''}{inp_0' + \bar{r}_1 \cdot inp_0''}$$

and because $z_2' = z_1' + \bar{r}_1 \cdot x$, we obtain

$$z_2' = \frac{\bar{r}_1 \cdot inp_0'}{inp_0' + \bar{r} \cdot inp''_0} \cdot z_0''$$

and

$$z_2'' = \frac{inp_0'}{inp_0' + \bar{r} \cdot inp_0''} \cdot z_0''$$

These expressions can be simplified if we introduce the symbol h for the stage ratio of outputs

$$h = \frac{z_0'}{z_0''} = \frac{inp_0'}{inp_0' + inp_0''}$$

We then obtain

$$z_2' = \frac{\bar{r}_1 \cdot h}{h(1 - \bar{r}_1) + \bar{r}_1} \cdot z_0'' \tag{19.1}$$

$$z_2'' = \frac{\bar{r}_1}{h(1 - \bar{r}_1) + \bar{r}_1} \cdot z_0'' \tag{19.2}$$

the stage ratio of outputs in the new equilibrium equaling the initial stage ratio h.

III

In assuming aggregate inputs as constant and in applying the fall in returns to the aggregate of Stage 1, we have placed the foregoing analysis in a stationary framework. However, we must now recall that our true frame of reference is dynamic equilibrium, that is, a state of affairs in which, in every period of production, labor supply is supposed to increase at the rate of α. This changes our problem into one in which the reshuffling of stages of production required to cope with the fall in returns coincides with an expansion of Sector II congruent with the growth rate α of the system. As was stated previously, to simplify exposition we shall confine ourselves to investigating the case in which the fall in returns affects the *aggregate* output of Stage 1 in Sector II and not only its increment.

Earlier we have assumed that the reshuffling of the stages induced by the fall in returns is to take two periods of production. By making use of the reduction coefficient of Equation 19.2, we obtain for the output of consumer goods in Period 2

$$z_2'' = (1 + \alpha)^2 \cdot \frac{\bar{r}_1}{h(1 - \bar{r}_1) + \bar{r}_1} \cdot z_0'' \tag{19.3}$$

At the same time the system's aggregate labor force has risen over two periods to

$$n_2 = (1 + \alpha)^2 \cdot n_0$$

so that per capita real wages have fallen to[11]

$$w_2 \text{ (real)} = \frac{\bar{r}_1}{h(1 - \bar{r}_1) + \bar{r}_1} \cdot \frac{z_0''}{n_0''}$$

IV

What is the effect of diminishing returns on the output of *equipment goods?* It stands to reason that the direct effect within Sector I resembles the result that we obtained for the fall in returns in Sector II. Whereas diminishing returns in Sector II do not, however, reduce demand for equipment goods and, thus, output and employment in Sector I, the reverse is not true. By curtailing the growth of output of both primary and secondary equipment, diminishing returns in Sector I impose a fall in the increase of the capital stock and, thus, of the growth rate in all three sectors – a fall that is bound to leave idle part of the steady increment of labor supply, bringing about a general distortion of the initial structure of production. It is formally similar to that caused by an increase in the rate of labor supply in a system in which the capital stock is fully utilized. Restoration of dynamic equilibrium then depends on a restructuring of the system along the lines discussed in Chapters 14 and 15.

In order to assess the extent of the structural change required, we must provide a measure of the quantity of labor that can no longer be steadily absorbed as a consequence of diminishing returns in Sector I.

---

[11] For the adjustment process in numerical terms, see Sections III–V of the Appendix to this chapter.

For this purpose, we again assume that the fall in returns affects the *aggregate* output of Stage 1 of both subsectors of Sector I and also that the reshuffling of the stages takes two periods of production.

The simplest way of ascertaining the fall in employment capacity of the system at large owing to a fall in returns in Sector I is by first determining the size of the aggregate capital stock F_2 as it shapes up after the lapse of two periods. The aggregate capital stock operating during the first period, F_1, is the result of the net output in Sector I during Period 0 when returns are still unchanged and the initial rate of growth is still in effect. Because net output of equipment goods in Period 0 equals gross output minus depreciation[12] or

$$\left(\frac{B}{k} - d\right) \cdot F_0$$

therefore

$$F_1 = \left(1 + \frac{B}{k} - d\right) \cdot F_0 = (1 + \alpha) \cdot F_0 \tag{19.4}$$

We assume that output issuing from that part of F_1 which consists of primary equipment is subject to diminishing returns. Thus the net output of equipment in Period 1 falls to

$$\left(\dot{r}_1 \cdot \frac{B}{k} - d\right) \cdot F_1$$

and

$$F_2 = \left(1 + \dot{r}_1 \cdot \frac{B}{k} - d\right)(1 + \alpha) \cdot F_0 \tag{19.5}$$

Dividing Equation 19.5 by the prevailing capital–labor ratio c, we obtain the employment capacity of F_2 or

$$n_2 \text{ (empl)} = \frac{[1 + \dot{r}_1 \cdot (B/k) - d](1 + \alpha)}{c} \cdot F_0 \tag{19.6}$$

The aggregate labor force available in Period 2 amounts to

$$(1 + \alpha)^2 \cdot n_0$$

[12] See Chapter 9, Section V, Model XII.

which equals

$$\frac{(1 + \alpha)^2}{c} \cdot F_0$$

By subtracting from this magnitude the right side of Equation 19.6, we obtain the quantity of idle labor in Period 2

$$n_2 \text{ (idle)} = \frac{1 + \alpha}{c} \cdot \left(\alpha - \bar{r}_1 \cdot \frac{B}{k} + d \right) \cdot F_0 \qquad (19.7)$$

Then the ratio of idle labor to total labor available amounts to

$$\frac{n_2 \text{ (idle)}}{n_2 \text{ (available)}} = \frac{\alpha - \bar{r}_1 \cdot (B/k) + d}{1 + \alpha} \qquad (19.8)$$

To gain a concrete notion of the unemployment effect caused by diminishing returns in Sector I, we make use of the numerical magnitudes that describe dynamic equilibrium in Chapter 15: $k = 2$; $d = 1/10$; and $\alpha = 1/100$. We further assume a fall of returns in Sector I to four-fifths of the initial state. This establishes the ratio of idleness in Period 2 at 2.7 percent of the total labor force available at that period, also indicating the minimum of additional capital formation required to restore dynamic equilibrium. However, we must be aware that, with the lapse of time, the need for additional capital formation increases. Because in the given structural setup the period rate of growth of labor supply is bound to exceed the period rate of absorption, the gap between available and employed labor and, thus, the ratio of idleness must steadily grow.[13]

---

[13] To be precise, aggregate labor supply rises by α, per period, that is by 4 percent, given the stipulated numerical setup. On the other hand, the rate of absorption in Period 2, as Equation 19.6 indicates, is only

$$\bar{r}_1 \cdot \frac{B}{k} - d$$

that is, 1.2 percent. From Section II, we know that, after the reshuffling of inputs among the strategic stages in Period 2, the rate of absorption rises to

$$(rc) \cdot \frac{B}{k} - d$$

where rc stands for the "reduction coefficient" as determined in Equation 19.2, that is, with $h = 0.5$ to 2.4 percent. It can stay at this level so long as $\bar{r}_1$ is unchanged and the destabilizing effect of the growing ratio of idleness is disregarded – a dubious motorial condition.

V

What *motorial conditions* assure the successful adjustment of the system to diminishing returns? In answering this question we shall confine ourselves to the simplest case, namely, the adjustment of the consumer-good sector in a stationary framework, because it fully illustrates the basic principles.

Speaking in terms of our numerical example, we do not encounter any motorial problem in the structural transition from Period 0 to Period 1, because the fall in output in both stages is a "mechanical" consequence of the fall in returns in Stage 1, as is the displacement of labor and equipment in Stage 2. The problem starts with the transition from Period 1 to Period 2, when the displaced factors are to be redistributed over the two stages.

Again, no particular difficulties stand in the way of adjustment in a collectivist system, in which the planners can calculate, along the lines of our structural analysis, the proportion in which the displaced labor and equipment are to be reassigned to the two stages. But, by what micro-decisions may we achieve the same result in a free market system?

What is required are decisions to invest in additional working-capital goods those business savings that accrue to the firms in Stage 2 from the reduction in payrolls and replacement expenditure. Such increase in demand for the output of Stage 1 will, first, raise prices and (under motivational conditions still to be examined) also quantities of primary output to be produced with the help of some of the displaced factors. Such increments of primary output can then be applied as inputs in Stage 2, attracting there additional units of idle labor and equipment. Once the idle factors have been fully reemployed in the proportions required for a new equilibrium, the structure depicted for Period 2 will be established and adjustment completed.

Speaking for a moment in "positive" terms, it is obvious that the new proportions of employment can be realized in practice only by a process of trial and error, even if the gradual fall of prices in Stage 1 back to the equilibrium level serves as a guide. Moreover, it is more than likely that such trial and error must extend over more than one period of production, causing additional complications if we transpose the analysis into a dynamic framework with steady growth in labor supply. In a word, in the real world the process of adjustment to a fall in returns seems to overtax the forces operating in a free market unless the change in returns is small and slow or public control takes over at the critical junctures.

Once more the instrumental character of the foregoing structural analysis is demonstrated. However, to serve as a pointer to effective control, this analysis now needs to be complemented by elaborating the motivational conditions required for eliciting the appropriate market behavior.

The first hurdle is the initial decision on the part of the firms in Stage 2 to invest in additional working capital goods. Again, taking the rule of the extremum principle for granted, our main concern is the expectations that are likely to stimulate a positive investment decision. As a matter of fact, the situation in which firms in Stage 2 find themselves at this point resembles the situation analyzed when we studied the initial investment decision required to start the absorption process induced by an increase in the rate of growth of labor supply.[14] Firms are again confronted with a set of unemployed resources, exerting contradictory influences on the decision process.

To the extent that excess supply of labor and equipment depresses prices of the employed factors, additional surpluses accrue to the firms and the required investment decision will be stimulated. For this to occur, we must assume that the elasticity of quantity expectations with regard to factor supply is positive and that the elasticity of factor price expectations is unity; in other words, excess factor supply is expected to continue and the fall in factor prices is regarded as permanent. There is, however, another side of the coin that complicates the decision. This is the effect of a general wage fall on aggregate demand for and, thus, on prices and outputs of consumer goods. In the short run the effect is bound to be unfavorable so that only negative elasticity of quantity and price expectations as to output will support a positive investment decision.[15] Given a general state of uncertainty, which is likely to arise from these conflicting tendencies, it seems that only public information supported by standby measures of investment control can induce goal-adequate expectations.

Once positive investment decisions have been taken, the next difficulty is connected with the need for redistributing the idle resources among the stages in the appropriate proportion. To do so the market possesses no mechanism other than price changes which, however, can pronounce only an *ex-post* verdict on actual investment. This is again the trial and error approach mentioned earlier as the only available investment procedure, but whose obvious *faux frais* can be avoided only by direct control.

---

[14] See Chapter 15, Section II.
[15] A similar effect on demand, prices, and output of equipment goods arises from temporary excess supply of secondary equipment, to be countered only with the same set of expectations. At this point we find a temporary spillover of changes in the consumer-good sector to the equipment-good sectors after all.

A final problem is posed by the fact that the necessary shift to Stage 1 of part of the labor and equipment displaced in Stage 2 is impeded by factor specificity. Even if we are willing to disregard this block so far as labor is involved, machinery suitable for the production of finished consumer goods cannot be employed in the production of primary output. Even if the capital "fund" embodied in the displaced equipment need not change, the physical form of part of the capital goods must change to permit their reinvestment. In other words, a technical process of capital formation must intervene before the new equilibrium can be attained – a process fraught with all the motorial difficulties expounded earlier.

In summing up, we arrive at the same conclusion for market adjustment to falling returns that we had to accept when we investigated the traverse of systems with both expanding and contracting rates of growth of labor supply. Then as now it has proved possible to outline a structural path of more or less frictionless adjustment. However, the motorial requirements for the realization of this path are in sharp conflict with the short-term incentives and the range of information that characterize a regime of decentralized decision making. One need only spell out these requirements to realize the need for public control or guidance at all critical turns.

Appendix to chapter 19

Traverse with diminishing returns illustrated on a numerical quantity model

I. A STATIONARY STAGE MODEL

	Sector Ia					Sector Ib					Sector II				
Stage	F	f	n	ω	o	F	f	n	ω	o	F	f	n	ω	o
(1)	(10)	1 ∪	4	4	→ 5	(40)	4 ∪	16	16	→ 20	(200)	20 ∪	80	80	→ 100
(2)	(10)	1 ∪	4	∪ 5	→ 10	(40)	4 ∪	16	∪ 20	→ 40	(200)	20 ∪	80	∪ 100	→ 200

II. EFFECT OF DIMINISHING RETURNS ARISING IN STAGE 1 OF SECTOR II

	Stage	F	f	n	ω	o
Period 0	(1)	(200)	20 ∪	80	80	→ 100
	(2)	(200)	20 ∪	80	∪ 100	→ 200
Period 1	(1)	(200)	20 ∪	80	80	→ 50
$(r = \frac{1}{2})$	(2)	(100)	10 ∪	40	∪ 50	→ 100
			displaced in Stage 2:100 F; $10f + 40n$			
Period 2	(1)	(266⅔)	26⅔ ∪	106⅔	∪ 66⅔	→ 66⅔
Readjustment	(2)	(133⅓)	13⅓ ∪	53⅓	66⅔	→ 113⅓

221

Appendix to Chapter 19 (*cont'd*)

III. A STAGE MODEL IN DYNAMIC EQUILIBRIUM

Stage	Sector Ia						Sector Ib						Sector II					
	F	f	co	I	ω	o	F	f	co	I	ω	o	F	f	co	I	ω	o
(1)	(90)	9 ∪	18 ∪	18	18	→ 45	(60)	6 ∪	12 ∪	12	12	→ 30	(100)	10 ∪	20 ∪	20	20	→ 50
(2)	(90)	9 ∪	18 ∪	18	45 →	90	(60)	6 ∪	12 ∪	12	30 →	60	(100)	10 ∪	20 ∪	20	50 →	100

IV. EFFECT ON SECTOR II OF TWO PERIODS OF GROWTH ($G = 20\%$) WITH CONSTANT RETURNS IN STAGE 1 OF SECTOR II

Stage	F	f	co	I	ω	o
Period 0 + 2 (1)	(144)	14.4 ∪	28.8 ∪	28.8	28.8	→ 72
(2)	(144)	14.4 ∪	28.8 ∪	28.8	72 →	144

V. EFFECT ON SECTOR II OF TWO PERIODS OF GROWTH ($G = 20\%$) WITH DIMINISHING RETURNS IN STAGE 1 OF SECTOR II

Stage	F	f	co	I	ω	o
Period 0 + 2 (1)	$(158\tfrac{2}{3})$	$\dfrac{238}{15}$ ∪	$\dfrac{476}{15}$ ∪	$\dfrac{476}{15}$		→ $64\tfrac{2}{3}$
(2)	$(129\tfrac{1}{3})$	$\dfrac{194}{15}$ ∪	$\dfrac{388}{15}$ ∪	$\dfrac{388}{15}$	$\dfrac{970}{15}$ →	$129\tfrac{1}{3}$

20

Recycling of production and consumption residuals and the structure of production

The rapidly rising concern with the ecological effects of industrial production and of the consumption style of modern life has so far found little resonance in economic theory. It has now been more than fifty years since Pigou called attention to the importance of "externalities" and, in particular, of diseconomies afflicting the general public, which arise from actions that benefit individual actors. In the tradition of his reasoning, it is still the partial equilibrium aspect and the emphasis on the "bads" rather than the "goods" emanating from such actions that dominate the discussion of these issues.

In a remarkable paper, Ayres and Kneese[1] have broken with this tradition. They present a general equilibrium model of the "material balance" approach to the production and disposal of residuals, with special regard to their recycling into newly usable resources. The following exposition will move along similar lines, but with two notable differences. First, our interest centers on the possibility of emancipating ourselves from the dependence on a given stock of *natural* resources and, thus, on the potential *benefits* that can be reaped from the proper treatment of production and consumption residuals. Second, rather than relating the recycling process to the Walrasian model of general equilibrium, which is the starting point of Ayres and Kneese, we shall try to incorporate the process of retransforming residuals into "artificial" resources as another circular flow in our original schema of production. A few comments are in order to justify this shift of emphasis.

Even if they are not the only sources of apprehension on the part of an ecologically minded observer of industrial society, the *falling resource–population ratio* and the *environmental pollution* due to the rapid growth of production and consumption residuals are probably the most urgent

---

[1] See Robert U. Ayres and Allen V. Kneese, "Production, Consumption, and Externalities," *American Economic Review*, June 1969, pp. 282–97. For their own sources the authors refer to a dissertation by F. Smith, *The Economic Theory of Industrial Waste Production and Disposal*, 1967, and also to K. E. Boulding's well-known paper, "The Economics of the Coming Spaceship Earth," in H. Jarrett, ed., *Environmental Quality in a Growing Economy*, Baltimore, 1966.

ones. Now it is easy to see that the recycling process holds a key position under both aspects. It removes from the living space of men, animals, and plants part of the production and consumption waste that the atmospheric and biological forces of the environment can no longer dispose of. It is true that the second law of thermodynamics would preclude total reliance on *recycled* materials even in a stationary system.[2] But even in a growing system the perfection and generalization of the recycling technology should substantially reduce the threat that depletion and transition to ever less productive resources would pose to the indefinite continuance of the industrial process.

For this reason recycling may in the long run prove to be one of the great innovations of our age. Of lesser importance for mankind at large, but highly intriguing to the economic theorist are its analytical implications. They amount to a partial resurrection of the classical model.

We saw earlier[3] that the unconditional predictions of the classical economists, including Marx, derived from the conception of the macroeconomic process as a closed system held together by a number of feedback relations, through which the major causal forces – labor supply, accumulation, technical progress – were supposed to be recreated and, in a predictable manner, to be transformed by the secondary consequence of their immediate effects on wage level, profits, and market expansion. We also pointed to the growing discrepancy between such a notion of a self-contained socioeconomic evolution and the reality of capitalist evolution. This discrepancy has led postclassical theory to draw the conclusion that the strategic forces ruling aggregate demand, labor supply, accumulation, and technical change must be treated as extrasystemic variables. The only factor for which the classical position could be maintained was real capital. Because it is both an input and an output, the maintenance and formation of capital can and, indeed, must be conceived in terms of a circular mechanism – the basis of the growth models that have occupied us so far.

Now, it should be remembered that the only factor of production that also in the classical system stood *outside* the network of feedback relations was precisely natural resources. Contrariwise, the introduction of the recycling technology leads to the methodological consequence that a factor that throughout the history of economic analysis has been treated as extrasystemic, is being transformed, in analogy with real capital, into an intrasystemic input–output–input phenomenon. Certainly this new methodological status of resource supply will not by itself restore classical

---

[2] For this reason full emancipation from what we call "natural" resources depends on the progress of applied synthetic chemistry.
[3] See Chapter 1, Section I.

determinacy to economic theory so long as labor supply and technical change retain their status as independent variables. It is, however, a step in this direction – a step that population control and public regulation of investment might conceivably enhance at some future date.

I

Correctly identifying a problem is half the solution. To accomplish this purpose we shall study the role of recycling in the structure of production in a highly simplified framework. First, we shall discuss it in the context of *stationary equilibrium* in which the inputs of basic resources are constant. Second, we shall disregard the effect of the second law of thermodynamics, and assume that the recycling process enables us to recover the initial quantity of resource inputs without any loss. Finally, we shall treat, in a first approximation, the residuals of both production and consumption as free goods.

On this basis recycling amounts to no more than a modification of the physical outputs and the substitution of some types of physical inputs for others. To be specific, we shall extend the concept of output by acknowledging that, at every stage of each one of our three sectors of production, there issues in every period not only some "good" in some degree of "completion," but also some "residual," namely, some physical leftover from the process of production. This residual may be the result either of the wear and tear of fixed-capital goods or of the incomplete utilization of working-capital goods that were employed in their production. To simplify further, we shall disregard the latter and thus identify the *production residuals* with "scrap" in the narrow sense of the term. Output in every stage and sector will then appear as a "joint product," consisting of a good plus some scrap.[4]

Now the scrap part of output represents the artificial resources which, when recycled into the process of production and combined with the appropriate type of machinery and labor, will be transformed into "ore," that is, into the raw material from which, through further technical transformations, new equipment goods can be produced in a steady circular process: equipment–scrap–ore–equipment. It thus closes the production circuit in the *equipment-good sectors*. How does this procedure

---

[4] Sraffa (*loc. cit.*, p. 63 ff.), following von Neumann's lead, also operates with a concept of "joint product," consisting of both a goods output and a residual of fixed equipment, a notion that is formally similar to our concept. However, he differs basically in the determination of the residual: He defines residual as that part of the equipment stock which, at the end of the period, is not yet worn out but available for further production.

differ from the procedure by which equipment is obtained in our original schema of production?[5]

In the previously described process, the basic (natural) resource is the mine from which ore is dug up with the help of extractive machinery and labor, to be transformed into the final output "equipment" by the same technical manipulations as just indicated. What distinguishes the recycling process from the conventional process of procuring the necessary raw material "ore," is the substitution of the artificial resource "scrap" for the natural resource "mine," and of a new type of machinery, called "recycling machinery," for the extractive machinery of old. Assuming that the available quantity of scrap yields the same quantity of ore as formerly did the mine and assuming also that the construction of the recycling machinery claims the same amount of inputs as formerly did the construction of extractive machinery, the structural order of production in the equipment-good sectors is clearly unchanged.

Turning now to the *consumer-good sector,* we find the same situation, so far as outputs are concerned. Again they consist in every stage of production of some good and some scrap, the latter representing the residual of consumer-good equipment. These additional quantities of scrap augment the pool of artificial resources available for steady reproduction in the equipment-good sectors and of such consumer goods as derive from the "inorganic" material. Yet, where are we to obtain the resources required for the production of consumer goods based on "organic" materials such as cotton and wheat? In our original schema the natural resources serving this purpose consisted of land, animals, and plants. What residuals can take their place?

To answer this question we must extend our original production schema by adding a *household sector.* In other words, we no longer regard the transformation cycle as completed once finished consumer goods leave the field of production and enter the households. Rather we now treat the households themselves as productive units, in which finished consumer goods form the inputs. But what are the outputs into which these inputs are "transformed"? They consist, first of all, of "utility" (u), "satisfaction," "welfare," or whatever term by which we denote the intangibles that are the ultimate motive for our preoccupation with economic activity. It is the very intangibility of these outputs, precluding intersubjectively valid calculation, that bars them from the conventional analysis of the structure of production. However, as we are more and more becoming aware, these intangibles do not exhaust the "total product" of the consumption process. In analogy with the production process, the utility output is associated with the output of

[5] See Chapter 3, Section II.

residuals, for which henceforth the term *consumption waste* will be used. They too have an intangible aspect, but now of "disutility," an aspect of great importance for the proper evaluation of economic welfare. At the same time they take on, however, the *tangible* form of material objects, open to productive manipulation through the technique of recycling. There, then, in the consumption waste accumulating over an interval measured by production periods, we have the artificial resources which, in the sector producing consumer goods, can take the place of the traditional natural resources.[6]

As is evident, the substitution of consumption waste for natural resources affects the structure of production in the consumer-good sector as little as does the introduction of scrap into the equipment-good sectors. Nothing changes except the type of equipment that transforms consumption waste into raw material: Recycling machinery takes the place of cotton gins, shears, and so forth.

However, what indeed has changed is the basic "structure of production." Resources, which in the form of *natural* resources were a datum such as labor and, thus, an input only, have become also an output, and a new circular mechanism analogous with that relating to real capital has been established. Speaking in terms of our original schema of production, of the four stocks – labor, resources, fixed capital, and working capital – the cooperation of which represents the productive process in an industrial system, now three instead of formerly only two are themselves outputs of an earlier phase of this process. How will this affect our basic quantity–price sum model?[7]

II

We shall answer this question in stages. As preparation for our main problem, namely the structure of a system using *priced* residuals as resources, we shall, to begin with, present two numerical flow models in which the resource inputs are treated as *free goods*. The first de-

---

[6] Realistically considered consumption waste includes also some scrap in the sense defined above, namely, as an artificial resource usable in the equipment-good sectors. Therefore the residuals arising in our new household sector supply resource requirements to all sectors of production, as, in turn, part of the flow of production residuals (scrap) is claimed in the consumer-good sector for the production of, say, automobiles. We propose to disregard this modification in our further deliberations, as we did with the waste products that accrue in the transformation of working-capital goods. Thus, in our simplified model scrap, arising in all production stages of all sectors, is postulated to be the only resource to be fed into the equipment-good sectors, whereas consumption waste forms the sole resource input in the consumer-good sector.

[7] See Models IV and IV.i in Chapter 4, Section II.

scribes a process of production using *natural* resources. It is a value model with the relevant quantities added in parentheses.[8]

	F	f	n	res	o
Ia	20(20)	2(2) +	8(8)	+ 0(2) =	10(10)
Ib	80(80)	8(8) +	32(32)	+ 0(8) =	40(40)
II	400(400)	40(40) +	160(160)	+ 0(40) =	200(200)

$$\text{(XIII)}$$

It is evident that the introduction of unpriced natural resources does not affect the value structure (sector ratios, intersectoral equilibrium conditions) of the system in any manner different from other "free gifts" of the environment, such as air or water.

Nor does this value structure change if next we substitute free *artificial* resources, scrap (*sc*) and consumption waste (*cw*), for the natural resources in the first model. To obtain the same quantity figures for resources input as in Model XIII, we assume that the output of scrap and consumption waste equals 20 percent of the total inputs in the production and consumption sectors, respectively.

	F	f	n	res	o	sc
Ia	20(20)	2(2) +	8(8)	+ 0(2) =	10(10) ∪	
Ib	80(80)	8(8) +	32(32)	+ 0(8) =	40(40) ∪	(10) (XIV)
II	400(400)	40(40) +	160(160)	+ 0(40) =	200(200) ∪	

$$\text{Household input} \longrightarrow \text{Household output}$$
$$200(200) \qquad U \cup (cw = 40)$$

However, if stationary equilibrium is to be maintained over time, some new equilibrium conditions must be fulfilled. They relate the output of scrap in all three sectors to the input of artificial resources in the two equipment-good sectors, and also the household output of consumption waste to the input of artificial resources in the consumer-good sector. In specific terms we have

$$sc_{(a+b+z)} = res_{(a+b)}$$
$$cw = res_z$$

$$\text{(20.1)}$$

Two comments on conditions 20.1 are in order. First, as we have already noted, the conditions disregard the second law of thermody-

---

[8] Because resources enter the system at the earliest stage of production, the mechanism becomes fully transparent only in a combined stage–sector model. For our purposes it suffices to add the values (in the present case equal to zero) and the quantities of the resource inputs to the aggregate inputs of labor and equipment in the respective sectors.

namics and are for this reason not fully realizable. Or, in other words, the new circular mechanism that connects scrap and consumption waste as outputs with resource inputs in the subsequent period can never cover all requirement of steady reproduction, but must be partially supplemented by a "linear" influx of natural resources into the system. On the other hand, so long as the *aggregate* output of scrap equals the attainable technical maximum, the relative size of the contribution of the individual sectors is immaterial.

III

In what manner does Model XIV change when we drop the assumption that residuals and, thus, artificial resources are to be treated as free goods? It stands to reason that, as a description of the *technical* structure of production, the parenthesized part of Model XIV fully retains its validity. Placing a price on the residuals and thus also on the resource inputs cannot change the quantities of equipment, labor, and of the resources themselves required to produce the respective output quantities. However, the model is in need of significant modifications, if we focus attention on the underlying *receipt–expenditure* structure. This will become manifest when we now elaborate the pertinent order of prices and sectoral price sums.

By taking again as our starting point the *quantities* as stipulated in Model XIV, we obtain the following structure in which all quantities are priced:

	F	f	n		res	o	sc	
Ia	25(20)	2.5(2) +	8(8) +	2(2)	= 12.5(10)	+ 0.4(0.4)		
Ib	100(80)	10(8) +	32(32) +	8(8)	= 50(40)	+ 1.6(1.6)		(XV)
II	500(400)	50(40) +	160(160) +	40(40)	= 250(200)	+ 8.0(8.0)		

$$\text{Household input} \atop 250(200) \quad \rightarrow \quad \text{Household output} \atop U \cup 40(40)$$

The first question concerns the manner in which the resource inputs are priced. Their prices are the result of a bargaining process on the part of the owners of residuals with the resource-requiring firms in the three sectors. More precisely, the owners of consumption waste bargain with the firms in Sector II, whereas the owners of scrap in Sectors II and Ib bargain with the firms in Sectors Ib and Ia (scrap accruing in Sector Ia is applied as resource input in the firms of Sector Ia). Because, as was already mentioned, part of the total resource requirements continue to be covered by natural resources, the prices of both scrap and consumption waste are affected by the competition on the part of the owners of natural resources.

Because the actual price of the artificial resources depends on the relative bargaining strength of the contracting parties, it cannot be derived analytically. For the sake of simplicity it has been assumed in Model XV that the unit price of any residual equals the wage unit. Stipulation of a specific number is necessary if we want to establish the relative purchasing power of wage earners and residual owners in terms of consumer goods. It has also been assumed that the money supply has been increased to the extent necessary to leave the wage unit unchanged.

As a consequence of our assumptions, the price sum of aggregate inputs and outputs, as compared with the values set down in Model XIV, has risen by 25 percent. This reduces real wages and, thus, the claim of labor on the quantity output of consumer goods to 80 percent of their former level, the difference now going to the owners of residuals. By what intersectoral shifts can this result be achieved?

A direct transfer occurs between the household sector and the consumer-good sector, by means of which 40 value units of consumption waste are exchanged for 40 value units of consumer goods, representing 40 quantity units of consumption waste and 32 quantity units of consumer goods. The exchange of scrap for consumer goods is more complex. It takes place through the medium of the systematic intersectoral transfers that we discussed in analyzing the structure of stationary equilibrium.[9]

First of all, in order to restore production equilibrium it is necessary to exchange a part of the output of Sector II equivalent to f_z for the output b of Sector Ib – in the present context, 50 value units and 40 quantity units on either side. Now, so long as resources were treated as free goods, the consumer goods thus acquired by Sector Ib could be divided up between the claims of labor operating in Sector Ib and in Sector Ia, the latter receiving their share by exchanging for it an equivalent amount of primary equipment to be applied in Sector Ib as capital replacement. In the present setup, labor in both sectors must share its claim on consumer goods with the owners of priced scrap accruing in all three sectors. As a consequence, payrolls in Sector Ib, as before amounting to 32 units, command at the increased unit price of consumer goods a quantity of only 25.6 units, whereas the difference of 6.4 quantity units accrues to the scrap owners in Sector II at a price sum of 8. In the same manner the remaining 10 value units of consumer goods, amounting to 8 quantity units, are dis-

[9] See Chapter 4, Section II.

tributed between payrolls in Sector Ia and scrap owners in Sectors Ib and Ia, amounting in quantity terms to 6.4, 1.28, and 0.32 units, respectively.[10]

Our discussion can be summarized in the following income–expenditure condition:

$$n_{a_v} + n_{b_v} + n_{z_v} + sc_{a_v} + sc_{b_v} + sc_{z_v} + cw_v = z_v \tag{20.2}$$

Condition 20.1 formulating the relationship between the output of residuals and the input of resources remains valid, and now extends also to the price-sum relations.

IV

Application of our results to the structure of *dynamic* equilibrium does not pose any new problems. All that changes is the addition to the original income-receiving factors, labor and profit recipients, of a third income-receiving factor, namely, the owners of residuals. Of course, in a steadily expanding system the receipts of the latter need not be fully or even partly spent on consumer goods; in principle, they can be saved and invested. In that case a new problem does arise. Because, with a given rate of growth, the required aggregate savings–investment ratio is fixed, we can no longer maintain one of the conditions stipulated for our two-strata model, namely, that all profits and only profits be invested – the "golden rule." Rather an amount of profits equal to the invested part of the receipts of the owners of residuals must now be consumed.

Nor would closer study of the *motorial* conditions for the maintenance of this extended structure of stationary or dynamic equilibrium yield new insights. The action directive and the expectations required for equilibrating behavior of the owners of residuals do not differ from those pertaining to the suppliers of other factors of production.

[10] The reader is reminded that the figures in Model XV depict only input values and quantities and output values and quantities. The real receipts of labor and owners of residuals are not registered. They will be found by dividing the quantity figures for labor and resources input by 1.25, that is, by the new, higher unit price of consumer goods.

PART IV
Changes in the rate of change

III. The dynamics of technological progress

21

The scope of the investigation

I

Speaking in the broader terms of social welfare, technological change is the true stimulus of economic growth. Rising labor supply, considered in isolation, forces capital formation on the system if its members are "to stay where they are," that is, if per capita output and consumption are to be maintained on the preexisting level. Only through the medium of technological progress in one of its many modalities can the members attain a rise in their material provision and can the notion of "growth" be extended beyond a mere aggregative concept.

In pointing to the many modalities under which technological change appears, I have mentioned a characteristic that will profoundly affect our treatment of the issue. There is, alas, no generally accepted classification for these modalities. Without offering an exhaustive listing, the following distinctions will help us in the selection of the problems with which we are going to deal.

There are, first of all, distinctions among invention, innovation, and technological change. Again we cannot fall back on a firm convention for the use of these terms.[1] As far as the first two are concerned, we shall follow Schumpeter's suggestion that *invention* is concerned with the discovery of new technical knowledge, whereas *innovation* refers to the economic application of such new knowledge. The knowledge itself concerns either "novel ways of making old goods" or "old ways of making novelties."[2] Accordingly, we can distinguish in the realm of economic application between "process-innovation" and "product-innovation." In what follows we shall identify *process-innovation* with *technological change,* which then becomes a subcategory of innovation generally.

This by no means commonly accepted definition of technological

---

[1] See, for example, V. Ruttan, "Usher and Schumpeter on Invention, Innovation and Technological Change," *Quarterly Journal of Economics,* November 1959, pp. 596–606.

[2] See M. Blaug, "A Survey of the Theory of Process-Innovation," *Economica,* February 1963, p. 13.

change follows from the earlier definition of technology as "the way of making goods," a way that remains unchanged in product-innovation. Even more important for this narrowly circumscribed definition is a practical reason, that is, product-innovation has so far proved refractory to economic analysis. This seems to be due to two complications. On the one hand, such innovations change simultaneously both the supply and the demand functions. On the other hand, because the product is "new," the associated supply function cannot be related to any previously existing supply function, thus destroying the continuity of economic relations – the precondition for analysis as we know it. In view of these considerations, we shall confine the Dynamics of Technological Progress to the study of process-innovation.

In principle, technological change faces in two directions as technical progress and technical regress. As we saw earlier, a fall in the rate of increase and even an absolute reduction of labor supply are, practically speaking, serious possibilities, and perhaps even future aims of public policy. Contrariwise, technical regress, and even a slowing down of the rate of technical progress seem unlikely for the foreseeable future. Even if ecological considerations might suggest public control of technological change, the aim of such control is likely to be "better" rather than "less" change. Therefore we shall limit our investigation to issues related to *technical progress,* or *progressive process-innovation.*

Technical progress in this sense amounts to such improvements of technology, more precisely, to such shifts of the production function, as will reduce average unit costs of output in the presence of unchanged input prices. Such improvements are not confined to changes in equipment, but also include plant reorganization, changes in working capital, direct improvements in labor efficiency, and so on. To keep our task within manageable bounds, we shall concentrate on *improvements due to changes in the input of equipment and/or labor.* This will make it possible to place again sector analysis in the center of the investigation, unhampered by the complications that, for example, simultaneous stage analysis (working capital!) would introduce.[3]

Even so the variety of conceivable changes is very large. This is mainly owing to the fact that we conventionally distinguish between neutral and nonneutral changes. In accord with our definition of innovational neutrality given earlier, we shall speak with Harrod of "a neutral stream of innovations as one which shall require a rate of increase of capital equal to the rate of increase of output engendered by it."[4] On

---

[3] However, for an exception, see Chapter 27.
[4] Harrod, *Toward a Dynamic Economics, loc. cit.,* pp. 26–77; see also Chapter 8, Section I, above.

the other hand, Harrod's definition of nonneutrality – a stream of innovations that require capital to increase at a greater rate, thus being labor-saving or capital-requiring, and, conversely, for an increase of capital at a smaller rate – does not seem to be precise enough. It conceals the fact that we are confronted there with no less than five cases: pure labor-saving; pure capital-saving; labor-saving and capital-saving; labor-saving and capital-attracting; capital-saving and labor-attracting. Any one of these changes or a combination of them may occur in one of the three sectors of production or simultaneously in two or even three. Furthermore, the technical change may be accompanied by steady or unsteady changes in the supply of other factors – labor and natural resources.

To find our way through such a bewildering maze of alternatives, we shall keep our analysis strictly within the limits set by the overall program of this study. We shall concentrate on the initial impact of neutral and nonneutral innovations on a preexisting dynamic equilibrium and on the structural and motorial conditions for their absorption, to the exclusion of the productivity effect, private and social,[5] and of the distributive effect of technological changes.

We shall begin by reexamining, as promised earlier,[6] the structure of dynamic equilibrium itself and especially therein the role of neutral innovations. Next follow four chapters that deal with nonneutral innovations. The first offers a general survey of the problem, the next two treat labor- and capital-displacing innovations, respectively, and the fourth, combined changes in labor and capital input. Up to this point the investigation will· be conducted under the assumption of constant returns of natural resources. The last chapter of this part will study the countervailing effect of innovations on diminishing returns.

The social organization that serves as the framework for our analyses will again be a closed laissez-faire market system. Differential effects on the adjustment processes, which a collectivist system would introduce, will be discussed when the occasion arises.

In practice, technological changes originate, as a rule, in individual firms and extend, even after generalization, at most over a particular stage of production. Nevertheless, as already indicated, we shall be almost exclusively concerned with the repercussions that such a change has on the sectoral order at large. However, we shall pay special attention to the difference it makes whether process-innovation affects the

---

[5] For a discussion of these effects, see Adolph Lowe, "The Social Productivity of Technical Improvements," *The Manchester School*, Vol. VIII, 1937, pp. 109–24.

[6] See Chapter 8, Section I.

consumer-good sector or one of the two equipment-good sectors. In this context we must be aware that any improved equipment good must initially be *produced* with the help of preexisting, that is, nonimproved equipment goods – one of the instances that justify our assumption of fixed coefficients within the Marshallian short period. Only when, in this manner, "old ways" have succeeded in making improved primary or secondary equipment, will the *application* of such novel equipment reduce average unit costs of output and, thus, satisfy our criterion for technological progress.

A final word needs to be added about the distinction between *autonomous* and *induced* innovations – a distinction that has played a prominent role in the literature since its first appearance in Hicks's theory of wages. Irrespective of the inherent merits of this distinction,[7] our interest centers on the *effects* rather than on the causes of technological change. This permits us to disregard completely the issue of invention and to treat all progressive process-innovations as autonomous, that is, as independent variables. One exception from this rule is Chapter 27, in which the introduction of innovations is treated as response to the diminishing return of natural resources.

II

We cannot conclude these introductory comments without taking up an issue to which we alluded before when we first discussed the various mechanisms of *saving* that are to provide the funds necessary to finance the real capital formation bound up with all types of economic growth.[8] All three available mechanisms, voluntary, involuntary, and forced saving, have, in principle, proved applicable when capital formation for the sake of absorbing a rise in *labor supply* is at stake. It is true that we conducted our analysis of the relevant adjustment processes mainly under the assumption of *involuntary* saving. We did so for the reason that only in this case can a causal relationship between the initiating stimulus of a rise in labor supply and the response of the system in terms of provision of investible funds be established through a fall in money wages and a corresponding rise in profits. No such link exists between the rise in labor supply and voluntary savings. Moreover, whatever link can be construed with forced savings brings in the

---

[7] So long as the "inducement" is related to a *change* in relative factor prices, it is difficult to separate out genuine labor-saving innovations from a mere substitution of capital for labor. See, however, C. Kennedy, "Induced Bias in Innovation and the Theory of Distribution," *Economic Journal*, September 1964, pp. 541–47.

[8] See Chapter 8, Section II, and Chapter 15, Section I.

uncertain factor of expectations. Because we were especially interested in highlighting, however, the hurdles that the adjustment is forced to take, it seemed only fair to select the case most favorable to equilibration.

When it now comes to the financing of *innovations,* we are confronted with a different constellation. A mechanism analogous with involuntary saving does not exist, because the mere "availability" of process-innovations, in contrast with the availability of additional labor, has no immediate effect on the prevailing price–cost relations and the wage–profit ratio bound up with them. Such an effect comes into operation only after the innovation has been embodied in new capacity. For this reason, only *voluntary* and *forced* savings can provide the means for the acts of investment whereby the technological improvement acquires tangible form.

In the context of our motorial assumptions, also in this case it is considerations of profit that induce investors to borrow from private savers or banks. These profits, however, are now the *anticipated result* of investment rather than, as in the case of involuntary savings, its *cause.* Considering the at least temporary competitive superiority of the technological pioneer, both borrowers' and lenders' risks are much lower than in the earlier case in which the growth stimulus took the form of additional labor supply. Therefore it is safe to assume that the willingness to lend will meet with an eagerness to borrow, irrespective of the manner in which the investible funds come into being – whether through voluntary reduction of consumption or through forced reduction as a consequence of a rise in consumer goods prices. However, in order to avoid the complications bound up with forced savings, we shall conduct the subsequent analyses under the assumption of a *voluntary* restriction of consumption.

22

Dynamic equilibrium once more

I

In agreement with prevailing opinion we have so far defined dynamic equilibrium as an economic process moving under the impact of two steady growth stimuli, more specificially of a constant rate of growth of labor supply and of capital-requiring neutral innovations.[1] Although we discovered that the conditions for the maintenance of dynamic equilibrium are stricter and its stability is firmer than the conventional interpretation of the Harrod-Domar formula contends, the basic validity of the formula itself was not questioned. In particular, it has been taken for granted that the procedure for providing the additional real capital required for the absorption of a labor increment is equally applicable to the provision of the capital in which the innovational change is to be embodied. This procedure consists, as we saw, in a reorganization of the stationary structure of production by shifting resources from the consumer-good sector to the equipment-good sectors. Such a shift is supposed to yield in each period of production a surplus of equipment goods in proportion with the combined period addition to labor supply and to technical productivity.

This notion that the steady expansion of the capital stock can be achieved by the steady *addition* of the *period net output* in the equipment-good sectors needs to be subjected to closer scrutiny. The procedure is unassailable so far as the steady absorption of a labor increment is concerned. In this case, homogeneous units of labor (homogeneous among themselves as well as with the preexisting stock of labor) are supposed to enter the system in a steady flow. They require for their employment additional homogeneous units of equipment of the preexisting type, which are supplied, together with the current replacement units, by the current output of the equipment-good sectors.

It is possible to visualize a type of innovation that logically parallels such addition of homogeneous labor units. Let us assume that, in

[1] See Chapter 8, Section I.

240

every period, a gadget is added to the preexisting units of equipment, increasing their productivity in proportion to the capital increment – a notion that is, although not nonsensical, to say the least, highly unrealistic. The normal case of a capital-requiring technical improvement calls for a piece of equipment that is *different* in size and, in most cases, also in form from the preexisting pieces. This, however, implies that we cannot add an "increment" to a capital stock that otherwise is left physically intact. Rather, in principle, the *entire* preexisting capital stock has to undergo *physical transmutation*. In addition, if a preexisting dynamic equilibrium is not to be disturbed, the entire transmutation must be carried out within *one period of production*.

Can dynamic equilibrium be attained at all, not to say, maintained through time, under these conditions? To answer this question we must form a quantitative estimate of the major variables involved, in particular of the *period* savings required. For this purpose we take our bearings from the Harrod-Domar formula. By isolating for the moment the innovational change from simultaneous changes in labor supply, we can write the required addition to capital stock as this formula assumes it, that is, F times π, where F stands for the original total capital stock, and π for the increment of productivity. We further denote the related savings ratio exclusively devoted to the financing of technological change as $\bar{s}$. If this addition is to be built in one period of production, we have the condition

$$\bar{s}(1 - kd) \cdot o = F \cdot \pi = \pi \cdot k \cdot o$$

or

$$\bar{s}(1 - kd) = \pi \cdot k = \text{the Harrod condition}$$

However, if in every period the *entire* preexisting capital stock is to be rebuilt (besides the provision of the capital required to absorb the improvement), the period "addition" to capital stock rises to F times $(1 + \pi)$. Fortunately the net savings ratio $\bar{s}$ required for an investment of this size need not cover the total investment demand, because part of the latter can be provided by changing the physical form of current replacements. That part of the new stock which can be provided in this manner amounts to $d \cdot F$, and the required net savings equal the difference between the investment necessary to build the new stock and that part of it which is procurable through the replacement process, that is,

$$\bar{s}(1 - kd) \cdot o = F(1 + \pi) - d \cdot F$$

or

$$\bar{s} = \frac{k(1 + \pi - d)}{1 - kd} \tag{22.1}$$

Dynamic equilibrium is feasible only if the right-hand expression of Equation 22.1 is smaller than 1, so that the required addition to capital stock can be provided by the savings of one period. To demonstrate that in practice this condition cannot be fulfilled, we set $k = 2$, $d = 1/10$, and π as low as 3/100. This yields for $\bar{s}$ the unworkable value of ca. 2.3. Conversely, for a realistic savings ratio of, say, 1/10 we obtain, for the same values of d, and π, a value of $k =$ ca. 1/10, which has never been encountered in any industrial system.[2]

II

Yet, are we not following on the trail of a red herring? Are there no attenuating circumstances or business strategies that might after all reduce the required savings and investment ratios to feasible levels?

An apparent objection to our radical proposition has been stated by Harrod himself.[3] Neutrality of innovations in the aggregate need not imply that all or even any one innovation bears that character, so long as the deviations from neutrality cancel out. This amounts to stipulating that labor-saving and capital-saving innovations are distributed over the system in such a manner that the surplus requirements of new capital in the labor-saving industries must balance the less than average capital requirements in the capital-savings industries. It stands to reason, however, that such an arrangement cannot reduce total requirements of capital below what they would be if neutrality prevailed in every industry.

Greater significance seems to attach to another expedient. Given an "equilibrium" age distribution and straight-line depreciation of all

---

[2] An explanation for the total disregard of this issue in conventional analysis can be found in the "oversaving bias" with which the entire discussion is burdened. In the wake of the Keynesian preoccupations, of which modern growth theory is a direct offspring, the savings ratio is treated as the independent variable to which the growth rate must adjust if dynamic equilibrium is to be maintained. Here the danger is that *ex ante* savings will outrun *ex ante* investment demand. In the climate of recent technological progress – to mention only atomic energy and automation as the most conspicuous applicants for real capital – the bias is toward undersaving, not to mention the capital demand of the developing regions. In other words, it is the desired growth rate that now represents the independent variable to which savings are to adjust.

[3] See Harrod, *Toward a Dynamic Economics, loc. cit.,* p. 23.

capital stocks in the system, can neutrality not be maintained by replacing, in every period, only the currently worn-out part of the stock by improved units of equipment? True, under these conditions, the units of real capital simultaneously employed in the respective industries and sectors are no longer homogeneous and, being introduced in successive periods, are of different productivity – a "vintage" structure of capital. Thus, if the number of depreciation periods is *n,* we have *n* technologies embodied in the operating equipment stock, their productivities being in inverse proportion with the age of the embodying equipment units. Disregarding the well-known objections to the aggregation of physically dissimilar units of real capital into a single measure, we can then conceive of an ensuing overall capital–output ratio that remains constant through time: The period net addition to capital stock is matched by the net addition to output.

Thus the criterion of neutrality seems fulfilled, provided only that the economic movement in which such "vintage neutrality" materializes, is a genuine dynamic equilibrium, namely, a *stable* process of steady growth. An interesting attempt has been made to demonstrate such stability by an analogy with Ricardo's notion of a secular process based on the different fertility of units of land: "Different vintage machines are comparable to Ricardo's acres of different fertility. The machine on the margin of being scrapped earns no quasi-rent and corresponds to Ricardo's no-rent land."[4]

Unfortunately, the comparison breaks down at the essential point. What we should compare with Ricardo's no-rent land is not the oldest machine to be scrapped at a given moment, but the newest machine about to be introduced. Then we realize that, in Ricardo's case, long-period prices of output are determined by the highest costs of production prevailing at that moment, whereas in the innovational case they are governed by the lowest costs of production. Therefore, Ricardo's growth process, being ruled by increasing costs, displays stability in every phase, whereas innovational growth proceeding under a regime of decreasing costs remains unstable until competition has eliminated all less productive machines—an operation of indefinite length considering the steady introduction of new innovations.

However, to overcome all these difficulties, could we not adjust the period rate of depreciation to the requirements of a continuous renewal of the capital stock or, more precisely, charge the capital stock in every period with an appropriate obsolescence allowance? This is the solution that Charles Kennedy has in mind, which, by raising the

---

[4] Hahn and Matthews, *loc. cit.,* p. 840; see also Joan Robinson, *The Rate of Interest,* London, 1952, pp. 56, 60–63.

rate of gross investment to output, is to perform the steady adjustment without any net saving or net investment.[5]

Perhaps an individual firm or even industry can avail itself of this procedure, that is, of writing off its total capital stock in every period of production. However, a moment's reflection tells us that, to be feasible for the system at large, the aggregate capital–output ratio must be below 1, otherwise all resources will have to be devoted to steady capital re-formation with nothing left for the production of consumer goods.

Thus our original result is fully confirmed: Neutral innovations in all empirically relevant instances are capital-requiring in the radical sense of a need for the steady reconstruction of the entire operating capital stock in every successive period of production.[6]

III

From this result a number of far-reaching consequences follow which will profoundly affect our subsequent analyses:

1. The concept of dynamic equilibrium must be modified as referring exclusively to the processes induced by a steady rate of growth of *labor supply*. A model in accord with this narrow interpretation will henceforth serve us as a frame of reference,[7] excepting certain didactic explorations that will be conducted in the framework of stationary equilibrium.

2. In studying the dynamics of labor supply, the need for real capital formation arose whenever the rate of change in labor supply *increased*. Now we have realized that such problems are in the center of the analysis of neutral technical progress even if the rate of change is *constant*.

3. Because neutral technical progress proves incompatible with dy-

---

[5] See Charles Kennedy, "Technical Progress and Investment," *Economic Journal*, 1961, pp. 292–99, and "The Character of Improvements and Technical Progress," *ibid.*, 1962, pp. 899–911.

[6] Our analytical result would not be affected if we were to drop the postulate of both amortization and replacement moving in straight-line fashion (see Chapter 9, Section V, footnote 17). With the stipulation that productive capacity is not to decline during the lifetime of equipment, the replacement ratio varies inversely with the growth rate. With straight-line amortization, about 40 percent of net capital formation can then be supported by excess amortization, assuming realistic values for both the rate of growth and the lifetime of the equipment. See also Domar, *loc. cit.*, p. 161, and R. F. Harrod, "Replacements, Net Investment, Amortization Funds," *Economic Journal*, March, 1970, pp. 24–31.

[7] In the interest of simplifying our exposition, we already applied this limited concept of dynamic equilibrium in all the investigations of Parts II and III.

namic equilibrium, the macrogoal on which instrumental analysis is to orient itself cannot, also in this case, be dynamic equilibrium. Whether treated in isolation or as superimposed on a steady rate of growth of labor supply, the effect of a steady stream of neutral innovation is a permanent distortion of the equilibrium structure of production. The optimum goal to be stipulated in the context of neutral technical progress can only be a setup in which the deviations from dynamic equilibrium are kept to a minimum, in particular excluding cumulative processes of deviation.

Paradoxically, it is only *neutral* innovations that are bound to distort any equilibrium structure, because they are supposed to affect *all* structural components of the system *simultaneously* and to be *currently* absorbed in their entirety. No such rigid constraints are imposed on nonneutral, that is, factor-displacing innovations. They initiate a *partial change* in factor utilization in some particular sector, stage, industry, or firm, the generalization of which may extend over *several periods of production.* Therefore, the additional savings and investments required *in any one period* are likely to be a small fraction of the amount predicated in Equation 22.1, well within the limits of feasibility. Furthermore, given the suitable structural and motorial conditions, the system can, in principle, be kept on the path toward a new dynamic equilibrium, even if continuous innovational shocks should prevent it from actually ever reaching the equilibrium level.[8]

[8] See Chapters 24–27.

23

Nonneutral innovations: a general survey

Because neutral innovations are characterized by "an equal rise of productivity on the part of all labor however far back or forward it may be between the inception and the final stage of production,"[1] they assure constancy not only of the capital–output ratio but also of the level of utilization of capital and labor. Now, nonneutral innovations change the relative application of the two resources. Therefore one might expect that the nature of nonneutral change is reflected in characteristic changes of the capital–output ratio.

Indeed, in the literature the proposition has been advanced that a fall in the capital–output ratio indicates "capital-saving" and its rise, "labor-saving."[2] However, such a sweeping generalization arouses suspicion simply because it fails to take notice of the great variety of possible combinations of the two factors, to which reference was made earlier.[3] Nor is it ever made clear whether the proposition concerns the *initial impact* on the innovating firm, industry, or sector or the *terminal* capital–output ratio for the system at large, after the initially "saved" factor has been brought back into utilization. Moreover, where in one of the equipment-good sectors are we to place a labor-"saving" innovation that reduces the replacement costs of secondary equipment and, thus, resembles capital-"saving" in the consumer-good sector?

From all this it follows that, to be able to read a particular type of nonneutral innovations in any indicator, we must, first of all, rigorously define the concepts of labor-saving and capital-saving. In other words, we must not use the notion of "factor-saving" indiscriminately as referring both to a *reduction of input quantities at constant prices* and to a *reduction of the prices of constant input quantities.* In the first category, we must further distinguish between the *initial displacement* of a quantity of capital and/or labor and a *permanent fall,* for the system at large, of the ratio between the total input quantity of a factor

---

[1] See Harrod, *Toward a Dynamic Economics, loc. cit.,* p. 23.
[2] *Ibid.,* pp. 26–77. See also Blaug, *loc. cit.*
[3] See Chapter 21, Section I.

and the quantity of aggregate output once full utilization of factors has been restored.

In line with our overall program, we shall concentrate on *factor-displacement* (and on *factor-attraction* as its systematic opposite), that is, on the structural and motorial requirements for a traverse that is to adjust the distortion of an original dynamic equilibrium caused by such displacement to a new dynamic equilibrium. To avoid any confusion of meanings, henceforth we had better shun altogether the term factor-saving. Instead, we shall speak of *factor-displacement* (*-attraction*) *whenever introduction of a nonneutral innovation reduces* (*raises*) *that input quantity of labor and/or capital that is technologically required to produce the original output quantity of a firm, industry, or sector.*

To generalize about *terminal* input–output ratios for the system at large after the restoration of dynamic equilibrium seems difficult whenever an innovation affects more than one sector. On the other hand, the *secondary price effects* of such innovations will be designated as such.

Furthermore, with regard to factor-displacement (-attraction) as defined here, we shall presently see that changes in the capital–output ratio, understood as *input quantity divided by output quantity,* by themselves fail to indicate the type of nonneutral innovation involved. For this reason, we have listed in the attached table the capital–output ratio, the capital–labor ratio, and the output–labor ratio for six categories of nonneutral innovations, limiting ourselves to possible combinations of fixed capital and labor to the disregard of working capital, which has no place in our sectoral analysis.[4]

It has already been emphasized that our ratios are to be understood as quantity ratios. This raises, of course, difficult aggregation problems, especially when a common measure is to be found for heterogeneous capital units. However, as we saw already, the other alternative, that is, working with value ratios involving actual market prices, is bound to blur the technological picture whenever more than one sector is affected by the innovation. To achieve comparability among our basic variables, we express them in fixed homogeneous wage units, stipulating that all changes in our aggregates so measured are to reflect quantity changes.

We furthermore require a measure for the displacement effect of nonneutral innovations. For this purpose we introduce the concept of a "displacement ratio" (or, conversely, "attraction ratio"), symbolized by

---

[4] Were we to disaggregate our sectors into successive production *stages,* our results would be also applicable to the effect that innovations occurring in a particular stage have on the respective ratios.

δ or -δ, respectively. It expresses the proportion of the displaced factor quantity to the quantity originally employed:

$$\delta_n = \frac{n_0 - n_1}{n_0} \quad \text{and} \quad \delta_f = \frac{f_0 - f_1}{f_0}$$

The subscripts refer to the periods before and after the introduction of the innovation.[5] If the ratios bear a negative sign we deal with factor attraction.

Effect of nonneutral innovations on capital–output ratio
(k), capital–labor ratio (c), output–labor ratio (o/n)
(initial quantitative impact on innovating sector)

		Effect on		
Type of innovation		k	c	o/n
1. Pure labor-displacing		0	+	+
2. Pure capital-displacing		−	−	0
3. Labor- and capital-displacing		−	+	+
$\delta_n > \delta_f$				
4. Labor- and capital-displacing		−	−	+
$\delta_f > \delta_n$				
5. Labor-displacing, capital-attracting		+	+	+
6. Capital-displacing, labor-attracting		−	−	−

By inspecting the table, we find that the conventional rule, that is, rising k indicating labor displacement and falling k indicating capital displacement, is confirmed in all cases of capital displacement, irrespective of any simultaneous change in the utilization of labor. Conversely, the rule fails to apply in cases of labor displacement, except when labor displacement is accompanied by capital attraction. In order to obtain an unambiguous result, we must consider more than one indicator. As a matter of fact, even the combination of any two of our indicators does not achieve a clear distinction. Only by using all three indicators can we identify each innovational type.[6]

[5] At first sight it seems to be more appropriate to express displacement and attraction ratios in terms of the stock variables N and F, especially so far as capital is concerned. We shall presently understand why expression in terms of flow variables is more convenient for our purposes.

[6] It is not without interest to compare the behavior of the three ratios, as shown in our table, with their behavior in the conventional interpretation of *neutral* innovations. In the latter case, both capital stock and output are supposed

II

Of the six categories listed in the table we shall submit categories 1 and 2 to detailed analysis. The procedure applied can easily be extended to the other cases in which changes in labor and capital input combine, as we shall demonstrate in some additional comments.

In every instance our task consists in examining the initial impact of the technological change on a preexisting dynamic equilibrium, and in elaborating the structural and motorial conditions for the establishment of a new dynamic equilibrium after the innovation has been absorbed. Again, issues of capital formation and capital liquidation will be in the foreground. This is obvious whenever the innovation is capital-attracting or capital-displacing, because in this case capital formation or liquidation must occur even *before* the innovation can have any impact on the preexisting equilibrium. Although this is not so in cases of pure labor displacement, we shall discover that when it comes to the establishment of terminal equilibrium, the creation of additional working places for the initially displaced units of labor and, thus, capital formation is a prime requirement. This is even true of certain capital-displacing innovations, namely, whenever average costs and sales prices of the innovating firm fall below the variable costs of competing marginal firms, and the elasticity of demand is too low to permit the transfer of all workers displaced in the marginal units to the innovating unit.

In fact, this secondary need for capital formation in the interest of "compensating" any initial displacement of labor and the complex of circumstances related to such compensation present the major structural problem in the macroeconomics of factor-displacing innovations. Of course, capital displacement creates additional problems. Yet because their solution involves as a rule liquidation rather than reutilization of the discarded equipment, they affect the structural reorganization of the process of production only indirectly through the motorial consequences of idle capacities.[7]

> to increase in the same proportion, the quantity of labor employed remaining unchanged. This yields the postulated constancy of the capital–output ratio, whereas capital–labor and output–labor ratios steadily rise – a constellation that indicates a pure labor-displacing innovation in the table. Nevertheless, there is no danger of confusing these two innovational types, because it is the very essence of a neutral change in the conventional interpretation that no factor is displaced and that dynamic equilibrium remains undisturbed.

[7] In contrast with its strategic position in the analysis of nonneutral *process*-innovations, technological unemployment and its subsequent compensation play a minor role in *product*-innovations. At any rate the "forward- and

By centering our investigation of the traverse on the *compensation of technological unemployment,* we emphasize an issue the relevance of which is highly controversial. It has been debated for more than 150 years and, considering the secular employment trend over this period, it is not surprising that, in the view of the majority of experts, technological unemployment is today regarded as perhaps an occasional irritant but not as an ever-present threat to the stability of the system. Moreover, in the heat of polemics, the arguments on either side have occasionally been overstated. What is still worse, the basic question at issue has been blurred. This question is neither whether, as a rule, nonneutral innovations initially create unemployment (they do) nor whether, given sufficient time, compensation is possible (it certainly is). The question is whether a free market is endowed with a *systematic mechanism that assures compensation within the Marshallian short period,* thus precluding any secondary distortions that could upset dynamic equilibrium. Perhaps there is no better way of clarifying the issue than a brief survey of the history of the problem, with special regard to the role played in the debate by capital formation for the sake of compensation.

III

As is well known, the issue was first introduced into respectable theory in the third edition of Ricardo's *Principles.* Its publication in 1821 was a profound shock to the whole body of progressive opinion. In a newly added chapter "On Machinery" the recognized head of liberal economics formally abandoned one of its basic tenets, namely, that industrial progress is necessarily beneficial to all classes of society. Reluctantly he had reached the conclusion "that the substitution of machinery for human labor is often very injurious to the interests of the class of labourers."

The proposition was not original with Ricardo. It played a considerable role in merchantilist literature and in the "underworld" of popular writings of the day. However, Ricardo was now claiming that it was in conformity with "the correct principles" of political economy.

backward-linkages" (see Albert O. Hirschman, *The Strategy of Economic Development,* New Haven, 1958, p. 98 ff.) so characteristic of many of these innovations, render their overall effect both labor- and capital-attracting rather than labor- and capital-displacing. Therefore, in practice, the labor-displacement effect of nonneutral process-innovations is most easily compensated by the simultaneous introduction of product-innovations. Because, however, no systematic reason can be adduced for such coincidence, this consideration will be ignored in the subsequent exposition.

One of these principles – the essential one – was the theory of the wage fund, according to which the system's capital stock at any moment contained a limited fund of wage goods. From this fund the maximum employment capacity of the system could be derived by a simple calculation, that is, by dividing the wage fund by the subsistence wage per worker. Moreover, because wages tended toward the subsistence level according to classical principles, any reduction of the wage fund must create unemployment. Now it is Ricardo's main argument that such a decrease of the wage fund is necessarily associated with the introduction of machinery. During the period of transition, factors that formerly produced wage goods produce machines. Thus, instead of replenishing the wage fund they transform it into fixed capital. As a result the system will be faced in the subsequent period with a deficit in wage goods, and part of the labor force hitherto employed will have to be dismissed.

Of course, the story need not end at this point. The machines would not have been introduced had they not increased the chances for larger profits. To the extent that these profits serve new capital formation, the wage fund may expand even beyond its previous size. In this manner additional saving and investment, to use modern terms, may bring about the compensation of the original displacement of labor, although no one can predict the length of the interval of underemployment.

The challenge was taken up by Ricardo's own school, which hit back at him with Say's law. If it is true that supply always creates its own demand, the proposition must be valid not only for the commodity market but also for the labor market. The optimistic argument used in this context is still quite popular and is, therefore, worth explicit statement. The technological unemployment under consideration is a consequence of technical progress. Such progress is bound to reduce the average costs of production, a change which manifests itself either in rising profits or in falling prices. Either way, additional real purchasing power is created that will show in an increase of aggregate demand. In supplying the commodities for the satisfaction of such additional demand the displaced workers will find new employment.

It was J. S. Mill who came forth with the pessimistic rebuttal that demand for commodities need not be demand for labor. He did not deny that cost reductions due to technical progress raised the purchasing power of either the technical pioneer and/or of the consumers. What he denied was that in this manner *aggregate* purchasing power can be raised. Once the system has lost the buying power of the displaced, then the best the buying increment of entrepreneurs and consumers can achieve is to balance this loss. In this way the production–consumption circuit will again be closed, but it is a circuit from which the displaced workers have been eliminated. Only simultaneous displacement or new accumulation of *capital,* neither of which is a necessary consequence of the technological change, would bring about compensation.

The case for "capital shortage" found its strongest expression in Marx. However, it was no longer considered that a deficiency of circulating capital in the form of an alleged wage fund caused the trouble, but rather a shortage of *fixed* capital. Ricardo had already discovered that it was somehow easier to absorb the displaced workers in "menial services" than in industrial production. Now Marx offered the explicit argument. To find productive employment for the displaced, new working places – plant and equipment – have to be provided. This requires a process of saving and investment which is by no means automatically assured by the existence of idle factors or even of surplus profits on the part of the technical pioneers. On the contrary, with growing capital intensity, that is, increasing capital per capita, the bottleneck of capital formation can be overcome only by a steadily increasing rate of investment or, more likely, by the continuous lengthening of the adjustment period required. In the interval, technological unemployment persists and exerts pressure on the wage level and on aggregate consumption. Such a fall in demand for mass consumption goods will in the end affect also investment unfavorably. Instead of gradual compensation we have to expect what today we would call a cumulative deflation and a cyclical downswing.

At this point the theory reached a new stage. What started out as an imperfection of the market mechanism had by then developed into a threat to the stability of the system at large, and technological unemployment was advanced as the main cause for the "underconsumption crisis." However, the underlying dispute by no means ended there. Neoclassical theory, for example in the writings of J. B. Clark, contains at least an implicit answer to the Marxian challenge. It would admit that compensation is conditional on the availability of capital. However, what it would not admit is the need for *additional capital formation.* The stock of capital as it exists at any moment is regarded as offering, at least in principle, unlimited employment opportunities.

This result was gained by the dropping of two classical premises. No longer are the coefficients of production taken as fixed, nor the long-period level of real wages as invariable. I refer, of course, to the marginal productivity theorem according to which varying quantities of labor can be combined with any given quantity of capital, provided that wages adjust themselves to the corresponding change in the marginal productivity of labor. Thus, any amount of technological unemployment can be absorbed by the available capital stock so long as money wages fall to the required extent. Moreover, such a fall in money wages need not even amount to a fall in real wages, if, for example, the preceding change in productive technique has cheapened wage goods. However, even if real wages have to fall, the general level of productivity in the modern industrial economy provides a wide margin for such reductions without bringing the wage level down to the subsistence level.

If I see it correctly this is still the prevailing theory of compensation. It is no longer quite so optimistic as was the proposition derived from Say's law, because a fall in the level of real wages is an admitted possibility. With regard to the *employment effect* of technical changes, however, the result is "harmonistic," because the marginal productivity mechanism, if only permitted free play, is supposed to bring about automatic self-correction of all temporary distortions of the full employment level.

Unfortunately, the neoclassical solution is applicable only under quite specific and largely unrealistic conditions relating to the shape and elasticity of the relevant production functions. If, as is the case, for example, in traditional farming or retail trade, prevailing technology permits the addition of more workers to the given equipment without prior adjustment of the physical form of this equipment or of the skills of the labor increment, absorption is easy. The situation looks quite different in most manufacturing industries. If we wanted to double the labor force operating a given number and type of looms or linotype machines, the marginal product would probably fall to zero or even turn negative. Before raising the employment capacity of the existing stock of fixed capital to any noticeable degree, we would have to *change its physical form,* not to mention the delay of adjustment in the labor market if, say, displaced steelworkers would have to be absorbed in textile production. Moreover, promptly to change the operating type of plant and equipment under the impact of a wage reduction would in most cases prove highly unprofitable, unless depreciation was already far advanced. Thus, in practice, it may take years before the marginal productivity mechanism can even begin to operate as a compensating force. In the interval, labor displacement will persist with all its dismal consequences for the wage level, aggregate consumption, and the overall stability of the system.

IV

In drawing some conclusions from this historical survey, we must be aware that all its statements bear a "positive" character, and may require modification before they can be incorporated in an instrumental analysis. Even so they will help us to demarcate the types of technological unemployment that can be compensated only over the long period, that is, after the formation of additional fixed capital.

Even if we disregard more fundamental objections, neither of the two systematic propositions that have been adduced in favor of short-period compensation, that is, transformation of the technological cost reduction into effective demand, on the one hand and, on the other hand, the marginal productivity theorem, can dispense with prior capital formation, except under quite special conditions. Only to the extent that the new demand turns toward "services" can the displaced workers be reemployed without complementary expansion of the equipment stock. This is apparently a secular tendency in industrial societies and, thus, a safety valve for the unemployment created by small and steady technological improvements, but it is not likely to suffice for the shocks arising from large and discontinuous innovations. Having granted the possibility of small variations of the coefficients of production without prior changes in the physical form of most operating equipment, we can apply the same reasoning to the marginal productivity mechanism. Although capable of accommodating small technological changes, it can absorb large displacements only by reconstructing the system's capital stock.[8]

Thus, it is the *large-scale distortions* that periodically unbalance the labor market under the impact of major innovations that make compensation conditional on prior capital formation. Such distortions themselves are related to a whole array of factors: the number and scope of simultaneously occurring innovations; the speed at which such innovations succeed one another; their productivity in terms of cost reductions; the "gradient" of average cost differences among the firms composing the industry in which the innovations occur, as well as among the firms composing any other industry affected by the technological change; and the distribution of aggregate employment over these gradients. Obviously the displacement effect is the greater the larger the cost reduction, and the more numerous the workers employed in the marginal firms, especially in those whose variable costs exceed the new average costs of the "pioneers." The last point is de-

---

[8] See Chapter 13, in which we also discussed the narrow limits of a multiple shift system for expanding the employment capacity of a given equipment stock.

cisive for the "bunching" of displacement at any given point of time. Although in the long run all firms will be eliminated whose average total costs exceed the sales price of the improved output, displacement will be "staggered" and, thus, the initial impact alleviated, so long as the marginal firms can cover their average variable costs.

It is clearly impossible to give even an approximate estimate of the relative strength of these factors in the totality of empirical innovations. We shall be on safe ground, however, in asserting that compensation requires capital formation whenever improvements of a high degree of productivity create large and bunched displacement in the marginal firms of the innovating industry or when an entire industry is reorganized reducing employment even in the innovating firms. It is to such cases that our subsequent analysis mainly refers. Because in practice these major innovational shocks turn up in discontinuous sequence, they will have to be treated as *once-over changes superimposed on a process of a steady growth of labor supply*. Such discontinuity does not exclude the possibility that a subsequent innovation gets under way before the system has been able to cope with all the repercussions of the preceding one. This complication will be disregarded in our analysis.

In view of the significance that the bunching of the displacement effect has on the manner of compensation, the question arises whether dynamic equilibrium is the most suitable framework for the study of the initial impact of such technological changes. During the 150 years preceding the Second World War, innovational activity was intimately related to certain phases of the business cycle – mainly to the phases of stagnation and revival – with the consequence of a postponement of displacement to the upper turning point when it coincided with a general reduction of employment, creating a large-scale bunching effect. Moreover, initial capital formation, the precondition for the introduction of all capital-attracting innovations, was greatly facilitated by the presence of idle resources during the early phases of the cycle. If, nevertheless, we shall retain dynamic equilibrium as our frame of reference, we do so in order to study the structural requirements for the absorption of nonneutral innovations in isolation from any other, especially cyclical distortions.

24

Pure labor-displacing innovations

The clearest case by which to demonstrate both the initial impact and the structural adjustments required for compensation is a pure labor-displacing innovation introduced in the consumer-good sector. More precisely, a capital stock equal to the original one in terms of wage units can now produce the original output with less labor input, because either the given physical stock is more efficiently organized or a new more efficient stock was built after the original stock was fully depreciated. The displacement effect is unambiguous, as is the need for additional capital formation so long as the displaced workers are supposed to be absorbed in industrial production. Subsequently, we shall also examine the effect of pure labor-displacing innovations occurring in one or the other of the equipment-good sectors. We are already prepared for additional complications that will then arise because of the secondary effect of this type of change on the price of capital inputs in the consumer-good sector.[1]

I

Our main task is to study the effect of pure labor-displacing innovations on a system in dynamic equilibrium. However, once again it will prove useful to start out from a stationary frame of reference. We then assume that in some firm(s) belonging to a particular industry in the consumer-good sector, production will be reorganized in such a manner that the available stock of secondary equipment can produce the original output quantity with a smaller input of labor.[2] As a consequence, a certain amount of labor will be initially displaced in the consumer-good sector, and our first problem is to establish the terminal structure of production in which the displaced workers can be reemployed.

[1] See Chapter 23, Section I.
[2] Because we are primarily interested in the structural consequences of the technological change, we disregard for the time being its effect on prices and profits and, therefore, also a possible expansion of output in the pioneer firms as a result of price reduction. Although partly shifting the displacement effect to other firms of the same industry or even to quite different industries, such expansion will not offset displacement as such, and, hence, it will not alter the structural consequences of the technological change. We shall return to the issue in the context of motorial analysis.

For this purpose we subdivide the aggregate labor force initially operating in the consumer-good sector into two parts: one part, $u \cdot n_z$, employed in a subsector comprising the pioneering firms and another part, $(1 - u) n_z$, employed in another subsector comprising all other firms and industries producing consumer goods.[3] By using symbol δ for the displacement ratio as defined earlier,[4] we obtain for the magnitude of labor displaced the expression $\delta_n u \cdot n_{z_0}$. In order to achieve compensation, this idle labor must be distributed over the system at large. In what proportions?

At first sight one might consider distributing the displaced labor among the two subsectors of the consumer-good sector in proportion to the magnitude of labor employed in each subsector after the technological change has occurred, that is, at the ratio

$$\frac{u(1 - \delta_n)}{1 - u}$$

However, because, in accord with our general presupposition, reemployment is conditional on prior formation of real capital, some part of the displaced labor must be channeled into the respective equipment-good sectors, first, for the construction and, ultimately, for the steady replacement of the additional capital stock. In other words, our division of the consumer-good sector into two subsectors must be extended to the system at large. We then have *subsystem* 1 composed of the innovating firms as consumer-good sector and of certain firms in the two equipment-good sectors required for the steady reproduction of the capital stocks operating in subsystem 1. Correspondingly, we have *subsystem* 2, comprising the remainder of the consumer-good and equipment-good sectors of the original total system. Our task is to determine the precise proportion in which the displaced labor will, terminally, have to be distributed over all three sectors of both subsystems if a new stationary equilibrium is to be established.

This proportion must equal the ratio of the total labor force in subsystem 1 after displacement to the total labor force employed in subsystem 2.[5] The former equals

$$\frac{u \cdot n_{z_0}}{1 - kd} - \delta_n u \cdot n_{z_0} \quad \text{or} \quad \frac{u[1 - (1 - kd) \cdot \delta_n]}{1 - kd} \cdot n_{z_0}$$

[3] As was stated earlier (See Chapter 23, Section I), we express labor input as a flow magnitude measured in homogeneous wage units.

[4] See Chapter 23, Section I.

[5] This must be so because, after the displacement of labor has occurred, the system as a whole, excluding the displaced, is again in equilibrium, as was pointed out by J. S. Mill (see Chapter 23, Section III). From this it follows that the displaced must be absorbed in the same proportions that would be valid if a system in stationary or dynamic equilibrium had to absorb an increment of labor supply.

$1 - kd$ enters in the denominator so as to account also for labor employed in the equipment-good sectors. For the same reason labor employed in subsystem 2 equals

$$\frac{1 - u}{1 - kd} \cdot n_{z_0}$$

Consequently, that part of the totality of displaced workers, $\delta_n u \cdot n_{z_0}$, which must find employment in subsystem 1 amounts to

$$\sigma_{1_n} = \frac{u[1 - (1 - kd) \cdot \delta_n]}{u[1 - (1 - kd) \cdot \delta_n] + 1 - u} \cdot u \delta_n \cdot n_{z_0} = \frac{\delta_n u^2 [1 - (1 - kd) \cdot \delta_n]}{1 - (1 - kd) \cdot \delta_n u} \cdot n_{z_0} \quad (24.1)$$

Correspondingly, we obtain for that part which must be shifted to subsystem 2

$$\sigma_{2_n} = \frac{(1 - u) \cdot \delta_n u}{1 - (1 - kd) \cdot \delta_n u} \cdot n_{z_0} \quad (24.2)$$

Within each subsystem the respective magnitudes σ_{1_n} and σ_{2_n} must be distributed in proportion with the prevailing sectoral employment ratios. Turning first to subsystem 2, the sectoral order of which has not been changed, the proportion equals the ratios in which labor is distributed over the three sectors in the original stationary equilibrium, so that

$$\sigma_{2_{n_z}} : \sigma_{2_{n_b}} : \sigma_{2_{n_a}} = 1 - kd : kd(1 - kd) : (kd)^2 \quad (24.3)$$

In establishing the analogous sector ratios for subsystem 1, we must remember that the labor force active in the innovating consumer-good sector has been reduced to

$$(1 - kd)(1 - \delta_n) \cdot n_{1_0}$$

Therefore we obtain[6]

$$\sigma_{1_{n_z}} : \sigma_{1_{n_b}} : \sigma_{1_{n_a}} = \frac{1}{1 - \delta_n(1 - kd)} [(1 - kd)(1 - \delta_n) : kd(1 - kd) : (kd)^2] \quad (24.4)$$

Knowing the manner in which the displaced part of the labor force will have to be distributed over the sectors of the two subsystems, we

---

[6] To obtain the new sector ratios as fractions of 1, the multiplicant

$$\frac{1}{(1 - kd)(1 - \delta_n) + kd} = \frac{1}{1 - \delta_n(1 - kd)}$$

must be added.

can proceed to ascertain the *additions to capital stock* in each sector, on the provision of which reemployment depends. This is easily done because we know for each sector the capital–labor ratio that must prevail in the new equilibrium. In fact, in five of the sectors (in all three sectors of subsystem 2 and in the two equipment-good sectors of subsystem 1), the original capital–labor ratio, *c*, remains unchanged. It changes only in the consumer-good sector of subsystem 1 to

$$c_z' = \frac{c_z}{1 - \delta_n}$$

The required addition to capital stock in each sector amounts then to the respective labor increment multiplied by the respective capital–labor ratio.

We illustrate the procedure on the critical consumer-good subsector in subsystem 1, in which the innovation has been carried through. From Equation 24.4, we know that the final addition to labor amounts to

$$\frac{(1 - kd)(1 - \delta_n)}{1 - (1 - kd) \cdot \delta_n} \cdot \sigma_{1_n}$$

or, in accord with Equation 24.1,

$$\sigma_{1_{n_z}} = \frac{(1 - kd)(1 - \delta_n) \cdot \delta_n u^2}{1 - (1 - kd) \cdot \delta_n u} \cdot n_{z_0}$$

Then the required addition to capital stock in the consumer-good sector of subsystem 1 (ΔF_{1_z}) amounts to

$$\Delta F_{1_z} = \frac{c_z(1 - kd) \cdot \delta_n u^2}{1 - (1 - kd) \cdot \delta_n u} \cdot n_{z_0}$$

We can translate this expression into our standard variables *k* and *d* by remembering that, in a stationary flow,[7]

$$n_z = (1 - kd)^2 \cdot o_0 \quad \text{and} \quad c = \frac{k}{1 - kd}$$

This yields

$$\Delta F_{1_z} = \frac{k(1 - kd)^2 \cdot \delta_n u^2}{1 - (1 - kd) \cdot \delta_n u} \cdot o_0$$

[7] See Chapter 4, Section III.

We need not follow up the structural adjustments leading to terminal equilibrium in detail. We deal here with a problem that is fully analogous to the problem posed by a once-over influx of labor supply. If we were to assume a steady sequence of labor-displacing innovations in the consumer-good sector (not a very realistic assumption), the adjustment process would be a perfect replica of the conditions analyzed earlier.[8] Nevertheless, so far as the structural processes are concerned, we can interpret the compensation process for this particular type of innovation as the traverse to an increased capital stock expanding under the impact of an excess supply of labor, irrespective of whether the labor increment originates outside or inside of the system.

II

When it comes to the motorial conditions for adjustment, this analogy holds only within limits. We can then no longer disregard the effect of the technological reduction of costs and its consequences for prices, profits, consumption, and investment.

In tracing these effects, we shall have to distinguish between three modalities. First (and this is the basis on which we have conducted our structural analysis), output on the part of the pioneering subsector 1 is kept constant with sales price unchanged. Second, in view of the quasimonopolistic position that the pioneering subsector holds at least temporarily, and assuming that the elasticity of demand for the improved output is above zero, subsector 1 can expand the improved output to the point of equality of the reduced marginal costs with marginal revenue, accompanied by a reduction in sales price. This will shift part of labor displacement to marginal firms in the pioneering industry and even to other consumer-good industries. Third, as the innovation generalizes over the entire pioneering industry, price falls to the level of the reduced average costs, with further output expansion which may, in extreme cases, shift the entire displacement effect to other industries. As a matter of fact, these three eventualities may well be regarded as successive stages on the way to terminal equilibrium. We shall now briefly examine them.

1. With output and sales price unchanged, the cost reduction is bound to turn into profit and, as we know from earlier considerations,[9] further developments depend on whether these technological profits will be hoarded, consumed, or saved and invested. If they are hoarded or consumed, they cannot induce a process of compensation. Under such

[8] See Chapter 14.
[9] See Chapter 8, Section II, and Chapter 15, Section II.

conditions, as is the case with an extrasystemic increment in labor supply, absorption depends on voluntary or forced saving or on the mechanism of involuntary saving, that is, on a general reduction of money wages, to provide the funds that, given appropriate expectations, will set the process of capital formation in motion.

If, however (again assuming appropriate expectations), the technological profits are saved, a second source of investment funds will be provided, speeding up the adjustment process. In fact, in this case we can also speak of "involuntary saving," because it is the former money wages of the displaced labor that turn into technological profits, and it is the vanishing of their demand for consumer goods that liberates part of the stock of equipment goods for self-augmentation. In other words, although the existence of technological profits extends the scope for capital formation, the mechanism thus set in motion does not differ from the one extensively discussed before under wage-induced profits.

2. The picture is quite different when we examine the second alternative, in which the pioneering firms are supposed to expand their output to the optimum size permitted by their temporary monopolistic position. Although the price of the improved output must fall, it is bound to stay high enough to yield technological profits above the level achieved under alternative 1. However, such expansion of output is feasible only if, first of all, the stock of secondary equipment in subsystem 1 is increased. We realize now the significance of alternative 1. Though under the given conditions, it does not offer maximum technological profits this maximum can be obtained only if the intermediary profits due to the reduced wage bill in the pioneering firms are saved and invested.

Expansion of the improved output is, of course, conditional on expansion of demand as a consequence of the fall in price. So long as the elasticity of demand is above unity, aggregate expenditure for the improved output rises above initial expenditure, which is equivalent to saying that demand for some unimproved output(s) must fall, with important consequences for the displacement effect.

Again it is essential to look at alternatives 1 and 2 as consecutive stages in the adjustment process. Initially the labor-displacing effect shows only in the pioneering firms. To the extent that the ensuing technological profits are invested – possibly supplemented by "wage profits" created by a general fall of wages throughout the system – part of the displaced labor force (with a high elasticity of demand, even all of it) will find reemployment in subsystem 1. It must be understood, however, that, far from being a short-period adjustment process, such reemployment can occur only *gradually* at the rate at which new secondary equipment is provided. Moreover, even in the extreme case when the entire originally displaced labor force can be absorbed again in subsystem 1, only part of it can return to the sector from which it was displaced, another part being required for the steady replacement of the addition to capital stock.

However, as was already indicated, an additional displacement problem arises whenever aggregate expenditure for the improved output increases and some demand is deflected from other industries. In the extreme case, displacement is entirely shifted to nonimproved industries, posing a compensation problem analogous with the one discussed in the context of alternative 1. Still, two important differences need to be pointed out. First, it is no longer true that the overall distribution ratio of the displaced labor is

$$\frac{(1 - \delta)}{1 - u} \cdot u$$

that is, the initial ratio between employment in the innovating subsector after displacement and employment in the rest of the consumer-good sector. With the expansion of output in the innovating sector under the influence of a high elasticity of demand, the numerator of the fraction is bound to increase and the denominator to decrease – to what extent can only be determined if the precise degree of demand elasticity is known. Second, displacement in unimproved industries sets free not only labor but the complementary capital stock in all three sectors. This "liberation" of additional capital stock, over and above that liberated as a result of the pressure of excess labor supply on money wages, is bound to facilitate compensation, always assuming suitable expectations.[10]

3. Turning finally to the third alternative, namely, the competitive generalization of the technological change that raises the improved output to the level of equality between average revenue and average costs, we shall find that all the building blocks for a solution have already been provided. Again such expansion of output can occur only step by step as capital formation increases. On the other hand, with the gradual disappearance of the technological profit as a consequence of the progressive fall in prices, the funds for the financing of capital formation are transferred to buyers of the improved output in the form of a rise in their real incomes.

As we saw earlier,[11] such real gains have played an important role in the discussion on compensation, and even today are sometimes ad-

---

[10] There is no need to spell out here the nature of suitable expectations because they are identical with the setup as detailed in Chapter 15, Section II.

[11] See Chapter 23, Section III.

duced as an argument in favor of a *short-term automatism* assuring reemployment of the displaced. It should by now be clear that J. S. Mill was right in asserting that demand for commodities is "a totally different thing from demand for labor." In other words, assuming perfect mobility of all factors as Mill does, the additional expenditures on consumer goods on the part of the beneficiaries of the cheapened output will only compensate for the lack of demand on the part of the displaced, without reestablishing the larger economic circuit based on their reemployment. Only to the extent that the addition to consumers' purchasing power will be saved and invested, during an interval long enough to build new working places for the displaced, will compensation be achieved. This certainly represents neither an automatic nor a short-period mechanism.

III

What difference does it make if a pure labor-displacing device is introduced in some industry producing *secondary equipment,* such as shoe machines, instead of in the industry producing the final consumer good, shoes?

We again subdivide the system into two subsystems. Subsystem 1 now contains not only the innovating part of the shoe machine industry as subsector 1 but also that part of the primary equipment-good sector which assures replacement of the capital-stock in subsector 1 and, in addition, the entire shoe industry, which, at some stage in the adjustment process, will be affected by the price reduction of its input of shoe machines. The complement is subsystem 2 containing the remainder of the aggregate system.

By applying the same symbols as used in Section I, we can express the magnitude of labor displaced in subsector 1 as $\delta \cdot u \cdot n_b$, a magnitude that must again be distributed over the entire system in the proportions as determined by the respective sector ratios prevailing in the two subsystems. To do so, the capital stocks in all subsectors must be increased in analogy with the structural and motorial processes as described for the same type of innovation taking place in the consumer-good sector.

The one and only difference concerns the secondary effect of the innovation occurring in the production of secondary equipment on prices and output in the related part of the consumer-good sector. What this difference amounts to can best be seen if we again examine the three modalities discussed in Sector II. These modalities were shown to be consecutive steps in the traverse to a new equilibrium.

The initial impact of the innovation is confined to labor displacement and the corresponding emergence of technological profits in subsector 1 of Sector Ib. Because initially the capital stock is fixed, output of shoe machines cannot increase and prices remain at the original level. In other words, for the time being there is no secondary impact on the consumer-good sector.

This is bound to change to the extent to which technological and wage profits are invested in additions to the equipment stock operating in subsector 1 of Sector Ib. Now output of shoe machines can increase and prices can fall, the limits of either movement again being determined by the prevailing elasticity of demand. But demand for what? Obviously the elasticity of demand on the part of the users of shoe machines is determined by the elasticity of demand for their own output, namely, shoes. Thus, it is again demand for the output of the consumer-good sector of subsystem 1 that determines the absorption ratio between the two subsystems.

With the last step, the generalization of the innovation in subsector 1, we approach terminal equilibrium. Prices in that subsector and the related consumer-good subsector have fallen in line with the cost reduction of secondary equipment, and we encounter the same situation as described previously.[12] The technological profits have been transformed into additional purchasing power on the part of the buyers of the cheapened output, and compensation is conditional on the temporary saving and investing of consumers' gains.

IV

Quite a different picture emerges if the pure labor-displacing innovation occurs in the *primary equipment*-good sector. Because the output of this sector is physically identical with its capital input, there is only one industry to consider, and the secondary impact of the innovation affects the entire system, including the primary equipment-good sector itself. In other words, such an improvement in the sector of primary machinery reduces prices of equipment input in both equipment-good sectors. As a consequence, prices for all types of secondary equipment can be reduced, although physically nothing has changed in the secondary equipment-good sector. This, in turn, will reduce the prices of capital input in the entire consumer-good sector, with a corresponding fall of prices of consumer goods.

Of course, this describes the required structure in terminal equilibrium, a state of affairs that will be reached only gradually through

[12] See Section II, 3.

the successive steps by now known to us, starting with capital formation in the primary equipment-good sector. The workers initially displaced in that sector will have to be distributed over all three sectors in accord with the respective additions to capital stock. These additions themselves and, thus, the ultimate distribution of the displaced over sectors and industries will depend on the elasticity of consumers' demand for the entire range of consumer-good output.

For the sake of simplicity, our analysis has been conducted within the framework of a stationary process. The steady increase of extra-systemic labor supply, which characterizes dynamic equilibrium and which accompanies the structural adjustment processes following the technological change, has been disregarded. We saw, however, that these latter adjustment processes can themselves be interpreted as conditions for the absorption of a labor increment, even if its source is now intrasystemic. So what we are dealing with in a dynamic framework is a steady increase in labor supply as analyzed in Chapter 9, superimposed by a once-over increase in labor supply – a limiting case of our general analysis of a steady change in labor supply, as studied in Chapters 14 and 15.[13]

[13] To be precise, what we are concerned with here is the Primary Model, as analyzed in Chapter 14, Sections I–IV. It has been construed under the assumption that capital formation as induced by a change in the rate of growth of labor supply can be analyzed while bracketing the effect that successive batches of additional labor have on the adjustment process – a true replica of the structural movements required to absorb a once-over increase. What in the earlier context served the didactic purpose of simplification, now turns out to be an appropriate model of the compensation process following technological unemployment. If we recall the various impediments to a successful traverse, especially those of a motorial nature as revealed by the model, we can certainly not take compensation for granted.

25

Pure capital-displacing innovations

I

Superficially considered, pure capital-displacing innovations appear as the reverse of pure labor-displacing innovations. Closer inspection, however, reveals fundamental differences. They begin with the standard of measurement applicable to displaced capital as compared with displaced labor. As we saw, the latter lends itself to the standard of homogeneous wage units that measure physically homogeneous labor units. On the other hand, it is difficult to imagine empirical cases in which capital-displacing innovations displace part of a homogeneous set of machines, while the remaining machines continue to operate in physically unchanged form. The normal case is a replacement of the original type of machinery in use by a new type, representing a smaller number of wage units, yet being capable of producing, with the original labor input, the same output as initially but at lower unit costs. In other words, a process of "capital transmutation"[1] must precede the actual introduction of a typical capital-displacing innovation.

Fortunately, one major obstacle, which stands in the way of speedy transmutation when a stream of neutral innovation is to be absorbed, namely, the need to transmute the entire stock in one period of production, is absent in the present case. Current amortization of the original capital stock provides the funds with the help of which the original stock can be *gradually* transmuted into the new one. This is at least so if the innovation occurs in the consumer-good sector. Investible funds of the same origin are available also when the innovation occurs in one of the equipment-good sectors. However, the new primary capital stock is then the result of a combined process of transmutation and self-augmentation.

When we now turn to the question of compensation, we encounter a paradox. We saw that in the case of labor-displacing innovations, the major concern is the reabsorption of the displaced labor in productive

---

[1] See Chapter 22, Section I. The change occurring is a typical case of "old ways" producing a "novelty."

activity. By contrast, the discarded machinery is not supposed to become active again but drops out of the economic circuit.[2] In other words, there is displacement of a factor but no problem of compensation.

On the other hand, capital-displacing innovations create a compensation problem for indirectly displaced *labor*. In analogy with what we discussed in the last chapter, this is the case when the lower price, owing to lower costs of the improved output, eliminates output in some marginal firms of the same or some other industry. An analogous effect on capital was noticed arising from labor-displacing innovations without, however, creating a compensation problem, for the reason just mentioned. Rather, simultaneous capital displacement in that case facilitates the reabsorption of the displaced labor – an effect which, as we shall see, operates *a fortiori* in the present case when capital displacement is the initial change.

However, there is another and generally valid reason for labor displacement as a consequence of pure capital displacement. It arises from the fact that, in contrast with labor, real capital is not only an input but also an output. Therefore, not only does capital displacement in one or both of the equipment-good sectors reduce prices of capital input and commodity output in the consumer-good sector, but capital displacement in the consumer-good sector is bound to reduce capital input and output in both equipment-good sectors. As a consequence we have there both capital and labor displacement – and as to the latter, there is now also a compensation problem – although no innovation has occurred in the equipment-good sectors. Because this is the most interesting case and the one in which both the similarities and the differences between capital-displacing and labor-displacing innovations stand out most clearly, we shall examine it more closely.

II

The early phases of the adjustment process following capital displacement in the consumer-good sector and, consequently, capital and labor displacements in the related equipment-good sectors, are a perfect replica of what we have encountered in the corresponding case of pure labor displacement. We again subdivide the total system into subsystems 1 and 2 at the ratio $u/(1 - u)$, where u represents the part in which the capital-saving innovation occurs. The magnitude of labor displaced in the two equipment-good sectors of subsystem 1 amounts

[2] Certain empirical cases in which discarded machinery is put to productive use again, for example, under conditions of war or of a strong boom, do not belong on the level of analysis along which our inquiry moves.

then to $\delta_n u \cdot n_{(a+b)_0}$. By again applying the reasoning that guided us in the earlier case,[3] we obtain for the magnitude of displaced labor reemployed in subsystem 1

$$\eta_{1_n} = \frac{\delta_n u^2 (1 - kd \cdot \delta_n)}{1 - kd \cdot \delta_n u} \cdot n_{(a+b)_0} \qquad (25.1)$$

and, correspondingly, for subsystem 2

$$\eta_{2_n} = \frac{\delta_n u (1 - u)}{1 - kd \cdot \delta_n u} \cdot n_{(a+b)_0} \qquad (25.2)$$

Within each subsystem, the respective quantities η_{1_n} and η_{2_n} must again be distributed in proportion with the prevailing sectoral employment ratios. So far as subsystem 2 is concerned, these are once more the ratios of stationary equilibrium. In subsystem 1 these ratios change as a consequence of the employment effect that capital displacement in the consumer-good sector has in the two equipment-good sectors. In Sector Ib employment falls to

$$kd(1 - kd)(1 - \delta_n) \cdot \eta_{1_0}$$

whereas in Sector Ia it is reduced to

$$(kd)^2 (1 - \delta_n) \cdot \eta_{1_0}$$

This yields the new sectoral employment ratios[4]

$$\eta_{1_{n_x}} : \eta_{1_{n_b}} : \eta_{1_{n_a}} = \frac{1}{1 - kd \cdot \delta_n} \lfloor (1 - kd) : kd(1 - kd)(1 - \delta_n) : (kd)^2 (1 - \delta_n) \rfloor$$

In determining the *additions to capital stock* on which reemployment of the displaced workers depends, we also can make use of the procedure elaborated in the context of pure labor displacement. As we remember, the size of these additions can be calculated as the product of the respective additions to prospective employment multiplied with the respective capital–labor ratios. Again the capital–labor ratios remain unchanged in all sectors of subsystem 2 and in the two equipment-good sectors of subsystem 1. In the consumer-good sector of subsystem 1, capital displacement reduces the capital–labor ratio c' to $c_z \cdot (1 - \delta_n)$.[5]

At this point the similarity between the structural adjustment of

---

[3] See Chapter 24, Section I.
[4] See Chapter 24, footnote 6.
[5] In the present context the ratio of fixed-capital displaced as a consequence of the innovation equals the ratio of *labor* displaced as a secondary effect of the initial capital displacement, so that we can continue using symbol δ_n in our formulas.

a pure labor-displacing with a pure capital-displacing innovation ceases. In the labor-displacing case, the required additions to capital stock in every sector had to be newly built, existing capacity in all equipment-good sectors being fully utilized. Now, owing to the initial act of capital displacement, we are confronted with idle capacity in both equipment-good sectors of subsystem 1. Furthermore, the question arises whether this capacity, which is immediately available without any capital formation, is sufficient to provide the additions to capital stock in both subsystems necessary for the absorption of the displaced labor.

To provide a generally valid answer, we must express the size of the required addition to capital stock and the immediately available capacity for producing that stock in symbolic terms. This is easily done for the *available stock of primary equipment in subsystem 1* $[F_{(a+b)}\text{av}]$. It equals the magnitude of labor displaced as a secondary effect of capital displacement, multiplied by the unchanged capital-labor ratio c, that is,

$$F_{(a+b)} \text{ av} = c \cdot u \delta_n n_{(a+b)_0}$$

or, by again substituting $k/(1 - kd)$ for c and $kd(1 - kd) \cdot o_0$ for $n_{(a+b)}$

$$F_{(a+b)} \text{ av} = k^2 d \cdot u \delta_n \cdot o_0 \qquad (25.3)$$

Determination of $F_{(a+b)}$ requ, that is, the *aggregate addition to primary capital stock required for compensation*, is more complex. It consists of two parts. For the addition to subsystem 2 we obtain

$$F(2)_{(a+b)} \text{ requ} = c \cdot kd \cdot \eta_{2_n}$$

Correspondingly for the addition to subsystem 1

$$F(1)_{(a+b)} \text{ requ} = c \cdot kd \cdot \frac{1 - \delta_n}{1 - kd \cdot \delta_n} \cdot \eta_{1_n}$$

By adding the two equations and substituting $k/(1 - kd)$ for c, we obtain

$$F_{(a+b)} \text{ requ} = \frac{k^2 d}{1 - kd} \left[\eta_{2n} + \frac{\eta_{1_n}(1 - \delta_n)}{1 - kd \cdot \delta_n} \right] \qquad (25.4)$$

In order to facilitate comparison with Equation 25.3, we transform Equation 25.4 into a multiple of o_0. This yields first

$$F_{(a+b)} \text{ requ} = \frac{k^2 d}{1 - kd} \left\{ \frac{\eta_{1_n} + \eta_{2_n} - \delta[kd \cdot \eta_{2_n} + \eta_{1_n}]}{1 - kd \cdot \delta_n} \right\}$$

$$= \frac{k^2 d}{1 - kd} \frac{(1 - u\delta_n) \cdot u \delta_n (1 - kd \cdot \delta_n)}{(1 - kd \cdot \delta_n)(1 - kd \cdot \delta_n u)} \cdot n_{(a+b)_0}$$

By substituting again $kd(1 - kd) \cdot o_0$ for $n_{(a+b)0}$, we finally obtain

$$F_{(a+b)} \text{ requ} = \frac{k^3 d^2}{1 - kd} \cdot \frac{(1 - u\delta_n) \cdot u\delta_n}{1 - kdu \cdot \delta_n} \cdot o_0 \qquad (25.4.1)$$

and the relationship between the available and the required capacity amounts to

$$\frac{F_{(a+b)} \text{ av}}{F_{(a+b)} \text{ requ}} = \frac{1 - kd \cdot u\delta_n}{kd(1 - u \cdot \delta_n)} \qquad (25.5)$$

Because kd is always smaller than 1, the expression (25.5) must exceed 1. In other words, capital displacement leads to the consequence that capacity in the equipment-good sectors made available through the displacement of capital must always be larger than the capacity required for providing the additional working places in which the displaced workers can be reemployed. No process of capital formation needs to intervene and given the appropriate expectations, compensation is concomitant with the current process of production.

What nevertheless complicates equilibrium is the fact that the excess of available capacity in the equipment-good industries of subsystem 1 represents a secondary displacement of capital. In contrast with the capital stock initially discarded as a consequence of the innovation, this secondary displacement concerns equipment goods of unaltered technical efficiency for which, however, there is no productive use within a stationary framework.

Nor will transition to dynamic equilibrium, which is our true frame of reference, alleviate the situation. True, there we encounter from period to period a steady increment of labor supply. However, as was shown earlier,[6] the structure of production of a system moving in dynamic equilibrium is arranged in such a manner that all additions to capital stock required for the absorption of the steady labor increment are currently produced. A collectivist system might "mothball" the idle equipment stock for unforeseeable contingencies. In a market system this excess stock can find employment only if capital displacement is not "pure," but is combined with labor displacement, thus creating a primary compensation problem in the solution of which the displaced capital stock can be profitably utilized.

III

Apart from the combination of transmutation and self-augmentation for the sake of providing the new type of primary equipment,[7] pure

[6] See Chapter 9, Section I.
[7] See Section I.

capital displacement in the sector producing *secondary equipment* does not pose any new problem. It resembles the situation prevailing when capital displacement occurs in the consumer-good sector, but with the modification that the secondary labor displacement is confined to the sector producing primary equipment and, thus, is proportionally smaller. However, we again end up with some excess capacity of primary equipment.

The secondary displacement effect dwindles with pure capital displacement occurring in the sector producing *primary equipment*. What effect still shows is connected with the current self-reproduction of primary equipment. According to our basic assumption the capital-displacing innovation makes it possible to produce the same output as in the original state with the original labor force. However, capital displacement in producing primary equipment reduces the replacement requirements in that sector and, therefore, makes it necessary to reduce output there *below* the original level, thus creating some labor displacement accompanied by some additional capital displacement. The relative magnitudes of the two displacements again point to some terminal excess capacity of primary equipment. Yet, the absolute magnitudes are quite small when compared with the other two cases of capital displacement, so that capital displacement in the primary equipment-good sector comes closest to rapid achievement of terminal equilibrium.

As in the analysis of pure labor-displacing innovations and for the same reasons, we have not explicitly spelled out any modifications that arise in a dynamic framework, nor the motorial conditions for a successful traverse. Both again coincide with the results obtained in Chapters 14 and 15.[8]

[8] See also Chapter 24, footnote 13.

26

Some comments on combined changes in the input of labor and capital

Pure labor-displacing and pure capital-displacing innovations supply us with the basic structural models from which the more complex and more realistic cases of combined changes in the input of labor and capital can be derived.

1. The most important case, which is also the center of Marx's macrodynamics, is represented by *capital-attracting, labor-displacing* innovations. So far as the traverse from the initial impact to the terminal equilibrium is concerned, this category presents the same problems that we discussed extensively under Pure Labor-Displacing Innovations. However, its capital-attracting nature requires an initial process of net capital formation combined with the gradual transmutation of the initial capital stock, before the innovational impact can even get under way. Again, in analogy with pure capital-displacing innovations, current amortization sums provide some of the funds required for transmutation. It depends on the degree of capital intensification by how much these amortization funds fall short of the total required for the necessary capital formation. If no additional voluntary or forced savings are provided, this process of the gradual transmutation of the old into the new capital stock will be long drawn out.

2. We find quite a different situation when we turn to *capital-displacing, labor-attracting* innovations. The capital-displacing effects and the requirements for their accommodation are similar to those studied under Pure Capital-Displacing Innovations. A new issue arises however, from the need to increase labor input per unit of output.

At first sight it looks as if the problem could be solved within an equilibrium framework only by introducing quite unrealistic assumptions, such as a prior labor-displacing innovation creating an excess supply of labor for which the subsequent labor-attracting innovation might act as welcome compensation. Or, because labor cannot be treated as an output, in contrast with capital, must we fall back on the still more fanciful notion that timely changes in the rates of population increase or of labor participation will close the gap?

In asking this question we imply that capital-displacing, labor-attracting innovations raise the system's employment in the aggregate. Fortunately, it can be demonstrated that this is not so because the act of capital displacement is bound, as a secondary effect, to displace more labor in the equipment-good sectors than is required for the profitable operation of such an innovation in the consumer-good sector.[1]

To see this we must realize that the displacement ratio of capital and the attraction ratio of labor are by no means independent variables. Because it is a prime condition for the introduction of any type of technological progress that unit costs of output be reduced, the addition to labor input in terms of wage units per unit of output must be smaller than the reduction of capital measured in the same terms. Thus, given the capital displacement ratio δ_f, we can determine the upper limit below which the addition to labor must remain if the innovation is to improve productivity. This upper limit amounts to the sum of original inputs of capital and labor (equal to the value of output) minus the initial input of labor minus the reduced capital input.

Arguing again in a stationary context, and denoting this upper limit by $\Delta n_z(\max)$, we obtain for such an innovation when introduced into the consumer-good sector

$$\Delta n_z (\max) = z_0 - (1 - kd)z_0 - kd(1 - \delta_f)z_0$$

or, when expressed in terms of the original aggregate output o_0,

$$\Delta n_z (\max) = (1 - kd) \cdot kd \cdot \delta_f \cdot o_0 \tag{26.1}$$

The innovation is technically feasible if the mechanism of capital displacement indirectly displaces labor in the equipment-good industries up to the maximum amount as determined by Equation 26.1. Taking both equipment-good sectors together, we obtain for the magnitude of labor displaced the identical amount of

$$(1 - kd) \cdot kd \cdot \delta_f \cdot o_0$$

Because for reasons of profitability the *actual* amount of labor required must be smaller than the *maximum*, as shown in Equation 26.1, not only can this additional working force be provided through shifts within the system, but there will always arise some excess supply of labor, to be dealt with in accord with our earlier discussion.

---

[1] *Mutatis mutandis* the proposition holds equally for capital-displacing, labor-attracting innovations in one of the equipment-good sectors.

3. Little needs be added concerning the structural analysis of combined *labor- and capital-displacing innovations*. It proceeds along the lines described for labor- and capital-displacing innovations appearing in isolation. The simultaneous displacement of capital obviously facilitates the compensation of labor displacement. However, a smooth traverse dispensing with new capital formation is possible only if the size of the displacement ratio of capital relative to the size of the displacement ratio of labor corresponds to the new capital–labor ratio in the innovating sector.

Again the motorial requirements of adjustment in all three cases are by now familiar problems to be solved in the manner discussed earlier. For the same reason we have not given extensive consideration to the modifications that the structural processes might undergo in a *collectivist system*. Within the limits previously delineated[2] cannibalization of the existing capital stock can serve as a substitute for capital formation, thus accelerating compensation. At the same time, savings and investment ratios can be brought in line with the amount of capital formation actually required and also conversely. This is an advantage that would facilitate the initial act of capital formation required for the actualization of capital-attracting innovations. Finally, as was already indicated, the current process of production can always be insulated from the effects of excess capacity.

[2] See Chapter 16.

27

Technical progress and diminishing returns

Up to this point we have strictly adhered to the methodological principle enunciated at the beginning of our deliberations about technical progress.[1] We have treated innovations as independent variables, the operation of which is supposed to distort a preexisting dynamic equilibrium. Our task has been to determine the responses of the system suitable to adjust it to the technological stimulus. Now we are going to change the focus of our investigation by treating innovations themselves as part of the *response* of the system – a device for counteracting the effect of diminishing returns in the area of natural resources and for restoring the initial per capita output.

This change in focus implies, first of all, a *specification of the macro-goal* which, in our previous analyses, served as the guidepost for all adjustment processes. It is no longer a process of production moving in dynamic equilibrium generally, but a process that achieves and maintains a *preordained level of per capita output of consumer goods*. Second, deviations from this stipulated level in the downward direction are supposed to induce innovations sufficiently productive to compensate for any decline of returns. Such inducement is conditional on the operation of a motorial mechanism, that is, on the presence of behavioral and motivational patterns that will assure innovating activity of the right size at the right time. Third, this motorial mechanism can be set in motion only if, at the outset, a set of blueprints (inventions) is available from which one or more goal-adequate ones can be chosen as innovations. To account for the availability, at the required moment, of such a catalog would involve us in a theory of invention, a little-explored topic that lies beyond the range of our investigation. For this reason we shall simply stipulate that the blueprints are freely available and can be embodied in new productive processes without delay.

In discussing earlier the effect of diminishing returns in the field of natural resources on the structure of production, we distinguished between two alternatives. In one instance, taking mining as prototype, it is assumed that returns diminish from period to period even under

[1] See Chapter 21, Section I.

stationary conditions when the quantity of ore to be obtained remains constant over time. The alternative situation prevails when it is only *growth*, that is, the expansion of output, that gives rise to falling returns, the latter affecting the incremental rather than the total output – a notion that underlies Ricardo's conception of land. To simplify exposition, we shall concentrate on the first alternative, but also assuming a steady period increase of labor supply by α.

I

Before embarking on the structural analysis of the manner in which innovations are capable of counteracting the decline in output owing to diminishing returns of natural resources, we are going to catalog the problems encountered in such an analysis. First of all, as already indicated, our present investigation can be seen as a continuation of our earlier study of the Dynamics of Diminishing Returns.[2] The results obtained there concerning the effect of diminishing returns on the output of consumer goods and equipment goods, respectively, will be our starting point in ascertaining the rise in productivity, π, required for restoring the initial per capita output. The combination of a three-sector and a two-stage model, which served us then, will remain the framework for our analysis, and we shall use the notation introduced there to the extent that the same variables occur in the present context.

One of the main findings of our earlier inquiry concerned the difference between the initial impact and the terminal effect of diminishing returns. By shifting capital and labor from the secondary to the primary stage where the actual fall in return occurs, it is possible to mitigate the initial impact and to arrive at a level of terminal output that lies somewhere between the original and the lowest level to which the initial impact reduces output temporarily. It stands to reason that the required magnitude of the offsetting π varies with the level of output to which the system has been restored at the moment when the innovation is introduced. Because after the initial impact output rises again until the terminal level is reached, it can be said that the required *size* of the productivity increase is inversely related to the *timing* of the innovation. To the extent that smaller increases in productivity are easier to achieve than larger ones, one might draw the conclusion that it will always be advantageous to postpone the balancing innovation until the initial fall in output has been partly offset by the resource shift. We shall see that this conclusion is not warranted.

Another set of problems is connected with the *location* of the in-

---

[2] See Chapter 19.

novation in the hierarchy of stages. The obvious place seems to be the primary stage where the distorting change occurs. The purpose of the new technology is then to restore the original quantity of the primary output of working-capital goods (wheat, ore) by a different combination of the inputs of labor, capital, and natural resources. However, we must remember that, under the aspect of restoring per capita output, we are interested in the output of *finished* goods rather than of any intermediate working-capital good. Therefore an innovation applied somewhere in the later stages of production, aggregated in our model into one secondary stage, will be equally effective if it succeeds in extracting from the reduced output of the primary stage a finished output of the original size, for example, by reducing "waste" in manufacturing. We are then dealing with innovations that reduce the quantity of working-capital goods required, possibly in conjunction with reducing the input of labor and/or capital. For reasons of analytical economy, we have so far excluded this type of innovation from our investigation.[3] In the present context it seems necessary to consider it.

Finally, the question arises of the *types* of innovations best suited for offsetting diminishing returns. Even disregarding the possible role of working capital, we are now confronted with three factors of production – labor, fixed capital, and natural resources – each one of which, singly or in varying combinations, can be the subject of a technological change. By excluding those cases that do not yield a reduction in unit costs, we still obtain no less than 19 varieties of possible changes in the primary stage. It is obviously beyond the endurance of the writer and the reader to follow up all these combinations. We shall see, however, that other criteria, especially timing, will help us in greatly limiting the practically useful range.

II

We begin by studying the conditions for technological balancing of diminishing returns in the *consumer-good sector*. Our first problem is to determine the required size of π in relation to the fall in returns. As before[4] we denote the two relevant *stages* of production by superscripts $'$ and $''$, and successive *periods* of production by subscripts $0, 1, 2, \ldots$ The *rate of return* that prevails in any period is again symbolized as $\bar{r}_0, \bar{r}_1, \bar{r}_2, \ldots$, the subscripts referring to the period in which the prevailing rate of return was first attained. If, for example, the rate of return falls from $\bar{r}_0$ in Period 0 to $\bar{r}_1$ in Period 1, it is possible, and is actually

[3] See Chapter 21, Section I.
[4] See Chapter 19, Section II,2.

assumed in our subsequent examples, that this rate $\bar{r}_1$ persists over a number of adjustment periods. As to the size of $\bar{r}$ it is again stipulated that $\bar{r}_0 = 1$ and $0 < \bar{r}_1, \bar{r}_2, \ldots < 1$.

1. It was already stated that the required value of π differs according to whether the balancing innovation in Stage 1 is introduced immediately after the rate of return has fallen there or whether such introduction is postponed until a shift of resources from Stage 2 to Stage 1 has again raised output in Stage 1 and, subsequently, in Stage 2 above the lowest level brought about by the initial impact. This entails a postponement by two periods according to the setup of our model for diminishing returns.[5] Assuming that returns fall from $\bar{r}_0$ in Period 0 to $\bar{r}_1$ in Period 1, output z_0' in the primary stage rises only to

$$(1 + \alpha) \cdot \bar{r}_1 \cdot z_0'$$

instead of $(1 + \alpha) \cdot z_0'$.

If this reduction is to be offset by a simultaneous innovation achieving output in Stage 1 equal to $(1 + \alpha)z_0'$ (Case I), we obtain for the required rate of improvement

$$\pi_{\text{I}} = \frac{(1 + \alpha)z_0' - z_1'}{z_1'} = \frac{(1 + \alpha)z_0' - (1 + \alpha)\bar{r}_1 \cdot z_0'}{(1 + \alpha)\bar{r}_1 \cdot z_0'} = \frac{1 - \bar{r}_1}{\bar{r}_1} \quad (27.1)$$

On the other hand, if the innovation is postponed for two periods (Case II), we obtain

$$\pi_{\text{II}} = \frac{(1 + \alpha)^2 z_0' - z_2'}{z_2'} = \frac{(1 + \alpha)^2 - (1 + \alpha)^2/[h(1 - \bar{r}_1) + \bar{r}_1]}{[(1 + \alpha)^2 \cdot \bar{r}_1]/[h(1 - \bar{r}_1) + \bar{r}_1]}$$

$$= \frac{h(1 - \bar{r}_1) + \bar{r}_1}{\bar{r}_1} \quad (27.2)$$

It should be added that Equation 27.2 also measures π_{III}, that, is, the rise in productivity required if the innovation occurs in Stage 2 with the aim of balancing the reduction in working-capital goods as a consequence of a permanent fall of output in Stage 1.

2. Our next issue concerns the choice of the *types of innovation best suited for Case I*, that is, when the fall in returns is simultaneously to be offset by technological progress in Stage 1. We must remember that we study our problem in a dynamic context in which labor supply steadily increases from period to period, and with it the demand for

---

[5] See Chapter 19, Section II. For a numerical illustration, see again the appendix to Chapter 19.

primary output. Therefore, unless the innovation is ready for operation at the end of Period 1, another labor increment enters the system and a new complication arises.

Now there are only two types of innovation that do not require installation time: pure labor- and pure land-displacing technological improvements. Contrariwise, whenever the physical capital stock needs changing, be it a capital-displacing or a capital-attracting change, a process of capital construction must be initiated, which is likely to extend over several periods of production. Furthermore, even for the two innovations that do not require adjustment time, only land-saving improvements spare the system further complications, because it can be assumed that the discarded areas are permanently taken out of circulation. As we know, this is not the case with displaced labor, the compensation of which requires capital formation along the lines discussed in earlier chapters.

3. What about *Case II* in which the innovation is postponed until a shift of resources from Stage 2 to Stage 1 has partly restored the initial level of output? Because the stage ratio of outputs, h,[6] must be smaller than 1, therefore π_{II} is smaller than π_I, although π_{II} takes into account the rise in primary output made necessary by the influx of additional labor over two periods. Thus, under the aspect of economizing investment in new technology, especially if the available innovations should be capital-attracting, Case II appears at first sight as the preferable alternative.

Closer examination shows that this is true only for a very special type of innovation. Any rise in productivity in accord with π_{II} is supposed to raise output in the primary stage in Period 3 to the initial level increased in proportion with the labor influx over two periods. Consequently, working-capital goods in the secondary stage, which coincide in our aggregated model with the output of the primary stage, must increase in the same proportion, requiring for their processing into finished output additional labor and capital. Now, the assumed shift of resources in Period 2 from Stage 2 to Stage 1 in combination with the innovation permanently alters the stage ratio of inputs in favor of Stage 1. Therefore Stage 2 lacks the active factors necessary to transform the increment of working capital into finished output, unless the innovation itself provides the required resources by displacing labor and capital in the right amounts, in this way restoring the original stage ratio of inputs. Thus any innovational type other than a combined labor- and capital-displacing device is incapable of offsetting the fall in returns under the conditions of Case II, if we

[6] See Chapter 19, Section II.

disregard the analytically uninteresting possibility that the resources complementary with the increment in working capital are supplied extrasystemically. In practical terms, postponing the balancing innovation beyond the moment of the immediate impact of diminishing returns holds little promise of success.

4. This is at least true so long as the innovation is located in Stage 1, serving the purpose of restoring the primary working-capital output to its original level. The situation changes under the conditions of *Case III*. There the innovation restores only the original level of *finished* output (always increased in proportion with the labor influx during the interval) on the basis of a lower level of working-capital output as brought about by the fall in returns. Any innovation that succeeds in extracting from this lower working-capital input the original level of finished output without requiring more labor and/or capital than the prior shift of resources to Stage 1 has left in Stage 2, will achieve the goal. The ideal condition is a pure working-capital-reducing device, which leaves the input of labor and capital unchanged. If the innovation is, besides, labor-displacing and/or capital-displacing, additional adjustments will become necessary. If it is either capital- or labor-increasing the same obstacles to a solution will prevail as have been described in the preceding paragraph 3.

Only in passing it should be added that Case III can be modified in such a manner that the innovation concerning more productive use of working-capital goods might be introduced under the immediate impact of the fall of returns, that is, before a shift of resources from Stage 2 to Stage 1 compensates at least partly for this fall. Because the quantity of working-capital goods available for processing in Stage 2 is now smaller than in the prior version of Case III, a larger increase in productivity will be required to offset the fall in returns. In other words, whereas formerly π_{II} measured the necessary rise in productivity, now the larger π_I comes into play. On practical grounds it appears that the limits for reducing working-capital input are narrow, so that the relevance of this modified version of Case III is small.

A word needs be added about offsetting diminishing returns in one or both of the equipment-good sectors. We remember that when we studied the Dynamics of Diminishing Returns in isolation, considerable complications arose in this instance because of the secondary repercussions of such a change in an equipment-good sector on inputs and outputs in the consumer-good sector.[7] No such repercussions arise in the present context if the fall in returns is offset by a simultaneous

[7] See Chapter 19, Section IV.

innovation – Case I. In this instance the results obtained in studying the effect in the consumer-good sector have full validity.

III

We must now take up the problem that distinguishes the focus of the present investigation from the instrumental analysis of the other innovational issues discussed. It concerns the fact that, in the present context, technological progress is treated as a dependent variable or, more precisely, as a structural requirement for attaining the goal of constancy of per capita output. What mechanism then induces the suitable innovational change?

In the framework of a free market system this can only be the price mechanism. Indeed, under the impact of diminishing returns, its signals are unmistakable. It is intuitively clear that a reduction of primary output with inputs remaining unchanged amounts to an increase in unit costs to be followed by a rise in unit price. Besides restoring the original output quantity, it is the purpose of the balancing innovation to counteract this price rise, and it is, therefore, of interest to find a general expression for this process.

We illustrate the procedure on the conditions prevailing in Case I, in which the fall in return in primary output is supposed to induce at once the offsetting innovation.[8] All we need then is to establish p_1', the price of primary output in Period 1 relative to p_0', its price in Period 0.

Generally speaking, we have $p = z_v/z_q$, where z_v refers to the value or price sum, and z_q to the quantity of output. As compared with Period 0, the quantity of output increases in Period 1 in proportion with the increment α of labor supply but decreases in proportion with the fall in returns to the level r_1. Thus we obtain

$$z_{q_1}' = (1 + \alpha) \cdot \bar{r}_1 \cdot z_{q_0}'$$

The price sum of this output, on the other hand, lies above the original price sum by the addition of costing inputs in proportion to increment α, that is

$$z_{v_1}' = (1 + \alpha) z_{v_0}'$$

Thus we obtain

$$p_1' = \frac{1 + \alpha}{(1 + \alpha) \cdot \bar{r}_1} \cdot p_0' = \frac{1}{\bar{r}_1} \cdot p_0' \tag{27.3}$$

[8] See Section II.

Obviously for $\bar{r}_1 < 1$, p_1' must exceed p_0'. The same result is obtained for the analogous determination of p_1' in Case II and of p_2'' in Case III.

Given the extremum principle as action directive, the rise in unit prices of primary or secondary output, respectively, will induce the introduction of a balancing innovation if the prospective innovators hold suitable expectations over an appropriate time span. The latter condition varies according to the type of innovation intended. With pure land-saving or pure labor-saving innovations, all that is required is that the elasticity of price expectations be positive; that is, prices must be expected to stay above the original level so as to make the innovation profitable. At the same time it is significant that the time horizon over which the innovator plans may be arbitrarily short, because by reemploying the displaced labor or by putting the abandoned land back into utilization, the previous technological organization can at any time be restored without loss.

This is not so whenever the innovation requires a physical change in the capital stock, be it capital-displacing or -attracting. In this case, positive elasticity of price expectation will induce innovational activity only if the expectational horizon covers the entire time span of capital formation or capital transmutation. On the other hand, as is true of all types of innovations, no such motorial problems are likely to arise in a collectivist system.

IV

In conclusion it might be pointed out that, if the fall in return of natural resources is offset through land-displacing innovations, this approximates the smooth expansion path that is conventionally attributed to the operation of neutral innovations. Such land-displacing innovations maintain steady increments in input and output in accord with the steady growth rate of labor supply, without any secondary distortions that labor-displacing or capital-displacing innovations applied for the same purpose could bring about.

However, we must not take leave of the issue of relating technical progress to diminishing returns of natural resources without briefly commenting on some recent attempts at linking innovations with diminishing returns to Capital.[9]

[9] See, in particular, the writings of W. Fellner, *Trends and Cycles in Economic Activity*, New York, 1956, especially pp. 220–23, and "Does the Market Direct the Relative Factor-Saving Effects of Technological Progress?" in *The Rate and Direction of Inventive Activity*, Princeton, 1962, pp. 171–88. Also Henry J. Bruton, "Contemporary Theorizing in Economic Growth," Bert F. Hoselitz, ed., *Theories of Economic Growth*, Glencoe, Ill., 1960, pp. 239–98, especially pp. 280–81 and 287.

Now any reasoning analogous with what has been discussed in the present chapter presupposes that the problem of diminishing returns on capital can be placed in a secular context.[10] Indeed, the representative example used in the writings quoted concerns a market system undergoing growth, in which the capital stock rises "at a greater proportionate rate than the labor force." This is supposed to diminish returns to capital indicated by a fall of profits. Suitable innovations, either labor-displacing or capital-attracting, are then regarded as compensating factors restoring a normal rate of profit.

In evaluating this theoretical construct, we shall disregard the recent objections to the particular concept of "capital" and to the "neoclassical parable" that underlie this argumentation.[11] We also grant that, in an uncontrolled free market, preservation of a normal rate of profit is a *motorial* condition for further accumulation and even for the mere maintenance of the existing capital stock, so that under these circumstances growth may, indeed, come to an end unless innovational profits fill the gap created by any fall of the marginal product of capital.

True or false, it should be obvious that the proposition just expounded moves on an analytical plane quite different from what we have been dealing with in this chapter. In either case, to speak of "diminishing returns" without further qualifications is bound to lead to confusion. What we have been concerned with is the use of innovations intended to compensate for a *fall in per capita real output* as a *physical* consequence of diminishing returns to natural resources, irrespective of the effect that such a fall may have on relative factor receipts. Contrariwise, a relative plenitude of capital in the framework of the neoclassical parable must lead to a *rise* in per capita real output – a rise that is all the greater the greater the disproportion between the rise of the capital stock and of the labor force (independently of any innovation). In fact, as was pointed out earlier,[12] accumulation up to the point of complete capital saturation is the very procedure by which "the maximum physically possible permanent level of output" (J. Robinson) can be attained.

Now we can construe an imaginary case in the realm of natural resources which truly parallels the case of growing capital intensification. Assume that, instead of having to bring steadily inferior areas into cultivation, more units of prime efficiency could be steadily opened up, putting more and more of the inferior grades out of operation. Not

---

[10] See Chapter 19, Section I.
[11] See Harcourt, *Some Cambridge Controversies in the Theory of Capital, loc. cit.*
[12] See Chapter 6, Section II.

only would per capita real output steadily rise but, as is the case with profits under progressive capital intensification, rents, the receipt obtained from natural resources, would steadily decline. This might induce resource owners progressively to reduce the supply of their resources – to be countered by labor- and capital-displacing innovations that restore rent at the expense of the otherwise steadily rising wages and profits!

The absurd consequences of this imaginary analogy shed light on the true difference between the meaning of the term "diminishing returns" in the resource case and the capital case. In the latter instance we deal with the motorial consequences of the *institutional structure of an uncontrolled free market*. These consequences can be easily avoided not only by a collectivist system but also by a market in which investment is "socialized" (Keynes). In the former case, we are confronted with a *universally valid natural constraint* that only technology can overcome. A social critic might well denounce the consequences of the institutional structure of capitalism by pointing to the consequences of diminishing returns to capital. Confronted with the diminishing returns to natural resources," he must strike the flag.

28

Some concluding remarks

It is not easy to sum up the gist of our deliberations. The main reason for this difficulty lies in the fact that, although the various topics discussed are all aspects of economic growth, they have been related to one another by a peculiar method of investigation rather than by the unity of their content. It is true, all these topics have as common denominator the analysis of "paths" and of "disequilibria" that must be overcome if the stipulated goal of balanced growth is to be attained. Still, this volume resembles a series of extensive monographs rather than the systematic exposition of one theme.

However, there may well be two questions left in the reader's mind to which at least a tentative answer should be given. One concerns our original claim that instrumental analysis has a better chance of arriving at empirically valid generalizations than the conventional techniques of positive reasoning.[1] I trust that this claim has been vindicated by the manner in which, for example, the traverses required to absorb a rise or a fall in the rate of growth of labor supply or to adjust labor-displacing or capital-displacing technical changes have been treated. Given a precise definition of both the initial and the terminal state of the system and also an exact circumscription of the path criteria, it has proved possible in each case to determine, step by step, the appropriate sectoral motions of the system. Because our results do not depend on the prior acceptance of any behavioral axioms, they are not refuted by deviations of the actual from the required course of economic processes. Their validity is instrumental, that is, the structural and motorial conditions so derived are true means for the stipulated end.

Yet, while insisting on the truth value of our findings, we may still be challenged as to their practical significance. Even if we know the suitable paths to a stipulated goal, and the behavioral and motorial patterns assuring the pursuit of that path, can such knowledge on the part of the scientific observer be translated into the behavior of the economic agents shaping the course of actual growth processes?

In principle, we can answer this question in the affirmative. How-

[1] See Chapter 1, Section III.

ever, we have to qualify this affirmation by two reservations. One refers to the level of abstraction at which our investigations have been conducted; the other concerns an intrinsic limitation of all social research.

It was stated in our methodological introduction[2] that, with the conception of a political economics underlying our analyses, the link between theory and practice is established by public controls – a link that belongs to both these worlds. The discovery of which controls are goal-adequate in a given situation is the final regressive step in instrumental analysis; their application is a political act. Yet, to make the theoretical findings amenable to practical application, they must first be specific enough to permit their translation into concrete measures of economic policy.

Now in order to keep a complex analysis within manageable bounds, we have been arguing on the highest possible level of abstraction. Thus only the essential variables have been taken into account: a production schema based on no more than three fully aggregated sectors; an institutional framework that depicts only the extreme opposites of sociopolitical organization: pure laissez-faire and complete collectivization; only one macrogoal, Balanced Growth; and a sparse number of path criteria. Certainly this setup is far removed from the order of the real world. However, there are no basic obstacles to overcoming this lack of realism by expanding the production schema in the direction of a comprehensive input–output matrix, by focussing closer attention on "mixed" socioeconomic systems, or by varying both the macrogoal and the path criteria in any number of ways. Incidentally, further disaggregation of the schema will stress some affinity of our procedure with a dynamic Leontief model, although even then the *aggregate* motions of the two equipment-good sectors relative to each other and to the consumer-good sector will remain strategically crucial.

The true limitations to the practical application of the findings of instrumental analysis lie elsewhere. As has been indicated before,[3] they arise from our imperfect understanding of "social causation," that is, the manner in which the sociopolitical environment and, especially, public controls affect economic behavior of the microunits. We have rejected any *a priori* knowledge of a "response mechanism" that is to link the extrasystemic force of control with the motivations of marketers. Even intrasystemic stimuli, such as changes in the quantities demanded or supplied and in the prices offered or charged, are no more than "suggestions" which may be accepted or rejected. The same is true

[2] *Ibid.*
[3] *Ibid.*

of the response to public controls, if we leave aside extreme cases of coercion. Improved information, manipulation of public opinion and other techniques of persuasion, measures of indicative planning, or even compensatory intervention will create the intended effect only if the purpose of such controls is, first, *understood* by the controlled, and, second, if the macrogoals pursued and the policy instruments applied are *approved* by those who are to be controlled. Universal approval can hardly be expected if the goals in question, for example, a radical change in the distribution of income and wealth, affect different strata of society in opposite directions. On the other hand, public controls will meet with much less resistance whenever their acceptance achieves a state of affairs that coincides with the aspirations of the controlled themselves.

Fortunately the macrogoal of Balanced Growth – the lodestar of our analyses – seems to fall in the latter category. Therefore, appropriate public intervention, guarding, for example, against malinvestment, or braking both expansion and contraction before they overshoot the mark stand a good chance of meeting with the desired response.

This cannot alter the conclusion that, although instrumental analysis can pronounce with certainty on goal-adequate paths and behavioral and motivational patterns, its statement on the goal adequacy of controls possesses at best a high degree of probability. There the linearity of cause and effect, characteristic for natural phenomena, yields to the "circularity of reason and consequence" – a lack of determinacy typical for social analysis generally. "Still, who but a professional manipulator or an incurable addict of 'scientism' would have it otherwise?"[4]

[4] *OEK,* p. 161.

Appendix

An alternative presentation
of Lowe's basic model
by Edward J. Nell

Adolph Lowe's Basic Model, on which he builds his analyses of various types of economic growth, is a new species of an increasingly familiar genus. Since the 1920s when Lowe first formulated his ideas,[1] Sraffa, von Neumann, Joan Robinson, Samuelson, Hicks, Goodwin, and Morishima, to name but a few of the best known, have developed fixed-coefficient models for the analysis of capital accumulation and, thus, implicitly or explicitly, of economic growth. Lowe's book is an important reminder that these efforts have grown out of a long and still largely unappreciated tradition of nonneoclassical thinking in continental Europe between the two world wars.[2]

The questions asked in this tradition, as well as the modes of analysis, differ significantly from the standard procedure of neoclassicism – a point that stands out clearly in the present work. Rather than studying the problems most prominent in recent discussions, such as pricing, income distribution, or the valuation of capital, Lowe is concerned with the almost totally neglected problem of the adjustment of a growing system using fixed-capital goods to a change in its parameters and, in particular, with the issue of "traverse" (Hicks) from a given to a higher or a lower rate of growth.

The purpose of this appendix is, first of all, to provide the basis for a comparison of Lowe's Basic Model of the structure of production and especially its technical foundations, with the framework of two other types of fixed-coefficient models most prominent in contemporary literature – the multisectoral models of von Neumann, Leontief, Sraffa, et al., on the one hand, and the two-sector models of Hicks, Spaventa, Good-

---

[1] See A. Lowe, "Wie ist Konjunkturtheorie ueberhaupt moeglich?" *Weltwirtschaftliches Archiv*, October 1926, pp. 166–97, especially pp. 185–92.

[2] In this context, see the work of F. A. Burchardt, cited in Chapter 2, footnote 6, of this book. See also Alfred Kaehler, *Die Theorie der Arbeiterfreisetzung durch die Maschine*, Leipzig, 1933, Ch. IV, for the detailed exposition of an input–output model formulated in arithmetical terms. The entire literature of that period and, in particular, the contribution of the Kiel School have been surveyed by D. L. Clark, Studies in the Origin and Development of Growth Theory, 1925–50, University of Sydney, Australia, 1974 (unpublished dissertation).

win, and Morishima, on the other hand. By translating part of Lowe's analytical apparatus into the symbolic language used in some of these models, essential similarities as well as differences can be seen. Second, it will be shown that by relaxing Lowe's very strong assumptions, his model can be developed to deal with some of the problems that he does not explicitly discuss in this book, in particular important and controversial topics of capital theory. Of course, it should be understood that to carry out the explicit comparison with other models, or the analysis of, for example, questions of modern capital theory and income distribution would require far more space than is available here.

To restate the main characteristics of Lowe's model, as expounded in Chapters 3 and 4, we deal with a tripartite structure of the economy. More precisely, in his conception every industrial system, that is, all systems that apply fixed capital, are to be subdivided into two broad sectors, I and II, the former of which is further subdivided into Subsectors Ia and Ib. Sector I taken as a whole serves the production of fixed-capital goods, Sector II that of consumer goods. Subsector Ia, on its part, produces the fixed-capital goods that enter as inputs in both Subsectors Ia and Ib; Subsector Ib, on the other hand, produces the fixed-capital goods used in Sector II.

This basic structure of production may be described in symbolic terms as follows:

$$
\text{I} \quad \begin{cases} a_a & 0 \cup n_a \to 1 \text{ unit of } a \\ a_b & 0 \cup n_b \to 1 \text{ unit of } b \end{cases} \text{capital goods}
$$
$$
\text{II} \quad \{0 \quad b_z \cup n_z \to 1 \text{ unit of } z\} \text{ consumer goods}
$$

a_a represents the amount of capital good a currently used up in order to produce 1 unit of capital good a; a_b is the amount currently used up to produce 1 unit of capital good b, and b_z, in turn, is the amount of capital good b currently used in producing the unit output of the composite consumer good z. Symbols n_a, n_b, and n_z stand for amounts of labor input required during the time needed to complete production. However, n_a, n_b, and n_z are expressed in terms of the amounts of the *consumer good* that, at an assumed basic standard of living, will support labor (workers and their families) for that amount of time; that is, we take as given a basic "subsistence" standard of living, permitting us to translate hours of labor into amounts of the consumption good. This has the advantage of allowing us to treat all input coefficients symmetrically as fractions of one or another of the outputs.

Lowe assumes that fixed equipment depreciates at the same rate in each sector. This assumption greatly simplifies the analysis because, as a result, the actual rate of profit on fixed capital will always equal the rate of depreciation times the rate of profit on current flow input.[3]

The contrast between this structural setup and the conventional two-sector models is striking. In the latter it is commonly assumed that fixed capital is transferable between sectors and especially between the capital-good and the consumer-good sectors. In the Lowe model, this transferability assumption is valid only in the relationship between the two subsectors of Sector I: Neither can the specialized equipment intended for use in the two fixed-capital-good subsectors be transferred to the consumer-good sector nor can equipment suitable for production in Sector II be transferred to Sector I. Such immobility of fixed-capital goods matters little so long as analysis is confined to the study of stationary or dynamic equilibria. It matters greatly during disequilibrating movements, in particular, during traverses from one rate of growth to another one, higher or lower. During such traverses inputs and outputs in the two subsectors of Sector I move inversely: Sector Ia expands while Sector Ib contracts and conversely. Not only can such countermovements not be recognized if fixed-capital production is aggregated into one sector, but the ensuing sectoral redundancies or shortages of capacity and labor supply must go unnoticed. In a word, only a tripartite model can reveal the essential fact that, with the use of fixed capital in production, no "full utilization" or "full employment" traverse is possible.

Nor will multisectoral models do better in this respect. They are by the nature of the case so complex, especially when they treat fixed capital as a kind of joint product,[4] that it is practically impossible to grasp the

---

[3] "Current flow input" is equivalent to what has sometimes been called "circulating capital." Unfortunately, the more traditional phrase has been given many different meanings at different times.

[4] The advantages of treating fixed capital as a kind of joint product for certain purposes are considerable and are well explained in Sraffa, *Production of Commodities by Means of Commodities, loc. cit.,* Ch. X. It is important to remember, however, that his ". . . investigation is concerned *exclusively* with such properties of an economic system as do not depend on changes in the scale of production or in the proportions of 'factors.' " (p. v; emphasis added.) In particular, when, as in Lowe's work, there is excess demand in some sectors and underutilization in others, varying from period to period, it becomes difficult to specify the quantity of equipment appearing in each period as joint product with the (varying) output. If equipment is underutilized will more of it appear as the joint product, or products? In what proportion? Moreover, plant and equipment can be underutilized in different ways. For instance, one part could be left idle, and the rest run at full blast, or, alternatively, all of the equipment could be run at less than peak intensity. Sometimes technology will dictate the way equipment is underutilized when demand is short, but sometimes managers may have a choice. Will these options be treated the same or differently in representing underutilized fixed capital as a joint product? Similar remarks apply to overutilization when and where it is physically possible. Such questions may

strategic relationships among the three aggregates depicted in a tripartite model. Therefore, it is not surprising that the analysis of changes in these models takes the form of comparative statics rather than of genuine dynamics.

Because of these limitations of the conventional models, we will have to confine our attempt at translating Lowe's model into the conventional notation to the investigation of stationary and dynamic equilibrium, respectively. In doing so, we shall interpret his model (contrary to the meaning bestowed upon it in the body of the book) as a construct in positive rather than instrumental economics. In other words, using Lowe's terminology, we will be concerned exclusively with "structural" relations, taking the equilibrating "forces," namely, the extremum principle of behavior and stabilizing expectations, for granted. This will make it possible to concentrate our inquiry on the subject matter discussed in Chapters 4 and 9 of this book.

I. THE STATIONARY STATE IN EQUILIBRIUM

1

Lowe's model is an offspring of the classical tradition emphasizing the "circular" relations in production – the use of the various commodities produced as input in the different sectors. This conception of production has at least three significant implications in Lowe's work. First, the pattern of interdependence virtually dictates the way the system can respond to, for example, a change in the growth rate of labor supply. This is perhaps the principal subject of Lowe's analysis, but need not be discussed here. Second, directly relevant here, interdependence in production creates the need for exchange, because, in producing, the different sectors consume each other's output, and so require mutual replacement supplies. Third, self-reproducing economic systems produce as output at least as much of each good, and usually more of some, than they consume in the aggregate during the course of production. (If the first condition, "at least as much of each" is not met, the system is not viable; if the second, "more of some," is not met, it is not productive.)

To see the implications of interdependence in production let us first write Lowe's system as a purely self-sustaining system that produces in the aggregate *exactly as much* (no more and no less) as is needed for replace-

be answerable, but it is unlikely that the simplicity and elegance of the "joint product" method of analyzing fixed capital will survive the inclusion of the answers in the model.

ment in each period. This means spelling out two points quite carefully: On the one hand, we must show the *exchange ratios* that must be established among the products of the different sectors and, on the other hand, we must establish the ratios of the outputs of the sectors. If the exchange ratios are wrong, then one sector may end up short while another has an excess, and, if the output ratios are wrong, then too much of one good may be produced and too little of another in relation to overall replacement needs. So, writing, p_a, p_b, p_z for prices and q_a, q_b, q_z for the quantities, and using the coefficients defined earlier, we can set out the following "dual" systems of equations:

Exchange values	Relative quantities	
$a_a p_a + n_a p_z = p_a$	$a_a q_a + a_b q_b = q_a$	
$a_b p_a + n_b p_z = p_b$	$b_z q_z = q_b$	(I.1)
$b_z p_b + n_z p_z = p_z$	$n_a q_a + n_b q_b + n_z q_z = q_z$	

The left-hand set of equations determines the price ratios that will enable each industry to obtain in exchange what it needs to carry out another round of production. The right-hand set of equations determines the relative sizes of output that must be produced so that in the aggregate total output will just match the replacement demands, with no shortages or surpluses. Each of the quantity variables is a ratio of two quantities. It is true, we cannot add wheelbarrows and pears, but we can carry pears in wheelbarrows. So the number of pears per wheelbarrow is a significant ratio and, indeed, must be known if we are to calculate how many wheelbarrows to produce to carry the crop of pears. Thus output *ratios* are significant independently of value, although, of course, output *sums* are not.

Next, as a check, let us write out the dimensions of the equations. Let the dimensional unit of A be *a*, of B be *b*, and of Z, *z*. Labor time is measured in hours, *h,* and we remember that the given subsistence standard of consumption yields an implicit equation allowing us to translate consumption goods into labor time.

Dimensions – value

$$\frac{a}{a} \cdot \frac{h}{a} \cup \frac{h}{a} \cdot \frac{z}{z} \to \frac{h}{a}$$

$$\frac{a}{b} \cdot \frac{h}{a} \cup \frac{h}{b} \cdot \frac{z}{z} \to \frac{h}{b}$$

$$\frac{b}{z} \cdot \frac{h}{b} \cup \frac{h}{z} \cdot \frac{z}{z} \to \frac{z}{z}$$

Dimensions – quantity

$$\frac{a}{a} \cdot \frac{a}{z} \cup \frac{a}{b} \cdot \frac{b}{z} \to \frac{a}{z}$$

$$\frac{b}{z} \cdot \frac{z}{z} \to \frac{b}{z}$$

$$\frac{h}{a} \cdot \frac{a}{z} \cup \frac{h}{b} \cdot \frac{b}{z} \cup \frac{h}{z} \cdot \frac{z}{z} \to \frac{z}{z}$$

Because hours of labor are equivalent to specific amounts of consumption the dimensions work out correctly.

Next let us examine the exchange equations:

$$p_a = \frac{n_a p_z}{1 - a_a}$$
$$p_a = \frac{p_b - n_b p_z}{a_b} \qquad \text{(I.2)}$$
$$p_b = \frac{p_z(1 - n_z)}{b_z}$$

Setting the first two equations equal, substituting for p_b, and dividing out p_z, we obtain

$$\frac{a_b}{1 - a_a} = \frac{1 - n_b b_z - n_z}{n_a b_z} \qquad \text{(I.3)}$$

which can be described as the condition for the system's *viability*.

By solving in a different way, we obtain the prices

$$p_a = \frac{n_a}{1 - a_a}$$
$$p_b = \frac{a_b n_a + (1 - a_a)n_b}{1 - a_a} \qquad \text{(I.4)}$$
$$p_z = 1$$

from which it follows that

$$\frac{p_a}{p_b} = \frac{n_a}{a_b n_a + (1 - a_a)n_b} \qquad \text{(I.5)}$$

showing that the price ratio of a to b is independent of the conditions of production in the consumer-goods sector.

By solving the quantity equations, we find

$$q_a = \frac{a_b b_z}{1 - a_a}$$
$$q_b = b_z \qquad \text{(I.6)}$$
$$q_z = 1$$

However, a subsistence level economy is only a special case of a stationary economy. Normally a surplus is produced, that is, more is produced than is required for replacement. The consequences of this will occupy our attention now, although the subsistence level system provides a convenient reference point.

2

Throughout his stationary analysis, Lowe does not distinguish between a subsistence system and one that produces a surplus. As a consequence, he must assume that, in systems producing a surplus, the latter is distributed, with the purpose of being consumed, among the labor force in proportion to the labor input in each of the three sectors. This makes Lowe's stationary state equivalent with Joan Robinson's "state of bliss." In such a state, labor is equipped with a stock of fixed capital capable of producing the maximum physical output attainable with the prevailing technique. This output consists of consumer goods and of equipment goods exclusively serving replacement purposes. The surplus, if one exists, forms then simply part of the wage bill.

Now, and this amounts to a generalization of the Lowe-Robinson model, it depends on the prevailing socioeconomic system to whom the surplus accrues. In precapitalist systems, it was directly appropriated by a dominant class. Under capitalism, part or even the whole of the surplus may, even under stationary conditions, be transferred to the owners of the means of production owing to their superior bargaining power in labor markets – a monopsonistic gain based on a class monopoly. Still, even then in physical terms the surplus consists exclusively of consumer goods. Moreover, because the output of fixed-capital goods is confined to period replacements, it is possible to conduct the analysis in terms of flows, bearing in mind that the corresponding capital stocks equal the size of the period flows of fixed capital multiplied by the inverse of the rate of depreciation.

Taking our bearings from Lowe's Basic Model, we are now going to incorporate an explicit expression for the surplus by presenting two new sets of equations – again a set of exchange value equations and a set of relative quantity equations. The first set determines the "net wage rate," θ, that is, the total wage rate minus subsistence wage rate, or the "rate of surplus value" together with exchange ratios. The second determines the "per capita net consumption rate," ζ, that is, total per capita consumption rate minus subsistence consumption rate, together with the relative size of the sectoral outputs.[5]

Exchange values	Relative quantities
$a_a p_a + (1 + \theta)n_a p_z = p_a$	$a_a q_a + a_b q_b = q_a$
$a_b p_a + (1 + \theta)n_b p_z = p_b$	$b_z q_z = q_b$
$b_z p_b + (1 + \theta)n_z p_z = p_z$	$(1 + \zeta)(n_a q_a + n_b q_b + n_z q_z) = q_z$

$$(\text{I.7})$$

[5] Where we have sets of equations, one for each sector, I will designate the entire set by one number, for example, I.7 here, and then refer to each by the letter designating the sector: I.7a, I.7b, and I.7z, respectively.

These exchange value equations show the exchanges that will ensure adequate replacement all around. They represent a generalization of Lowe's model because they are consistent either with paying the maximum possible wage rate to labor or with paying surplus value (over and above what is needed to acquire the goods to support labor at a subsistence level) to the dominant class at a rate uniformly proportional to the labor required in each sector. (Thus, the surplus might go in per capita feudal dues to a nobility, or in tithes to the priesthood.)

The relative quantity equations show the relative amounts that must be produced to replace the amounts used up, while producing a surplus consisting exclusively of the consumption good.

For a complete picture of stationary equilibrium, multiply the value equations (which I will call the V equations) by the equilibrium quantities, and the quantity equations (Q equations) by the equilibrium exchange ratios:

$$q_a[a_ap_a + (1+\theta)n_ap_z] = q_ap_a \qquad\qquad p_a(a_aq_a + a_bq_b) = p_aq_a$$
$$q_b[a_bp_a + (1+\theta)n_bp_z] = q_bp_b \qquad\qquad p_b(b_zq_z) = p_bq_b \qquad (I.8)$$
$$q_z[b_zp_b + (1+\theta)n_zp_z] = q_zp_z \qquad p_z[(1+\zeta)(n_aq_a + n_bq_b + n_zq_z)] = p_zq_z$$

Several important relationships follow at once from this. First, we can see at once that

$$\theta = \zeta \qquad\qquad (I.9)$$

Add the equations on the left together; then add the equations on the right. Both sets are equal to $q_ap_a + q_bp_b + q_zp_z$ and consist of the same terms differently arranged, the only difference being that θ appears in the left-hand set and ζ in the right. Hence the net wage ratio in value terms must equal the ratio of the surplus of the consumption good to necessary consumption, a purely quantitative ratio.

Second, subtract Equation I.8a(Q) from Equation I.8a(V):

$$(1+\theta)q_an_ap_z = p_aa_bq_b \qquad\qquad (I.10)$$

The right-hand side is the replacement capital needed in Equation I.8b(V), that is, Sector Ib. *Thus the wage bill in Sector Ia equals the replacement capital in Sector Ib.*

Third, given the preceding equality, we can see from Equations I.8b(V) and I.8a(Q) that *the replacement capital* in Equation I.8z(V), that is, *in Sector II is equal to the combined wage bill of Sectors Ia and Ib.* We have just seen the $q_ba_bp_a = (1+\theta)q_an_ap_z$, and from the two sides of I.86

$$q_ba_bp_a + (1+\theta)q_bn_bp_z = p_bb_zq_z$$

Hence

$$(1 + \theta)(q_a n_a p_z + q_b n_b p_z) = p_b b_z q_z \tag{I.11}$$

Relationships I.10 and I.11 show the intersectoral flows necessary to reproduce the system, and they are strongly reminiscent of Marx's schemes of reproduction. We will return to them later; now it is necessary to look more closely at the p's and q's.

First let us solve the *quantity equations*. From Equation I.7a(Q)

$$q_z(1 - a_a) = a_b q_b = a_b b_z q_z$$

because from Equation I.7b(Q)

$$q_b = b_z q_z$$

From Equation I.7z(Q) we see that ζ is not dependent on q_z; for

$$q_z[1 - (1 + \zeta)n_z] = (1 + \zeta)\left(\frac{n_a a_b b_z q_z}{1 - a_a}\right) + (1 + \zeta)n_b b_z q_z$$

Here q_z appears in every term and, consequently, cancels. It is, therefore, an appropriate candidate to serve as *numéraire*. The three quantities are then

$$\begin{aligned} q_a &= \frac{a_b b_z}{1 - a_a} \\ q_b &= b_z \\ q_z &= 1 \end{aligned} \tag{I.12}$$

Notice that these are *the same* as the quantities in the subsistence level economy.

For Lowe the economy contains (and constrains) its own possibilities of technical change. To change any of the coefficients is a major undertaking involving rebuilding or scrapping and replacing fixed equipment. We cannot, therefore, examine "technical progress" by taking partial derivatives. It is useful, however, to find the way in which the relative quantities vary, providing we interpret such variation as the *comparison of differences*. Taking the total differential of Equation I.12a,

$$dq_a = \frac{b_z}{1 - a} \, da_b + \frac{a_b}{1 - a_a} \, db_z + \frac{a_b b_z}{(1 - a_a)^2} \, da_a \tag{I.13}$$

Here the partial derivatives can readily be seen. The q_a varies directly with all three coefficients, which is to say that "technical progress" in any sector would reduce the size of Sector Ia relative to the rest. This can also be seen by combining Equations I.12a and I.12b, giving the ratio

$$\frac{q_a}{q_b} = \frac{a_b}{1 - a_a} \tag{I.14}$$

which shows the same relation in an intuitively obvious form. Note also that the relative sizes of Sectors Ia and Ib *depend only on the capital-good coefficients in those sectors*. Neither their own labor coefficients nor any coefficients from Sector II play any part in determining the relative size of Ia and Ib.[6]

If we look back at Equation I.7z(Q) as rewritten, we have

$$1 = (1 + \zeta) \left[\left(\frac{n_a a_b b_z}{1 - a_a} \right) + n_b b_z + n_z \right]$$

Hence, by rearranging,

$$\zeta = \frac{1 - a_a}{n_a a_b b_z + (1 - a_a)(n_b b_z + n_z)} - 1 \tag{I.15}$$

So long as $1 - a_a > 0$, that is, so long as a surplus is produced, both numerator and denominator of the ratio will be positive. For $\zeta \geq 0$, however, this ratio must be greater than 1. To put it another way, the condition for the system to be just self-replacing is that $\zeta = 0$, which, in turn, entails that

$$1 - a_a = n_a a_b b_z + (1 - a_a)(n_b b_z + n_z)$$

or

$$1 - a_a = \frac{n_a a_b b_z}{1 - n_b b_z - n_z} \tag{I.16}$$

or, alternatively,

$$\frac{a_b}{1 - a_a} = \frac{1 - n_b b_z - n_z}{n_a b_z}$$

The left-hand side is the net output of Sector Ia; the right-hand side gives the composite demands for that output, for *use both as capital and,*

---

[6] Notice the important implication: whereas labor-saving technical progress, which reduces the n coefficients, in one or more sectors, will affect prices (as we shall see), it will not affect quantities.

eventually transformed, as consumption. This, then, is the condition for the *viability* of the system, and is the same as that for the subsistence level economy.

New let us turn to the *value equations.* From Equations I.7a(V) and I.7b(V)

$$\frac{p_a}{p_b} = \frac{n_a}{n_b(1 - a_a) + n_a a_b} \tag{I.17}$$

Observe that the exchange ratio between a and b depends only on the coefficients in Sectors Ia and Ib; it is entirely independent of the technology or productivity of Sector II. Notice also that p_a/p_b is the same here as in the subsistence level economy, although we will see shortly that p_a and p_b are not the same as there. Intuitively, it is clear that p_a/p_b will vary directly with a_a and inversely with n_b and a_b; the effect of n_a is not so obvious, but, in fact,

$$\frac{\delta(p_a/p_b)}{\delta n_a} = \frac{n_b(1 - a_a)}{[n_b(1 - a_a) + n_a a_b]^2} > 0$$

so that p_a/p_b varies directly with n_a.

To obtain the net *wage rate,* we substitute from Equations I.7a(V) and I.7b(V) into I.7z(V)

$$(1 + \theta) \frac{a_b n_a b_z p_z}{1 - a_a} + (1 + \theta) n_b b_z p_z + (1 + \theta) n_z p_z = p_z$$

Clearly p_z has no effect on θ, and like its counterpart, q_z, is a good candidate for the role of *numéraire.* Rearranging the foregoing equation,

$$\theta = \frac{1 - a_a}{n_a a_b b_z + (1 - a_a)(n_b b_z + n_z)} - 1 = \zeta \tag{I.18}$$

Clearly θ and ζ will vary inversely with all the coefficients.[7] The result that $\theta = \zeta$ we reached earlier by a different route; this time, however,

[7] All the coefficients except a_a are obvious. In the case of a_a,

$$\frac{\delta\theta}{\delta a_a} = \frac{-n_a a_b b_z - 2a_a(n_b b_z + n_z)}{D^2} < 0$$

(where D is defined in Equation I.19). See also footnote 8.

$$\frac{\delta\theta}{\delta n_z} = \frac{-(1 - a_a)^2}{D^2} = -\theta^2$$

we have the exact expression for θ and ζ in terms of the coefficients. Using this we can now write out the prices in full. First, let us rewrite the net *wage* rate equation as[8]

$$\theta = \frac{1 - a_a}{D} - 1 \tag{I.19}$$

where

$$D = n_a a_b b_z + (1 - a_a)(n_b b_z + n_z)$$

Then, using Equations I.7a(V), I.7b(V), I.7z(V) and substituting Equation I.19,

$$p_a = \frac{(1 + \theta)n_a}{1 - a_a} = \frac{n_a}{D}$$

$$p_b = a_b \left(\frac{n_a}{D}\right) + (1 + \theta)n_b = \frac{a_b n_a + n_b(1 - a_a)}{D} \tag{I.20}$$

$$p_z = \frac{b_z(a_b n_a) + n_z(1 - a_a) + n_z(1 - a_a)}{D} = 1$$

These are *not* the same as the subsistence level economy's prices. Now bearing these equations in mind, let us look at the matter rather differently. The direct and indirect labor embodied in a unit of each good is given by the following equations:

$$\begin{aligned}
\Lambda_a &= n_a + a_a \Lambda_a \\
\Lambda_b &= n_b + a_b \Lambda_b \\
\Lambda_z &= n_z + b_z \Lambda_z
\end{aligned} \tag{I.21}$$

Here Λ_i stands for the embodied labor in a unit of each good; the first term gives the direct labor, and the second the indirect. Solving, we find for the labor values

$$\begin{aligned}
\Lambda_a &= \frac{n_a}{1 - a_a} \\
\Lambda_b &= \frac{a_b n_a + (1 - a_a)n_b}{1 - a_a} \\
\Lambda_z &= \frac{n_a a_b b_z + (1 - a_a)(n_b b_z + n_z)}{1 - a_a} = \frac{D}{1 - a_a}
\end{aligned} \tag{I.22}$$

[8] Symbol D will be used throughout the Appendix to refer to the denominator of the net wage rate–rate of profit tradeoff (or the net consumption–growth rate tradeoff), a special case of which is given here in Equation I.19, where the rate of profit is zero. The D always refers to the same mathematical expression, regardless of the particular values assumed by the coefficients or variables.

Hence, we find that ratios of labor values equal prices:

$$\frac{\Lambda_a}{\Lambda_z} = \frac{n_a}{D} = p_a$$

$$\frac{\Lambda_b}{\Lambda_z} = \frac{a_b n_a + (1 - a_a)n_b}{D} = p_b \qquad (I.23)$$

$$\frac{\Lambda_z}{\Lambda_z} = 1 = p_z$$

Thus, in full equilibrium in the stationary state, the labor theory of value correctly describes the prices that must obtain for replacement to be possible consistently with uniform earnings in proportion to direct labor.

3

Now let us turn to the derivation of what Lowe calls the "sectoral ratios," that is, the ratios of the value of the output of each sector to the value of the total gross output o. First, the expressions for the value of the output of each sector can be written as

$$q_a p_a = \frac{n_a a_b b_z}{(1 - a_a)D}$$

$$q_b p_b = \frac{n_a a_b b_z + (1 - a_a)n_b b_z}{D} = \frac{(1 - a_a)n_a a_b b_z + (1 - a_a)^2 n_b b_z}{(1 - a_a)D} \qquad (I.24)$$

$$q_z p_z = 1$$

The value of total output is

$$q_a p_a + q_b p_b + q_z p_z = \frac{(1 - a_a)D + n_a a_b b_z(2 - a_a) + (1 - a_a)^2 n_b b_z}{D(1 - a_a)} \qquad (I.25)$$

$$= \frac{(3 - a_a)(n_a a_b b_z) + (1 - a_a)[(2 - a_a)(n_b b_z) + n_z]}{(1 - a_a)D} \qquad (I.26)$$

and the sectoral ratios then are

$$\frac{q_a p_a}{q_a p_a + q_b p_b + 1} = \frac{n_a a_b b_z}{(3 - a_a)(n_a a_b b_z) + (1 - a_a)[(2 - a_a)(n_b b_z) + n_z]} = \frac{o_a}{o}$$

$$\frac{q_b p_b}{q_a p_a + q_b p_b + 1} = \frac{(1 - a_a)(n_a a_b b_z) + (1 - a_a)^2 n_b b_z}{(3 - a_a)(n_a a_b b_z) + (1 - a_a)[(2 - a_a)(n_b b_z) + n_z]} = \frac{o_b}{o} \qquad (I.27)$$

$$\frac{1}{q_a p_a + q_b p_b + 1} = \frac{(1 - a_a)D}{(3 - a_a)(n_a a_b b_z) + (1 - a_a)[(2 - a_a)(n_b b_z) + n_z]} = \frac{o_z}{o}$$

The aggregate capital flow–gross output ratio (in Lowe's notation k_d, where k measures the capital stock–gross output ratio) will equal

$$\frac{q_a p_a + q_b p_b}{q_a p_a + q_b p_b + 1} = \frac{(2 - a_a)(n_a a_b b_z) + (1 - a_a)^2 n_b b_z}{(3 - a_a)(n_a a_b b_z) + (1 - a_a)[(2 - a_a)(n_b b_z) + n_z]} \quad (I.28)$$

and the capital to *net* output ratio will equal

$$\frac{q_a p_a + q_b p_b}{1} = (2 - a_a)(n_a a_b b_z) + (1 - a_a)^2 n_b b_z \quad (I.29)$$

These relationships are awkward and obviously not very easy to work with. Lowe therefore proposes a striking simplification: He assumes that the capital–labor ratios are the same in all three sectors, which also implies that the capital–output and labor–output ratios are the same everywhere. Some care has to be taken with these assumptions; even though the model makes it possible to express capital–labor ratios directly, because each sector has only one capital good, the ratios cannot be compared dimensionally unless they are expressed in value terms. The same obviously holds for capital–output and labor–output ratios. The assumptions can be written

$$
\begin{array}{cccc}
\text{Labor–capital} & \text{Output–capital} & \text{Output–labor} & \\[4pt]
\dfrac{n_a}{a_a p_a} = \dfrac{n_b}{a_b p_a} = \dfrac{n_z}{n_z p_b} & \dfrac{1}{a_a} = \dfrac{p_b}{a_b p_a} = \dfrac{1}{b_z p_b} & \dfrac{p_a}{n_a} = \dfrac{p_b}{n_b} = \dfrac{1}{n_z} & (I.30)
\end{array}
$$

By manipulating these equations, we can find expressions for the prices:

$$
\begin{aligned}
p_a &= \frac{n_a}{n_z} = \frac{(a_a)^2}{a_b b_z} \\[4pt]
p_b &= \frac{n_b}{n_z} = \frac{a_a}{b_z} \\[4pt]
p_z &= 1
\end{aligned}
\qquad (I.31)
$$

It follows that

$$n_a a_b = n_b a_a \qquad n_b b_z = n_z a_a \qquad n_a a_b b_z = n_z (a_a)^2 \qquad (I.32)$$

With these equations in mind, we can rewrite the preceding relationships.[9]

---

[9] Notice that the prices are not necessarily unity. If $p_a = p_b = 1$, then we would have the "one-commodity" case, where the products of the sectors exchanged one for one; but this need not be the case here. Even though the "organic composition of capital" is everywhere the same, exchange need not be one for one. This is *not*, strictly speaking, a one-commodity model.

First write out the expression for D:

$$D = n_a a_b b_z - n_b a_a b_z + n_b b_z - n_z a_a + n_z \qquad (\text{I.33})$$

(If we apply expressions I.32, $D = n_z$.)

Now looking back at the equations for labor values in the set I.24, we rewrite them using Equations I.32. The expressions showing the amounts of direct and indirect labor embodied in unit outputs are

$$\Lambda_a = \frac{n_a}{1 - a_a}$$

and as before

$$\Lambda_b = \frac{a_b n_a + (1 - a_a) n_b}{1 - a_a} = \frac{n_b}{1 - a_a} \qquad (\text{I.34})$$

$$\Lambda_z = \frac{n_a a_b b_z + (1 - a_a)(n_b b_z + n_z)}{1 - a_a} = \frac{n_z}{1 - a_a}$$

Hence, the labor theory of value holds in an extremely simple form:

$$\frac{\Lambda_a}{\Lambda_z} = \frac{n_a}{n_z} = p_a$$

$$\frac{\Lambda_b}{\Lambda_z} = \frac{n_b}{n_z} = p_b \qquad (\text{I.35})$$

$$\frac{\Lambda_z}{\Lambda_z} = 1 = p_z$$

Next, observe that the assumptions expressed in Equation I.30 have no effect on quantities, which remain as described in Equation I.12. Putting together quantities and prices (Equation I.31), we have

$$q_a p_a = \frac{a_b b_z}{1 - a_a} \cdot \frac{(a_a)^2}{a_b b_z} = \frac{(a_a)^2}{1 - a_a}$$

$$q_b p_b = \frac{b_z a_a}{b_z} = a_a \qquad (\text{I.36})$$

$$q_z p_z = 1$$

Hence, the total gross output is

$$q_a p_a + q_b p_b + 1 = \frac{1}{1 - a_a} \qquad (\text{I.37})$$

and the sectoral ratios then reduce to the manageable ratios

$$\frac{q_a p_a}{0} = (a_a)^2$$

$$\frac{q_b p_b}{0} = (1 - a_a)a_a \qquad (I.38)$$

$$\frac{1}{0} = (1 - a_a)$$

Notice that a_a is the capital–output coefficient in Sector Ia. Hence these equations are exactly the same as Lowe's but are expressed in terms of the physical coefficients.

Now recalling the "reproduction" conditions I.10 and I.11, it was shown in Equation I.10 that the wage bill in Sector Ia equalled the value of the replacement capital in Sector Ib, and in Equation I.11 that the wage bill in Sectors Ia and Ib together equalled the value of the replacement capital in Sector II:

$$(1 + \theta)(q_a n_a) = a_b p_a q_a$$
$$(1 + \theta)(q_z n_a + q_b n_b) = b_z p_b$$

By using Equations I.12a and I.12b, the expressions for q_a and q_b, and by drawing on Equation I.32, we rewrite Equations I.10 and I.11, under conditions of equal capital–labor ratios,

$$(1 + \theta)\left(\frac{n_a a_b b_z}{1 - a_a}\right) = \frac{n_a a_b b_z}{n_z}$$

which implies

$$\theta = \frac{1 - a_a}{n_z} - 1 \quad \text{and} \quad (1 + \theta)n_z = 1 - a_a \qquad (I.10')$$

and

$$(1 + \theta)\left(\frac{n_a a_b b_z}{1 - a_a} + n_b b_z\right) = \frac{a_a b_z}{b_z}$$

which then becomes

$$(1 + \theta)\left(\frac{n_a a_b b_z - a_a n_b b_z + n_b b_z}{1 - a_a}\right) = a_a \qquad (I.11')$$

In turn, this expression implies (because from Equation I.32, $a_b n_a = a_a n_b$) that

$$(1 + \theta)(n_b b_z) = (1 - a_a)a_a \tag{I.11''}$$

This is another expression for the ratio of the output of Sector Ib to total gross output. Also Equation I.10′ gives another expression for the output ratio of Sector II to total output or, alternatively, for the gross wage rate. Note also that from Equation I.32 again, $n_b/n_z = a_a/b_z$, hence

$$\frac{n_b b_z}{a_a} = n_z$$

so that Equation I.11″ reduces to $(1 + \theta)n_z = 1 - a_a$, which is the expression for the gross *wage rate*.

More generally, we can write Equations I.10 and I.11

$$(1 + \theta)\left(\frac{n_a a_b b_z}{1 - a_a}\right) = a_b b_z\left(\frac{n_a}{D}\right)$$

$$(1 + \theta)b_z\left(\frac{a_b n_a + n_b - a_a n_b}{1 - a_a}\right) = b_z\left(\frac{a_b n_a + n_b - a_a n_b}{D}\right)$$

using the general price equations (I.25a and I.25b). Clearly both of these simplify to

$$(1 + \theta) = \frac{1 - a_a}{D}$$

which is the wage equation (I.19). The reproduction conditions therefore imply and are implied by the existence of a uniform "rate of surplus value" in all sectors.

II. DYNAMIC OR GROWTH EQUILIBRIUM

1

The surplus produced in the stationary state was wholly consumed and was appropriated in the same proportion to direct labor in every sector, either by labor itself, as a net "wage," or by a dominant class, as a rate of exploitation. Now, in a growing economy, we shall consider the investment of all or part of the surplus, adding to fixed capital, and, corresponding to this, the appropriation of the value of the surplus as profit, in the same proportion in each sector to the value of the fixed capital. This requires rewriting the equations, introducing both the *rate of growth* and the *rate of profit*. However, the situation is a little more complicated now: We must recognize that the surplus must be divided, on the one hand, between investment and consumption, and, on the other hand, between capitalists who receive profit and workers who earn net wages. It will be necessary to find the general relationships among the net wage rate, the rate of profits, and prices, on the one hand, and among net consumption per head, the rate of growth, and relative outputs, on the other.

As before, we shall write the coefficients in terms of the amounts used in the annual circuit of production. Because depreciation is assumed to be physical and to take place at the same rate in all three sectors, we can convert the profit and growth rates relative to current flow input directly to the fixed-capital rates. The rate of profit on current flow input is

$$\rho = \frac{\text{profit}}{d \times \text{fixed capital}}$$

where d is the annual rate of physical depreciation. Hence the true rate of profit on fixed capital is $R = d \times \rho$. An exactly analogous conversion holds for the current flow input growth rate, g, and the true growth rate on fixed capital, G: $G = d \cdot g$. Notice that this depends heavily on the assumption of "straight-line" depreciation. With any other depreciation assumption, this will not work. (If, for example, the rate of depreciation increased with the age of the capital, then the size of the current flow input coefficients would rise over time, and the rate of growth and rate of profit would both fall.)

Remembering Lowe's concept of fixed capital, however, we shall have to be very careful how we interpret our results. In his system, a *net wage–rate of profit tradeoff* does not represent a curve along which the economy could move, nor does the net consumption–growth tradeoff. To move from one growth rate to another or, analogously, from one distribution to another *requires rebuilding the capital stock*. Once capital is installed there is only one set of outputs that can be produced consistently with full utilization and full employment. Lowe's question is precisely, How, given these circumstances, can the economy move from one position of steady growth to another?

What meaning then can we give to the wage–profit and consumption–growth tradeoffs, and to their derivatives? The point should be familiar from Joan Robinson's writings – it is the same as her complaint about the production function where she sees fixed capital locking the economy into a particular *technique*. Lowe certainly accepts this idea: The main part of his analysis concerns an economy operating with a given technique.

However, he goes a step further and argues that fixed capital locks the system into a particular pattern of *output* as well. To move, to change outputs, means investing, because the system cannot change output unless it first changes inputs. Yet to change inputs is to *draw on the output of the input-producing sectors*. The system itself determines its own capacity for change; the capital-goods sector must provide the goods necessary to change the inputs to produce the new pattern of output. In turn, it is implied that the capital-goods sector must produce different goods, or deliver them to different investors, than it did previously. Moreover, this change will necessarily entail shortages and/or surplus capacity in some parts of the economy, relative to the previous full capacity utilization.

Thus, each point on the wage–profit and consumption–growth trade-offs implies a particular structure of fixed capital. (The capital is *physically* fixed on the growth–output side. However, corresponding to this on the profit-value side are *fixed legal claims* – fixed costs. Thus we have both fixed physical equipment and fixed claims and obligations. To change the first we must draw on the capital-goods sector; to change the second, we must renegotiate loans in the capital market.) *Hence these curves represent comparisons of economies using the same technique but operating under different distributions or growth patterns.* Consider a sunny archipelago filled with identical island economies, all using the same technique. At the dawn of history each island established a pattern of growth and distribution. The wage–profit and consumption–growth curves are simply *orderings* of the island economies according, respectively, to their net *wage rates* and their per capita net consumption, and the derivatives of these curves are simply comparisons of differences. Lowe's principal analytical problem could then be put this way: What would one island have to do to make its growth and consumption pattern like that of another?

2

Now let us write out the equations, remembering that we are writing them for current input flows, so that the rates of profit and growth will have to be converted.

Exchange value	Relative quantities

$$(1 + \rho)a_a p_a + (1 + \theta)n_a p_z = p_a \qquad (1 + g)(a_a q_a + a_b q_b) = q_a$$
$$(1 + \rho)a_b p_a + (1 + \theta)n_b p_z = p_b \qquad (1 + g)b_z q_z = q_b \qquad (\text{II.1})$$
$$(1 + \rho)b_z p_b + (1 + \theta)n_z p_z = p_z \qquad (1 + \zeta)(n_a q_a + n_b q_b + n_z q_z) = q_z$$

These are the basic equations. Thus we can refer to Equation II.1a(V) or Equation II.1b(Q), designating each member of the set II.1 by the letter standing for its product. Now multiply the value equations by the corresponding quantities and the quantity equations by the corresponding prices, just as we did for the Stationary system.

$$q_a[(1 + \rho)a_a p_a + (1 + \theta)n_a p_z] = q_a p_a$$
$$q_b[(1 + \rho)a_b p_a + (1 + \theta)n_b p_z] = q_b p_b$$
$$q_z[(1 + \rho)b_z p_b + (1 + \theta)n_z p_z] = q_z p_z$$
$$p_a[(1 + g)(a_a q_a + a_b q_b)] = p_a q_a$$
$$p_b(1 + g)b_z q_z = p_b q_b$$
$$p_z[(1 + \zeta)(n_a q_a + n_b q_b + n_z q_z)] = p_z q_z$$

(II.2)

First add the equations on the top; then those on the bottom. Because the sum of each set of equations equals $p_a q_a + p_b q_b + p_z q_z$, they equal each other. Now looking at the terms in which θ and ζ appear, respectively, it can be seen that each of the three terms is identical to a corresponding term from the other side, except for the variable θ or ζ. The same can be seen to be true for the terms containing ρ and g. Assume that $\theta = \zeta$; the column of wage bills then adds up to exactly the amount of consumption goods. However, because the equations *as a whole* add up on both sides to total gross output, the remaining sum of gross profit on the left-hand side must equal the gross investment on the right-hand side. Also, because the terms differ only in having ρ on the one side where g appears on the other, it follows that $\rho = g$ when $\theta = \zeta$. By exactly analogous reasoning, we can prove that when $\rho = g$, then $\theta = \zeta$.

Next look at Equations II.2a(V) and II.2a(Q), and subtract them. The result is analogous to the stationary state; that is, the wage bill in Sector Ia equals the gross profit of Sector Ib.

$$(1 + \theta)q_a n_a p_z = (1 + g)q_b a_b p_a$$

(II.3)

From Equations II.2a(V), II.2b(V), and II.2b(Q), we find that

$$(1 + \theta)[q_a n_a p_z + q_b n_b p_z] = (1 + g)q_z b_z p_z$$

(II.4)

The combined wage bills of Sectors Ia and Ib equal the gross investment of Sector II – again a relationship very similar to the reproduction condition holding in the stationary state.

Before we analyze this any further, we had better examine, first, quantities in relation to consumption and growth and, then, prices in relation to wages and profits.

From Equations II.1a(Q) and II.1b(Q) we obtain

$$q_a = \frac{(1 + g)^2 a_b b_z}{1 - (1 + g)a_a}$$

(II.5)

Next we provisionally set, $q_z = 1$, taking it as the *numéraire* by analogy with the stationary state. We will return to this point. Differentiating the quantities with respect to the growth rate gives

$$\frac{dq_a}{dg} = \frac{2(1+g)a_b b_z}{1 - (1+g)a_a} > 0 \qquad \text{(Any increase in } g \text{ raises } q_a.)$$

$$\frac{dq_b}{dg} = b_z > 0 \qquad\qquad \text{(Any increase in } g \text{ raises } q_b.) \qquad\qquad \text{(II.6)}$$

However,

$$\frac{q_a}{q_b} = \frac{(1+g)a_b}{1 - (1+g)a_a} \quad \text{and} \quad \frac{d(q_a/q_b)}{dg} = \frac{a_b}{[1 - (1+g)a_a]^2} > 0 \qquad \text{(II.7)}$$

so that any increase in g raises q_a/q_b. Faster growth requires the expansion of machinery making machines, relative to the other sectors.

Now let us find the relation between g and ζ. From Equations II.1a(Q) and II.1b(Q),

$$q_b = \frac{q_a[1 - (1+g)a_a]}{(1+g)a_b} = (1+g)b_z$$

and from Equation II.1z(Q),[10]

$$q_a = \frac{1 - (1+\zeta)n_z - (1+g)(1+\zeta)n_b b_z}{(1+\zeta)n_a}$$

Then by substituting,

$$(1+g)b_z = \frac{[1 - (1+g)a_a][1 - (1+\zeta)n_z - (1+g)(1+\zeta)n_b b_z]}{(1+g)(1+\zeta)a_b n_a}$$

and multiplying out and rearranging,

$$\zeta = \frac{1 - (1+g)a_a}{n_z + (1+g)(n_b b_z - a_a n_z)(1+g)^2(a_b n_a - a_a n_b)b_z} - 1 \qquad \text{(II.8)}$$

---

[10] Note that the equation initially comes out as

$$q_a = \frac{q_z - (1+\zeta)n_z q_z - (1+g)(1+\zeta)n_b b_z q_z}{(1+\zeta)n_a q_z}$$

and that q_z cancels out on the right-hand side.

It is easily seen that the numerator will be positive so long as $g < (1 - a_a)/a_a$. The denominator, however, is not so obvious, but it can be rewritten

$$n_z[1 - (1 + g)a_a] + (1 + g)n_b b_z[1 - (1 + g)a_a] + (1 + g)^2 a_b n_a b_z$$

which will also be positive so long as $g < (1 - a_a)/a_a$. To see the economic meaning of this restriction observe that if ζ falls to -1, the left-hand side will be zero, when the unit term is moved over. Hence, when $\zeta = -1$,

$$g = \frac{1 - a_a}{a_a} = g_{max} \qquad (II.9)$$

Under these conditions, *gross* consumption has fallen to zero. This is the maximum *technically* possible accumulation rate, where the workers, so to speak, "live on air." To see that any level of consumption higher than this implies a lower growth rate, we find the first derivative (letting N be the numerator, and D the denominator of Equation II.8):

$$\frac{d\zeta}{dg} = \frac{D(dn/dg)}{D^2} \qquad \frac{N(dD/dg)}{D^2}$$

$$= \frac{-a_a D - [1 - (1 + g)a_a][(n_b b_z - a_a n_z) + 2(1 + g)b_z(a_b n_a - a_a n_b)]}{D^2}$$

By multiplying out, cancelling like terms, and then, regrouping, we obtain

$$\frac{d\zeta}{dg} = \frac{-n_b b_z[1 - (1 + g)a_a]^2 - (1 + g)a_b n_a b_z[2 - (1 + g)a_a]}{[n_z + (1 + g)(n_b b_z - a_a n_z) + (1 + g)^2(a_b n_a - a_a n_b)b_z]^2} \qquad (II.10)$$

The denominator is >0, and because, ex hypothesi, $g < g_{max}$, both terms in parentheses are positive, the numerator is negative. Hence,

$$\frac{d\zeta}{dg} < 0$$

Now let us return to q_z, which we provisionally set equal to 1. From Equation II.1z(Q), we have

$$q_z = (1 + \zeta)(n_a q_a + n_b q_z + n_z q_z)$$

Hence

$$q_z = \frac{(1 + \zeta)(n_a q_a + n_b q_b)}{1 - (1 + \zeta)n_z}$$

Substituting from Equation II.8 and simplifying

$$q_z = \frac{[1 - (1 + g)a_a](n_a q_a + n_b q_b)}{D - n_z[1 - (1 + g)a_a]}$$

Then substituting for $n_a q_a$ and $n_b q_b$, and simplifying:

$$q_z = \frac{(1 + g)^2 n_a a_b b_z + [1 - (1 + g)a_a](1 + g)n_b b_z]}{(1 + g)n_b b_z[1 - (1 + g)a_a] + (1 + g)^2 n_a a_b b_z} = 1 \qquad \text{(II.11)}$$

Thus we are not arbitrarily setting q_z equal to 1. Given the concept of the net wage and the fact that n_a, n_b, and n_z are expressed as the amounts (fractions) of the consumption good needed to support the required labor for the necessary work time, q_z is *determined*. That is, it is a theorem of the model, not an assumption, that the relative quantities are expressed in relation to the consumption good, and we will show shortly that in the same way, relative prices are expressed in relation to p_z.

Intuitively, it makes economic common sense that if a positive level of net consumption per head, $\zeta > 0$, can be produced under stationary conditions, a system with the same technology but different fixed capital (producing a different combination of outputs) could establish a positive net rate of growth, $g > 0$. Furthermore, an intuitive proof based on the continuity of the ζ,g function can easily be given.

Let the level of per capita net consumption when $g = 0$ be ζ_m, and the level of the rate of growth when $\zeta = 0$ be q_m. We remember that when $\zeta = -1$,

$$g = g_{\max} = \frac{1 - a_a}{a_a} > 0$$

From the ζ,g tradeoff, $d\zeta/dg < 0$, and we *assume* the the ζ,g function is continuous. Hence, in the interval $-1 \leq \zeta \leq \zeta_m$, where $\zeta_m > 0$, g falls in the interval

$$\frac{1 - a_a}{a_a} \geq g \geq 0$$

Yet $\zeta = 0$ falls between -1 and ζ_m; hence, for $\zeta = 0$, $g = g_m > 0$.
QED.

The only difficulty here is that we have had to assume the continuity of the ζ,g function, on which everything depends. To prove continuity is notoriously arduous. More importantly, the idea is foreign to the spirit

of Lowe's work, in which rigidities and discrete changes are highly significant. Instead, let us establish the proposition that when $\zeta_m > 0$, $\zeta = 0$
implies $g = g_m > 0$, by ordinary algebra.[11]

When $\zeta = 0$, we have[12]

$$1 = \frac{1 - (1 + g_m)a_a}{[1 - (1 + g_m)a_a][n_z + (1 + g_m)n_b b_z] + (1 + g_m)^2 n_a a_b b_z} \tag{II.12}$$

This can be rewritten

$$\frac{a_b}{1 - (1 + g_m)a_a} = \frac{1 - n_z - n_b b_z - g_m n_b b_z}{(1 + g_m)^2 n_a b_z}$$

Because a_b, $1 - (1 + g_m)a_a$, and $(1 + g_m)^2 n_a b_z$ are all > 0, it follows that

$$(1 - n_z - n_b b_z - g_m n_b b_z) > 0$$

whether or not $g_m \gtrless 0$ so long as

$$g_m < g_{\max} = \frac{1 - a_a}{a_a}$$

As we saw earlier when $g = 0$, then $\zeta = \zeta_m$, which can be written

$$\frac{a_b}{1 - a_a} = \frac{1 - n_z - n_b b_z - \zeta_m n_z - \zeta_m n_b b_z}{(1 + \zeta_m)n_a b_z} \tag{II.13}$$

Because a_b, $1 - a_a$, and $(1 + \zeta_m)n_a b_z > 0$, therefore

$$(1 - n_z - n_b b_z - \zeta_m n_z - \zeta_m n_b b_z) > 0$$

---

[11] An exact analog of this holds for wages and profits – the value side of things.
There it can be interpreted as saying that a positive *rate of surplus value*,
$\theta_m > 0$, implies that when the entire surplus goes to profit, $\theta = 0$ (that is,
the net wage rate is zero), then a positive uniform rate of profit can be
established.

[12] This yields the following expression for g:

$$g = \frac{-n_b b_z - a_a(1 - n_z) \pm \{[n_b b_z + a_a(1 - n_z)]^2 - 4b_z(n_a a_b - a_a n_b)(n_z - 1)\}^{1/2}}{2b_z(n_a a_b - a_a n_b)}$$

because

$$(1 + g)^2 b_z(n_a a_b - a_a n_b) + (1 + g)[(n_b b_z - a_a n_z) + a_a] + n_z - 1 = 0$$

This expression is not easy to work with and inspection yields no obvious
clues.

Now for notational convenience, let

$$X = 1 - n_z - n_b b_z - \zeta_m n_z - \zeta_m n_b b_z$$
$$Y = 1 - n_z - n_b b_z - g_m n_b b_z$$

and

$$X - Y = (g_m - \zeta_m) n_b b_z - \zeta_m n_z \qquad \text{(II.14)}$$

We can write

$$\frac{a_b}{1 - a_a} = \frac{X}{(1 + \zeta_m) n_a b_z} \qquad \text{(II.15)}$$

Then, because

$$a_b = \frac{(1 - a_a - g_m a_a) Y}{(1 + g_m)^2 n_a b_z}$$

we can write

$$\frac{a_b}{1 - a_a} = \frac{\{1 - g_m [a_a/(1 - a_a)]\} Y}{(1 + g_m)^2 n_a b_z} \qquad \text{(II.16)}$$

This shows clearly that g_m must be $< (1 - a_a)/a_a$.
From Equations II.15 and II.16, clearly

$$\frac{X}{1 + \zeta_m} = \frac{\{1 - g_m [a_a (1 - a_a)]\} Y}{(1 + g_m)^2} \qquad \text{(II.17)}$$

so that

$$\frac{1 + g_m}{1 + \zeta_m} X = \frac{1 - g_m [a_a/(1 - a_a)]}{1 + g_m} Y \qquad \text{(II.18)}$$

By assumption $\zeta_m > 0$. Can g_m be ≤ 0? First suppose $g_m = 0$. Then from the definition $X < Y$, but obviously, then

$$\left(\frac{1}{1 + \zeta_m}\right) X < Y$$

Hence $\zeta_m > 0$ is inconsistent with $g_m = 0$.

Next suppose $g_m < 0$. Again $X < Y$, but

$$\frac{1 + g_m}{1 + \zeta_m} < 1 \quad \text{and} \quad \frac{1 - g_m[a_a/(1 - a_a)]}{1 + g_m} > 1$$

Hence again Equation II.18 cannot be satisfied; $\zeta_m > 0$ is inconsistent with $g_m < 0$. Only $g_m > 0$ is compatible with Equation II.18. QED.

It would be hard to overemphasize the importance of these propositions, although they may seem common sense. When there is a surplus of consumption over and above the level of necessary consumption, then, if the economy can alter its fixed capital, it can grow. Moreover, the rise in the ultimate level of the growth rate depends precisely on the extent to which consumption is curtailed. Again we must remember that in Lowe's model, movement along the ζ, g function is not possible. There the function shows different possible states, and the derivative compares differences. Function ζ, g, nevertheless, provides the essential framework for Lowe's analysis, for it exhibits the various possible steady growth states between which "traverse" may take place.

Next we can see very quickly that the relationship between the growth rate and the rate of net consumption per head has its exact counterpart in the tradeoff between the rate of profits and the net wage rate. Looking back at the value equations (II.1), we can solve first Equation II.1a(V) and then Equations II.1b(V) and II.1z(V) together for p_a; hence

$$p_a = \frac{(1 + \theta)n_a}{1 - (1 + \rho)a_a} \cdot = \frac{1 - (1 + \theta)n_z - (1 + \rho)(1 + \theta)n_b b_z}{(1 + \rho)^2 a_b b_z}$$

By cross-multiplying, we obtain

$$(1 + \rho)^2(1 + \theta)n_a a_b b_z = 1 - (1 + \theta)n_z - (1 + \rho)(1 + \theta)b_z - (1 + \rho)a_a$$
$$+ (1 + \rho)(1 + \theta)a_a n_z + (1 + \rho)^2(1 + \theta)a_a n_b b_z$$

and by collecting terms, rearranging, and dividing out:

$$\theta = \frac{1 - (1 + \rho)a_a}{n_z + (1 + \rho)(n_b b_z - a_a n_z) + (1 + \rho)^2(a_b n_a - a_a n_b)b_z} - 1 \qquad \text{(II.19)}$$

Or, rewriting the denominator,

$$\theta = \frac{1 - (1 + \rho)a_a}{n_z[1 - (1 + \rho)a_a] + (1 + \rho)\{n_b b_z[1 - (1 + \rho)a_a] + (1 + \rho)^2 a_b n_a b_z\}} - 1$$
$$\text{(II.20)}$$

This equation is the same as Equation II.8, except that θ appears here in places of ζ, whereas ρ replaces g. The maximum technically possible is $\rho = \rho_{max} = g_{max} = (1 - a_a)/a_a$. It occurs when $\theta = -1$. If $\rho = -1$, then $\theta = \theta_{max} = \zeta_{max} = 1/n_z$. Neither of these levels is maintainable, however. In the first case, no replacements would be available for depreciated equipment in Sectors Ib and II, whereas the second case is not even feasible on Lowe's assumptions, for it would require decumulating capital equipment at an impossible rate, and/or transferring it from Sector I to Sector II, which is not possible, owing to the specificity of equipment. Hence the feasible maximum rate of profit occurs when $\theta = 0$, and will be given by the same expression that gives the maximum feasible growth rate when net consumption per head is zero. The maximum feasible net wage rate occurs when $\rho = 0$ and is

$$\theta_m = \frac{1 - a_a}{(1 - a_a)n_z + n_b b_z(1 - a_a) + a_b n_a b_z} - 1 \qquad (II.21)$$

an expression we have already met in the analysis of stationary conditions. The proof that if $\theta_m > 0$, then when $\theta = 0$, $\rho > 0$, follows exactly as in the consumption–growth case. The first derivative $d\theta/d\rho$ will be the same as $d\zeta/dg$, with ρ replacing g throughout. Hence we can write

$$\frac{d\theta}{d\rho} = \frac{-n_b b_z[1 - (1 + \rho)a_a]^2 - (1 + \rho)a_b n_a b_z[2 - (1 + \rho)a_a]}{[n_z + (1 + \rho)(n_b b_z - a_a n_z) + (1 + \rho)^2(a_b n_a - a_a n_b)]^2} < 0 \qquad (II.22)$$

A rise in the net wage rate always brings a corresponding fall in the rate of profits. Or, putting it correctly (for Lowe's assumptions do not permit easy movement from one steady state to another), a higher net wage rate can only be established in conjunction with a lower rate of profit.

3

Now we must consider how prices vary with the rate of profits. Solving the original value equations, we have

$$p_a = \frac{n_a}{D} > 0$$

$$p_b = \frac{n_b[1 - (1 + \rho)a_a](1 + \rho)n_a a_b}{D} > 0 \qquad (II.23)$$

$$p_z = 1$$

Given the wage–profit equation, these formulas are arrived at by the same procedure as in the analogous equations for stationary conditions.

The equation for the consumption sector is particularly interesting. From Equation II.1z(V),

$$p_z = \frac{(1 + \rho)b_z p_b}{1 - (1 + \theta)n_z}$$
$$= \frac{(1 + \rho)n_z b_z[1 - (1 + \rho)a_a] + (1 + \rho)^2 n_a a_b b_z}{D - n_z[1 - (1 + \rho)a_a]} = 1 \tag{II.24}$$

That is, given the method we have taken in solving the model, prices are automatically and necessarily expressed in terms of the price of the consumption good.

An important related fact is that the prices of goods A and B are independent of the method of production of the consumer good. From the preceding,

$$\frac{p_a}{p_b} = \frac{n_a}{n_b[1 - (1 + \rho)a_a] + (1 + \rho)n_a a_b} \tag{II.25}$$

which contains no terms from Sector II.

The connection of the prices of A and B with the rate of profit is readily seen:

$$\frac{\delta p_a}{\delta \rho} = \frac{D(\delta n_a/\delta \rho) - n_a(\delta D/\delta \rho)}{D^2}$$

where

$$\frac{\delta D}{\delta \rho} = n_b b_z[1 - 2(1 + \rho)a_a] - a_a n_z$$
$$= \frac{-n_a[n_b b_z - a_a n_z + 2(1 + \rho)b_z(a_b n_a - a_a n_b)]}{D^2} \tag{II.26}$$

This can clearly be either positive or negative, but it is worth noting also that it could *change* sign, as ρ increases. For at the point where

$$\rho = \frac{n_b b_z - a_a n_z}{2b_z(a_a n_b - a_b n_a)} - 1$$

the derivative

$$\frac{\delta p_a}{\delta \rho} = 0$$

That is, this value of ρ marks a stationary point in the value of the first derivative, so that having risen it begins to fall or vice versa.

Similarly,

$$\frac{\delta p_b}{\delta \rho} = \frac{D(n_a a_b - a_a n_b) - n_b[1 - (1 + \rho)a_a] + (1 + \rho)n_a a_b(\delta D/\delta \rho)}{D^2}$$

so that,

$$\frac{\delta(p_a/p_b)}{\delta \rho} = \frac{n_a(a_a - a_b)}{\{n_b[1 - (1 + \rho)a_a] + (1 + \rho)n_a a_b\}^2}$$

This menas that p_a/p_b will move directly with ρ if $a_a > a_b$, and inversely, if $a_a < a_b$; but, in any case, nothing depends on the coefficients in the consumer-goods sector.

A very striking feature of Lowe's model is now evident: The relationship between prices and the rate of profits is not at all symmetrical with the relationship between quantities and the rate of growth. Both q_a and q_b always increase with the rate of growth, but p_a and p_b can vary either directly or inversely with the rate of profit. Moreover, q_a/q_b always varies directly with the rate of growth, whereas p_a/p_b may take either sign, or may even change signs. However, one feature is common to both the quantity and price equations: The relationships among q_a, q_b, and g, and among p_a, p_b, and ρ are wholly independent of the coefficients in the consumption goods sector.

4

For Lowe technical progress is the process of changing the technical coefficients. In certain very special cases this might be done easily and costlessly, but as a general rule changing the coefficients will be a major enterprise, similar to, and normally involving investment. Hence we cannot examine the effects of technical progress on the rate of profit by, for example, totally differentiating our equations. We can, however, *compare* economies producing the same goods with the same resources, and the same methods, except that one coefficient differs. In other words, we cannot examine technical *change,* but we can compare technical *differences.* Here again the purpose of such an analysis is to determine whether, and to what extent, it might be worth while to move from one position to another.

We have already seen, in our examination of stationary conditions, that ζ_m varies inversely with the coefficients. It is evident by inspection that

$$g_{max} = \frac{1 - a_a}{a_a} = \rho_{max}$$

$$\zeta_{max} = \frac{1}{n_z} = \theta_{max}$$

depend only on the ratio of their own output to their own input. In this respect they are the analogues of the maximum rates of profit (growth) and of net wages (net consumption) in the Hicks-Spaventa model. However, we have seen that these are not in fact feasible. The true maxima, ρ_m, g_m, and ζ_m, θ_m, do depend on all the coefficients, and will be increased by a decrease of any of them. We know this for ζ_m and θ_m; we must now prove it for ρ_m and g_m.

The demonstration will have to be a little roundabout, for the direct expression for g_m (ρ_m is the same, of course) is intractable. So we shall make use of the expression relating ζ_m and g_m which we developed above to show that $\zeta_m > 0$ entailed $g_m > 0$. First, rewrite that expression

$$\left(\frac{1}{1 + \zeta_m}\right) X = \left\{\frac{1 - g_m[a_a/(1 - a_a)]}{(1 + g_m)^2}\right\} Y \tag{II.27}$$

where X and Y are the same as before. Here the left-hand side consists only of terms in which ζ_m appears, whereas the right-hand side has only terms with g_m. There are six coefficients – a_a, a_b, b_z, n_a, n_b, n_z – and they divide into three cases.

Case I refers to the behavior of a_b, n_a. Neither appears in the preceding equation, but we know that

$$\frac{\delta\zeta_m}{\delta a_b} < 0 \quad \text{and} \quad \frac{\delta\zeta_m}{\delta n_a} < 0$$

For simplicity, we will assume that the difference we are considering is a *decrease* in a coefficient, which therefore "raises" ζ_m. Clearly when ζ_m rises, both X and $1/(1 + \zeta_m)$ decrease; hence the equation would no longer hold. To maintain the equality, g_m must rise, diminishing both Y and

$$\frac{1 - g_m[a_a/(1 - a_a)]}{(1 + g_m)^2}$$

Case II refers to the behavior of a_a. A decrease in a_a raises ζ_m; it also decreases $a_a/(1 - a_a)$ because

$$\frac{[a_a/(1 - a_a)]}{a_a} = \frac{1}{(1 - a_a)^2} > 0$$

So on the left-hand side, both X and $1/(1 + \zeta_m)$ decrease, whereas on the right-hand side

$$1 - g_m \left(\frac{a_a}{1 - a_a}\right)$$

increases, exacerbating the inequality. To maintain the equation, g_m must increase.

Case III refers to the behavior of n_b, b_z, n_z. A decrease in any of these will raise ζ_m; but the effects on X and Y are more complicated. By taking n_z first, we obtain

$$\frac{\delta Y}{\delta n_z} = -1 \qquad \frac{\delta X}{\delta n_z} = -1 - \zeta_m - n_z \left(\frac{\delta \zeta_m}{\delta n_z}\right)$$

However,

$$\frac{\delta \zeta_m}{\delta n_z} = \frac{-(1 - a_a)^2}{D^2} = -\zeta_m^2$$

so, in fact, $|n_z \zeta_m^2| < |\zeta_m|$ because $\zeta_m < 1/n_z$. Consequently,

$$\frac{\delta Y}{\delta n_z} = -1 > \frac{\delta X}{\delta n_z} = -(1 + \zeta_m - n_z \zeta_m^2),$$

because

$$1 + \zeta_m - n_z \zeta_m^2 > 1$$

Hence both the effect on ζ_m and the effect on X compared to that on Y, will reduce the left-hand side compared to the right-hand side. Furthermore, to preserve equality, there must be an offsetting increase in g_m. Exactly parallel considerations hold for n_b and b_z because in each case the partial derivative of X is less than that of Y, with respect to the coefficient.

We must now return to the wage–profit and consumption–growth curves. However, before we can draw them and examine the variation of the value of capital as the rate of profit differs (from island to island), we need to know more about their shape. All we know so far is that they are downward-sloping. What about the second derivative? Let D stand for the denominator, N for the numerator of the wage–profit curve, then

$$\theta = \frac{N(\rho)}{D(\rho)} \quad \text{and} \quad \frac{d\theta}{d\rho} = \frac{\bar{N}}{D^2}$$

where

$$\bar{N} = D\left(\frac{dN}{d\rho}\right) - N\left(\frac{dD}{d\rho}\right)$$

so that

$$\bar{N} = -n_b b_z[1 - (1+\rho)a_a]^2 - (1+\rho)a_b n_a b_z[2 - (1+\rho)a_a] < 0$$

where

$$\begin{aligned}
\frac{d^2\theta}{d\rho^2} &= \frac{[D(dN/d\rho) - N(dD/d\rho)][D - 2(dD/d\rho)]}{D^3} \\
&= \frac{\bar{N}[D - 2(dD/d\rho)]}{D^3} \\
&= \frac{d\theta}{d\rho}\left[\frac{D - 2(dD/d\rho)}{D}\right]
\end{aligned} \qquad (\text{II}.28)$$

We know that $\bar{N} < 0$; hence $d\theta/d\rho < 0$, since $D > 0$. The sign of $d^2\theta/d\rho^2$ will, therefore, depend on the term in parentheses. Moreover, $d^2\theta/d\rho^2 = 0$ whenever $D = 2(dD/d\rho)$. At such points of inflexion, the curvature of the $\theta - \rho$ (or $\zeta - g$) function changes. The question now is, How many points of inflexion can there be?

The answer is quite straightforward. The equation, $D = 2(dD/d\rho)$, can be rewritten:

$$n_z + (1+\rho)(n_b b_z - a_a n_z) + (1+\rho)^2 b_z(a_b n_a - a_a n_b)$$
$$= 2(n_b b_z - a_a n_z) + 4(1+\rho)b_z(a_b n_a - a_a n_b)$$

which becomes

$$n_z + (n_b b_z - a_a n_z)(1 + \rho - 2) + (1+\rho)^2 - 4(1+\rho)b_z(a_b n_a - a_a n_b) = 0$$

and rearranged in standard form, this is

$$(1 + \rho)^2(a_b n_a - a_a n_b)b_z + (1 + \rho)(n_b b_z - a_a n_z - 4b_z(a_b n_a - a_a n_b)$$
$$+ n_z - 2(n_b b_z - a_a n_z) = 0 \quad \text{(II.29)}$$

Let $x_1 = a_b n_a - a_a n_b$ and $x_2 = n_b b_z - a_z n_z$, so the equation reads

$$(1 + \rho)^2 x_1 b_z + (1 + \rho)(x_2 - 4b_z x_1) + n_z - 2x_2 = 0$$

The general solution is given by the quadratic formula:

$$1 + \rho = \frac{-(x_2 - 4b_z x_1) \pm [(x_2 - 4b_z x_1)^2 - (4b_z x_1)(n_z - 2x_2)]^{1/2}}{2b_z x_1} \quad \text{(II.30)}$$

By examining the discriminant first, we obtain

$$x_2{}^2 - 8x_2 x_1 b_z + 16x_2{}^2 b_z{}^2 - 4b_z n_z x_1 + 8x_1 x_2 b_z = x_2{}^2 + 16x_1{}^2 b_z{}^2 - 4n_z b_z x_1$$

This will necessarily be positive when $x_1 < 0$; but it can easily be positive otherwise, although it can take negative values, too. There may be two real roots, but there need not be. The next question is whether these roots when they exist are both positive, and this is easily resolved. Let the coefficients of the quadratic be designated α, β, γ:

$$(1 + \rho)^2\alpha + (1 + \rho)\beta + \gamma = 0$$

where

$$\alpha = x_1 b_z \qquad \beta = x_2 - 4b_z x_1 \qquad \gamma = n_z - 2x_2$$

The condition for both roots to be positive is that either

$$\alpha > 0, \beta < 0, \gamma > 0 \quad \text{or} \quad \alpha < 0, \beta > 0, \gamma < 0$$

Clearly $x_1 < 0$ is by no means sufficient for both roots to be positive. However, it is certainly compatible. In the second case, if $x_1 < 0$ and $x_2 > 0$, then $\beta > 0$ is assured.[13] For $\gamma < 0$, then, it will be necessary for $n_b b_z > n_z + (a_a/n_z)$. This is certainly a possible case; hence we have established that there may be as many as two inflexion points in the second derivative of the wage–profit tradeoff. (It should also be evident that there may be only one or none.) In economic terms, the case we have considered

[13] When $x_1 > 0$ and $x_2 < 0$, the first case of the signs of the coefficients is automatically filled, but it is not necessary that the discriminant be positive. If it is, then the two real roots will both be positive.

occurs when Sector Ia is capital-intensive compared to Sector Ib, but Sector Ia's capital to Sector Ib's labor is less than the capital–labor ratio in Sector II. To put it another way, Sector Ia is capital-intensive compared to Sector Ib, but Sector II is capital-intensive compared to the "crossways" capital–labor ratio of Sector I.

We can now draw the complete net wage–profit or net consumption–growth diagram. Here $\zeta_{max} = 1/n_z$ and $g_{max} = (1 - a_a)/a_a$. Symbols

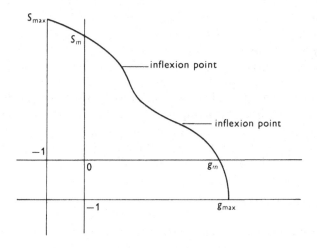

ζ_m and g_m were defined previously. We have shown that $d\zeta/dg$ is always negative, and that $d^2\zeta/dg^2$ may have as many as two points of inflexion. Further, we know that ζ_m and g_m will increase with reduction in input, whereas ζ_{max} and g_{max}, by contrast, depend only on their "own" input.

As the preceding discussion has shown, the analysis of the growing economy presents formidable difficulties. Lowe cuts through these with the important, although obviously unrealistic simplifying assumption (which we examined earlier) that all sectors employ labor and capital in the same ratio. As a consequence, from $n_b b_z p_b = n_z a_b p_a$, and because $a_a p_b = a_b p_a$, it follows that $n_b b_z = a_a n_z$. Then clearly because $a_b n_a = a_a n_b$, the net wage–profit and net consumption–growth tradeoffs reduce to

$$\theta = \frac{1 - (1 + \rho)a_a}{n_z} - 1 \qquad \zeta = \frac{1 - (1 + g)a_a}{n_z}$$

So that, when $\rho = 0$,

$$\theta_m = \frac{1 - a_a}{n_z} - 1 \qquad \zeta_m = \frac{1 - a_a}{n_z} - 1 \qquad (II.31)$$

and when $\theta = 0$,

$$\rho_m = \frac{1 - n_z}{a_a} - 1 \qquad\qquad g_m = \frac{1 - n_z}{a_a} - 1$$

where

$$\frac{d\theta}{d\rho} = \frac{a_a}{n_z} \qquad \frac{d\zeta}{dg} = \frac{a_a}{n_z}$$

and

$$\frac{d^2\theta}{d\rho^2} = 0 \qquad \frac{d^2\zeta}{dg^2} = 0$$

Following Lowe's procedure, we can calculate the "sectoral ratios." As before we define the sectoral outputs

$$q_a p_a = \frac{(1 + g)^2 a_b b_z}{1 - (1 + g)a_a} \cdot \frac{(a_a)^2}{a_b b_z} = \frac{[(1 + g)a_a]^2}{1 - (1 + g)a_a}$$

$$q_b p_b = (1 + g)b_z \left(\frac{a_a}{b_z}\right) = (1 + g)a_a \qquad\qquad \text{(II.32)}$$

$$q_z p_z = 1 \cdot 1 = 1$$

Then, by using Lowe's symbol for output, we have

$$o = q_a p_a + q_b p_b + q_z p_z = \frac{1}{1 - (1 + g)a_a}$$

and the sector ratios are

$$\frac{q_a p_a}{o} = [(1 + g)a_a]^2$$

$$\frac{q_b p_b}{o} = [(1 + g)a_a][1 - (1 + g)a_a] \qquad\qquad \text{(II.33)}$$

$$\frac{q_z p_z}{o} = [1 - (1 + g)a_a]$$

Now let us look back at the discussion of the intersectoral equilibrium conditions, Equations II.3 and II.4 (Section II,2). These can be rewritten (assuming $\rho = g$) :

$$\frac{1 + \rho}{1 + \theta} = \frac{q_a n_a p_z}{q_b a_b p_a} = \frac{\text{labor in Sector Ia}}{\text{capital in Sector Ib}} \qquad\qquad \text{(II.3′)}$$

$$\frac{1 + \rho}{1 + \theta} = \frac{(q_a n_a + q_b n_b)p_z}{q_z b_z p_b} = \frac{\text{total labor in Sector I}}{\text{capital in Sector II}} \qquad\qquad \text{(II.4′)}$$

Because the left-hand sides of Equations II.3′ and II.4′ are the same, it follows that in growth equilibrium, regardless of the coefficients, the "cross-sectoral" capital–labor ratio of the whole system exactly reflects that of the two parts of Sector I, the capital–goods sector.[14] Moreover, by putting these equations together, cancelling p_z, and rearranging, we obtain

$$\frac{p_a}{p_b} = \frac{q_a n_a b_z}{q_b a_b (q_a n_a + q_b n_b)} \tag{II.34}$$

This gives the relation between prices and quantities necessary for growth equilibrium.

CONCLUDING REMARKS

We have now examined the connection of Lowe's model to the traditional labor theory of value, the meaning and implications of his assumption of growth equilibrium, and we have given a complete analysis of both the net wage–profit and net consumption–growth tradeoffs, showing their shapes and how they depend on the coefficients of input. This provides a translation into modern terms of the framework within which Lowe poses his questions concerning the movement of an industrial system using fixed capital from a given growth path to a higher or lower one. It also provides the tools for an examination in his terms of many of the principal questions of modern capital theory. However, it would be inappropriate to carry this discussion any further. The purpose of this appendix has been to provide a guide to the reader familiar with modern growth theory, and I hope this guide will encourage him to develop the argument for himself.

[14] Letting K stand for capital and L for labor, in an obvious notation, this means that in growth equilibrium:

$$\frac{L_A}{K_B} = \frac{L_A + L_B}{K_Z} \quad \text{or} \quad \frac{K_Z}{K_B} = 1 + \frac{L_B}{L_A}$$

Glossary of recurring symbols

Symbol	Interpretation	First Reference
a	Output of Sector Ia – Primary Equipment Goods	Chapter 4, Section I
a_a	Period Input of Primary Equipment Goods per Output of Primary Equipment Goods	Appendix, Introduction
a_b	Period Input of Primary Equipment Goods per Output of Secondary Equipment Goods	Appendix, Introduction
b	Output of Sector Ib – Secondary Equipment Goods	Chapter 4, Section I
b_z	Period Input of Secondary Equipment Goods per Output of Consumer Goods	Appendix, Introduction
c	Capital–Labor Ratio	Chapter 4, footnote 9
d	Rate of Depreciation	Chapter 4, Section I
e	Value Productivity	Chapter 9, Section I
f	Period Input of Fixed Capital	Chapter 3, Section III
g	Flow Rate of Growth	Appendix, Section II
i	Net Investment Ratio	Chapter 9, Section I
inp	Input	Chapter 5, Section I
k	Capital–Output Ratio	Chapter 4, Section III
m	Average Period of Maturation	Chapter 5, Section I
n	Period Input of Labor	Chapter 3, Section III
o	Aggregate Output	Chapter 4, Section II

Symbol	*Interpretation*	*First Reference*
p	Price	Chapter 4, Section II
$\bar{p}$	Profit Ratio	Chapter 9, Section V
q	Quantity	Chapter 4, Section II
r	Period Input of Natural Resources	Chapter 3, Section III
$\bar{r}$	Rate of Return of Natural Resources	Chapter 20, Section II
s	Net Savings Ratio	Chapter 9, Section IV
t	Period of Observation	Chapter 4, Section I
u	Ratio of Innovating Subsystem to Total System	Chapter 24, Section I
v	Value	Chapter 4, Section II
w	Wage Unit	Chapter 4, Section II
z	Output of Sector II – Consumer Goods	Chapter 4, Section I
A	$k(G + d)$	Chapter 9, Section III
B	$kd + s(1 - kd)$	Chapter 9, Section V
B'	$kd + (s + s')(1 - kd)$	Chapter 14, Section II
C	Stock of Total Capital	Chapter 5, Section I
D	Quantity Demanded	Chapter 7, Section III
F	Stock of Fixed Capital	Chapter 3, Section II
G	Stock Rate of Growth	Chapter 9, Section III
I	Net Investment	Chapter 9, Section I
N	Stock of Labor	Chapter 3, Section II

Symbol	Interpretation	First Reference
P	Profit	Chapter 9, Section V
R	Stock of Natural Resources	Chapter 3, Section II
$\bar{R}$	Rate of Self-Augmentation of Primary Equipment	Chapter 14, Section V
S	Quantity Supplied	Chapter 7, Section III
Sa	Net Savings	Chapter 9, Section V
W	Stock of Working Capital	Chapter 5, Section I
α	Rate of Growth of Labor Supply	Chapter 9, Section I
β	Number of Maturation Periods of Secondary Equipment	Chapter 14, Section VIII
γ	Number of Maturation Periods of Primary Equipment	Chapter 14, Section V
δ	Displacement Ratio	Chapter 23, Section I
ζ	Per Capita Net Consumption Rate	Appendix, Section I
θ	Net Wage Rate	Appendix, Section I
ρ	Flow Rate of Profit	Appendix, Section II
π	Rate of Growth of Productivity	Chapter 9, Section I
ϕ	Density Coefficient of Working Capital	Chapter 5, Section I
ω	Flow of Working Capital	Chapter 3, Section II

Name index

Abramovitz, M., 4, 6
Aubrey, H., ix
Ayres, A. U., 223

Blaugh, M., 235
Bloch, E., 169
Boehm-Bawerk, E. von, 23, 30, 48
Boulding, K. E., 7, 223
Britto, R., 3–4, 7
Bruton, H. J., 282
Burchardt, F. A., ix, 23, 31, 290
Burmeister, E., 3
Butler, S., 31

Clark, D. L., 290
Clark, J. B., 23, 35, 48, 75, 252–3

Dobell, A. R., 3
Domar, E., 22, 78, 87, 91–3, 94, 100, 123, 143, 240–1, 244
Dorfman, R., 34
Dosso, 34, 47, 59, 105

Eisner, R., 87
Engels, F., 23
Erlich, A., 175

Fellner, W., 282
Friedman, M., 12

Gaitskill, H. T. N., 23
Galbraith, J. K., 7
Goodwin, R. M., 290

Haberler, G., 182
Hahn, F. H., 3, 7, 16, 96, 243
Hanson, N. R., 13
Harcourt, G. C., 60, 283
Harrod, R. F., 19–20, 70–1, 78, 87, 91–3, 96, 99, 100, 123, 143, 235, 236–7, 240–1, 242, 244, 246
Hayek, F. A., 30
Heilbroner, R. L., 8, 14
Hicks, J. R., 4, 7–8, 10, 11, 48, 67, 182, 238, 290
Higgins, B., 182

Hirschman, A. O., 250
Hoffmann, W. G., ix

Jaffé, W., 22
Jevons, W. S., 48
Johannson, A., 177
Jonas, H., 14

Kaehler, A., 290
Kalecki, M., 10
Kennedy, C., 238, 244
Keynes, J. M., 19, 22, 42, 48, 59, 67, 73, 127, 242
Kneese, A. V., 223
Kurihara, K. K., 96–9
Kuznets, S., 6

Lange, O., 67
Leontief, W., 22, 290
Lewis, W. A., 6, 61
Lowe, A., ix, x, 6, 23, 103, 237, 290–7, 298, 302–3, 307–8, 313, 316, 318, 323, 325
Lundberg, E., 48, 176, 177

Machlup, F., 12, 21
MacIver, R. M., 14
Marshall, A., 6, 9–10, 20–1, 115, 210
Marx, K., 5–6, 23, 30, 41, 48, 75, 182, 224, 252, 272
Matthews, R. C. O., 3, 7, 16, 96, 243
Mill, J. S., 6, 210, 212, 251, 257
Mises, L. von, 30
Modigliani, F., ix
Moore, W. E., ix
Morishima, M., 23, 59, 73, 290

Neisser, H. P., ix, 48
Neumann, J. von, 225, 290
Nurkse, R., ix

Peirce, C. S., 13
Pigou, A. C., 223
Polya, G., 13

Quesnay, F., 22

Ricardo, D., 5, 48, 60, 182, 210–11, 243,
  250–1, 252, 276
Robertson, D. H., 48
Robinson, J., 10, 58, 59–60, 70–1, 73,
  89, 106–7, 243, 290, 296, 307
Ruttan, V., 235

Samuelson, P. A., 7, 34, 47, 59, 61, 105,
  210, 296
Schumpeter, J. A., 59, 73, 210, 235
Simon, H. A., 7
Smith, A., 5–7, 48, 182
Smith, F., 223

Solow, R., 34, 105
Spaventa, L., 290
Sraffa, P., 34, 40, 225, 290
Steuart, J., 210

Taussig, F. W., 48
Tinbergen, J., 12
Turgot, A. R. J., 210

Walras, L., 22
Weber, M., 26
Wicksell, K., 97
Wyler, J., 48, 51

Subject index

Action directive, 66–7
Aggregation, 22–3, 36, 151, 247

Balanced growth, *see* Growth, balanced
Behavior patterns, 12–13, 20–1, 62–5, 95
  see also Model, behavioral
Bunching of labor-displacement, 255
Business cycle, 8–9, 161, 183, 204, 255

Cannibalization of capital stock, 110,
  169, 170–5, 274
Capital
  defined, 25–6
  fixed, defined, 25, 35; *see also* equip-
    ment goods
  malleability of, 75, 93, 107
  money, defined, 25–6
  real, defined, 10–11, 22, 25–6
  speculative, defined, 26
  vintage structure of, 171, 243
  working, defined, 25–6, 35; flow, 28–
    9, 52–4, 112–14, 178–80, 212–14,
    277–80; stock, 24–5, 49–52
Capital formation, 9–11, 104, 109–10,
  112–13, 122, 124, 249
  see also Investment
Capital–labor ratio, 44, 75, Chap. 13
  (115–22)
Capital liquidation, 11, 104, 150, 182–3
Capital-output ratio, 43–4, 57, 85–6
Capital saturation, 58–60, 72, 283
Capital shortage, 75–6, 104, 204, 252–3
Capital transmutation, 241, 266, 270,
  272, 282
Causation, social, 14, 286–7
Circular mechanism, *see* Methodology
Coefficients of production
  fixed, 9–10, 60, 104, 106–7, 238, 252
  variable, 60, 75, 106–7, Chap. 13
    (115–22), 252–3
Communication, 17, 63–4
Compensation of factor displacement,
  249–55, Chaps. 24–27 (256–284)
  passim

Consumption waste, 227, 228–31
Control, public, 12–14, 15–16, 17, 69,
  108, 134, 144, 161, 169, 200, 203–
  4, 218–20, 225, 286–7
Critical time span, 171–5

Decline, *see* Growth, rate of, falling
Density of inputs, 51, 57
Depreciation, rate of, 36, 43, 57, 83,
  116, 171
Diminishing returns
  to capital, 282–4
  to natural resources, 118, 120, 209,
    Chap. 19 (209–22) *passim*, Chap.
    27 (275–84) *passim*
  to scale, 210
Displacement ratio, defined, 247

Economic growth, *see* Growth
Economic systems
  collectivist, 17, 63–4, 71–2, 84, 95,
    107–8, Chap. 16 (168–75), 203,
    237, 270
  free market, 17, 64–9, 72–6, Chap. 10,
    107–8, 122, Chaps. 14–15 (123–
    167), Chap. 18 (182–206), 218–20,
    231, 249–50, 251–5, Chaps. 24–27
    (256–84)
Efficiency, 21, 38, 58, 87, 105–6, 124,
  183–4
  technical, 58
Elasticity
  of demand, 260–1, 262, 264–5
  of expectations, *see* Expectations,
    elasticity of
Ends–means relationship, 11–16, 285–7
  see also Instrumental analysis
Engineering rules, 12, 13
Equilibrium
  dynamic, 20, 21–3, 70, Chaps. 9–10
    (77–100), 103–6, 214–18, 231,
    237
  inter-sectoral conditions of, 41, 80
  inter-temporal conditions of, 41, 82–3

Equilibrium (*continued*)
  stationary, 20, 21–2, 38–9, Chaps.
    6–7 (55–69), 178–81, 212–14,
    221–2, 225–31, 256–65, 267–71,
    273–4
  see also Growth, balanced, steady
Equipment goods, 25, 26–8, 30, 31–4,
    75, 109–12
  see also Capital, fixed
Expectations, 67–9, 95–6, 100, 147–8,
    149–51, 156–60, 197, 199, 201–4,
    219, 282
  elasticity of, 67–9
  price, defined, 67
  quantity, defined, 67
Externalities, 223
Extremum principle, defined, 66

Feedback mechanism *see* Methodology
Finished goods, 24–5
Force analysis, *see* Methodology

Growth
  balanced, 105–6, 185–6, 286–7
  classical theory of, 5–6, 7
  defined, 19, 103
  discontinuous, 9–10, 104–5
  historical and sociological study of, 4,
    7
  instrumental theory of, 11–13, 285–7
  once-over, 19–20, 255, 265
  patterns of, 19–21
  positive theory of, 3–4, 7–8, 96–100,
    105
  rate of, actual, 96; falling, 182–3,
    Chap. 18 (182–206); natural, 99;
    labor supply, defined, 77; produc-
    tivity, defined, 77; rising, 2, 70,
    236; warranted, 96
  steady, 20–1; *see also* Equilibrium,
    dynamic
  stimuli, 5, 9, 16, 104

Homeostatic principle, 66
Household sector, 226–7, 228–30
Hypothetico–deductive method, *see*
    Methodology

Input-output analysis, 46–7, 286
Instrumental analysis, *see* Methodology
Instrumental theory of growth, *see*
    Growth
Interest, 58–9, 72, 73
Invention, 235, 238, 275
Innovation
  autonomous, 238
  capital-attracting, 247–48, 272

capital-displacing, Chap. 25 (266–
    71), 272–3
  definition, 235
  factor-saving, 237, 246–8
  induced, 238
  labor-attracting, 248, 272–3
  labor-displacing, 247, Chap. 24 (256–
    65), 272
  neutral, 70, 236, 240–5, 248
  nonneutral, 236–7, Chap. 23 (246–
    55)
  process, 235–6
  product, 235–6, 249–50
Investment
  decision, 84–5, 148–51, 156, 159–61,
    197–8, 200–201, 218–19, 252,
    261–4
  gross, 78–9, 127
  net, 78, 83, 87
  ratio, 77–9, 84–5, 87, 91, 133

Joint products, 225

Law of variable proportions, 210

Machine tools, 30, 34, 113, 177, 181
Macrogoal, 8, 11–15, 21, 36, 38, 55,
    58, 62–3, 85, 105, 124, 168, 183–4,
    237, 249, 275
Marginal productivity theorem, 252–4
Maturation, *see* Period of maturation
Maturity hypothesis, 182
Maximum expansion from within, 130,
    Chaps. 14–15 (123–67) *passim*
Maximum principle, *see* Extremum
    principle
Methodology, 3–6, 7–8, 11–16, 62–3,
    103–6, 224–5, Chap. 28 (285–7)
  circular mechanism, 5–6, 10–11, 13,
    224
  descriptive analysis, 8
  feedback mechanism, 5–6, 10–11, 224
  force analysis, defined, 17
  hypothetico–deductive method, 12
  instrumental analysis, 12–16, 21,
    Chap. 28 (285–7)
  normative analysis, 11
  political economics, 14–16, 286
  positive analysis, 4, 7–8, 12, 20–1, 59,
    69, 85, 96–100, 105, 250–4
  prescriptive analysis, 8, 11
  pure economics, 15
  structure analysis, defined, 17
  systems analysis, 5
Microgoals, 65–7

Minimum period of construction, 173–5
Model
  behavioral, 65, 95
  dynamic equilibrium, 81, 84, 88
  expenditure, 88, 152, 229–31
  Harrod-Domar, 78–9, 89, 91–3, 96–100, 132, 241–2
  primary, 123–34, 135, 146, 265
  production, *see* Model, quantity, value
  quantity, 38, 40, 79, 81, 152, 162–3, 205–6, 222–3, 228–9
  receipt, 88, 152, 229–30
  secondary, 123, 134–45, 146, 162–3, 188, 194
  sector, 31–4, 44–5, 65–6, 89–91, 97–100
  stage, 28, 31–4, 49–51, 212–15, 218–22
  stationary equilibrium, 38, 40, 56
  three-sector, 23, 30–4, 98
  value, 40, 81, 152, 162–3, 205–6, 222–3, 228–9
Motivational patterns, 66–9, 95
Multiplier, 120, 127–9, 130, 151, 153–5, 156–7

Normative analysis, *see* Methodology

Optimization, 11, 58
Output–labor ratio, 248
Overbuilding of capital stock, 111, 124, 131, 159, 161, 169

Path
  analysis, 12, 16–17, 20, 103–6, 144
  criteria, 13, 105–6, 124, 183–4
Period
  of maturation, 50–4, 123, 134–6, 137–43, 152, 157, 159–60, 173–5, 186, 188, 193–6
  of observation, 43, 52, 53
Planning, *see* Control, public
Political economics, *see* Methodology
Positive analysis, *see* Methodology
Positive theory of growth, *see* Growth
Prediction
  conditional, 6–7
  unconditional, 5–6
Primary equipment goods, 30, 35; *see also* Fixed capital
Process innovation, *see* Innovation, process
Production, 24
  industrial, 24, 30, 31–4
Productivity
  rate of, 77–8
  value, 77

Profit, 58–60, 66, 72–6, 86–9, 96, 153–5, 159, 160, 162–4, 166–7, 205–6, 251, 260–3
  rate of, 87, 154, 159, 162–3, 198–201, 205–6
  ratio, 87, 88

Rate of growth, *see* Growth
Reduction coefficient, 214, 215, 217, 278
Replacement, rate of 23, 37, 39–40, 57, 86–8, 244
Residuals
  consumption, 227, 228–31
  production, 225–6, 228–31
Resources
  artificial, 223, 228–31
  natural, 24, 28–9, 31–3, 37–8, 209, 210–12, Chap. 19 (209–22) *passim*, 223–6, 228–9, Chap. 27 (275–84) *passim*
Rock bottom, 127–30, 151, 155–6, 163

Sanction, 17, 63, 64
Saving, 30, 72, 85, 170, 197, 238
  forced, 72, 110, 148, 197, 239
  involuntary, 72, 73–6, 125, 147, 197–8
  voluntary, 72, 76, 96, 98–9, 110, 148, 161, 197
Savings ratio, 79, 85, 87, 88, 91, 93
Schema of production, 27–34, 35, 49, 112–14, 178–80, 223–7
Scrap, 225–6, 227, 228–31
Secondary equipment goods. 30, 35; *see also* Capital, fixed
Sector ratios
  dynamic, 85–6, 89
  stationary, 43–6
Sectoral coefficients
  equal, 44, 46, 56–7, 75, 91–3, 106
  unequal, 45, 89–91, 259
Services, 252, 254
Solidarity dilemma, 151, 161, 169
Spectrum of techniques, 60, 106–7
Structure
  analysis, *see* Methodology
  of expenditure, 42, 86–9, 229–31
  physical, 35–9, 78–81, 86
  of production, *see* Schema of production
  of receipts, 42, 86–9, 229–31
  value, 39–42, 78–81
Surplus value, 75
Systems analysis, *see* Methodology

Technological change, *see* Innovation, process

Technological progress, *see* Innovation, process
Technological unemployment, *see* Innovations, labor-displacing
Transformation problem, 75
Traverse, defined, 10
Theory, *see* Methodology

Underbuilding of capital stock, 111, 124, 131, 136, 161

Value judgments, 14–15

Whirlpools, 34
Working capital, *see* Capital, working
Work shifts, 116, 120–1, 254